Touching Base

Sport and Society

Series Editors
Benjamin G. Rader
Randy Roberts

A list of books in the series appears at the end of this book.

TOUCHING BASE

Professional Baseball and American

Culture in the Progressive Era

Revised Edition

Steven A. Riess

University of Illinois Press
Urbana and Chicago

The epigraph to chapter 1 is reprinted from
The Celebrant: A Novel by Eric Rolfe
Greenberg by permission of the University
of Nebraska Press. Copyright © 1983 by
Eric Rolfe Greenberg.

© 1999 by the Board of Trustees of the University of Illinois
Manufactured in the United States of America
1 2 3 4 5 C P 5 4 3 2 1

This book is printed on acid-free paper.

Library of Congress Cataloging-in-Publication Data
Riess, Steven A.
Touching base : professional baseball and American culture in the
progressive era / Steven A. Riess.—Rev. ed.
p. cm.—(Sport and society)

Includes bibliographical references and index.
ISBN 0-252-02467-2 (cloth : alk. paper)
ISBN 0-252-06775-4 (pbk. : alk. paper)
1. Baseball—Social aspects—United States—History—19th century.
2. Baseball—Social aspects—United States—History—20th century.
I. Title. II. Series.
GV867.64 .R54 1999
796.357'0973—ddc21
98-58018
CIP

To my mother and in memory of my father

Contents

Illustrations follow page 98

Acknowledgments

During the long period of time that the first edition of this book was in preparation, I developed many intellectual debts that I am pleased to acknowledge. All historians of baseball owe a great deal to the pathbreaking work of Harold Seymour and David Q. Voigt. The early direction for this study was strongly influenced by the wisdom and candor of Neil Harris. Several good friends during my years of study at the University of Chicago constituted a true community of scholars, and they aided me considerably. Morris Vogel and James Wunsch were both kind enough to provide me with valuable data that they had come across in the course of their research. Kenneth Chern and James Pzystup spent many hours with me discussing and criticizing various hypotheses. Later on sections of the work were read by some of my Northeastern Illinois colleagues, and I thank Larry Dial, Gregory Singleton, and June Sochen for their assistance. My good friend Melvin Adelman read the entire manuscript, and I benefited greatly from his unique expertise. My dear wife Tobi also read the final drafts, and my obligations to her are legion. I thank her profusely for everything. Many librarians in Atlanta, Chicago, and New York aided me in my research. I particularly want to thank the staffs of the Atlanta Historical Society and the New York Public Library and individually Clifford Kachline of the National Baseball Library, the Baseball Hall of Fame, Coqperstown, New York; Evangeline Mistaras, of Northeastern Illinois University; Archie Motley of the Chicago Historical Society; and Helen Smith of the University of Chicago. My maps were drawn by David Morrow and Brian Harms of the Department of Graphics at Northeastern Illinois University. The editors of the *Journal of Ethnic Studies*, the *Journal of Sport History*, the *Maryland Historian*, and

Stadion: Journal of the History of Sports and Physical Education kindly gave me permission to utilize material that appeared in their journals in different forms. I also want to thank the editor and the staff at Greenwood Press for their invaluable assistance in the first edition, and for allowing the rights to the book to revert to me.

The revised edition of this book was also a long time in coming. In that interval two wonderful children were born, Jamie and Jennie, who between homework and soccer games allowed their dad to scribble away. My eldest daughter, Jodi, grew up in the interval, got married to a wonderful guy, and had her own babies, but continued to help her old man out with his computer. I want to thank Larry Malley, who first urged me to bring the study up to date and to work with the University of Illinois Press toward that end. At the press, I was championed and aided by director Richard Wentworth, and the co-editors of the Sport and Society series, Randy Roberts and Benjamin Rader, and I thank them all for their help. The excellent staff members at the National Baseball Hall of Fame in Cooperstown were very helpful, particularly in assisting me with photographs. Also helpful with photographs were the Atlanta Historical Society, the Chicago Historical Society, and the New York Historical Society. Debbie Siegel of Northeastern Illinois University helped with interlibrary loan requests. Various members of the Society of American Baseball Researchers were most supportive, particularly Jerry Malloy, who shared with me much of his extraordinary research into African-American history. William Akin and several anonymous scholars read the entire revised manuscript, and I thank them all for their suggestions and criticisms. Of course, I alone am responsible for any errors.

Introduction

Baseball and the Cultural Approach to History

> Whoever wants to know the heart and mind of America had better
> learn baseball, the rules and realities of the game—and do it by watch-
> ing first some high school or small-town teams. . . . The wonderful
> pouring of the passions that we all experienced in the fall of '51, the
> despair groaned out over the fate of the Dodgers, from whom the league
> pennant was snatched at the last minute, give us some idea of what
> Greek tragedy was all like. . . .
>
> That baseball fitly expresses the power of the nation's mind and body
> is a merit separate from the glory of being the most active, agile, varied,
> articulate, and brainy of all our group games.
>
> —Jacques Barzun, "The Underentertained"

In 1954 Jacques Barzun urged all who wanted to know the American character to study baseball, but a generation passed before scholars
really rose to his challenge. Baseball was well over one hundred years old
before any serious and erudite analysis of the national pastime was written. Historians were hesitant to study not just baseball, but sport history
in general. With the exception of three books published between 1929
and 1940 and a pioneering 1917 essay on the rise of sport in the *Mississippi Valley Historical Review* (now the *Journal of American History*),
sport was virtually shunned by professional historians. It was not until
1953 that the leading journal of American history published its second
essay on sport. In 1960, Harold Seymour published his seminal *Baseball:
The Early Years*, the first academic volume on baseball and only the
fourth scholarly book on American sport history.[1]

Historians disdained studying institutions of mass culture like base-ball because they believed there were more important topics to examine and because they were snobs. Scholars believed such institutions were well understood by the public who participated in them and that detailed analysis would not foster new knowledge or explain broad historical problems. After all, ten year olds could discuss baseball intelligently with their elders and might well have a better command of esoteric sta-tistics to back up their opinions.[2] Furthermore, historians who wanted to study sport were often deterred by professional concerns. Novice schol-ars were afraid they would never get a job if they wrote dissertations on sport, and even recognized historians worried that writing about sport would label them as frivolous. As the noted historian Carl B. Cone remi-nisced in 1979: "I wrote some sports history forty years ago, but strictly as an extra-curricular interest. . . . These publications could not earn brownie points to influence tenure, promotion, and merit decisions. I would not have dared to include these writings in my dossier; they might have counted against me as indicative of a young assistant professor who was not seriously engaged with the discipline of history as it was then understood."[3]

Academic interest in sport history slowly developed in the early 1970s when I was in graduate school, and people were often bemused when I told them that I was writing a dissertation on the history of baseball. It was difficult to get that study published in the late 1970s be-cause publishers had little idea about what to do with a scholarly study of sport. The academic community was unprepared for the emerging fas-cination with sport that resulted from such factors as the democratiza-tion of the historical profession, the demands of students in the late 1960s for a more relevant curriculum, the rise of the New Social history, the growing importance of interdisciplinary studies, influenced in partic-ular by cultural anthropology, and the organization of the North Ameri-can Society for Sport History (1972), which created a supportive intellec-tual community for sport historians. But the fundamental reason the study of sport history achieved acceptance was that historians were real-izing that the analysis of the internal history of sport and the history of its interaction with the broader society could elucidate such central pro-cesses of American history as urbanization and industrialization and such variables as politics, class, ethnicity, race, and gender.[4]

Building on the pioneer work of historians such as John R. Betts, Harold Seymour, and David Quentin Voigt, a host of bright scholars moved into the field, and by the late 1980s a veritable flood of high quality scholarship had begun. Ken Burns, creator of the monumental *Civil War* documentary, was similarly influenced to produce his 1994 18.5-hour television chronicle *Baseball:* "The story of baseball is . . . the story of race in America, of immigration and assimilation; of the struggle between labor and management, of popular culture and advertising, of myth and the nature of heroes, villains, and buffoons; of the role of women and class and wealth in our society. The game is a repository of age-old American verities, of standards against which we continually measure ourselves, and yet at the same time a mirror of the present moment in our modern culture."[5]

From its modest origins, sport history has blossomed into a booming field, particularly strong in the history of baseball and boxing and the genre of biography. Sport history is no longer simply social history, but may be economic history, urban history, political history, educational history, or cultural history, depending on the topic and the questions under consideration.[6] Several scholarly journals around the world specialize in sport history, led by the pioneering *Journal of Sport History*, and many prestigious presses publish sport history and have sports studies series. Yet sport remains a stepchild in history departments, which have never advertised a position in that field.

In this book I examine the myths and realities of professional baseball during the Progressive Era to evaluate how the sport influenced and at the same time mirrored the broader society. I also seek to employ baseball as a lens to better view the nature of American society in the early twentieth century. I present a structural functionalist analysis of Progressive Era professional baseball. The use of such a paradigm for sport history was first employed by the colonial historian Timothy Breen in his classic essay "Horses and Gentlemen: The Cultural Significance of Gambling among the Gentry of Virginia." Breen asserted that "a specific, patterned form of behavior, such as gambling, does not become popular in a society or among the members of a subgroup of that society unless the activity reflects or expresses values indigenous to that culture." Breen's employment of a sport model was based on the scholarship of cultural anthropologists, who analyze preliterate societies by studying their principal cultural artifacts to expose basic patterns of thought and behavior. Cultural anthropologists define culture as the "pattern of constructs of modes of meaning, values, and ideas about acting, inferred from noninstinctive . . . human action and the products of action." They believe that a culture's components reflect the society's fundamental characteristics. Thus, cultural anthropologists study myths, rituals, and symbols, which are regarded as expressions of implicit or explicit sets of values. The classic anthropological study of play is Clifford Geertz's work on Balinese cockfighting. Geertz saw these highly ritualized spectator contests as intense social dramas. The fights involved the honor of social leaders and their families, reflected the entire social structure, and represented the way Balinese perceived social reality. Geertz demonstrated how the elements of the rituals, that is, the rules, betting patterns, and reactions of opponents, helped elucidate the intricacies of Balinese culture.[7]

Similarly, the study of professional baseball's myths, realities, symbols, and rituals provides a means to better understand American mores, values, and beliefs. The game of baseball supplanted cricket as the most popular American team sport in the 1850s and toward the end of the decade was already gaining consideration as *the* national pastime. Shortly after the Civil War, baseball was universally recognized as the preeminent American game.[8]

Baseball's popularity as a participatory amusement transcended its entertainment value. As historians have demonstrated, the game provided an opportunity to gain recognition for prowess and promoted a sense of community among a "brotherhood" or "fraternity" of baseball players. Boys and young men in the nineteenth century appreciated its ability to display their manliness through toughness, aggression, physicality, and skill. As the historian Ronald Story points out, team members of formalized clubs played cohesively by batting in turn, playing for a run at a time, employing the "long sequence" offense, and defending as a team, with each player covering his designated territory. Membership offered new urbanites a sense of community ("home base")—indicated by their uniforms, which set them apart from nonmembers—a well-ordered space in a chaotic and distended environment, and physical and emotional releases. The ball club provided a more uplifting "family" for young men than such alternatives as street gangs.[9]

The professionalization and commercialization of baseball began in the 1860s when the first players were paid to play and fields were enclosed so that promoters could charge admission fees to spectators. The National Association of Professional Base Ball Players, the first professional league, was started in 1871, supplanted five years later by the National League of Professional Base Ball Clubs (NL). Then in 1877 the loosely organized seventeen-team International Association was established. The Northwestern League, the first so-called minor league, was created in 1879, and the American Association, a second major league, in

1882. Thereafter several leagues were organized with varying success, primarily in the East and Midwest. By the end of the century only the NL and thirteen minor leagues remained.

After the turn of the century the professional game reached its peak of popularity as the country's leading sport. Its fast, exciting, and dramatic action captured the public's imagination, nearly monopolizing the interest of sports fans. By the early 1900s, when boxing and horse racing were operating, if at all, under severe legal and social restrictions, and football was an amateur sport mainly limited to the college crowd, professional baseball teams played in nearly every city. Baseball did not encounter vigorous competition from other spectator sports until the "Golden Age of Sports" in the 1920s. It has remained the national pastime pretty much ever since despite competition from horse racing (which actually outdrew baseball from the early 1950s to the mid-1980s) and from professional football, which temporarily supplanted baseball in the 1970s.[10]

Baseball's dominance of the Progressive Era's sporting scene was reflected by the growing number of leagues, the large crowds at games, the total attendance statistics, and the enormous attention it received in newspapers and periodicals. Between 1903 and 1908 major league attendance doubled to over seven million, and minor league attendance increased even more rapidly, a growth rate that encouraged major league owners to build expensive new fireproof parks seating upwards of forty thousand fans.[11] Beginning in 1903, each year except for 1904 was highlighted by the postseason World Series between the American and National Leagues, which was rivaled for national interest only by presidential election campaigns. Baseball fans came from every social class, race, ethnic group, and gender, although most spectators were middle-class men. Baseball news dominated the newly established sports sections in the daily press, and articles on the national pastime appeared in popular magazines with growing frequency. Journalists had a hard time satisfying the public appetite for baseball during and after the season, reporting not just game outcomes, but writing feature stories, short fiction, and even poetry. The press turned stars like Christy Mathewson into role models for youngsters who idolized them.

Professional baseball's prominence was not simply a result of its manifest function of providing exciting amusement for spectators, fans who read about it in the press, and children who admired its stars. The national pastime's eminence was also a consequence of the ideology developed by cooperative writers that made the sport appear to be directly relevant to the needs and aspirations of middle America. Baseball was portrayed in such a way that it supplied some of the symbols, myths, and legends society needed to bind its members together.

The United States in the early 1900s was undergoing significant social changes as it emerged as a modern nation. This highly nationalistic country was gaining recognition as an international power. The economy was booming, and it was the leading industrial nation in the world. Government and private organizations were increasingly bureaucratized and criteria of expertise and efficiency began replacing familial, social, and political connections in hiring and promoting. Policies were also heavily influenced by the enormous immigration of eastern and southern Europeans, who came looking for jobs and refuge from oppression. These newcomers moved primarily into ethnic neighborhoods in eastern and midwestern cities. The combination of European immigrants and urban-bound folk from the countryside transformed the United States from a primarily rural country in 1890 (64.6 percent of the population), to a mainly urban nation thirty years later (51.4 percent).

These social changes further distended what was already a highly stratified society, and the nation appeared to be drifting toward a dangerous future. Poverty was widespread in urban areas, and men, women, and children were employed in backbreaking, brutal, and hazardous factory jobs. Community ties were weak and anomie was on the rise, particularly in the overcrowded and crime-heavy ethnic sections of cities, where newcomers tried as best as they could to adapt to America by maintaining old institutions and establishing new ones. Urban politics was dominated by corrupt and powerful political machines that delivered goods and services to their mainly immigrant constituencies in return for votes. Bureaucratization threatened old values such as rugged individualism and self-reliance by encouraging new values such as teamwork and cooperation.

A broad-based social movement known as progressivism developed in an attempt to alleviate some of these problems and to bring order to the country. Progressives were optimistic reformers who believed that once social, economic, or political problems were identified, studied, and understood, they could then be rectified. The movement was mainly led by white Anglo-Saxon Protestants, but drew supporters from a wide political and social spectrum. Certain progressives promoted a wide variety of social reforms out of altruism, while others supported just one or two particular reforms because of their personal or corporate interest. The progressive coalition included settlement house workers who wanted social justice for the urban poor; highly trained professionals such as economists, engineers, lawyers, and sociologists who wanted to use their expertise to make business, government, and industry more efficient by employing their research and by placing the best people, namely experts like themselves, into positions of responsibility; sagacious business leaders who supported government regulation when it could be controlled by business-minded bureaucrats favoring the rationalization of commerce; liberal machine politicians who tried to make life more comfortable for their constituents through such reforms as public bathhouses; and middle-class native-born white Americans who worried about the future of their culture and their country and were hopeful of preventing radicalism and anarchy by acculturating and exercising social control over the new immigrants and their children through such institutions as the public school and the national pastime and such reforms as immigration restriction and Prohibition.[12]

Professional baseball's ideology spoke directly to white Anglo-Saxon Americans and their need to secure order. According to the baseball creed, the sport was one of our finest national institutions whose latent functions contributed to both individual and public welfare. This credo claimed that baseball was an indigenous American game that had originated in the countryside, and that it typified all that was best in our society. It asserted that crowds included people from all walks of life, that owners were benevolent citizens who operated their franchises out of concern for the public interest, that players were predominantly from rural origins, and that the sport was open to anyone with talent and perseverance. The game's principal functions were purportedly its ability to teach children "traditional" American values and to help newcomers assimilate into the dominant WASP culture through their participation in the sport and its rituals. In addition, by encouraging fans to identify with the home team, baseball was expected to encourage a sense of community by promoting hometown pride and boosterism.[13]

This construction of baseball reality was accepted without question by the public and became the conventional wisdom. The ideology encompassed values and goals many small-town Americans and WASP progressives wanted to maintain, particularly those associated with the well-integrated village and those that sought to homogenize and control the immigrant-dominated cities.

My major purpose in writing this book is to examine the realities of the baseball creed by analyzing the sport's three main elements—spectators, owners, and players—in three cities—Atlanta, Chicago, and New York. New York and Chicago, both major league cities, have received considerable attention from urban historians, while Atlanta, which had only a minor league team during the Progressive Era, has probably been more thoroughly studied than any other southern city.

Atlanta, the Gate City of the South, was the third largest city in the region in 1900 after New Orleans and Memphis and had a population of 89,872. It was known as the "Chicago of the South" because of its ties to the railroads that had stimulated post–Civil War development. By 1920 its 200,616 inhabitants made it the second largest city in the region, with an economy more equally balanced between manufacturing and commerce than those of major northeastern and midwestern cities. Professional baseball came to Atlanta in 1885, but several early teams failed. In 1902 it finally got a stable franchise with the founding of the Crackers in the Southern League.

After merging with Brooklyn in 1898, New York had a population of 5.6 million, largely immigrants, which made it the largest city in the United States. The financial, industrial, and cultural capital of the country, it was an early center of professional baseball after the Civil War and a charter member of the NL in 1876. It had two major league franchises in 1900, and three years later became the only city with three major league clubs.

Chicago was the nation's shock city, growing from a virtually empty prairie in the 1830s to a metropolis of about 300,000 in 1870, when it was the leading commercial center of the West. Despite the Great Fire of 1871, which destroyed two-thirds of it, at the turn of the century Chicago had a population of about 1 million, making it the second largest city in the nation. Chicago had two major league teams in 1901, each a charter member of its respective league.

My research indicates that the key aspects of the baseball creed were myths that can be categorized as either agrarian, democratic, or integrative. The agrarian and democratic myths encapsulated many important ideals of nostalgic native-born Americans who looked back to an idealized, pristine past and worried about the future of their society, while the integrative myth suggested a way to secure that future. But although most of the ideology's basic elements did not accurately reflect American culture, fans accepted its veracity, and that perception helped shape their attitudes and behavior.[14]

The public saw baseball as an accurate reflection of contemporary society. If one accepted the fundamental assumption that baseball was a democratic sport epitomizing the best in America, then it made a lot of sense that the national pastime should and could be utilized symbolically and instrumentally to preserve a familiar social order and indoctrinate youngsters into the traditional value system. Baseball's symbolic function was to demonstrate the continuing relevance of old values and beliefs in an increasingly modern and urban age. Its instrumental function was to teach the dominant WASP belief system and serve as a bulwark against those social developments that seemed to challenge or threaten the core culture. Baseball did this through the rituals of spectatorship and by being transformed into a moral equivalent of the frontier that provided heroes and role models for its young fans.

The myths and realities of professional baseball will be analyzed in five chapters. I focus on the fans in chapters 1 and 4. In chapter 1 I discuss public perceptions of the ideology of baseball, the social functions ascribed to the national pastime, the social composition of crowds, factors that influenced the opportunity of fans to attend games, and the behavior of crowds. In chapter 4 I examine the relationships between Sunday blue laws and professional baseball, which varied sharply in different geographic regions. In chapters 2 and 3 I am concerned with the owners and their work as sports entrepreneurs. In chapter 2 I examine the social origins of baseball club owners, their political connections, and how they operated their franchises as business ventures. This chapter is followed by one on the history of professional baseball parks. In chapter 5 I examine the career of the professional baseball player around the turn of the century. Here I explore the conventional wisdom about major leaguers, who were presumed to be predominantly uneducated, unsophisticated, rural young men. Through the technique of collective biography, I compare the popular image of ballplayers to their actual social backgrounds, their careers on the diamond, and their opportunities after retirement. Finally, in the conclusion I analyze the social functions of professional baseball in the Progressive Era.

"Take Me Out to the Ball Game"
The Crowd and the Ideology of Baseball

His delight was to invite guests to the local ballpark. He'd staked this out as his personal form of business entertainment, leaving the burlesques and bawdy houses to his fellows of the selling trade. Here professional calculation matched his personal inclination. For himself, Eli Kapinski of New York, no fancy out-of-town attraction could rival those of home, but a major league ballgame in any city carried a sort of guarantee. For his clients—what a disarming suggestion! An afternoon at the ballpark, so refreshing, so American!

—Eric Rolfe Greenberg, *The Celebrant*

Professional baseball enjoyed extraordinary growth and expansion during the Progressive Era, although there were no crucial innovations in the game on the field, which had achieved its modern form by the 1880s. Attending a professional game was fun and offered an experience that seemed uniquely congruent with both modern and traditional attitudes, behavior, and values. Matches were manly contests played by excellent athletes and filled with exciting, dramatic moments and frequent shifts between offense and defense. Ball games were generally played rapidly, but with frequent breaks in the action to facilitate friendly banter among spectators or the purchase of peanuts and popcorn from vendors. It was not time grounded (perhaps providing an escape from time-work discipline), but based on a fixed number of innings, between which fans could run to the concession stands for beer. Since fans had played base-ball as youngsters, attending a pro game brought back fond memories of their youth.[1]

The game's swift development as a commercialized spectacle also de-pended on such modernizing external factors as urbanization, economic prosperity, and transportation and communication innovations. Rapid urbanization meant a significant increase in the number and size of po-tential markets for professional baseball. An improved standard of living, particularly among the middle and upper lower classes, provided many urbanites with discretionary income and leisure time that many chose to spend at ballparks. Mass transit advancements, particularly electrified streetcars, enabled fans from all over the city and nearby suburbs to get to playing fields swiftly and cheaply. And the emergence of well-illustrated penny newspapers helped disseminate information about the national pastime.

Finally, the growing popularity of professional baseball depended on a vigorous public relations campaign waged by baseball magnates and sportswriters to promote the game. Journalists promulgated an ide-ology of baseball based on the American sports creed that advocated clean, recreational athletics. Such sports supposedly promoted sound morality, developed good character, enhanced public health, and pro-vided a substitute for the lost world of small-town America.[2] The base-ball creed asserted that participation in the rituals of baseball contrib-uted to both individual self-improvement and national betterment. It proved to twentieth-century urbanites that attending baseball games was not a waste of time but an enjoyable and edifying leisure activity.

The Popularity of Professional Baseball

The enormous growth of professional baseball's popularity after the turn of the century was reflected by a remarkable increase in the number of professional teams and leagues, the size of crowds, and the extent of media coverage. Professional baseball was originally largely limited to the Northeast and Midwest. The South and Far West had no organized associations until 1885, when the Southern League and state leagues in Virginia and California were established. By 1900 organized baseball was ready to expand into untapped or underexploited markets. Evidence of profitable franchises coupled with hometown pride encouraged business leaders and local politicians to organize new teams and leagues all across the country. The minor leagues rose from 13 in 1900 to 34 in 1907 to 47 in 1912. They were also increasingly stable operations. While 5 of 13 leagues folded in 1900, four years later all 23 completed their seasons. By 1913 there were over 300 teams in 43 leagues employing 5,000 professional players.[3]

There are only modest data for nineteenth-century crowds. In 1879, for example, Providence drew 43,000, and two years later the Philadelphia Phillies drew a total of 55,890 over 51 games. In 1884 when "Hoss" Radbourne's Providence American Association (AA) club won the championship, some home games drew fewer than 1,000 fans. Attendance varied by quality of team (contenders usually did best), market size, and pricing. In 1883 when the Phillies started out charging 50 cents for tickets, most fans went to the new Athletics club of the AA, which charged only 25 cents. When the NL permitted the Phillies to cut prices in half to meet the competition, attendance at their games rose by 400 percent.[4]

Attendance peaked in 1889, a record-setting year for most teams, led by pennant-winning Brooklyn (AA), which ended the year with an attendance of 353,690, a daily average of 5,126 spurred by cheap seats. The Giants led the NL with an average of 3,201. Beginning in 1893 big league daily attendance typically was about 2,000, a drop induced by the Great Depression and the merger of the American Association with the NL in 1892. The amalgamation cut the number of teams from sixteen to twelve and reduced the number of those charging under 50 cents. In 1894 the New York Giants led the NL in attendance, averaging about 2,500 per game, though thereafter the most successful draw was the Philadelphia Phillies, who charged as little as 25 cents for admission. Their home attendance surpassed 250,000 each year from 1893 to 1898, peaking in 1895 with a record 460,000. On the other hand, in 1899, the Cleveland Spiders drew an all-time low of under 200 a game after owner Stanley Robison sent his best players to St. Louis to bolster his brother Frank's newly purchased team. Cleveland was barely half the size of St. Louis, had a smaller ballpark, played no Sunday games, and had a terrible team. Cleveland, now nicknamed the "Misfits," spent the bulk of the season on the road, ending up 20-134, the worst in major league history. A recent study of eleven nineteenth-century teams found they averaged 2,651 spectators per game, ranging from 3,352 in Chicago to 1,468 in Cleveland.[5]

Opening day, weekends, and holidays were the most popular days for baseball. By the mid-1880s, holiday and Sunday games in the biggest cities drew from 5,000 to 10,000 spectators. The single largest crowds turned out on Memorial Day or the Fourth of July. On Memorial Day 1887, a total of 30,000 New Yorkers attended morning and afternoon games at the old Polo Grounds. Chicago had several large crowds, including a record 34,942 for two contests (22,913 for the afternoon game alone) on 4 July 1895, and four years later a record 27,489 attended a Sunday afternoon game. On those occasions when seating capacities were taxed, owners accommodated fans by selling standing room on the perimeter of the playing field.[6]

Total attendance grew dramatically after the turn of the century, in part because the number of games increased to 154 from 140. In 1901, when the National and American Leagues were in competition, their audiences reached 3.6 million and virtually doubled by 1908. An average club drew about 3,400 per game, but crowds were unevenly distributed because of a team's metropolitan population, ticket prices, availability of Sunday baseball, and especially quality of play. If attendance had been equally divided among the teams, then each would have drawn 12.5 percent of the total number of spectators. However, the Giants drew 20.2 percent of the total NL gate in the period 1901–10 (including a record 910,000 in 1909), and the Chicago Cubs brought in 17.5 percent, but the Boston Braves had only 6.2 percent. In the next decade the Giants' share rose to 21.0 percent. The Giants' success was a result of the large home market, the capacity of the field, and the team's high quality. On the other hand, nearby Brooklyn had a smaller share of attendance (9.64 percent in 1901–10 and 11.16 percent in 1911–20) than its population would predict because of the Dodgers' poor play. They finished in the second division every year from 1902 to 1915. During the same decades, the White Sox were the top American League (AL) draw (17.1 percent and 18.2 percent) and the most popular team in baseball between 1910 and 1919 with an attendance of 5,577,496. The club benefited from a new park, a highly competitive team, a large section of seats for a quarter, and Sunday baseball. Washington was the worst draw in the AL during this period (6.8 percent and 7.6 percent), reflecting its small population and poor teams. The Highlanders (later known as the Yankees) were only average draws (11.4 percent and 13.4 percent) despite their Manhattan location because they fielded inferior teams.[7]

Beginning in 1909 potential crowd sizes were greatly enhanced by the construction of comfortable and attractive, albeit short-lived, fire-resistant parks. Attendance for major league games fluctuated during the middle of the next decade because of competition from the Federal League. Major league attendance dropped from 6.4 million in 1913 to 4.5

million in 1914. Attendance was also drastically cut in 1918 with the nation at war and the season shortened by a month. The Dodgers set a modern record low with a total attendance of 83,381. Following World War I total major league attendance rose to 6.5 million in 1919 and one year later increased dramatically to 9.1 million. The surge in 1920 was led by the Yankees, who with Babe Ruth and Sunday baseball for the first time drew 1,289,422, double their previous attendance.[8]

Minor league attendance also grew rapidly because of the greater interest in baseball and the absence of commercial entertainments in smaller towns. Even Saugerties, New York, population 7,000, had a team in the Class D Hudson River League. Among the most successful minor league franchises was Columbus, which in 1904 drew 254,156 spectators, more than five major league clubs. Smaller cities such as Atlanta drew more modestly. The Atlanta Crackers' attendance rose from 40,000 in 1902, its first year in the Class A Southern Association, to 86,818 by 1910. This made the Gate City's team fourth in the league, well behind New Orleans and Birmingham, which each sold over 130,000 tickets. It charged typical minor league prices, 10 cents for children and 25 cents for adults, plus another quarter for a grandstand seat. In 1920 Atlanta's attendance reached 221,638, or over 150 percent more than in 1910. This was far below minor league leader San Francisco, who had 371,931. The Class AA Pacific Coast League was the most successful minor league with large member cities, high quality play, and the longest playing season in organized baseball, resulting in a total annual attendance of 1.9 million in the 1920s, one-sixth of the total minor league audience.[9]

The mania over professional baseball was reflected, and promoted, by widespread newspaper and magazine coverage that fans relied on for their vicarious baseball enjoyment. Sports departments were established in the 1880s in mass-oriented newspapers and were busy year round trying to satisfy their readers' demands for detailed baseball coverage, including in-depth reports of ball games, trade rumors, and players' off-season activities. Reportage was supplemented by poetry and short fiction. The percentage of newsprint devoted to sport rose from 4 percent in 1890 to 17 percent in 1923.[10]

Henry Chadwick, an English immigrant, was the first baseball writer and became known as "the father of baseball." As a sportswriter in 1856 he focused first on cricket but shortly thereafter specialized in the new game of baseball for the *New York Herald* and the *Brooklyn Eagle*. Chadwick also wrote for the leading sporting periodicals, particularly the highly regarded *Clipper* (1858–89), and edited various baseball guides, including

Spalding's Official Baseball Guide (1881–1908). He was the sport's leading historian and statistician, helped devise the rules of the game, established the scoring system, and fought rowdyism and gambling.[11]

Modern baseball journalism emerged in Chicago's competitive newspaper market around 1887, led by Leonard Washburn of the *Chicago Inter-Ocean*, twenty-year-old Finley Peter Dunne ("Mr. Dooley") of the *Chicago Daily News*, and Charles Seymour of the *Chicago Herald*. Instead of bland game summaries, they emphasized crucial and spectacular plays and wrote stories filled with colorful prose, baseball slang, and humor. By the 1910s, New York's leading baseball writers, including Fred Lieb, Irwin Cobb, Bozeman Bulger, Heywood Broun, Grantland Rice, Charles Van Loan, and Damon Runyon, were counted among the most outstanding journalists. They avoided cliches and supplied readers with interesting stories and new angles. They employed satire with relish and enjoyed making fun of colorful contemporary characters such as Bugs Raymond of the Giants. Yet they were among the biggest boosters of the national pastime and originated the "Gee Whiz" school of sportswriting. Among the leading baseball writers outside of New York were Chicago's nationally syndicated columnist Hugh Fullerton of the *Chicago Examiner*, best known for his critical analysis of the 1919 World Series, and Ring Lardner, a popular syndicated columnist who eventually earned forty thousand dollars a year writing on baseball. His widely read publications such as "Alibi Ike" and *You Know Me Al* caricatured the ingenuous bumpkin players and utilized the institution of baseball to explore the problems of Americans unable to cope with their changing environment.[12]

Baseball was also a common topic in popular periodicals, whose baseball coverage increased exponentially in the early 1900s. As *Bookman* noted in 1910, "it has . . . [become] almost impossible to pick up a magazine that did not contain some kind of an article on baseball." Magazine coverage peaked between 1910 and 1914, when the *Reader's Guide to Periodical Literature* listed 249 baseball publications. Stories discussing pennant races, salary disputes, and scientific explanations for the curve ball appeared in such prestigious middle-class serials as *American Magazine*, *Collier's*, *Harper's Weekly*, the *Independent*, *Outlook*, *Scientific American*, and *Scribner's*. There were also specialized sports weeklies mainly devoted to baseball, most notably *Sporting Life* (1883–1920) and the *Sporting News* (1886–), as well as the monthly *Baseball Magazine* (1908–57).[13]

Many books were written about baseball, including fiction and nonfiction. The most prominent historical narratives were Albert G. Spalding's hyperbolic and self-congratulatory *America's National Game* (1911) and Francis C. Richter's *Richter's History and Records of Baseball* (1914). Spalding's well-promoted book reportedly sold over ninety thousand copies. He emphasized the role of the NL in popularizing baseball among the middle classes and the value of the game in building manliness, character, and an ethic of success. His alliterative list of American virtues included "Courage, Confidence, Combativeness; . . . Dash, Discipline, Determination; . . . Energy, Eagerness, Enthusiasm; [and] . . . Vim, Vigor, Virility." Baseball fiction was mainly aimed at youths, and the genre of juvenile baseball literature boomed, mainly through the pulp novels of Burt L. Standish (Gilbert Patten), best known for his Frank Merriwell series. Also immensely popular was the Baseball Joe series, written by Lester Chadwick of Tom Swift and Rover Boys fame.[14]

Contemporaries attributed the national pastime's popularity to its speed, excitement, outdoor venues, and American origins and character.[15] In 1905, Albert Spalding, an early professional star of the 1870s who pitched for and later owned the Chicago White Stockings and the A. G. Spalding and Brothers Sporting Goods Company, initiated a project to prove that baseball was an indigenous sport and not a descendant of the English game of rounders as Henry Chadwick had long claimed. A blue-ribbon commission of seven leading citizens, including two U.S. senators, was established to determine the sport's true origins. The committee concluded in 1907 on the basis of limited and dubious testimony, primarily that of octogenarian Louis Graves, that baseball was invented in 1839 by Abner Doubleday, who laid out the first diamond in Cooperstown, New York. Doubleday was a Civil War hero who in his autobiography had never even mentioned baseball. At the time of his alleged innovation, he was a West Point cadet. This alleged genesis immediately entered the baseball legend.[16]

Commentators also believed baseball was popular with adult males because watching games reminded them of playing the sport as youngsters. As Edward B. Bloss noted in *Outing:* "The man who sits in the grandstand does not want to forget those days picturesquely linked with his youth. He remembers the farm lad hurrying his work to practice awhile in the cool of the evening. He may have a vision of battle royals in vacant lots about town, with sentinels impatiently charged to watch for the police."[17]

Historians recognize this as part of baseball's cyclical history, which has been defined by Warren Goldstein as generational and repetitive (rather than chronological, linear, and cumulative) and "chronicles the game's emotional relationship." Fans watched what was virtually the same game and experienced the same emotions as earlier fans. Adult judgments were shaped by personal memories of a sport lived in the hearts and minds of people. As Bruce Kuklick points out, baseball and its institutions enabled people to "associate . . . themselves with cherished people who came before and after them; and . . . enabled men and women to give their lives a deeper significance by joining them to matters of consequence [e.g., a pennant race or a no-hitter]. The integrity of the[ir] souls depended on a semisacred collection of beliefs, handed-down stories, and recollections."[18]

For many men the game of their youth was not just a memory, since they continued to play competitively as adults. In Chicago, for example, there were 194 teams in the Inter-City Association, all of which played at least once a week. They included leagues of businessmen (bankers, jewelers, druggists, wholesale milliners) and religious groups (presbyterians, Columbian Knights, christian church members). There were also twenty high-caliber semipro teams whose Sunday games averaged about 1,000 spectators. By 1905 some contests drew as many as 7,000. In 1906 there were 400 teams, including those in youth associations, such as the West Side Sunday School League. Three years later there were over 550 registered amateur teams and twenty-six semiprofessional clubs. Neighborhood papers and the major dailies gave some coverage to the semipros and occasionally published box scores of the top amateur games. One old-timer estimated that toward the end of the decade, notable semipro matches played by the black Leland Giants and the Logan Squares drew over 15,000 on Saturday and Sunday mornings.[19]

Baseball was said to be well suited to the American lifestyle because it was an exhilarating game that took under two hours to complete and thus did not prevent fans from a full day's work. By comparison, the British game of cricket, the first popular American team sport, was so leisurely that it sometimes took days to complete. Cricket was perceived as more consonant with the pretensions of a leisured aristocracy than the aspirations of bourgeois Americans.[20]

The timelessness of baseball may have seemed troublesome to middle-class Victorians for whom time was money, but games were played relatively rapidly. On the other hand, it may have been appealing to fans who were uncomfortable with the imposition of time-work discipline at their workshops and factories.

The national pastime was praised by people from all walks of life, including such prominent figures as Cardinal Gibbons and William Howard Taft, who wanted to identify themselves with this popular and prominent mass institution. The president, whose brother, Charles P. Taft, was an important investor in major league clubs, was quoted in *Baseball Magazine:* "Baseball takes people into the open air—it draws out millions of factory hands, of tradesmen and interior laborers of all kinds, who spend their afternoons whenever possible in a healthful, genuinely inspiring contest in the warm sunshine and fresh air, when many other sports and in fact all natural tendencies conspire to keep them indoors engaged in various kinds of unwholesome and unhealthful pastimes."[21] Famed Boston rabbi and ethical culturist Charles Fleischer enjoyed going to games so that he could get out of the office and into fresh air and a community of his "fellow beings." Furthermore, "the game itself is so keen, so clean-cut, so complex, so scientific, that the pleasure of watching it is like that derived from observing the interplay of vast and complex machinery, but in this case incalculably more admirable because carried out by the cooperating men, and as a rule, by superb specimens of physical manhood."[22]

The Social Functions of Baseball

A crucial reason for baseball's expanded popularity was that the public identified it with certain basic American concepts. This resulted from owners' and sportswriters' public relations campaigns to improve the sport's image and combat competition from other amusements. Both groups cared about the success of baseball because they were fans and because their personal careers depended upon it. Proponents sought to demonstrate that besides providing entertainment, baseball was not a frivolous misuse of valuable time, but benefited the broader society.

Baseball was portrayed as a valuable vehicle to promote community integration because it supposedly instilled civic pride in fans. Club owners took advantage of traditional urban rivalries and the booster spirit to generate attention and affection for hometown teams. This localism was especially ardent if the team succeeded in a league deemed appropriate for the city's perceived status. Fans equated the team's fate on the diamond with their own success or failure. Furthermore, they rooted for the local stalwarts to defeat out-of-town opponents, or, in large metropolises, teams from different sections of town, to defend their community's honor. This was a highly satisfactory, albeit temporary, way to resolve interurban and intraurban rivalries. When teams were composed of amateurs who lived in the regions they represented, localism was a reasonable emotion, but after the demise of the National Association of Professional Base Ball Players, which lasted from 1871 to 1875, and the loosely organized Interstate League (1877–79), few professionals came from the towns in which they played.[23]

Dispassionate commentators argued that it was irrational for spectators to get overly excited about a team composed of mercenaries from elsewhere who might be traded at any moment to a rival and thus transformed overnight from hero to villain. *New York Times* editorials repeatedly decried the principle of localism:

> It has often enough been pointed out that it is quite absurd that there should be any local patriotism around about baseball. The players are mercenaries who make no pretense of playing for anything but money, and who play where they are paid best. So that the team which local patriotism requires the local patriot to cheer for one season may require him to execrate the next. Nevertheless, local patriotism is at the bottom of the business which baseball has come to be, and is the sentiment to which the managers appeal.[24]

Yet the *New York Times* could decide that it was worthwhile to solicit local pride for local ball clubs: "We hold that anything whatsoever that can excite local pride of New York is so far a good thing. For local pride is much the same as public spirit, which at least cannot exist without it, and there is no city in the world that is more deficient in public spirit than New York, or that ought to welcome anything that tends to stimulate that quality."[25] The editors felt that sports fans were about the only enthusiastic, civic-minded people around, but unfortunately fans wasted their energies yelling at mercenary athletes instead of seeking municipal improvements.[26]

The local baseball franchise was regarded by the public as a reliable index of a town's status. A city was not seen as much of an urban area unless it had a professional nine, and furthermore, it should be in the best league possible. If the team was in an association with larger cities, that was taken as a sign of its progressive and growing character. However, if the club was in a league that included smaller cities, then the town might be seen as stagnant and backward.

Smaller cities with few notable attractions relied on their baseball teams, often their only readily identifiable local institutions, to publicize their communities. Results of local games were reported in national sports weeklies and occasionally in the sports pages of leading newspapers across the country. For example, the *San Antonio News* recommended that local folk support the ball club: "Purely as a matter of advertising . . . whether one has any love for base ball or not, . . . a base ball team is the cheapest advertisement any city can have. . . . Reports of . . . games are telegraphed all over the country, and the constant keeping of a city's name before the people of a nation, as is done by a ball team, has an effect that can scarcely be estimated."[27] The publicity a franchise obtained for the hometown was important because it was expected to attract business and trade, lure new inhabitants, and consequently raise property values.

Atlanta baseball owed a great deal to the booster spirit that pervaded the Gate City, a community whose population quadrupled between 1870 and 1900. Atlanta's team was a charter member of the Southern League, organized in 1885 by booster Henry Grady, editor of the *Atlanta Constitution*, the league's first president. His goals were to provide recreation for Atlantans and prove that the New South cities had matured as reflected in their ability to support professional baseball. There was also the potential for developing a local institution around which a sense of community could be developed. Civic pride in Atlanta's team manifested itself through local ownership, public support at the box office, and pennants in the first two seasons. Except for 1902–5, when Abner Powell of New Orleans owned the Crackers, the franchise was always controlled by local interests. Atlantans resented foreign control, ardently believing that profits should remain at home.[28]

Community support in the Gate City was reflected by crowd sizes, particularly on opening day. The Southern Association annually awarded a trophy to the franchise with the largest opening day attendance, and the city's white community made a special effort to win the cup. Interurban railroads offered excursion rates and local transportation lines made special stops. Mayors frequently declared half-holidays for municipal workers so they could go to the game, while such companies as Coca-Cola, the city's most powerful corporation, closed its plant for the day and gave away tickets. Businesses that released their workers to attend were cited by the press. The Crackers won the attendance trophy several times even though it was far from the largest city in the league, an indication to townsfolk that their hometown was the most progressive and prosperous city in the South.[29]

The Crackers were almost universally regarded as a fine advertisement for Atlanta. In 1895, as the team departed on a western road trip, the *Atlanta Constitution* remarked, "Every member of the team will not only be a marked advertisement for the Gate City of the South, but everyone will be a walking sign depicting the push, the nerve and the energy of the state house town of the Empire state of the South." In 1906, when the club's president, Walthal Joyner, was elected mayor, he continued to travel with the ball club. "My purpose is to work for the good of Atlanta," he explained, "and I think I can do more good encouraging the home team to do some pennant winning than I can by sitting in my office at City Hall."[30] Local business leaders demanded a winning team. The chamber of commerce president commented during one losing season: "It is extremely unfortunate that a city holding the position that Atlanta does in the south should be more represented throughout this country by a tail-end team. The advertising that a city gets by supporting a winning team is of more importance than is commonly supposed. A tail-end team, on the other hand, casts a decided reflection on the city it represents."[31]

The prestige and reputation of leading metropolitan areas were also affected by their professional clubs, although less so than those of smaller towns were, since large cities had more well-known institutions and accomplishments. Detroit had no major league franchise from 1889 until 1901, and many local folk felt that hurt its prestige. The absence of major league teams in Baltimore, Buffalo, and Milwaukee after 1902 was considered a bad reflection on those cities as well.[32] Between 1903 and 1952, however, only ten cities had major league clubs. Boston, Chicago, Philadelphia, and St. Louis had two major league teams each, but only New York had three, which certified its stature as the leading American city.

Journalists writing in general circulation periodicals contributed to the baseball mythology by trying to convince their middle-class readership of the social functions of baseball. At a time when professional baseball was at its zenith, they wanted to explain and justify the sudden surging interest in the game. As Allen Sangree wrote in 1907, "A tonic, an exercise, a safety valve, baseball is second only to death as a leveler. So long as it remains our national game, America will abide no monarchy, and anarchy will be slow."[33] Six years later, *American Magazine* asserted, "Baseball has given our public a fine lesson in commercial morals. It is a well paying business . . . for it must be above suspicion. Nobody dreams of crookedness or shadiness in baseball. . . . Some day all business will be reorganized and conducted by baseball standards."[34]

The baseball creed was a product of the ideology of sport that emerged in the Jacksonian era, which justified sport and physical culture as useful and moral activities that promoted good health, sound morals, and an honorable character. Prior to the Civil War, the *Detroit Free Press* described baseball as a "healthy exercise counteracting the growing tendency to visit saloons and other places of resort with which [Detroit] abounds, thus saving them [fans] from early immorality." By the late 1860s, the game's ability to teach such Victorian values as thrift, sobriety, virtue, and hard work was widely recognized, and this realization encouraged business leaders to organize company teams and give players time off for practice and matches. Bosses also expected the formation of teams would improve worker loyalty and publicize their companies.[35]

The typical middle-class Victorian man worked hard, remained faithful to his wife, and provided well for his family. In antebellum America, most middle-income men were independent farmers, small business owners, or artisans. However, as society bureaucratized in the late nineteenth century and middle-class workers lost their autonomy and feelings of accomplishment, they often turned to sport to demonstrate their physical prowess and masculinity and to escape Victorian confinement. They were concerned about their courage, loss of sexual identity, and the perception of the feminization of mass culture. Baseball provided a means for middle-class men to prove their masculinity, which they could not demonstrate by working at physically demanding jobs. Baseball had been recognized as a manly sport since the 1860s, when rule changes had made playing more difficult (particularly the fly out rule of 1863 that required fly balls to be caught before bouncing to count as an out). Furthermore, as baseball became increasing competitive, it required considerable courage to bat against a hard-throwing pitcher or to guard a base against a speedy runner bearing down with sharpened spikes. In the 1880s, Henry Chadwick described the game in the military grammar of the post–Civil War era (pitcher and catcher constituted the "battery"; the team captain was "the commander of the field") and identified it with martial characteristics. At the turn of the century, however, the more violent game of football was recognized as the moral equivalent of war and thus *the* manly game.[36]

The most penetrating and comprehensive essay of this period analyzing baseball was H. Addington Bruce's "Baseball and the National Life," published in *Outlook* in 1913. A nationally renowned journalist who had authored several books on psychology and other subjects, Bruce discussed with considerable clarity and insight most of baseball's alleged latent functions. Bruce was primarily concerned with identifying the sport as a source of tension management—the widely accepted concept that baseball was a safety valve dated back at least to the 1880s—and as a factor in molding youngsters.[37]

Bruce argued that since most city dwellers worked long and arduous hours in boring, repetitive jobs, they needed an opportunity to relax and relieve themselves of built-up aggressions that might otherwise be directed toward their families or employers:

> An instinctive resort to sport [was] a method of gaining momentary relief from the strain of an intolerable burden, and at the same time finding a harmless outlet for pent-up emotions, which unless thus gaining expression, might discharge themselves in a dangerous way. . . .
> Baseball, then, from the spectator's standpoint, is to be regarded as a means of catharsis, or perhaps better, as a safety-valve. And it performs this service the more readily because of the appeal it makes to the basic instincts, with resultant removal of the inhibitions that ordinarily cause tenseness and restraint.[38]

Bruce and his contemporaries believed that baseball helped fans relax and forget about the rigors of daily life and relieved the pressures attending great public crises. During World War I, baseball's proponents argued that play should continue so that stress and strain on the home front could be alleviated. Frederick C. Lane, editor of *Baseball Magazine*, and others such as William Lyon Phelps, a literary critic and Yale professor, wrote that the country was tired of war news and that readers usually turned first to the sports pages to help them forget the calamities of the day.[39]

A second function Bruce attributed to baseball was its improvement of players' and spectators' character. He argued that baseball developed traits that would be important in the business of life, including fair-mindedness, honesty, judgment, patience, quick thinking, self-control, and temperance. Furthermore, the sport encouraged the development of traits that would eventually benefit the entire nation, such as respect for authority, self-sacrifice, and teamwork. These sentiments were echoed by Henry S. Curtis, a playground movement leader, in the *Journal of Education* (1916) and in the report of the 1920 Chicago grand jury investigating the connections between baseball and gambling. Baseball became closely identified with the idea of team spirit, a concept that was vitally important in an increasingly bureaucratic society. The sport was often used as a metaphor by people discussing cooperation. For instance, when Warren G. Harding was campaigning for the presidency in 1920, he delivered a speech on 2 September entitled "Team Play" that castigated President Woodrow Wilson's individualistic handling of foreign affairs, promising that if elected to employ collective methods instead.[40]

Young men were supposedly taught to become better people by watching and playing baseball and by emulating the conduct of professionals. Ballplayers encountered a myriad of situations requiring quick decisions, learned to sacrifice to help their team win, and were taught to accept the authority of the umpire. Boys and other spectators learned to be competitive but also to be good sports. The historian Neil Harris argues that spectators' ability to learn to subordinate their intense desire for victory "into a regularized code of behavior, indicated the possibilities of self-restraint in a divided society." While umpires were often the target of abuse from disgruntled fans, the crowds seldom interfered with games, especially by the late 1900s.[41]

Boys were fed a pabulum about baseball in the formula-ridden juvenile baseball fiction that was enormously popular at the turn of the century. These texts, like many other children's books, taught the importance of such values as pluck, "clean living" (no smoking or drinking), loyalty, fair play, modesty, hard work, and resiliency. The big breakthrough for baseball in boy's literature began in 1896 when Gilbert Patten's Frank Merriwell stories first appeared in the 5-cent *Tip Top Weekly* that sold over 500,000 copies a week. Merriwell was an all-around superstar at Yale, who stood up for the right of the weak, led a virtuous life, was always an honorable sportsman, and invariably led his team to victory with an extraordinary play in the bottom of the ninth or the last minute of the fourth quarter. Over 200 Merriwell books were eventually published, and 125 million copies circulated. Nearly as successful in this genre as Patten was Ralph Henry Barbour, whose 150 titles emphasized physical prowess, morality, and fair play. Barbour's vision of future success depended upon traditional values learned on the playing field.[42]

Boys were encouraged to imitate the play and behavior of their idols. The progressive *Outlook* reported in 1912 that professionals had a "thoroughly wholesome" influence on boys, who were inspired to play "proficiently." The pros were reportedly clean-living men since such deportment was indispensable for continued success. Naive youths were misled by pulp novelists and an obsequious press into believing that all players upheld traditional Christian values, while in reality some—like Bugs Raymond, Rube Waddell, and, later, Babe Ruth—were remarkable cases of dissipation. Ty Cobb was a crude misanthrope who fought with players, fans, and friends. Giants pitcher Bugs Raymond used his time in the bullpen to trade balls with fans for beer. When Manager John McGraw placed guards there to prevent this, Raymond lowered a rope and bucket from the clubhouse to a waiting confederate, who filled it at a nearby saloon. It was not unusual for players to suffer from venereal disease—one team alone had five players with gonorrhea—but newspapers would report that the players had been stricken by other ailments, such as malaria or rheumatism.[43]

Babe Ruth was the outstanding hero of the 1920s and perhaps the greatest player of all time. His success came naturally, unlike Cobb, a fierce competitor who worked hard and thought fast. Ruth grew up as a wayward child in Baltimore, and his parents sent him off at seven to St. Mary's Industrial School for Boys, a combination orphanage and reformatory. He developed into a great athlete and made his first appearance in the majors as a pitcher for the Boston Red Sox at age nineteen in 1914. Belying our image of him from later in his career, the young Ruth was 6'2", slender, and muscular at 198 pounds. He went 65-33 with a 2.02 ERA during his first three full years in the majors (1915–17), including 9 shutouts in 1916 (setting an AL record for lefthanders) and led the AL with a 1.75 ERA. But his skills were hardly limited to pitching. He was one of the fastest men on the Red Sox and their most powerful batter. In 1919 when Ruth played the outfield full-time, he hit a record 29 homers. Ruth was traded one year later to the Yankees and hit 54 homers, more than any entire major league club during the season. During his tenure with the Yankees he was a man of legendary accomplishments and consumption. In an era of low taxes, he earned about $3 million from baseball and outside endeavors. Ruth epitomized anti-Victorian standards of behavior, enjoying immediate gratification and excesses with food, liquor, and women.[44]

In contrast to these dissolute ballplayers, the athlete who especially represented Victorian ideals was tall, blond, college-educated Christy Mathewson of the New York Giants, winner of 373 games, the most in NL history up to that time. Matty was an outstanding moral hero and the model for Lester Chadwick's Baseball Joe stories. Considered the ideal Christian gentleman, Mathewson was often called upon to speak to youth organizations on clean living and fair play. "Big Six" was extremely competitive and successful at everything he tried, ranging from checkers to poker. Mathewson started playing baseball at the YMCA and never pitched on the sabbath because of his strong religious beliefs. Matty first gained athletic fame at Bucknell College, where he played baseball and football, was president of his class, and married his college sweetheart.[45]

When Mathewson got to the majors he did not fit in with his working-class teammates, who found him conceited and morally overbearing.

However, he soon won them over. Catcher Chief Meyers remembered: "How we loved to play for him! We'd break our necks for that guy. If you made an error behind him or anything of that sort, he'd never get mad or sulk. He'd come over and pat you on the back." Mathewson won 20 games in his first full season in 1901, and then 94 over the next three seasons. In the 1905 World Series he won 3 games, all shutouts. Matty was renowned for his "fade-away" (screwball) and exceptional control. He once pitched 68 straight innings without a single walk. When Mathewson's playing days ended, he managed the Cincinnati Reds for 2.5 years, resigning during World War I to become a captain in the army's Chemical Warfare Division. Mathewson's lungs were severely injured after the armistice, when he inhaled poison gas while inspecting German trenches, and subsequently contracted tuberculosis. John McGraw appointed him assistant manager of the Giants, and in 1923 he was appointed president of the Boston Braves.[46] When he died two years later, Matty was eulogized in newspapers and magazines across the country. *Commonweal* remembered him thus: "Certainly no other pitcher ever loomed so majestically in young minds, quite overshadowing George Washington and his cherry tree or even the transcendent model of boyhood, Frank Merriwell. . . . Such men have a very real value above and beyond the achievements of brawn and sporting skill. They realize and typify in a fashion the ideal of sport—clean power in the hands of a clean and vigorous personality."[47]

According to conventional wisdom, baseball was a panacea for the problems of American youths. Yet there were a few critics. Norman W. Bingham argued in *The Book of Athletics and Out-of-Door Sports* (1895) that boys overemphasized sports while neglecting academics and intellectual and moral abilities and he singled out baseball for promoting trickery and dishonesty. He was seconded by the noted progressive educator George Counts, who blamed baseball for a decline in morality and criticized it for teaching that stealing was good. Finally the psychologist Mary Brownell astutely pointed out in 1925 that "there is nothing inherent in the activity of baseball which *in itself* would make a participant develop along social, physical or mental lines. One can be made a cheat and a poor sport just as well as one can develop the desirable character traits." According to these critics, making juvenile delinquents into avid baseball fans and players did not automatically produce better citizens with improved characters.[48]

The third theme Bruce discussed was the democratizing value of baseball. The sport was regarded as a wonderful leveler of people. "The spectator at a ball game is no longer a statesman, lawyer, broker, doctor, merchant, or artisan," Bruce explained, "but just a plain everyday man."[49] Sportswriters were continually pointing out that ballplayers and fans were drawn from all levels of society and that spectators mingled together on equal terms. Edward B. Moss, sports editor of the *New York Sun*, wrote in *Harper's Weekly*, "Businessmen and professional men forget their standing in the community and shoulder to shoulder with the street urchin 'root' frantically for the hit needed to win the game." Hugh Fullerton examined crowds in the nation's capital and found "the Cabinet, Supreme Court, and Senate touch elbows with department clerks and discuss plays with porters and bartenders."[50]

The democratic character of the baseball crowd at ballparks and sandlots was considered a means to promote a sense of community in the distended cities. Jane Addams applauded the popularity of Saturday sandlot ball games in Chicago when it seemed that all the menfolk were enjoying themselves watching baseball and forgetting about their problems:

> The enormous crowd of cheering men and boys are talkative, good-natured, full of the holiday spirit, and absolutely released from the grind of life. They are lifted out of their individual affairs and so fused together that a man cannot tell whether it is his own shout or another's that fills his ears; whether it is his own coat or another's that he is wildly waving to celebrate a victory. He does not call the stranger who sits next to him his "brother" but he unconsciously embraces him in an overwhelming outburst of kindly feeling when the favorite player makes a home run. Does not this contain a suggestion of the undoubted power of public recreation to bring together all classes of a community in the modern city unhappily so full of devices for keeping men apart?[51]

The fourth and final latent function Bruce analyzed was baseball's contribution to public health. Theodore Roosevelt's strenuous life theory struck a chord with progressive reformers at the turn of the century. They promoted physical culture through the small parks and playground movements, offering clean, healthy, adult-supervised recreation to inner-city youths. Playing baseball was considered an ameliorative activity and a sound alternative to escapist entertainment at saloons, amusement parks, and cheap theaters. Participants would learn discipline and respect for figures of authority and be kept out of trouble.[52]

But how could professional baseball, a spectator sport, contribute to the physical well-being of fans, who sat in the stands watching players work? Baseball's proponents claimed that "a fairly large proportion of the people who pay for the support of the professional clubs play the game themselves to the benefit of the national health and the development of the national muscle."[53] Furthermore, they contended that the mere presence of fans at ball games contributed to health. As Bruce indicated, "it is a psychological commonplace that pleasurable emotions, especially if they find expression in laughter, shouts, cheers, and other muscle expanding noises, have a tonic value to the whole bodily system. So that it is quite possible to get exercise vicariously as it were; and the more stimulating the spectacle that excites feelings of happiness and enjoyment, the greater will be the resultant good. Most decidedly baseball is a game well-designed to render this excellent service."[54] This weak logic was supported by a 1914 report in the *New York Medical Journal* indicating that many physicians believed a man's health was improved merely by sitting out in the fresh air, shouting at the top of his lungs, and waving his arms in excitement. These doctors found such exercise sufficient for the typical male adult and doubted that his well-being could be significantly affected by participating in sports, since that merely developed his inherited capacities without creating new ones.[55]

Another social function journalists frequently attributed to professional baseball was its ability to acculturate the children of new immigrants. Baseball was said to be second only to the public schools as a teacher of American mores to immigrant children. Young boys were far more interested in American customs and habits than their parents, and observers rightly believed that they were receptive to baseball's appeal. It was a common sight to see kids playing stickball on city streets, using a rubber ball and a broomstick for their equipment. The respected sportswriter Hugh Fullerton wrote, "Baseball, to my way of thinking, is the greatest single force working for Americanization. No other game appeals so much to the foreign-born youngsters and nothing, not even the schools, teaches the American spirit so quickly, or inculcates the idea of sportsmanship or fair play as thoroughly."[56] Fullerton cited correspondence from Chicago settlement house workers in a Czech-Jewish neighborhood: "We consider baseball one of the best means of teaching our boys American ideas and ideals." Schools, YMCAs, and other youth agencies used baseball to ameliorate urban problems. In 1904, for example, the Chicago public schools made adult-supervised ballplaying a centerpiece of elementary physical education.[57]

Merely playing baseball, however, did not necessarily promote structural assimilation because youths often played on teams sponsored by church groups, fraternal organizations, and single ethnic associations

like Chicago's Polish League, founded in 1913 to promote ethnic identification and counter assimilationist trends. When French Canadians in
the predominantly francophone industrial town of Woonsocket, Rhode
Island, became baseball fans in the 1890s, their ethnic identification did
not weaken. They read box scores in the local French-language newspaper to follow their hero, Napoleon Lajoie, the premier second baseman
of the early 1900s, and when local francophone teams played Anglo nines,
players often gave signals in French. Baseball could be as much a means of
promoting ethnic pride and cultural pluralism as Americanization.[58]

The theory of baseball's latent functions strongly appealed to mainstream, middle-class Americans because it touched base with their own
beliefs, values, and social needs. Playing and watching the game seemed
to provide a progressive education, enabling children to learn from life
experiences and not merely from rote memorization. Furthermore, as
Kuklick points out, contests provided many fans with "their only experience of physical contest and victory, of valor and endurance, of grace
under pressure and dignity in defeat."[59] Professional baseball was welcomed as a moral, healthful recreation for hard-working men. The sport
demonstrated the apparent reality of the fundamental American ideal of
democracy and reassured old stock Americans of the relevance of their
rural-based value system in a modern world. The national pastime purportedly taught traditional qualities such as individualism, yet simultaneously instructed participants and audiences in the newer trait of teamwork, a quality vital for success in a bureaucratized society. Baseball
resolved for many Americans the apparent paradox of team play and
individualism by showing that winning squads got their nine players to
work together as a unit—exemplified by the hit and run, the sacrifice
bunt, and the double play—while taking advantage of individual talents
to achieve the collective goal of victory.

Baseball Crowds

The baseball ideology claimed that people from all segments of society
attended baseball games, where they participated in the rituals of the
sport and enjoyed a rare opportunity to mingle. Judges supposedly rubbed
shoulders with bootblacks, merchants with bakers, and so on. In reality
classes rarely intermingled since the audience was divided up by price
differentiated seats, but the national pastime did attract the broadest
audience of the major spectator sports, and crowds included people of all
ages, ethnicities, races, genders, and classes. As one St. Louis journalist
claimed in 1883:

A glance at the audience on any fine day at the ball park will reveal the presence of representatives of all respectable classes. Telegraph operators, printers who work at night, traveling men who go out on the road at nightfall, men of leisure, . . . men of capital, bank clerks who get away at 3 P.M., real estate men who can steal the declining hours of the afternoon, barkeepers with night watches before them, hotel clerks, actors and employees of the theaters, policemen and firemen on their day off, strangers in the city killing time, clerks and salesmen temporarily out of work, steamboat captains, clerks and mates, merchants in a position to leave their stores with a notice to the bookkeeper that they will not be back today, call board operators who need recreation after the experience of the noon hour, baseball players, semi-professional and amateur, workingmen with the lame hand, butchers, bakers, candlestick makers, mechanics out on strike, lawyers in droves, an occasional judge, city officials, . . . and . . . doctors.[60]

Journalists repeatedly harped on the democratic character of the crowds, frequently pointing out the variety of people they saw and the assortment of accents overheard at ballparks. Baseball provided a focus for the development of a community of fans. Artists' sketches drawn in the late nineteenth century indicated that fans were drawn from all ethnic and social backgrounds.[61] Yet in the crowd description above there is no mention of factory workers, unskilled workers, African Americans, or women. The cost of tickets, accessibility of ballparks, game times in the mid- or late afternoon, and the infrequency of Sunday games meant that most spectators at the turn of the century were white native-born male white-collar workers. "The wonder to a man who works for a living," mused a New York reporter in 1887, "is how so many people can spare the time for the sport. They are obliged to leave their offices downtown at 2 or 3 o'clock in order to get to the Polo Grounds in time."[62]

White-collar workers had higher incomes and worked shorter hours than manual workers and could more readily vary their schedules to accommodate their recreational interests. Furthermore, by 1890 white-collar employees were commonly working just a half-day on Saturdays. Better paid manual workers could afford to go to games, but the absence of Sunday ball in many cities and the daytime start of games made it difficult for them to attend unless they worked unusual shifts, took off from work, or were laid off or unemployed, yet could still afford a ticket. The elite *Boston Evening Transcript* in 1887 accurately identified the baseball crowd as composed of "the merchant and banker, the salesman, clerk and office boy, the contractors and his men and boys on Saturday half holidays [and] even women and girls by the hundreds."[63]

Middle-Class Fans

Baseball was from its earliest days primarily a middle-class sport. The first well-known club was the New York Knickerbockers, an upper middle-class social club, founded in 1842, and led by Alexander Cartwright, who in 1845 codified the rules of the sport. By the mid-1850s when there were about a dozen teams in New York and Brooklyn, three-fourths of the players were white-collar, equally divided between high- and low-level nonmanual workers, and the rest were skilled workers. As the sport boomed in metropolitan New York before the Civil War, and afterward spread elsewhere, players remained predominantly middle class, though increasingly artisan. Few players were of lower socioeconomic origins, even in industrial Newark, where only a small proportion (6.5 percent) of ball club members were semiskilled or unskilled workers. Amateur baseball clubs did not originate in high status communities, but were associations of future-oriented, hard-working, respectable men, known as the baseball fraternity, who joined teams to gain a sense of self-worth and of community (certified by the wearing of uniforms), important for residents of dynamic urban centers undergoing unprecedented social changes. These men enjoyed the excitement and exercise of playing a rational, competitive game, the opportunity to demonstrate prowess (becoming more difficult at the workplace for clerks and artisans), and the camaraderie offered by team sports, which included the sociability of postgame drinking and dining.[64]

Spectators at the earliest games were usually friends of players, but as the sport gained popularity, matches in Brooklyn between top clubs would draw a few thousand fans. In 1858 a ten-cent admission plus an additional parking fee was charged for the first time for a three-game all-star series between Brooklyn and New York at the Fashion Race Course in Long Island. Within two years major games were drawing from five thousand to ten thousand spectators, encouraging William H. Cammeyer, a reputed associate of Tammany boss William Tweed, in 1862 to convert his Williamsburg ice-skating rink in Brooklyn into the enclosed fifteen-hundred-seat Union Grounds at a cost of twelve hundred dollars. He rented it for free to the city's most prominent nines, charging spectators a dime. Ticket prices increased to a quarter in 1867, and doubled three years later for important contests like the Brooklyn Atlantics versus the Cincinnati Red Stockings. The higher fees went toward compensating players and promoters, improving facilities for the comfort of middle- and upper middle-class men, and discouraging lower-class spectators, who were considered too rowdy. The 1860 championship game between the Atlantics and the Excelsiors had to be stopped because the former's working-class supporters abused the umpire and the opponents. However, George Kirsch found that building enclosed stands and charging admission fees did not halt unruly behavior outside the ballpark or even inside, where fans got into fights, interfered with play, drank, gambled, and shouted derogatory epithets when the game did not go their way.[65]

Baseball lagged behind the performing arts, which had restrained audiences by segmenting spectators at musical and theatrical entertainment into high and mass culture groups and teaching proper conduct. This was far more difficult to do for spectator sports, particularly those that catered to the single male subculture. Baseball tried to polish its fans without destroying such boisterous, clean fun like cheering for the home team and booing visitors and the umpire. Management drew the line at rowdyism, which harmed the game's public image and deterred many potential fans. Disorderly fans were presumed to be lower-class spectators, although that was not always the case.[66]

When the NL was founded in 1876, owners vigorously encouraged the patronage of the "respectable classes," who had the leisure time to attend games and the money to afford the high admission fee, partly designed to keep out the lower classes, who management believed had not internalized such bourgeois norms as discipline and civility. Teams were required to bar liquor sales and provide police to preserve order and prevent gambling. The league originally eschewed Sunday baseball because owners thought that the middle classes would not patronize baseball if it defiled the sabbath. Albert Spalding was convinced that these policies worked and that his team's "audiences are composed of the best class of people in Chicago, and no theater, church, or place of amusement contains a finer class of people than can be found in our grandstands."[67]

Club owners tried various schemes to encourage middle-class enthusiasm, such as leaving passes for politicians, prominent businessmen, and clergymen; organizing ladies' days; telephoning suburbanites to advise them of field conditions; and discouraging unruly behavior. Magnates hoped to promote the sport by attracting clergymen and women spectators, whose presence might alleviate fears of disorderly crowds, gambling, and heckling and inspire a higher level of behavior among players and spectators. Consequently, clerics in nearly every town received season passes, and in the early 1900s the New York Giants reportedly distributed about 150 passes to religious leaders.[68]

Female spectators were not regarded as knowledgeable about the game, and men often resented their presence as intruders into their sphere and as nuisances whose hats obstructed the view of fans seated behind them. However, owners supported their presence in an attempt to curb crowd behavior, enhance business by inducing men to escort them to the game, and possibly improve the quality of play. Club executives made special efforts to modernize their facilities so that women could sit in clean, comfortable seats, be protected from vulgarity and harassment, and thereby enjoy the game and want to return. Security was bolstered, women's restrooms with attendants were provided, and certain grand-stand sections were often set aside for women and their companions. In Cincinnati a series of enclosed steps were built in the park leading from the carriage area directly to the grandstand so women could bypass the boisterous crowds on the way to their seats.[69]

The ladies' day custom derived from a tradition originated by the Knickerbockers, who in 1867 set aside the last Thursday of every month to invite their wives, sweethearts, or daughters to the field. When the NL began in 1876, women were admitted free any day when escorted by a man. This policy was soon discontinued, though women could still buy tickets at special rates. In 1883 the practice of ladies' day was introduced to bolster attendance and improve the status of the sport. Arrangements differed from town to town, but most teams admitted a woman for free or for a token payment on selected dates, typically Thursdays, when es-corted by a man. In St. Louis in 1883, fifteen hundred women were re-portedly in the grandstands each Thursday, while Saturday was ladies' day in Louisville. The Brooklyn Grays made all dates in 1885 and in 1889 ladies' day except Sunday and holiday games. In 1897 the Washington Senators tried to take advantage of handsome pitcher Winnie Mercer's popularity with women to increase attendance of female fans by ad-mitting them free to one game Mercer started. Unfortunately, after the fifth inning he was thrown out of the game by umpire Bill Carpenter, who was attacked after the contest by female spectators, while other women ripped out seats and broke windows. Carpenter was escorted away by the players and left the ballpark in disguise. This marked the end of ladies' day in Washington.[70]

Most minor leagues also made special provisions to encourage female spectators. In late nineteenth-century Atlanta, women were admitted free to the grounds and charged twenty-five cents for grandstand seats. After the Southern Association was established in 1901, every team ex-cept Shreveport had ladies' days. Women were admitted free every day in three cities, and in Atlanta and Nashville a one-dollar season pass entitled women to grandstand seats at twenty-five predesignated games. The system was so popular in Atlanta that in 1908 nearly one thousand women took advantage of ladies' days on Tuesdays and Fridays.[71]

By 1900 middle-class women were attending ball games throughout the United States. Press accounts of opening day festivities commonly remarked on the presence of women. They usually sat in the grandstands or box seats, but almost never in the bleachers near lower-class fans.[72]

Women's interest in baseball was reflected by a song written in 1908 by Jack Norworth and Albert Von Tilzer entitled "Take Me Out to the Ball Game." Neither one had ever attended a major league game, but they captured its spirit well. Baseball fans today are familiar with the refrain, which many assume is about a boy who wants to see a ball game. The long-forgotten verses actually told the story of a young Irish woman whose boyfriend wanted to take her out on a date to a show. However, Katie preferred the ballpark, where she felt completely at home. There she could fully participate in the rituals of the game—rooting for the hometown players, whom she knew by sight, and munching on peanuts and Cracker Jack. The song, sung by Norworth's wife, the renowned Nora Bayes, became a big hit among sheet music buyers.

Take Me Out to the Ball Game

Katie Casey was baseball mad,
Had the fever and had it bad;
Just to root for the home town crew,
ev'ry sou Katie blew.
On a Saturday, her young beau
Called to see if she'd like to go,
To see a show but Miss Katie said "no,
I'll tell you what you can do:

Chorus:
Take me out to the ball game,
Take me out to with the crowd.
Buy me some peanuts and Cracker Jack,
I don't care if I never get back.
Let me root, root, root for the home team.
If they don't win it's a shame,
For its one, two, three strikes, you're out,
At the old ball game.

Katie Casey saw all the games
Knew the players by their first names;
Told the umpire he was wrong,
All along, good and strong.
When the score was just two to two,
Katie Casey knew what to do,
Just to cheer up the boys she knew,
She made the gang sing this song:

Chorus

In the same year George M. Cohan wrote a song entitled "Take Your Girl to the Ball Game," which further reflected the potential interest of young women in the national pastime.[73]

In 1909 the NL discontinued ladies' day, claiming that women were sufficiently interested to pay their own way, but the AL continued the practice. In 1912 the St. Louis Browns admitted escorted women on certain dates free. Some women, however, abused this privilege by asking men outside the park to act as their dates just so they could get in free. Five years later the Browns simplified the matter by letting in all women for free. The NL restored ladies' day that year and admitted women for a reduced rate or for free. Thereafter women were estimated to comprise over 10 percent of the spectators.[74]

Women utilized their interest in baseball for political purposes, invading a major province of the male subculture to promote the suffrage movement. They were emulating the behavior of the more radical British women who in 1913 burned down racetrack grandstands and interfered with races. Suffragists occasionally sponsored professional ball games to gain publicity for their cause, starting with a minor league game in Newark on 25 June 1914 at which two thousand suffragists heard the feminist Ella Reeve Bloor lecture. The regular game was preceded by a match between an all-girl and an all-boy team. The most successful suffragist games were held at New York's Polo Grounds, where reformers purchased blocks of tickets for 65 percent of the regular price and resold them at face value. A 1915 game raised about three thousand dollars for the suffrage movement and twenty-five hundred dollars for the Giants. Club owner Harry Hempstead enthusiastically recommended the venture to Cincinnati Reds president August Herrmann as a means of attracting women spectators and making money. On 3 June 1916 suffragists sponsored another game at the Polo Grounds that drew about twenty-eight thousand spectators, one-fourth of them women.[75]

Besides trying to make the sport respectable, management further appealed to the middle classes by setting the starting time of games at a convenient hour for them. They could put in a full day at the office, travel to the ballpark, enjoy a two-hour ball game, and get home in time for dinner. In Chicago, where the Board of Trade closed at 1:30 and the Stock Exchange at 2:00, starting time was 3:00, typical for most cities. Atlanta games began promptly at 2:00 until 1896, when the owners realized that was too early and pushed the starting time back to 3:30. Ball games in New York traditionally started at 4:00 to give the Wall Street crowd an hour to take public transportation north to the Polo Grounds. In 1912 the starting time was moved forward thirty minutes in response to the complaints of fans getting home late for dinner. The latest starting time was 4:30 in Washington, D.C., to allow government clerks who finished work at 4:00 to get to the local ballpark.[76]

The strong middle-class presence at ballparks is reinforced by crowd photographs that suggest a largely male, middle-class audience during the Progressive Era. Nearly all fans wore the clothing associated with white-collar workers—dark jackets and ties topped with either a derby or a straw hat.[77] Of course, dress alone is not conclusive evidence because it was customary then to dress formally in public, even at Coney Island. Blue-collar workers who could change clothes at their workplaces would probably commute while wearing jackets, although they might wear caps rather than derbies. The development of mass-produced, ready-to-wear apparel had brought the cost of a handsome suit or a lovely dress within most people's budgets. It is likely that many spectators, especially bleacherites, were manual workers outfitted in their best Sunday church-going suits. James T. Farrell, the novelist and Chicago baseball fan, remembered that when his working-class grandmother took him to a Friday ladies' day game at Comiskey Park on the South Side of Chicago, she would wear a new hat and the same black silk dress that she wore to Sunday mass.[78]

Major league baseball's best-known fans were politicians, actors, and other celebrities, whose presence was often noted in the press. Few urbanites had as much leisure time as they did, and they often spent their idle time at the local ballpark. Politicians frequently could count on passes because they were friends or business associates of club owners or because magnates wanted to assure their good will. Professional politicians regularly attended games and were such ardent fans that it was not unheard of for city council members to cut short deliberations in time to head out to the ballpark. At a game they could demonstrate their civic spirit and identify themselves with the electorate. Political figures often tossed out the symbolic first ball to start each baseball season, a tradition President Taft initiated in Washington.[79]

Actors also enjoyed ball games, and some, such as DeWolf Hopper, David Warfield, and George M. Cohan, became well acquainted with owners and ballplayers. New York magnates were only too happy to provide thespians with passes because they believed their presence would attract their own fans. The public was advised on those days when there was no matinee that their favorites would be out at the Polo Grounds.[80]

Working-Class Fans

Although professional baseball was mainly oriented toward a middle-class market, commentators insisted that the sport was also extremely popular with the lower classes, who went to games in droves and followed their local heroes in the penny press. They respected the prowess, courage, and manliness of top ballplayers. Certain writers asserted that early baseball must have been a poor man's entertainment since there were so many roughnecks and gamblers in the crowds. However, working-class men were substantially underrepresented because of their limited leisure time, the expenses of attending, and the large proportion of indigent new immigrants who were uninterested in baseball. In 1886 a leading union periodical speculated that if an eight-hour workday could be mandated, there would be greater attendance at ball games. The syndicated columnist W. I. Harris in discussing mass sympathy with the Players' League of 1890, a cooperative venture sponsored by the Brotherhood of Professional Base Ball Players, baseball's first union, pointed out that "the laboring men as a rule have more heart than money, and are really not the people who support baseball because they cannot afford to do it. On holidays they will turn out in force, but they cannot naturally be every day patrons."[81]

Manual workers' limited leisure time in the industrial era was mainly a function of their long working hours. The factory system boomed in the late nineteenth century with the introduction of costly machinery and strict supervision by bosses. Workers were forced to learn time-work discipline, regulating their life according to the dictates of the factory manager, who required employees to be present at a certain time and remain there for a prescribed workday to efficiently operate the expensive machinery. Unskilled workers labored the longest hours for the least pay.[82]

When professional baseball was organized in the 1870s, the average manufacturing employee worked about 10.5 hours a day, 6 days a week, and 20 years later the average work week still exceeded 60 hours. The load was lighter for those in the unionized trades, who toiled about 8 hours a week less than nonunionized unskilled laborers. Artisans found it difficult and unskilled personnel found it almost impossible to attend ball games unless they worked unusual hours—like bakers did—took time off from work, were unemployed, had a rare holiday, or lived in a city that permitted Sunday baseball. In 1877 Louisville's German working-class fans complained to the Grays that the 4:00 starting time interfered with their work schedule. The owners said they were sympathetic, but would not shift the starting time, which was convenient for local businessmen.[83]

Sunday was the most popular day for all fans to attend games, followed by Saturday, but Sunday ball was barred in most eastern and southern cities. The *New York Times* estimated in 1906 that one-third of the total attendance in western major league cities came on Sundays. The conventional wisdom was that the composition of sabbath crowds differed from those on weekdays because a greater proportion of spectators were from the working classes. However, the columnist W. I. Harris argued as early as 1891 that over 80 percent of Sunday spectators could afford to go during the week if they chose, and just 10 percent had only Sunday off.[84]

A study by Dean Sullivan of late nineteenth-century Cincinnati crowds suggests that the working-class proportion of Sunday audiences was only slighter higher than their representation on other days, since fans from all social backgrounds attended on Sundays in rates similar to those during the rest of the week. Between 1886 and 1888, Cincinnati's Sunday crowds were 2.9 times larger than weekday crowds. There were 3.0 times as many fans in the cheap 25-cent terrace seats, 2.8 times as many in the 40-cent pavilion, and 2.6 times as many in the 50-cent grandstand.[85]

After the turn of the century the work week for manufacturing employees declined significantly. Average hours spent working dropped from 57.5 in 1899 to 53.5 in 1914 and then to 50.4 in 1920. Artisans continued to work about 8 hours a week less than unskilled workers. By 1920, skilled employees worked 8-hour shifts, and those in the construction trades had a half holiday on Saturdays. The change in the work week and the liberalization of Sunday observance patterns provided manual laborers with more discretionary time and a greater opportunity to pursue the amusement of their choice.[86]

Along with the work week and Sunday blue laws, working-class attendance was also shaped by costs. In 1876 the NL established 50 cents as the standard price of admission. A bleacher seat cost another dime and a grandstand seat an additional quarter. The *Clipper* recommended that tickets for nonleague games be cut to 25 cents because "people cannot afford it." Owners justified high prices as necessary to pay their highly skilled players, cover other expenses, and make a profit. If fans wanted to see first-rate baseball, Harry Wright, the renowned manager of the Boston Red Stockings, had previously argued, they would have to pay for it: "A good game is worth 50 cts, a poor one is dear at 25 cts."[87]

Harold Seymour, baseball's preeminent historian, claimed that compared with other commercial amusements, baseball ticket prices were not out of line. A seat at a popular theater cost from 25 to 75 cents, and a ticket for an important lecture, 50 cents. There was a great deal of opposition to the 50-cent minimum, which was regarded as a big expense for skilled workers. In 1876 the *New York Mercury* estimated that it cost an artisan $2.47 to take a family to see the New York Mutuals play a ladies' day game at their Brooklyn field, which included the cost of transportation, tickets, and the $1.25 lost by taking a half day off. Since the average manufacturing worker earned only $427.00 in 1890, one could see why the *Chicago Times* contended that NL pricing policies meant the almost total exclusion of mechanics and laborers from baseball games. Hence, many fans had to get their sport vicariously from the press and conversations with friends at neighborhood saloons. Better-paid artisans had greater options than less-skilled workers. A typical Cincinnati artisan who headed a family of five earned $623.00 and spent about $13.00 on entertainment, primarily alcohol, which did not leave a lot for baseball. In the early 1900s low wages, underemployment, and unemployment meant that about 40 percent of families lived below the poverty level ($500.00 a year) unless several people in the family worked. As Peter Shergold has pointed out, unskilled laborers were impoverished workers "to whom leisure was sleep, to whom recreation was a half hour at the nickelodeon, or a drink in the salon after work, to whom contentment was a full pipe of tobacco or a Sunday afternoon spent gambling at cards."[88]

The demand for cheap, high-quality baseball was temporarily filled in 1882 by the creation of the American Association (AA) as a rival major league. The association was founded by beer barons and barkeepers, who saw an opportunity to enrich themselves by obtaining ball clubs and selling their products to thirsty fans. These "interlopers" introduced several important promotions, including 25-cent tickets, Sunday baseball, and the sale of alcoholic beverages. The owners planned to fill their parks by catering to the lower classes, unlike the NL, who sought middle-class fans. In its very first season, the AA outdrew the senior circuit, although gross receipts were smaller because of the cheaper prices. Before the start of the next season, these two major leagues, along with the Northwestern League, signed the National Agreement, recognizing the sanctity of each other's contracts, establishing a postseason championship series, and allowing each to set its own policies regarding admission fees and Sunday baseball.[89]

The AA survived for ten seasons until 1891, when four of its clubs merged with the NL. It had drawn well with the working classes; in 1886 and 1887, for instance, almost half (49.2 percent) of Cincinnati's crowds sat in the cheap 25-cent seats. The enlarged NL set the basic ticket price at 50 cents, although Chicago and others could sell quarter tickets if they wished. The cheap seats were distant from the playing field and were often in bad condition. A typical big league park at the turn of the century would have about 1,600 quarter seats, or about one-tenth of its capacity. This severely limited the attendance of the lower classes, especially since on holidays Pittsburgh and certain other clubs sold the cheap seats for 50 cents.[90]

The paucity of cheap seats was decried by newspapers such as the *Brooklyn Eagle,* which believed that cheap baseball would enable more people to attend games, thereby providing a broad-based community service as well as greater profits. The paper felt that cheaper and more accessible entertainments, such as saloons and vaudeville, or resorts like Coney Island had baseball at a competitive disadvantage. Not only did baseball tickets cost more but "the ball game is held on the outskirts of the town, the seats are hard, the stand is open to the wind and snow and rain, there are no reliefs of scenery or music—nothing but sandwiches and frankfurters—and no legal guarantee that a poor, spiritless show may not be given."[91] Professional baseball also competed with amateur and semiprofessional baseball. In heavily industrialized Cleveland, for instance, working-class attendance was lower than expected on Saturdays because of competition from amateurs who played at cheaper and more accessible fields than the Indians' Lake Park. On 20 September 1914 the city's amateur championship between Telling's Strollers and Gus Hanna's Street Cleaners was attended by eighty-three thousand spectators. The Indians played on Sundays beginning in 1911, but needed good teams to draw working-class fans.[92]

When the AL was founded in 1900, its standard admission fee was 25 cents. The low price policy was maintained after the AL proclaimed itself a major league until 1902, when it raised the standard minimum to 50 cents. Boston, Chicago, and Philadelphia, however, were permitted to sell quarter seats to help them compete with local NL teams. The influential *Chicago Daily News* noted, "Heretofore, the young organization has sought the favor of the public largely on the score of half rates to see as good ball as in the National League, but now that the patronage has come its way, and it has had to pay the high salaries to players, having most of the stars of the game enrolled on its teams, the magnates have decided that the time for asking the public to pay more has come."[93]

By 1910 $.50 was the standard price for a bleacher seat, $.75 for the grandstand, and $1.00 for box or reserved seats. As David Nasaw points out, at a time when other commercialized amusements, like the movies, were heading in the direction of one-price admission policies, baseball was emphasizing pricing differentials that reflected the quality of the accommodations and distance from the action. The average amount spent for a ticket between 1909 and 1916 was $.66. While one-fourth of all admissions in 1910 were at the quarter rate, only Chicago's Comiskey Park, with seven thousand bleachers seats, and Philadelphia's Shibe Park, with thirteen thousand, had more than two thousand cheap seats. President Ben Shibe of the Athletics believed that those "who live by the sweat of their brow should have as good a chance of seeing the game as the man who never had to roll up his sleeves to earn a dollar." Working-class men may have comprised the majority of spectators in the low-priced sections, but inexpensive seats were also purchased by middle-class fans like New York's Frank B. "Well, Well" Wood, an electrical engineer who preferred sitting in the bleachers.[94]

Most owners phased out the cheap sections when they built their huge new sport palaces in the period 1909–16. The new Polo Grounds, for instance, had a token two hundred quarter seats out of thirty-one thousand when it was completed in 1911, and Ebbets Field, built two years later, had just one thousand. Magnates justified their seating policies by claiming the public was willing to pay more for better seats since few spectators still sat in the bargain sections (which was not true) and because they needed additional revenue to offset higher salaries and the overhead costs of their new fire-resistant ballparks. Journalists opposed eliminating low-priced seats in an effort to protect working-class fans, whom they regarded as the backbone of the spectatorship. In 1916 when Charles Ebbets announced plans to get rid of quarter seats, he was castigated by the *Sporting News*, traditionally a mouthpiece for organized baseball, which opposed making "baseball a game for the classes and denying it to the masses."[95]

Ticket prices increased during World War I after the federal government imposed a 10 percent surcharge on admissions to all commercialized entertainments. Baseball executives at first opposed the wartime levy, but realized they could use it to boost ticket prices. The tax was just a few cents, but owners announced that handling pennies would be cumbersome for ticket clerks, and so raised prices by a nickel or a dime, pocketing the difference. The cheap seats were completely eliminated after the war. By 1920 typical prices for major league seats were $0.50 for the bleachers, $1.00 for the grandstand, $1.25 for reserved seats, and $1.65 for box seats.[96]

World Series tickets were the most expensive, averaging about $2.00 between 1903 and 1920. A typical ticket for the first series in 1903 cost just $.50, but the National Commission (the ruling body of organized baseball, composed of the league presidents and a chairman they chose together) quickly recognized the enormous popularity of this postseason event and raised prices. Tickets for the 1906 World Series in Chicago cost approximately double the normal minimum at White Sox Park ($.50 for the bleachers, $1.00 for the pavilion, $1.50 for the grandstand, and $2.00 for box seats). By 1913 series tickets were again doubled, except for box seats, which were increased by 150 percent. Fans were further chagrined when the National Commission initiated a new ticket-selling policy. Individual ticket sales at the box office were banned, and customers had to purchase tickets in blocks for all home games or purchase single tickets from brokers or scalpers. By 1920 series prices ranged from $1.10 for the bleachers to $6.60 for box seats. Such high costs and the system of selling tickets to preferred customers prevented many die-hard fans, particularly those from the working classes, from attending the postseason classic.[97]

The Behavior of Crowds

Compared with the frenzied crowds that attended boxing matches or European soccer games, baseball audiences were far less rowdy. Nonetheless, as George Kirsch has pointed out, crowd control was an important problem as far back as the 1860s. Some disorder occurred outside the park among fans milling about or jostling each other as they waited to purchase tickets, but the more serious problems resulted inside. Spectators might become nuisances by standing up in their seats or walking up and down the aisles, obstructing the view of other fans, or, even worse, getting into arguments and fights with other spectators and players. Some unruly patrons threw dangerous objects on the field or at the umpires or even rushed onto the playing field and interfered with the game. In 1904 White Sox fans were taken to task by journalists for their misbehavior at a Sunday game when they hurled seat cushions at the Athletics' catcher chasing a foul ball and "indulge[d] in making targets of the first and third basemen and outfielders, using empty pop bottles for ammunition."[98]

One of the first chaotic episodes at a professional game came in 1869 at a game between the undefeated Cincinnati Red Stockings and the Troy Haymakers, backed by team president, Tammany politician, gambler, and former American boxing champion John Morrissey. The contest was tied at 17 in the fifth inning when Troy's captain and Morrissey got into such a big argument with the umpire that the game was forfeited to the visiting Red Stockings. Cincinnati journalists blamed the affair on Morrissey, who they believed instigated a riot to halt the game and save his bets and those of his friends.[99]

Full-blown riots broke out on occasion, mainly caused by crowd reactions to umpires' unpopular decisions that "robbed" the home team. There were many episodes of violence against umpires, especially in the 1880s when umpires had not yet earned public respect. In 1882 alone, major league umpires were mobbed in ten different episodes. A popular refrain of the day began:

> Mother, may I slug the umpire
> May I slug him right away?
> So he cannot be here, Mother
> When the clubs begin to play?

Boston's team installed barbed wire around its field to increase security.[100]

The general presumption was that the rioters were lower-class fans, but Dean Sullivan found that a disturbance in Cincinnati attributed to them actually occurred in the higher-priced seats. And in Louisville, he found that upper-class "crank" organizations like the 500-strong "Rooter's Club" were just as rowdy as the "twenty-five cent men," booing the umpires and even throwing eggs one afternoon.[101]

Crowd control problems got worse before they got better, abetted by the lack of respect players gave umpires and the rowdy style of play first popularized in the 1890s by the Baltimore Orioles. In 1902, for instance, Baltimore manager John McGraw provoked hometown bleacherites to attack umpire Jack Sheridan. As late as 1910 the journalist George Nathan claimed that umpire baiting, or "killing the umpire," was an American sport, and noted 355 cases of physical molestation the year before. The worst episode occurred in 1907 when AL umpire Billy Evans almost died from a soda bottle tossed by a teenage fan. Thereafter AL president Ban Johnson made a concerted effort to protect umpires and promote security. He heavily fined abusive players and required owners to eject obnoxious fans and secure arrests of the most violent spectators. In 1911 Johnson added a second umpire to help arbitrate all games. Once players and fans were socialized to respect the authority and integrity of umpires, and enlarged ballparks put seats further from the field, crowd behavior modulated. Spectators could still see the umpires as villains and dispute their close calls ("Let's Get the Umpire's Goat" was a popular song before 1920), but when they screamed "Kill the Umpire," they no longer meant it literally.[102]

Fans learned to accept unfavorable decisions and live with defeats because they no longer had their entire worldview wrapped up with their hometown teams. The players lived in different cities (only New York had two teams in the same league), and fans were spared face-to-face confrontations. Furthermore, all baseball fans pretty much shared the same basic values and beliefs. Consequently, contests did not symbolize deep-rooted antipathies or national rivalries. Fans could sit in the stands together, argue about their heroes, chastise the umpires, and shake hands once the contest was over, far different from soccer crowds in Glasgow, Scotland, where Rangers and Celtics represented ethnic, religious, and class rivalries.[103]

Overcrowding was the other major cause of riots. In the wooden-park era, teams had no qualms about selling more tickets than they had seats and letting spectators stand in the aisles, obstructing lines of vision and means of egress. Overflow crowds, often a problem in New York on opening day, were given standing room on the playing field, where they obstructed the vision of seated patrons and occasionally interfered with the game. A riot occurred at New York's Hilltop Park on 22 April 1905 when an imprudent promotion let in fans for free. In preparation, 150 police officers were assigned to the park along with 15 fire fighters with hoses and 24 Highlander employees with buckets to protect against fire. When too many boys appeared and got into fights, the police and management decided to let in only boys with adult companions. In Chicago,

which was generally spared disorderly crowds, the most notable riot occurred at the crosstown 1906 World Series when a crowd far in excess of
White Sox Park's capacity went amok trying to get in, knocking down
sections of the fence. Order was eventually restored by over 300 uniformed and plainclothes police officers.[104]

Problems caused by overcrowding were largely solved by the construction of large modern ballparks that had sufficient seating capacities
to satisfy ticket demands and by enforcement of new fire codes that regulated overcrowding. Thus, when the Giants played the 1911 World Series
at the new Polo Grounds, the structure had sufficient seats to satisfy
ticket demands. However, seating was inadequate for a 15 August 1919
doubleheader with the league-leading Reds, which drew a full house of
thirty-eight thousand plus ten thousand who could not get in. Lines of
fans waiting for tickets extended five blocks. So many people arrived by
el that the gates leading from the station into the park had to be closed for
safety. There was considerable chaos and many fans with tickets never
got to the box office. When the crowd outside became unmanageable, police reserves were called in. The throng at one turnstile was so great that
the police allowed hundreds to jump the gate and get in without tickets.
Other fans climbed the center field fence and jumped down twenty feet
to the bleachers. At one entrance fans crashed the gates and knocked
down an iron railing onto the runway leading to the grandstand's upper
deck, causing several injuries.[105]

Ethnic and African-American Baseball

Ethnic Fans

Blue-collar fans in the late nineteenth century and lower-class fans in
the early twentieth century were presumed to be mainly of WASP origins
or else second-generation Irish or German fans who had played baseball
in their youth. The latter were usually skilled artisans, while the former included bartenders, delivery drivers, city workers, and others who
worked unusual shifts. Club owners tried to appeal to Germans' interest
in baseball by advertising in German-language newspapers and by providing beer and Sunday games in cities heavily populated by German
immigrants, like Cincinnati and St. Louis. Interest by the Irish was so
great that sportswriters gave sections of some ballparks specific names,
such as "Burkeville" at the Polo Grounds.[106]

Working-class men enjoyed taking their young sons to the ballpark as a rite of passage into boyhood, but seldom brought their wives. In the thinking of these fans, the ballpark was a bastion of manhood, and women belonged at home, not in the manly sphere of sport. James T. Farrell recalled growing up as a poor Irish boy in Chicago during the early 1900s:

> Obviously, because I was born on the South Side of Chicago, I became a White Sox fan. Since baseball took such a strong hold upon me, it permeated my boyish thoughts and dreams. It became a consuming enthusiasm, a part of my dream or fantasy world. The conversations about baseball which I sometimes heard at home, the nostalgic recollections of players who have passed out of active play, the talk of players' names in an almost legendary way, all this was part of an oral tradition of baseball passed on to me, mainly in the home, during the early years of this century. It was a treat to a little boy to be taken to a ball game and also to sit while his elders talked of the game. Along with this, my elders approved of my interest in baseball and encouraged me. . . . Baseball was a means of an awakening for me, an emergence from babyhood into the period of being a little boy.[107]

Baseball was an important topic of conversation among working-class fans that helped transcend age, ethnicity, and class differences. Baseball was a subject through which fathers and sons could relate to each other as friends, an unusual situation in patriarchal families.

New immigrants from eastern and southern Europe generally did not become baseball fans. They were primarily concerned with earning a living, taking care of their families, and sustaining their cultural and social traditions. They worked at the most onerous, arduous, and poorest paying jobs and had little time or money for diversions. Their leisure time was generally spent with others of similar origins at ethnic clubs and taverns. In Abraham's Cahan short novel *Yekl: A Tale of the New York Ghetto*, Jake (Yekl) the tailor tried to become an expert on baseball, only to be ridiculed by his fellow workers for devoting so much time to a children's game in which men run around in short pants. Manliness for these immigrants meant taking care of familial and religious duties, not playing sports.[108]

Foreign-language newspapers gave little attention to baseball or other American sports. If a sports item appeared, it was usually about a matter of ethnic pride, although a paper might introduce readers to this important American institution.[109] In 1907, for instance, Cahan's prestigious *Jewish Daily Forward* printed an article entitled "Der iker fun di baseball game, erklert far nit keyn sports layt" (The Fundamentals of Baseball Explained to Those Unfamiliar with Sports) accompanied by a diagram of the Polo Grounds.[110]

Despite the lack of interest shown by most new immigrants, club owners tried to secure their attention by scouting ballplayers from these ethnic groups. Chicago teams recruited Slavic players to attract the city's large Czech and Polish communities. The New York Giants in the 1920s made a notable effort to discover Jewish athletes to draw the interest of middle-class Jews moving into the neighborhood near the Polo Grounds.[111]

Immigrants who lived in the crowded inner city learned to play ball games in school and on city streets, where they had to adapt the sport to their narrow playing field. They were more likely to play street games like punchball, stickball, or stoopball than baseball. George Burns remembered how his pals adapted baseball to their limited space on the Lower East Side: "Our playground was the middle of Rivington Street. We only played games that needed very little equipment, games like kick-the-can, hopscotch, hide and go seek, follow the leader. When we played baseball we used a broom handle and a rubber ball. A manhole cover was home plate, a fire hydrant was first base, second base was a lamp post, and Mr. Gitletz, who used to bring a kitchen chair down to sit and watch us play, was third base. One time I slid into Mr. Gitletz; he caught the ball and tagged me out."[112]

Inner-city boys, in particular, were enthusiastic fans who carefully followed their favorite teams and heroes in the daily press, and baseball was an important topic of conversation among the second generation, who wanted to show that they were "real Americans." However, they seldom attended games because tickets—at least the youth rate of fifteen cents—and transportation were expensive. Boys who really wanted to could get in for free if they retrieved balls hit out of the park, cleared the trash in the stands before a game, begged passes from a ballplayer, or sneaked in. In addition, teams occasionally distributed free tickets to youth groups to demonstrate their civic consciousness. A young Morris Raphael Cohen used to walk from his Brownsville home in Brooklyn to nearby Eastern Park in the 1890s to watch the Dodgers through a knothole in the fence. Two decades later, Al Schacht, a future major leaguer, watched Giants games for free from nearby Coogan's Bluff, while young Harry Golden attended games because he shared a job with friends delivering pretzels to the Polo Grounds. On days when it was his turn to bring the snacks, he arrived at the park around ten o'clock and lounged about the clubhouse running errands for players until game time.[113]

African Americans and Baseball

Unlike new immigrants, African Americans were familiar with baseball as both players and fans. Over seventy African Americans played in professional white leagues in the late nineteenth century, and black semipro teams became important community institutions. However, African Americans made up only a small segment of spectators at professional games because of the expenses, the inconvenient scheduling of games, and prejudice. In 1900 only about 10 percent of American blacks lived in the North, where they were legally allowed to sit wherever they wanted, although they usually sat in the cheap bleachers, while seating in the South was segregated by law. African Americans entered southern parks through separate entrances and sat in separate sections. In St. Louis, for instance, seating was segregated until the late 1940s.[114]

Chicago's first African-American professional team had its origins in the Unions, an amateur club founded by Henry Jones, who later became renowned in the gambling business. In 1894 the Unions claimed the black championship of the West with a 53-7 record. Two years later, the Unions, under Frank Leland and William S. Peters, became a semiprofessional squad. Leland was active in local Republican politics and was later elected Cook County commissioner. The Unions toured extensively during the week, playing at home on Sundays, the day most African Americans were off work. In 1900 after the five-year-old Page Fence Giants of Adrian, Michigan, a corporate-sponsored squad, lost its financial backing, several players moved to Chicago and provided the core for the new Columbia Giants, sponsored by the Columbia Club, which was comprised of the city's black business and professional leaders. Managed by John W. Patterson, the Columbia Giants became the dominant African-American club in the West, and Chicago became the midwestern center of black baseball. The team played at the minor league White Sox field at Thirty-ninth and Wentworth, a few blocks from an emerging African-American neighborhood. The Columbia Giants drew well on Sundays, but not when they played out of town. Chicago's thirty thousand African Americans were insufficient to support both clubs. The Giants went out of business in 1901, and the best players joined Leland (who split from Peters) to form the Union Giants. The club played at Sixty-first and St. Lawrence and became one of the finest semipro teams in the Midwest.

Renamed the Leland Giants, they won 112 of 122 games in 1905, including 48 straight.[115]

Leland did not fare well financially and sought support from the city's new black elite. In 1906 the club was purchased by Republican politicians Robert R. Jackson, a future state representative, and the attorney Beauregard F. Moseley. Leland remained as manager and part owner and was responsible for booking games. In 1907 the enterprise was incorporated as the Leland Giants Baseball and Amusement Association, which also included a skating rink and dance hall/restaurant. The team remained at Auburn Park (Seventy-ninth and Wentworth) on the Far South Side, where they had played since 1904. The field was owned by semipro promoter and bar owner John Schorling. By 1907 the Leland Giants were the preeminent midwestern African-American team, led by their new star pitcher and future Hall of Famer Rube Foster, who joined the team as player-manager. He brought with him seven teammates from the Philadelphia Giants, which up to then had been the top African-American team in the United States.[116]

Foster led the Leland Giants to the city semipro championship, and they became a symbol of community pride. One year later they joined the otherwise all-white City League, the finest semiprofessional association in the country, and amassed an overall record of 110-10. *Spalding's Official Baseball Guide of Chicago* described their play "as good as the Major Leagues." The team was so popular and talented that in 1909 it played a three-game postseason series with the Cubs, attracting fifteen thousand fans of both races. This was one of the first matches between an African-American nine and a major league team since the 1880s. While the Cubs swept the series, the Leland Giants acquitted themselves well, losing twice by just one run.[117]

Faced with the loss of control of his own team, Leland left the club in October 1909 and, financed by Jackson, organized a new Leland Giants nine that included several of his old players. A lawsuit prevented Leland from keeping the name of his old team for his new nine, but the new Chicago Giants did keep the lease to Auburn Park and the membership in the City League, which expelled the Leland Giants, now owned by Moseley and Rube Foster, who managed the club and booked its games. The club played at five-thousand-seat Normal Park (Sixty-ninth and Halsted) and reputedly went 123-6 that year. In the fall they played a ten-game series in Cuba against the top local teams, winning 5, losing 4, and tying 1. Four Leland Giants, including the new star outfielder, John

Henry Lloyd, were then recruited to play for a Havana club in a series against Ty Cobb and the Detroit Tigers, which the teams split.[118]

In 1911 Foster broke with his old club, formed the American Giants, and, with majority partner John M. Schorling, relocated to the recently abandoned White Sox field at Thirty-ninth and Wentworth. Schorling Park was a new wooden structure with a nine-thousand-seat capacity, but the club was so popular that one Sunday in 1911 it drew eleven thousand fans, surpassing crowds for both the Sox and Cubs, who were also in town that day. The American Giants' quality of play, Foster's leadership, the field's proximity to an African-American neighborhood, and special attention to community relations enabled the team to quickly corner the local African-American market.[119]

Semiprofessional black baseball in northern cities attracted white as well as black fans, and occasionally white spectators outnumbered blacks. In the South, whites attending black games sat in segregated sections.[120] African-American teams played at such accessible fields as New York's twenty-six-hundred-seat Harlem Oval (142d and Lenox) and Chicago's Schorling Park. Youths were charged fifteen cents, while adults paid a quarter for a bleacher seat and fifty cents for a grandstand seat. The top black teams were so popular before 1920 that they played occasionally at major league parks. The first game between African Americans at a major league ballpark since the 1880s occurred in 1906 at Philadelphia's Columbia Park, when the Philadelphia Giants clinched the championship of the eastern African-American ball clubs. Prior to 1910, black New York teams rented the Polo Grounds, Hilltop Park, and Washington Park. In 1911 four black clubs played a doubleheader at the Polo Grounds attended by thirteen thousand spectators, who were charged regular major league ticket prices.[121]

The leading semiprofessional African-American teams played at home on Sundays and toured nearby towns during the week. Sunday ball was legal in most communities near Chicago, but not back East. However, New York's police seldom interfered with semiprofessional games because they attracted less public attention than major league games, and politically connected promoters circumvented the blue laws or were protected from interference.[122] The black press gave cursory coverage to baseball and other sports until about 1909, when the *New York Age* established a rudimentary sports section. Before then, papers such as the *Chicago Defender* and the *Chicago Broad Ax* carried only scores and items pirated from other papers. The main exception was the *Indianapo-*

lis Freeman, which gave substantial coverage to African-American baseball because the paper's editors considered it an important community
institution. As late as 1919 Robert Abbott, publisher of the *Chicago
Defender,* was castigating other black papers for their limited sports coverage. The black press had an ambivalent attitude toward the segregated
professional leagues and African-American ballplayers, printing major
league standings and feature stories about the big leagues alongside comments such as "all race loving and race building men and women should
support the negro teams." As Abbott proclaimed, "I have made an issue
of every single situation in which our people have been denied their
rightful share of participation."[123]

Professional baseball in the Progressive Era was primarily a middle-class
spectator sport. The crowds consisted mainly of white-collar workers
who had the necessary leisure time and could afford the expense of going
to a game. The rest of the spectators were largely skilled men or service workers who earned adequate salaries and had greater free time
compared with most working-class people. However, in the 1920s, improved living standards and the curtailment of Sunday blue laws enabled nearly everyone to attend professional games. In 1920 construction
trades workers earned $2,404, industrial workers were up to $1,424 (on a
par with clerks), and even unskilled laborers made $1,014. These Ameri-
cans, with sufficient leisure time and discretionary income to enjoy their
spare time as they wished, were ready to join the consumer society, and
many chose to attend baseball games. This development was reflected by
enormous Sunday crowds and a big increase in postwar attendance at
games. People from all classes became enthusiastic participants in the
rituals of baseball.[124]

The middle-class sport of baseball was easily the leading spectator
sport of the early twentieth century, and its preeminence reflected its
broader social significance. Baseball had achieved that success because it
was an exhilarating, exciting sport to watch and its ideology stirred the
imagination of native-born Americans and other acculturated people.
This creed demonstrated how baseball made a positive contribution to
American society and fit with the prevailing progressive spirit of civic
improvement. Attending a ball game was hardly a waste of time, but was
instead an educational experience and a civic obligation for men like
Sinclair Lewis's quintessential bourgeoisie, George Babbitt. Babbitt was
not a big fan, but rooted for the home team because his peers expected

him to participate in one of his class's most popular rituals. As the noted philosopher Morris Raphael Cohen argued in 1919, baseball had become America's national religion, full of rituals and ceremonies that provided for its spectators "redemption from the limitations of our petty lives and the mystic unity with a larger life of which we are part."[125] Mainstream Americans blindly accepted the game's rhetoric without questioning its assumptions or assertions because the doctrines fit in so well with their worldview. The national pastime was supposed to remind native-born white Americans of their halcyon past, while at the same time giving them faith in the future and their country by protecting and propagating mainstream American verities and by integrating disparate elements of the society. Many aspects of the baseball ideology regarded as reality were actually myths, but this discrepancy had no bearing on the way Americans related to the sport. Certain segments of the baseball creed, particularly those dealing with youngsters playing sandlot baseball, did not really have any applicability to the professional sport as such, but organized baseball successfully grafted those elements onto the public's perception of the sport.

Professional Baseball and Urban Politics

"Meyer Wolfsheim? . . . he's a gambler. He's the man who fixed the
World's Series back in 1919."
"Fixed the World's Series?" I repeated.
The idea staggered me. . . . It never occurred to me that one man
could start to play with the faith of fifty million people—with the
single-mindedness of a burglar blowing a safe.
"How did he happen to do that?" I asked after a minute.
"He just saw the opportunity."
"Why isn't he in jail?"
"They can't get him old sport. He's a smart man."

—F. Scott Fitzgerald, *The Great Gatsby*

According to conventional wisdom in the early 1900s, team
owners were intelligent, hard-working, public-spirited citizens whose
primary concern was the welfare of their community. They were usually
portrayed by the media in favorable terms regardless of prior business
activities, abuse of players, or political manipulating. One periodical
put them "in a class with the Wall Street broker or the operator on the
Chicago Board of Trade." Sportswriters rarely explored the behind-the-
scenes business maneuvering in professional baseball despite the vigorous contemporary muckraking tradition. Investigative sports journalism
at this time was virtually nonexistent primarily because of the inces-
tuous relationship between writers and professional baseball. Writers
were beholden to club owners, who often paid their expenses and employed them for public relations work. Furthermore, several baseball

executives were themselves former journalists, including AL founder Ban Johnson.[1]

The absence of critical media commentary gave fans no reason to doubt the carefully designed image of magnates as outstanding civic-minded business professionals and selfless philanthropists devoted to providing clean and wholesome amusement. However, the reality was that professional baseball was not dominated by benevolent people, but by entrepreneurs out to make money. Each owner had three tangible assets—a franchise in a league, contracted players, and a ballpark—and an intangible fourth asset, the loyalty and good will of hometown fans.

Nearly all professional baseball teams in the nineteenth century had direct and indirect connections to urban politics. The historian Ted Vincent examined the occupations of 1,263 officials and stockholders of major and minor league teams and found that nearly half of them were politicians, including 50 mayors and 102 state legislators. They were typically professional politicians seeking to profit from a new business by using their connections while picking up votes from grateful fans who appreciated their sponsorship of a popular entertainment. Owners were often civic boosters, such as Aaron Champion, a Cincinnati businessman and politician, who together with other town promoters, including Democratic boss and publisher of the *Cincinnati Enquirer*, John R. McLean, organized the Cincinnati Red Stockings in 1869—the first all-salaried team—to advertise the Queen City. Nineteenth-century baseball teams were risky businesses: 650 of the 850 professional franchises (76.5 percent) lasted two years or less and only 50 survived for six or more seasons.[2]

In towns like Atlanta, Chicago, and New York, politicians operated local professional clubs just as they would any other enterprise. They were in a good position to assist their teams by making influential connections at city hall and securing valuable inside information about such matters as transportation plans, real estate developments, and preferential treatment in fees, taxes, and police protection. Magnates with political ties protected their investments against potential competitors and cumbersome municipal regulations and used their franchises for political purposes by manipulating them into a source of patronage and a public relations tool to enhance their public images.

Baseball and Politics in Atlanta, 1885–1921

Although turn-of-the-century Atlanta was dominated by its commercial elite, its baseball teams were controlled by politicians and politically connected enterprises. A series of joint stock companies led by transportation executives controlled the city's first professional teams. In 1894 the president of the syndicate operating the Southern League franchise was Joseph Hirsch, a wealthy clothing merchant, leading member of the Jewish community, and city council member. The Crackers needed his political influence because opponents were seeking to close down their playing field, Athletic Park, as a public nuisance. Their adversaries failed to get an injunction that year, but petitioned the city council in 1895 to deny the Crackers a license, charging that baseball crowds were disagreeable and that order could not be maintained. Despite Hirsch's guarantees not to tolerate disorder and promises of high-quality police protection, the council did not renew the license.[3]

The press attacked the decision, urging reconsideration since baseball was the town's finest summer amusement, attracting over half the city's population. Editorials argued that the owners were gentlemen who deserved special consideration since they had invested their own money for the community's welfare. The *Atlanta Constitution* claimed that the loss of the club would be a severe blow to the city's prestige and that "Possum Trot and all the other provincial villages of the country will point the finger of ridicule at us."[4] The city council reconsidered the license question and granted the team a trial period to prove it could keep order. The club won the Southern League pennant with a 70-37 record. In 1896, in a move sponsored by the Atlanta Traction Company, the Crackers relocated to Brisbine Park, supposedly better serviced by public transportation. Local residents protested loudly, but the club had no problem renewing its license.[5]

The ball club lost a lot of money in 1896 and was dismantled in midseason. One year later, the attorney W. T. Moyers organized a new team that lasted just two months in the Southeastern League. Early in 1898 Moyers met with local transportation officials and tried to interest them in helping finance a new club. Streetcar executives were heavily involved in urban politics because of their need for inside information, right-of-ways, and long-term leases. Baseball teams everywhere received assistance from local transit companies, which reaped good profits from transporting passengers to and from games. Moyers believed that Atlanta's streetcar companies should not benefit from baseball without contributing a fair share to its upkeep.[6]

Transportation firms owned recreational sites such as amusement parks and baseball fields because they were regarded as excellent attractions for riders. Ted Vincent estimated that 15 percent of nineteenth-century business professionals involved in baseball were transportation executives. He found that public transit lines in seventy-eight cities were financially involved in professional baseball. In 1899 there was even a New England Trolley League. Streetcar executives knew if they did not promote a ball club, their competition would. Some were even willing to support a baseball team at a loss because of anticipated profits from increased ridership. Streetcars headed in the direction of the ballpark would have signs on the front cars announcing scheduled games. In the late 1890s fans of the Cleveland Spiders arriving by trolley could buy a round-trip fare and admission ticket right on board. Both were owned by the transportation magnate Stanley Robison. Transit lines were particularly prominent sponsors of teams in smaller cities, where they were one of the few sources of local capital sufficient to maintain a professional nine.[7]

Clubs in southern cities such as Augusta, Birmingham, Charleston, Macon, Mobile, Montgomery, and New Orleans received substantial financial backing from transportation companies. In New Orleans, for example, a streetcar line built a new ballpark in 1898 and subscribed an additional fifteen hundred dollars to the Pelicans. In Montgomery bitter competition for control of the city's team erupted between the two main transit companies because each owned a baseball field at the end of a route.[8]

In 1898 Moyers persuaded the Atlanta Street Railway Company to aid his new team. Superintendent F. M. Zimmerman of the streetcar firm purchased stock in the franchise and was made its vice president, and a local judge was appointed secretary-treasurer. The company had made $600 on its ballpark route during the abbreviated 1897 season and was afraid of losing money if the team failed again. Zimmerman anticipated profits of about three thousand dollars, but the Southern League collapsed in midseason.[9]

Professional baseball resumed in Atlanta in 1902, when E. T. Peter and Abner Powell moved their Selma team in the year-old Class A Southern Association to the Gate City. In 1901 the National Association of Professional Baseball Leagues adopted a classification system to rationalize salary limits and a draft system in which teams in higher classifications could draft players from lower leagues. Player mobility was also facilitated through working agreements with major league clubs that sent surplus players, and sometimes money, to Atlanta in return for first crack on promising players.[10]

Abner Powell, a former player-manager and owner of the New Orleans Pelicans, had already been an enormously inventive executive. In 1887 he introduced the ladies' day custom in the Deep South and also rainchecks. Two years later he became the first executive to cover the playing field with tarpaulin to protect the infield from rain. He also introduced the Knothole Gang, which admitted children for free once a week, and such gimmicks as free sodas and gate prizes. The Crackers drew 39,808 in 1902, only sixth best in the league, far behind leader New Orleans with 98,000, resulting in an eighteen-hundred-dollar loss. In December Powell bought out his partner, making his total investment in the Crackers about four thousand dollars, and subsequently turned the Crackers into a profitable venture that made six thousand dollars in 1903. Attendance rose substantially under Powell's imaginative leadership, zooming to 135,000 in 1904. Profits came mostly from admissions, abetted by player transfers and the sale of the concessions privilege, which brought in two hundred dollars in 1902 and five hundred dollars by 1905. The *Atlanta Journal* claimed that Powell took in about sixty thousand dollars in four seasons of baseball, including nearly twenty thousand dollars when he sold the franchise, a very healthy return.[11]

Powell's success aroused the ire and jealousy of local fans, who were displeased that profits went to an outsider. In 1904 a clique of powerful politicians decided to drive Powell out by introducing an exorbitant license fee. The city council considered a fifty-dollar fee plus a 5 percent tax on gross receipts, which the *Atlanta Journal* denounced as unfair and unbearable: "There is no case on record where a team in any league or town is taxed outside of the license." The drastic measure failed, but the council did set a two-hundred-dollar license fee plus one hundred dollars for police protection. Fulton County added its own three hundred dollars assessment.[12]

Abner Powell's difficulties were compounded after the city purchased the 189-acre Piedmont Park (site of the 1895 Cotton States Exposition), where the Crackers had played since 1902, for ninety-nine thousand dollars. Powell still had a year on his lease and had just signed an option to renew, but feared the municipality would make it difficult for him to remain. Powell was also plagued by transportation interests, who refused him financial assistance and charged him five dollars a game to guarantee their service. In 1905 Powell acceded to public pressure and sold the franchise for seventeen thousand dollars to a syndicate headed by the twenty-one-year veteran fire chief Walthal R. Joyner, who became mayor, then largely an honorific position, one year later. Joyner had baseball experience, serving as team president back in 1889. The Crackers were one of six Southern Association teams to make money in 1905.[13]

In 1906 Joyner convinced Preston Arkwright, president of the Georgia Railway and Electric Company (GREC) (later renamed the Georgia Railway and Power Company), that supporting the Crackers would be an asset by virtue of the traffic baseball would generate, and Arkwright agreed to purchase stock in the team. One year later the team moved to Ponce De Leon Park, which had been built by the company. The streetcar company gained complete control of the team in 1908 and installed the famed Georgia Tech football coach J. W. Heisman as president and a GREC vice president as treasurer. The club achieved success on the field as Manager Will Smith led the Crackers to pennants in 1907, 1909, and 1913. Among its most memorable games was a thirty-two-minute contest on 19 September 1910, the shortest in professional baseball history.[14]

Despite the Crackers' accomplishments on the diamond, the GREC found the ball club more trouble than it was worth, and in 1911 announced its intent to sell out. Walthal Joyner organized a partnership to purchase the Crackers, but found the forty-thousand-dollar asking price too steep. Another potential syndicate included executives from Coca-Cola, a leading local enterprise. Coca-Cola was not sold at the ballpark because the exclusive concession privileges had been awarded in 1910 to the rival Red Rock Ko-nit Company. Coke executives decided that buying the Crackers would be good public relations—and profitable since they could resume selling their beverage to thirsty baseball spectators—but the price was too high. The franchise remained unsold until 1915, when a partnership led by City Councilman Frank H. Reynolds and the realtor J. W. Goldsmith Jr., son of a former city council member and nephew of the city comptroller, bought it for thirty-seven thousand dollars, although the park remained with the streetcar company. The new owners enjoyed championships under Manager Charley Frank in 1917 and 1919, but sold out in 1921 to the concessionaire R. J. Spiller.[15]

Baseball and Politics in Chicago, 1869–1920

The influence of politics and politicians on Chicago baseball was even more important than it was in Atlanta. In the fall of 1869 the real estate tycoon Potter Palmer, the *Chicago Tribune* publisher and future mayor Joseph Medill, General Phil Sheridan, and the department store owner and future U.S. senator Charles B. Farwell established the Chicago Base Ball Association and raised twenty thousand dollars to hire a professional nine. They anticipated that a successful club would bolster the city's reputation just as the Red Stockings had done for Cincinnati. The management recruited top players and offered salaries of up to twenty-five hundred dollars. The White Stockings began play in 1870 with City Treasurer David A. Gage as president and W. F. Wentworth, a son of the city's most famous early mayor, as vice president. Gage was indicted three years later for a $507,000 misappropriation of funds. Manager Tom Foley, a well-known amateur ballplayer, owned the city's leading billiard parlor. At the time there were about thirteen professional nines, half of which were fully salaried, while the rest compensated players with either a political sinecure or a share of the gate. Highlights of the first White Stockings season included a victory over the Red Stockings and a 157-1 rout over Memphis. One year later, the club was a charter member of the National Association of Professional Base Ball Players and came in second at the end of the season, even though it had to finish on the road after its ballpark burned down during the Great Chicago Fire. Chicago did not rejoin the National Association until 1874, when coal merchant and Board of Trade member William Hulbert, a shareholder since 1870, took over. An ardent hometown booster, Hulbert claimed he "would rather be a lamp post in Chicago than a millionaire in any other city."[16]

In 1876 Hulbert was the principal organizer of the NL, which promised to make baseball a money-making business. President Morgan Bulkeley, owner of the Hartford franchise and son of the founder of Aetna Life Insurance, was just a figurehead, and Hulbert, the real power, became president in 1877. The NL awarded franchises for a hundred-dollar fee only to well-financed teams in cities with over seventy-five thousand residents, had a fixed schedule arranged by the league, and in 1879 placed reserve clauses in player's contracts.

Hulbert had rebuilt the White Stockings well in advance of the 1876 season. During July 1875, he signed advance contracts for the following season with six star players, including four champion Boston Red Stockings players.[17] They included pitcher Albert G. Spalding, who in one season had won 57 games, including 24 straight. He was made player-manager and club secretary and was paid $2,000 plus one-fourth of gate profits. Another top recruit was Philadelphia Athletics first baseman Adrian "Cap" Anson, a future Hall of Famer. Anson was already a five-year major league veteran, and from 1879 to 1897 was the team's player-manager.

Led by Spalding, who went 47-13 with a 1.74 ERA, Chicago won the first NL pennant in 1876, providing a new opportunity to demonstrate the city was not remiss in municipal distinctions. Spalding quit the playing field after the next season, still in his prime, to enter business. He borrowed eight hundred dollars from his mother and established the A. G. Spalding and Brothers Sporting Goods Company, which soon dominated the athletic equipment business. When Hulbert died in 1882, Spalding became the club's president and chief stockholder. His partners included the noted politico John R. Walsh, president of the Chicago National Bank and executive of the American News Company, and Charles T. Trego, a Republican grain merchant, banker, and former director of the Board of Trade.[18]

Spalding made the White Stockings into the dominant team of the NL's first fifteen years, and according to the historian Peter Levine was the key figure in ensconcing baseball as a respectable middle-class recreation: "Aggressive, enthusiastic, and occasionally ruthless, he manipulated ballplayers, attracted publicity, and appealed for respectability as he shaped his conception of a professional sport that would allow both personal profit and public acceptance by a Victorian middle class." Spalding tried to gain middle-class respectability by not pushing for Sunday baseball and trying to improve his players' behavior: he fined heavy drinkers, imposed morals clauses in contracts, and hired private detectives to spy on the team. He curried favor with local politicians by generously providing season passes in the general admission section for city council members and box seats for mayors and department commissioners. Spalding also tried to spread baseball around the world through his 1888 international tour.[19]

The White Stockings were extremely successful under Spalding's capable direction, dominating the NL with five pennants in seven years (1880–82, 1885–86), and dividends often exceeded 20 percent of capital investment. In 1883 the club reportedly earned $20,000, in 1886, $15,000, in 1887, $80,000 (by which time the franchise had accumulated a surplus of about $100,000), and in 1888, $60,000. Overall, NL teams reportedly made a total of $750,000 between 1885 and 1889. However, they suffered huge losses in 1890 fighting the rival Players' League (PL); the White Stockings alone lost $65,000.[20]

A few months after the 1890 season, Spalding and his partners—Edward Talcott, who had operated the New York PL club, and Edward A. McAlpin, former president of the PL—purchased the local PL club for $25,000 from the Chicago contractor John Addison, vice president of the soon defunct league. Addison also received $15,000 in New York Giants stock.[21]

The White Stockings fared poorly in 1891 and even worse in 1892. Management blamed losses on conflicts with the rival AA, which in

1891 had awarded a local franchise to a Chicago group for $50,000. The war with the AA had started over the rights to former PL players and led to the AA dropping out of the National Agreement governing rules of ownership and salaries. The conflict ended late in 1891 with the NL buying out the Chicago franchise and four AA teams. The remaining four AA clubs joined the NL to form a twelve-team circuit.[22]

Spalding reorganized his baseball operations in 1892. He combined his Congress Street ballpark with other real estate holdings to form the A. G. Spalding Land Association. He withdrew from day-to-day supervision of the White Stockings, now a $100,000 corporation, and made Secretary James A. Hart the new president. Hart had been active in baseball since 1882, first as Louisville's manager and vice president and then as Milwaukee's manager and president. Hart, Trego, and Walsh became officers of the realty company, the latter two dropping their connection to the ball club. Spalding's new minor partners in the team included Ed Barrett, a Board of Trade member elected county sheriff in 1902, and the popular Cap Anson, his star first baseman and manager, who was elected city clerk in 1905. The club struggled at the gate in 1893 and 1894, attributed by Hart to competition from the world's fair and the cost of maintaining baseball fields in both the West and South Sides, but more obvious causes were the 1893 economic depression and the team's modest performance on the diamond. The club regained its profitability in the latter 1890s, averaging total dividends of 20–25 percent between 1895 and 1901 when few teams made money. In 1899, the last year the NL operated as a twelve-team league, the White Stockings reportedly made $20,000.[23]

Profit estimates varied widely, and must be treated cautiously (see table 1). White Stockings profits in 1899 were assessed by the *New York World* at $35,000, the *Chicago Times-Herald* at $20,000, and the *New York Herald* at 0. The *New York World* estimated the average team made $29,333, while the *New York Herald* reported no profits at all. Since the NL dropped four teams after the season, the *New York World*'s and *Chicago Times-Herald*'s estimates appear fanciful.

Baseball's enormous popularity in Chicago encouraged the fledgling American League to plant a franchise on the South Side in 1900. The team was owned by native Chicagoan Charles Comiskey, a former major league star of the 1880s, whose $6,200 salary as player-manager of the St. Louis Browns was among the highest in that era. He was one of seven children of Irish immigrant John Comiskey, a self-made man who was elected to the city council from a predominantly Irish West Side ward

Table 1. Estimated National League Profits in 1899

Team by Rank in 1899 Season	New York World	New York Herald	Chicago Times-Herald
Brooklyn	$50,000	$15,000	profit
Boston	60,000	20,000	$50,000
Philadelphia	75,000	40,000	15,000
Baltimore	15,000	10,000	15,000
St. Louis	50,000	20,000	50,000
Cincinnati	20,000	−5,000	profit
Pittsburgh	15,000	−10,000	15,000
Chicago	35,000	0	20,000
Louisville	12,000	−10,000	profit
New York	12,000	−40,000	loss
Washington	8,000	−10,000	profit
Cleveland	0	−30,000	loss
	$352,000	$0	unavailable

Sources: *Sporting Life,* 21 Oct. 1899; *Chicago Times-Herald,* 15 Oct. 1899.

that he represented for eleven years. He also served as clerk of the county board of commissioners. In 1890 Charles Comiskey left the Browns for Chicago's PL nine and became its player-manager. In 1894 after retiring from the diamond, he obtained the Sioux City franchise in the Western League, which he moved to St. Paul one year later.[24]

Under the driving leadership of Ban Johnson, the Western was soon recognized as the strongest minor league. It was renamed the American League in 1900 to indicate its growing ambitions, with franchises in Buffalo, Chicago, Cleveland, Detroit, Indianapolis, Kansas City, Milwaukee, and Minneapolis. Comiskey moved the St. Paul club to his hometown only after getting the local NL club's permission. He agreed to locate south of Thirty-fifth Street and to allow the Chicago Colts to draft two players after the season. Comiskey appropriated the familiar old nickname "White Stockings," shortened to White Sox two years later, but was not allowed to include the word *Chicago* in front of *White Sox.* The Sox were successful right from the start, winning the pennant in 1900 and making a $10,900 profit. They were one of only three AL teams to finish in the black and earned more than the other money-making teams, Detroit and Kansas City, combined.[25]

In 1901 when the AL proclaimed itself a major league, the White Sox again won the pennant. When it won again in 1906 the squad was known as the "hitless wonders," batting a league low .230. The team was carried by an excellent pitching staff, led by spitballer Ed Walsh, that compiled 32 shutouts. The Sox were huge underdogs in the World Series against the Cubs, who had gone 116-36 that season, the best record in major league history, and had won 23 more games than the Sox. In perhaps the greatest upset in World Series history, the American Leaguers won 4 games to 2.[26]

The White Sox were extremely profitable for Comiskey, who by the end of the 1908 season was said to have earned $400,000 from the team. He made an average of $100,000 the next three seasons, and $150,000 in 1912. Comiskey may have been the only major league magnate to own all his team's stock. He was a public figure and celebrity, reflected by his leadership in the Woodland Bards, a private club of politicians, journalists, civic leaders, and entertainers.[27]

In 1905 Albert Spalding sold his share in the Cubs to their press agent, Charles W. Murphy, for $105,000, but kept the West Side Grounds, where the team had played since 1893. Spalding had been out of the limelight with the ball club for several years, devoting himself to other business interests, and the public did not realize he was still the principal owner. Charles Murphy was a former sports editor of the *Cincinnati Enquirer*, assistant city editor of the *Cincinnati Times-Star*, and press agent for the New York Giants. A fine example of baseball's incestuous relationship with sportswriters, Murphy had just been hired as the Cubs' press agent when he discovered they were up for sale. Murphy rushed to his former publisher, Charles P. Taft, who agreed to lend him $100,000 to make the deal.[28]

Taft was the older brother and political advisor of Secretary of War William Howard Taft, the future president. He was an important power in Republican politics as publisher of the *Cincinnati Times-Star* and served a term in Congress. He aspired to a Senate seat in 1909, but instead devoted himself to helping brother William get elected president. Taft was married to the heiress Anne Sinton and was among the few upper-class families that invested in baseball. Taft became a minority stockholder in Murphy's Cubs, and was rumored to have capital invested in Brooklyn and Louisville, while in 1909 his wife became a minor partner in the Philadelphia Phillies. However, they did not take an active role in baseball and generally remained behind the scenes.[29]

Murphy's investment was an immediate success, and he quickly repaid Taft's loan. The Cubs made $165,000 in 1906, undoubtedly a result of their outstanding pennant-winning season that brought in large crowds. Murphy made considerably more in his first season than he had just paid for control of the club.[30]

The Cubs dominated the NL in the early years of the century under

Manager Frank Chance, the "Peerless Leader," with at least 99 wins each year from 1906 through 1910. They won three straight pennants (1906–8), including two world championships over the Detroit Tigers, came in second in 1909 with 104 wins, and won the pennant again in 1910, losing the series to the Athletics. They had an excellent pitching staff, led by Mordecai "Three-Finger" Brown, who won 20 or more games six times. Their infield of Tinkers to Evers to Chance (plus Steinfeldt at third) was one of the most famous of all time, memorialized by Franklin Adams's poem. Joe Tinkers and Johnny Evers, forever linked by Adams's verse, actually were not close, and for two years did not speak to each other following a quarrel over cabfare.

The highlight of the exciting 1908 pennant race was Fred Merkle's baserunning error in a crucial game between the Cubs and his Giants, ever since then referred to as "Merkle's Boner." The genesis for that play likely came from a letter in the *Chicago Tribune*'s "Inquisitive Fans" column on 19 July. A fan asked if a runner driven in by a base hit to the outfield in the bottom of the ninth counted if the batter did not bother to run to first base. The response was that it did not, if a play was made at first base. When a similar situation occurred at a Cubs game in Pittsburgh on 4 September in the bottom of the tenth at a game tied 0-0, the Cubs were ready. With two out, and runners at first and third, Honus Wagner stroked a single into center field to apparently win the game. However, as was customary then, Warren Gill, the runner at first base, never bothered to touch second base. The Cubs center fielder retrieved the ball and threw it to second baseman Johnny Evers for a force-out. But Hank Day, the only umpire working the game, did not see the play and let the winning run count. A protest filed with the league office was disallowed.[31]

On 23 September virtually the same incident occurred again in a crucial game between the Cubs and the first place Giants, who were ahead by three games. The contest was tied in the bottom of the ninth with Giants runners on first and third. A rocketing single up the middle drove in the apparent winning run, and the runner at first base, nineteen-year-old rookie Frank Merkle, did not bother to touch second base, joining everyone else leaving the field. Thereupon center fielder Art Hofman retrieved the ball and returned it to the infield to force out Merkle at second base. But he overthrew Evers, and the ball was retrieved by Giants pitcher Joe "Iron Man" McGinnity, who threw it in the direction of the left field fence. Shortly thereafter, Evers was seen standing on second base with a ball in his hand, not necessarily the actual game ball, claiming a force-out that would negate the winning run. Second base umpire Bob Emslie, who was almost hit by the batted ball, never saw the play. However, home plate umpire O'Day did, and on his ruling, Emslie declared Merkle forced out at second. O'Day then suspended the game, ostensibly on account of darkness, but mainly because the large crowd had already covered the field and chaos would have resulted had fans learned the game was not over. The Cubs then went on to win eleven of their last twelve games and at the end of the season tied the Giants for first place. Consequently the called game had to be replayed. About thirty-five thousand attended the playoff game at the Polo Grounds. Journalists guessed that over two hundred thousand people were outside the park on "roofs, fences, 'L' structures, electric light poles and in the distance on smokestacks, chimneys, advertising signs, and toppings of apartment houses." The Cubs won the replayed game, 4-2, and took the pennant.[32]

Success on the field resulted in huge profits. Taft estimated that the franchise earned $1,260,000 between 1906 and 1915, with total dividends on capital stock from 1907 to 1913 reaching 810 percent. But competition from the Federal League, which had a team in Chicago, and resentment against Murphy's management caused profits to plummet to 20 percent in 1914 and 5 percent in 1915. Only two other NL teams made a profit in 1915, however, so the returns were still pretty good.[33]

The public's disenchantment with Murphy was partly due to his apparent cooperation with ticket scalpers, a reflection of the strong ties that existed between sport, urban machine politics, and organized crime. Speculators never seemed to have any problem securing tickets, and fans believed they were protected and supported by prominent politicians. It was illegal for anyone standing on public property to sell admission tickets for prices higher than face value, but legal loopholes enabled scalpers to operate with impunity inside semipublic buildings like hotels. Furthermore, speculators with political pull sold tickets right outside ballparks with little fear of getting arrested or punished with more than token fines.[34]

The scalping of baseball tickets received great notoriety during the 1908 World Series between the Cubs and the Tigers. Chicagoans were informed they could purchase tickets at the downtown Spalding Sporting Goods Store, and thousands assembled there on the morning of the sale. By noon a rumor passed through the crowd that tickets were being sold at Cubs headquarters. Fans flocked to the team's offices to hear that the sale was postponed for a day. Actually, someone in the Cubs' front office had already distributed most of the tickets to scalpers, including one who got

630 tickets. The public was outraged, especially since similar shenanigans had occurred during the 1907 World Series. Some business leaders considered seeking injunctions to compel the Cubs to sell them tickets. Republican mayor Fred Busse, piqued that the Cubs had failed to supply him with passes, threatened to halt the series because of alleged building code violations at the ballpark. Busse announced he was going to put four hundred police officers on the streets around the field to block people from going to the game, but the city's corporation counsel, Edward Brundage, interceded for the Cubs, and the mayor got his tickets. Attendance at the games was unexpectedly light, which hurt the scalpers. Many fans boycotted the games to protest their inability to get reasonably priced tickets.[35]

Murphy further alienated Cubs fans by refusing to spend money for top players, by trading several local heroes, and by relating poorly to his popular managers. Manager Frank Chance resigned after the 1912 season, disgusted with Murphy's cheapness. The "Peerless Leader" had been eminently successful. Between 1905 and 1912, his teams won .667 percent of their games, and their *lowest* winning percentage was .595. His Cubs finished only once as low as third (in 1912). Chance was replaced by the star second baseman and future Hall of Famer Johnny Evers, who lasted only one season.

Murphy was on bad terms with his fellow owners for creating ill will in Chicago and for habitually making indiscreet public comments that reflected poorly on organized baseball. They decided Murphy had to go and convinced him in 1915 to sell his controlling interest to Charles P. Taft for about five hundred thousand dollars. Murphy kept a half-share in West Side Park, which he and Taft had jointly purchased from Spalding in 1908.[36]

Taft saw himself as only an interim owner and hoped to soon sell out. Several syndicates were formed to purchase the Cubs, each including at least one prominent political figure. For example, one clique of prominent Republicans consisted of future mayor William Hale Thompson, the promoter and Thompson's political confidant James A. Pugh, the taxi executive and prominent politician Charles A. McCulloch, and the restaurateur and former county treasurer John R. Thompson. Taft was dissatisfied with all proposals, including a reported top bid of $770,000, and decided to hold on for a while longer. Prospective buyers were discouraged from going higher by two pressing problems. They feared hostile legislation since patients from Cook County Hospital, located across the street from West Side Park, were sometimes disturbed by noise from the games. More importantly, the physical plant was in poor shape and needed new bleachers and a grandstand costing $250,000.[37]

Taft sold the franchise after the 1915 season to a syndicate headed by the owners of the rival Federal League team. The ChiFeds, or Whales, were owned by Charles Weeghman, a cafeteria chain mogul, and William Walker, a prominent Republican and leader in the fish industry. Weeghman had started out as a coffee server in a downtown Chicago restaurant in the 1890s and worked his way up to head waiter. He then opened up his own lunchroom and eventually owned fifteen in Chicago. The ChiFeds had done well on the diamond, contending for the championship in 1914 and winning the pennant in 1915, and did fairly well at the box office. Their roster included several former local stars, including Cubs veteran "Three-Finger" Brown, and was managed by former Cubs shortstop Joe Tinker.[38]

The ChiFeds initiated an anti-trust suit against organized baseball in 1915 that was tried before Federal Judge Kenesaw Mountain Landis, who had gained a national reputation in 1907 for fining the Standard Oil Company $29.4 million for violating the Sherman Anti-Trust Act. However, he dragged his feet in the baseball case, hoping for an out-of-court settlement. Following the 1915 season representatives from the Federal League and organized baseball met to halt the costly competition. They came to an agreement that called for the disbandment of the Federal League in return for $600,000 in compensation. In addition, Chicago and St. Louis Fed owners were given options to purchase major league teams in their respective cities, with the big leagues contributing 10 percent of the purchase price.[39]

The Baltimore Feds balked at the agreement and sued organized baseball for violating antitrust laws. The case was not decided until 1919, when a district court ruled for the plaintiffs, awarding $240,000 in damages. Organized baseball appealed the decision to the Supreme Court, which in 1922 overturned the prior judgment. The venerable justice Oliver Wendell Holmes Jr. explained that although baseball was a business, it was not commerce or trade as commonly defined, and while teams crossed state lines to play games, their movement was incidental to the business. This seminal decision meant that organized baseball was not subject to antitrust statutes and thus was permitted to operate virtually free of federal interference.[40]

Early in 1916, following the signing of the National Agreement by the Federal League and the major leagues, Taft sold the Cubs to Weeghman, Walker, and several other investors for about $500,000. The principal stockholder was the Jewish businessman and philanthropist Albert D. Lasker, head of the giant Lord and Thomas Advertising Agency. Other partners included such notable Chicagoans as J. Ogden Armour, scion of the meat-packing family, taxi magnate Charles A. McCulloch, contractor Al Plamondon, lumber baron A. D. Schuttler, and chewing gum king William Wrigley, who in 1918 became the principal stockholder. The Cubs roster consisted of a consolidated team of the best players from the old Cubs and the ChiFeds. In addition, the club moved from its old West Side Park to the two-year-old Federal Park on the North Side. The new owners also paid Taft two years' rent as compensation for the loss of his tenants. Two years later the Cubs won the NL championship in the war-shortened 1918 season with an outstanding 84-45 record, but lost to the Boston Red Sox in the World Series, 4 games to 2. Half of Boston's victories went to their youthful left-handed pitcher, Babe Ruth, who established a World Series record of 29⅔ consecutive scoreless innings that lasted until 1961. The postseason series was not played at the new Cubs Park, but at Comiskey Park because its seating capacity was more than double that of the North Side park.[41]

Lasker, McCulloch, Plamondon, Walker, and Wrigley were all important Republicans who lunched daily to plot political strategy. Lasker was a member of the Republican National Committee and along with Wrigley was a staunch supporter of California governor Hiram Johnson for their party's presidential nomination in 1920. But after Harding was nominated, Lasker served as his public relations director. Lasker countered Harding's public image as a golfer—and thus a rich man—by publicizing Harding's ownership of a minor league team. Lasker sent the Cubs to play an exhibition in Harding's hometown of Marion, Ohio. Harding took advantage of the moment to deliver his "Team Play" speech that criticized President Woodrow Wilson's individualistic style in foreign affairs. The New York Giants had been originally scheduled to compete, but Manager John J. McGraw withdrew his team at the last minute because of the club's close ties to Tammany Hall.[42]

Baseball and Politics in New York, 1870–1920

Baseball's far-reaching political ties in Chicago, a city whose early political machines were mainly local ward organizations, were minor compared with those in New York City, which had a powerful, seemingly omnipotent citywide machine. Amateur and professional baseball always had close links to Tammany Hall. Several prominent politicians, including boss Charles F. Murphy, even got their start in politics through Tammany-sponsored amateur baseball teams, which provided a means to attract ambitious, athletically inclined young men to politics.[43]

The Mutuals, the first prominent Tammany-sponsored team, was organized in 1857 by Tammany boss William M. Tweed and other politicians. In 1865 three players were discovered to have fixed a game against the Eckfords and were expelled by the amateur National Association of Base Ball Players. However, within five years they were all reinstated. The scandal, along with the club's close ties to Tammany, gave the Mutuals a bad reputation.

The Mutuals were originally an amateur nine, but within a few years they were supported by patronage jobs through club president John Wildey, the city coroner, or the sanitation department. These positions were sinecures that gave the Mutuals time to practice and play an extensive schedule. By 1867 some players shared in gate receipts. One year later several were on salary, and all were by 1869, making the club one of three professional teams in metropolitan New York. Tammany contributed generously to the team's upkeep. In 1869 New York city council members voted fifteen hundred dollars for the Mutuals, and one year later Tweed donated seventy-five hundred dollars out of his own pocket.

In 1871 the Mutuals became a charter member of the National Association of Professional Base Ball Players (NA) and played at Brooklyn's Union Grounds; Wildey served a term as NA president. They were one of only three clubs to play all five seasons that the NA was in operation. The Mutuals joined the new NL in 1876, but were expelled after deciding not to make the final western road trip because of anticipated financial losses.[44]

Following the demise of the Mutuals New York had no major league team until 1883, when the Metropolitan Exhibition Company was awarded franchises in both the NL and the year-old AA. The owners were Jim Mutrie, a former player in the New England League, the Tammanyite and manufacturer John B. Day, and Day's brother-in-law, the realtor and assistant Democratic district leader Joseph Gordon. Three years earlier Mutrie and Day had established the New York Metropolitans, an independent professional club that was the first professional team to actually play in New York City. The NL club, the Gothams, was based on the Troy Haymakers, which Day and Mutrie had purchased and moved to New York. The Mets (AA) were a modest box office success in their inaugural season, finishing fourth with an estimated five-thousand-dollar profit, well below the AA average of nearly twenty-three thousand dollars. The Mets won the AA pennant the following year, led by pitchers Jack Lynch and Tim Keefe, who each won 37 games. However, the club lost eight thousand dollars, while the Gothams made twelve thousand dollars. The Mets participated in the first World Series that season, falling to the Providence Grays of the NL in three straight games.[45]

Before the next season Day moved three of the Mets, manager Mutrie, star pitcher Keefe, and Tom "Dude" Esterbrook, who had batted .408, to his NL club. Day wanted to build up attendance for the Gothams because the senior circuit charged twice as much for tickets as the AA did. The Gothams, later renamed the Giants because of their players' physical stature, became immediate contenders, coming in second with a .759 winning percentage and taking pennants in 1888 and 1889. The club followed up each pennant with postseason victories against the AA champions. The revamped Giants were very profitable, netting a reputed $120,000 in 1885, $80,000 in 1886, $110,000 a year later, and $90,000 in 1889.[46]

The Mets, on the other hand, went in the opposite direction. The Mets fell to seventh in 1885 following the loss of their top players, with a record of 44-64. The AA convinced Day to sell the team to someone who would try to make it competitive, so he sold it to the transportation magnate Erastus Wiman for $25,000. Wiman moved the team from New York to his Staten Island amusement park, which was accessible to Manhattanites via his ferry line. Wiman had an ulterior motive in buying the ball club: he was negotiating with Baltimore and Ohio Railroad executives, who intended to make Staten Island their New York terminal, for use of his ferries and other facilities he owned. The rates were to be based on the average ferry traffic over a period of several years, and Wiman expected the ball club would help boost his traffic. However, Wiman ended up losing about $30,000 in just two seasons of baseball. Consequently, he got out of the baseball business in 1887, selling the team to the Brooklyn AA club for $18,000. The Brooklyn squad kept the better players and returned the franchise to the league.[47]

In 1890 New York got a new major league team in the upstart PL. New York had been a major center of sentiment for the Brotherhood of Professional Base Ball Players, and many of the finest Giants jumped to the new league's local franchise, including Buck Ewing, an outstanding first baseman, and shortstop John Montgomery Ward, the president of the brotherhood. Financing for the local PL nine came from several Republican politicians, including Edward Talcott, who was also a stockbroker, Cornelius Van Cott, who was leader of the Fiftieth Assembly

District and a former fire commissioner and state senator, and General Edward A. McAlpin, who was also a realtor and former mayor of Ossining. The PL made an excellent showing on the field and drew well at the box office since it included the preponderance of professional baseball's stars. The bitter war between the three major leagues left several franchises nearly bankrupt. In July Day secretly informed his NL colleagues he needed $80,000 or would have to sell out to the PL. They came to his rescue. Day sold $25,000 worth of stock to Albert G. and J. W. Spalding and the same amount to Arthur Soden of the Boston Beaneaters. In return for stock in the Giants, John T. Brush of the Indianapolis team erased a $25,000 debt Day owed him. Finally Day sold $6,250 in stock to both Ferdinand Abell and Al Reach of Philadelphia. Day was left with just a $20,000 interest in the Giants.[48]

The baseball war ended when NL magnates co-opted the capitalists behind the PL by offering several an option to purchase an NL or AA club in their hometown. Talcott and his partners were able to gain control of the Giants, whose owners had been all but bankrupted by the costly competition. The team lost $20,000 in 1891 and at least $30,000 in 1892, requiring a subsidy from the league. Press reports indicate that the team made a profit in 1893 and a healthy return of $38,000 in 1894, but was still heavily in debt. Then in January 1895 Andrew Freedman, a rising young Tammanyite businessman and political ally of John Day, purchased the controlling interest in the Giants for $54,000.[49]

Freedman was born in New York City on 1 September 1860 to German-Jewish parents. He graduated from City College with a law degree, but went into real estate. Freedman first became financially involved in sports in 1893 as the owner of Manhattan Field, the Giants' ballpark in 1889 and 1890. Freedman was an intimate friend of Richard Croker, the Tammany boss, and this relationship helped him secure many choice business opportunities. He advised the boss on business affairs and they were partners in several ventures. Freedman never held any governmental position, yet had enormous political influence through his association with the boss and as a member of Tammany's policy-making board, the finance committee, and treasurer in 1897 of the national Democratic party.[50]

Freedman was castigated for running his club as if it were a Tammany appendage. He was a remarkably unpopular owner, among the most hated ever, a status earned by constantly interfering with his team, repeatedly firing managers without cause (sixteen in seven years), encouraging rowdyism on the field, fighting with ballplayers and sportswriters, and treating his players miserably. In 1895 Freedman barred Sam Crane of the *New York Commercial Advertiser* from the ballpark after he wrote that the young owner was ruining New York baseball, and one year later Freedman assaulted Edward Hurst of the *New York Evening World* because of his critical comments.[51]

Some of Freedman's problems with owners and players stemmed from anti-Semitism. In the summer of 1898 when former Giant outfielder Ducky Holmes of the Orioles was belittled by his old teammates, he retorted, "Well, I'm glad I'm not working for a sheeny any more." Freedman demanded the umpire kick Holmes out for his vulgar language, but Tom Lynch demurred, claiming he had heard nothing. Freedman then took the Giants off the field, forfeited the game, and returned the fans' money. He was fined by the league, which also suspended Holmes for ten games.[52]

Freedman's fellow owners were mad at him for ruining the lucrative New York market and were frightened that he would employ his great political influence to bend the league to his will. The league paid him fifteen thousand dollars a year just to maintain control of Manhattan Field and help protect the league against potential interlopers seeking to invade the remunerative New York market.[53]

Freedman's presence discouraged the AL from moving into New York because through leases or options he controlled most of the locations suitable for baseball fields. Possible investors knew that even if they secured a good site, Freedman would use his political clout to halt them, possibly by cutting streets through their grounds. The AL badly wanted a New York franchise to certify its major league status and add to its profits. League executives followed the 1901 mayoralty election with great interest since the Fusion ticket was given a good chance of beating Tammany in the light of revelations connecting the machine to police corruption and gambling. AL owners figured that if the vote went poorly for Tammany, then Freedman would lose his power to prevent their invasion.[54]

The reformers defeated Tammany in the November elections, electing the reformer Seth Low as mayor. Several newspapers predicted that the American League would soon establish a club in the city. However, President Ban Johnson could not secure an adequate site because Freedman still controlled most of the appropriate locations, and Tammany still had a lot of influence, despite Croker's exile to England. The election had a deleterious impact upon Freedman's strength within league councils because it encouraged other owners to finally stand up to him.[55]

While Freedman may have been a loose cannon, he was an astute businessman, who tried unsuccessfully to get fellow magnates to cooperate in establishing a national baseball trust to make major league baseball operate as a true monopoly. Freedman proposed in December 1901 to reorganize the NL into a syndicate that could move franchises and shift reserved players wherever they would best promote competition and profits. The so-called Brush Plan proposed that a cartel be established in which the Giants got a 30 percent share and 12 percent went to each of Freedman's allies: Brush of Cincinnati, Soden of Boston, and Robison of St. Louis. The remaining 34 percent would be divided among the four other teams. Freedman's plan was defeated by his bitter rivals, led by Albert Spalding, who then were blocked in an attempt to ostracize him and take away his franchise.[56]

On 7 July 1902 Freedman signed John McGraw of the Baltimore Orioles to a four-year contract to manage the Giants for an annual eleven-thousand-dollar salary. McGraw had been an outstanding player in the 1890s, when the Orioles were renowned for rowdy and rough play, and was currently the manager and a minority stockholder. McGraw had done a lot of spade work in preparing an anticipated Orioles move to New York for the 1903 season, but was unpopular with Ban Johnson for his umpire-baiting. Johnson suspended McGraw several times in 1902, including five days for inciting spectators to attack umpire Jack Sheridan during a game in Baltimore, and then on 28 June was suspended indefinitely. McGraw knew that Johnson was not going to let him bring an AL club to New York. He secured his release from Baltimore in return for canceling a seven-thousand-dollar debt owed him and jumped to the rival NL.[57]

In the meantime, McGraw and John T. Brush, the principal owner of the Cincinnati Reds and the stockholder in the Giants closest to Freedman, acting as Freedman's agents, arranged for a purchase of a majority interest in the Orioles. On 16 July, a majority share in the Orioles was transferred to them. The new owners promptly released six of the fourteen-man Orioles roster, four of whom, including star catcher Roger Bresnahan and pitcher "Ironman Joe" McGinnity, then joined the Giants. A former boilermaker, McGinnity was also an "ironman" on the mound. During the 1900 pennant race he had won six games in six days, and over the length of his career would win nine doubleheaders. Brush's Reds picked up the other released Orioles, outfielders Cy Seymour and Joe Kelley, and Kelley became their new manager. Ban Johnson then ordered the Orioles franchise forfeited to the league since not enough players remained to field a team. The league operated the club for the remainder of the season with a rag-tag lineup that finished in last place.[58]

Freedman sold most of his Giants stock for $125,000 to Brush because he was disappointed that his investment had never reached its potential and was tired of all the abuse heaped upon him for his mismanagement and encouragement of rowdy baseball. The team's most profitable year under his leadership was 1897, when it made at least $50,000. The Giants finished in the first division only once under Freedman's tenure. In 1902 the Giants finished in the cellar, with their lowest winning percentage (.353) and most games out of first place (53.5) in their history. A third reason for the sale was that Freedman had more pressing matters to attend to, principally the construction of the New York subway. He was on the executive board of the Interborough Rapid Transit Construction Company, which was building the underground, and his security firm was part of the syndicate bonding the construction firm. He was also a member of the Interborough Rapid Transit Company, which would operate the subway, and used his influence as a director to block the Interborough Rapid Transit line from subsidizing an AL team in January 1903 and later prevented construction of a station on the Fourth Avenue line close to the Brooklyn Dodgers' field.[59]

Brush, the new Giants owner, was originally an Indianapolis clothier who had gotten into baseball in 1887 when he acquired the hometown AA franchise for a nominal sum. The team survived just one year in the majors and in 1888 joined the Western Association. Three years later he purchased the Cincinnati Reds for $25,000 and used his minor league team as one of the original "farm teams." Brush sold the Reds in 1902 for $146,000, ostensibly because he needed money to buy the Giants.[60]

A different scenario was that Brush had been forced to sell the Reds by the Cincinnati Republican machine. Brush paid off the machine for years so that his team could play Sunday baseball games. A rumor allegedly reached Brush that a street was going to be extended through his ballpark as part of a series of municipal improvements. Naturally upset, Brush visited a local politician and requested advice. He was told to sell out to certain powerful Republicans for a price well below market value. Brush denied these allegations, but did sell out to a consortium consisting of Republican boss George B. Cox, Cox's right-hand man and Water Commissioner August Herrmann, and Mayor Julius Fleischmann.[61]

Brush took over the Giants at their nadir, but in retrospect, the future was bright because of the former Orioles Freedman had brought to New York and the maturation of young Christy Mathewson. The club made a quick turnaround in 1903, finishing second, led by McGinnity and Mathewson, who combined for 61 victories. The Giants won the pennant in

1904 with 106 wins, led by their star hurlers, who won 68 games. McGinnity alone won 35 and also completed 38 games. But when the season was over, John McGraw refused to play the "inferior" AL champion Boston Red Sox in the World Series, which had been inaugurated the previous year. The snub enabled him to get back at Ban Johnson for having suspended him two years earlier. McGraw's men repeated in 1905 and this time played in the World Series, which they won—thanks in part to Mathewson's three shutouts—defeating the Philadelphia Athletics.

The Giants remained competitive for the next several years and were among the most profitable NL clubs, earning over $500,000 between 1906 and 1910. They won three straight (1911–13) NL crowns, but lost each World Series. The bitterest defeat came in 1912, when the Giants and Red Sox were tied after seven games with three wins apiece (one contest had ended in a draw). In the decisive game, Mathewson took a 2-1 lead going into the bottom of the tenth inning when Clyde Engle's high fly to left center was dropped by center fielder Fred Snodgrass, with the batter ending up at second. Harry Hooper then hit what seemed a certain triple, but Snodgrass made an extraordinary catch that stunned everyone, including Engle, who failed to advance. However, the Sox persevered to score twice and win the game. Snodgrass's muff became forever inscribed in World Series lore. This disappointment only heightened fan interest in 1913, which led to a profit estimated at $150,000–$300,000. The Giants remained contenders for most of the decade, but did not win the pennant again until 1917, when they were defeated in the series by the White Sox.[62]

Brush died in 1912 and his son-in-law Harry Hempstead took over the Giants. The club made an average of $250,000 between 1912 and 1917. Hempstead sold 58 percent of the franchise seven years later for $1.03 million to Tammanyite Charles Stoneham in a deal orchestrated by the infamous gambler Arnold Rothstein. Stoneham was a curb market broker of dubious integrity and was also involved in ticket scalping, bookmaking, and rum running. Stoneham was allied with Governor Al Smith and the powerful Second Assembly District leader Tom Foley, who was also a former sheriff and Stoneham's partner in several shady business deals. Stoneham's partners included John McGraw and Magistrate Francis X. McQuade, the team treasurer, best known for his sympathetic handling of Sunday baseball cases. McQuade resigned from the bench in 1934 under pressure from the Seabury Commission investigating political corruption in New York.[63]

Stoneham made a wise investment because baseball was about to boom in New York with the legalization of Sunday games. In 1920 the Giants made a huge profit of $296,803, the most in NL history to that time. His National Exhibition Company earned dividends of 400 percent by 1930 and was worth $3.75 million. Stoneham's tenants at the Polo Grounds, the Yankees, outdid their landlord, earning $373,862, a new major league record, which generated a lot of jealousy from Stoneham. The Yankees' big attraction was their new right fielder, Babe Ruth.[64]

New York's other NL franchise was the Brooklyn Dodgers. Prior to its merger in 1898 with New York, Brooklyn was the fourth largest city in the United States with a population of 806,343 in 1890. Professional baseball in Brooklyn dated back to the Atlantics and Eckfords of the late 1860s. The Eckfords appeared briefly in the NA in 1871 and 1872, while the Atlantics played in the NA from 1872 to 1875, reportedly with financial assistance from the deputy tax collector.

The team that became the Dodgers began in 1883 as the minor league Grays of the Interstate Association. They won the pennant, made a profit, and moved up to the AA one year later. Stockholders included president Charles Byrne, a realtor and former sports journalist, manager George J. Taylor, night city editor of the *New York Herald*, Byrne's brother-in-law Joseph J. Doyle, his partner in a New York gambling house, and Ferdinand Abell, proprietor of a Narragansett, Rhode Island, gambling emporium, who put up most of the capital. The club finished ninth in a twelve-team league, earning a ten-thousand-dollar profit, and soon became one of the AA's more profitable franchises.[65]

The team was mediocre until after it purchased the Mets following the 1887 season and was further strengthened when it acquired three St. Louis Browns stars. Brooklyn, now known as the Bridegrooms after six players got married, became contenders, coming in second in 1888 and winning the pennant the following year. They lost the championship series to the Giants, however, six games to three.[66]

There was considerable turmoil in the AA during the 1889 campaign. Following the season, two factions fought for control of the league, and after the Brooklyn-led group was defeated, the Bridegrooms and Cincinnati dropped out of the AA and switched to the NL. The Bridegrooms were replaced in the league by the short-lived Gladiators, owned by James C. Kennedy, a prominent and politically connected New York sports enthusiast. Brooklyn also had a club in the fledgling PL financed by Brownsville boosters: banker E. F. Linton, politico Wendell Goodwin, who was also an executive with a local streetcar line, and George Chauncey, a wealthy, prominent realtor and the principal partner, who owned

Eastern Park, where the Bridegrooms played. President Goodwin and his colleagues hoped that a team in their community would encourage people to travel there on Goodwin's transit route and possibly even move to Brownsville. The Bridegrooms lost at least twenty-five thousand dollars during the PL war. In the winter of 1891 following the PL's collapse, Linton and Goodwin purchased 49.6 percent of the Bridegrooms for forty thousand dollars. Byrne then moved the team from its Red Hook location in South Brooklyn to the more sparsely populated Brownsville. The team became known as the Trolley Dodgers because fans walking to Eastern Park had to avoid the trolley and streetcar lines. The move was a big mistake. Attendance in the 1890s averaged 184,000, barely half of the record attendance in 1889. In 1892 Abell bought out some of his partners and by the mid-1890s had 51 percent of the club; Byrne was left with 12 percent and the old PL group had the rest. They all took a beating in the late 1890s, Abell alone losing one hundred thousand dollars by 1898.[67]

Byrne died in 1898 and was succeeded by Charles Ebbets, who purchased half of Chauncey's shares for a one-fourth interest in the team. Born in 1860, Ebbets originally worked as a draftsman, drawing the blueprints for Niblo's Gardens and the Metropolitan Hotel, and then became a printer. But he was dissatisfied with these occupations, and in 1883 his brother helped him get a job with friends who owned the Brooklyn Grays, and Ebbets worked as a general factotum whose duties included printing scorecards, selling tickets, and bookkeeping. Ebbets did such a good job that he was soon promoted to club secretary. Ebbets became active in many volunteer organizations, including national bowling associations, cycling clubs, and secret fraternal societies as well as the Democratic party. In 1895 he was elected to the state assembly, but two years later lost a city council race by one vote. In 1904 Ebbets was buried in a bid for the state senate in the Roosevelt landslide, but was subsequently elected to the city council.[68]

Ebbets's first major decision was to move the ball club back to Red Hook. The move received considerable financial support from local transportation magnates, particularly Al Johnson, brother of Cleveland mayor Tom Johnson, whose Nassau Railroad had a route that passed by the old ballpark site. Because of his transit interests in Cleveland, Johnson had been the president of its team in the Players League in 1890. "I had seen streetcars on the opposite street road loaded down with people going to games," he explained, "and it occurred to me there was a chance for a good investment if I could get grounds on a streetcar line owned by my brother and myself." The Nassau line and the Brooklyn Heights Railroad purchased the lot across the street from the old Red Hook ballpark site for about fifteen thousand dollars and then leased it to the Dodgers for five thousand dollars--one-third less than the rent at Eastern Park.[69]

Ebbets kept his hands in all aspects of the Dodgers operations and even managed the Dodgers for several months. His career got off to a rocky start when the Dodgers ended up in tenth place and attendance was down by 40 percent. The team made a remarkable turnaround in 1899, however, after he formed a syndicate with the Baltimore Orioles, owned by the brewer Harry Von der Horst. The Orioles were an outstanding club, having won consecutive championships from 1894 to 1896 and coming in second the next two years. Yet they were losing money. In the new partnership, Von der Horst obtained 40 percent of the Dodgers and kept 40 percent of the Baltimore club. Orioles president Edward Hanlon got 10 percent of the Brooklyn nine and kept 10 percent of his old team. He became the Dodgers' manager, yet remained president of the Orioles. Ferdinand Abell ended up with 40 percent of each team, and Charles Ebbets got 10 percent of both clubs. The owners decided to concentrate their best men in Brooklyn, and consequently Hanlon brought with him six top players, including star hitters Willie Keeler, Hughie Jennings, and Joe Kelley and pitchers Jay Hughes and Doc McJames. One year later, Ironman Joe McGinnity also joined the Dodgers. Bolstered by these additions, the Dodgers won pennants in 1899 and 1900. The club became known as the Superbas after the popular vaudeville act known as Hanlon's Superbas. But their finest players jumped to the new AL, and the team fell into mediocrity.[70]

Ebbets purchased most of Von der Horst's stock in 1905, financed by an old friend, the furniture manufacturer Henry W. Medicus. In 1907 he bought out Hanlon and controlled 80 percent of the stock, and Medicus the balance. Ebbets became sole owner in 1912 just before he began to build Ebbets Field. The Dodgers under his control were a profitable team. In 1899, for example, when the club won the pennant, attendance rose by 120 percent and earnings were estimated at between $15,000 and $50,000. In the early 1910s, annual profits were about $100,000, reaching $250,000 in the pennant-winning 1916 season. In 1920, Ebbets's final pennant-winning year, the club made $139,785, averaged $138,172 for the next three years, and nearly doubled that in 1924 to $265,670. By then the club was worth an estimated $2.0–$2.5 million.[71]

New York became the site of a third major league team in March 1903 when the AL finally succeeded in landing a franchise there. AL President Ban Johnson had tried for some time to find a suitable Manhattan location without granting a franchise to local politicians, who were adamant in demanding control of any new club. Rumored candidates included the sports promoter James Kennedy, the owner of the Gladiators in 1890, and his political backer, State Senator Tim Sullivan, leader of the Lower East Side Third District and the number two man in Tammany Hall. Sullivan had been a prominent boxing promoter in the late 1890s and was a lead figure in the poolroom business (illegal off-track horse race gambling). They did not get the ball club, but Johnson did accede to political pressure when he awarded the local franchise to a shady Tammany syndicate.[72]

The partnership was presided over by Joseph Gordon, a figurehead and former stockholder in the Giants. Gordon had recently lost his position as deputy superintendent of buildings and wanted the recognition given to a major league club president to help out his coal business. He supposedly named the club the Highlanders after his favorite British regiment, the Gordon Highlanders. The real owners were the gambling impresario Frank Farrell, who soon replaced Gordon as president, and former police chief William Devery. Their political backers included former mayor Robert Van Wyck, Tim Sullivan, Tom Foley, and the retired police inspector Thomas McAvoy, head of Tammany's Twenty-Third A.D. District, where the new park was to be located.[73]

The year before, Farrell, reportedly worth $750,000, had agreed to furnish capital to move the Baltimore AL team to New York, but could not find a place to play. He had important interests in New York poolrooms and owned a luxurious casino designed by Stanford White that was frequented by high society. During the 1901 election campaign William Travers Jerome, the reform candidate for district attorney, named Farrell as a leader of the notorious New York gambling trust that included Devery, Police Commissioner Joseph Sexton, City Clerk J. F. Carroll, Mayor Van Wyck, and Big Tim Sullivan. Farrell lost his police protection following Tammany's debacle at the polls, began to diversify, and purchased Empire Racetrack in Yonkers for $217,000. Farrell resumed his prominence in gambling in August 1902 when he opened an elegant gambling house at 33 W. Thirty-Fourth Street. It had state-of-the-art security, including a double iron front gate and a secret button that turned off the light and closed all windows and doors. A concealed iron door on the fourth floor led to the building next door, where gambling apparatus was maintained. Nonetheless, Jerome had it raided in December and closed down. Three months later Farrell was back in business eleven blocks uptown.[74]

Farrell was originally regarded by the media as an infamous character.

But after Farrell obtained his baseball franchise, sold his new gambling parlor, and announced his decision to curtail his racing interests, the press attitude toward him changed radically. Newspapers devoted less attention to his illegal businesses and more to his new role as an ostensible public benefactor. He became a "sportsman" instead of a "gambler." Farrell was henceforth portrayed as a civic-minded citizen who was spending his own money to give his townsfolk an exciting baseball team. Compared with Freedman, Farrell was a model owner who treated his players well, was cordial to the press, and was generous to the fans. While Freedman appeared greedy, Farrell was seen as willing to invest to build a contender. The *New York American* claimed he spent 250 percent more on his ball club in 1907 ($98,000) than on his racing stables. The *New York Tribune*, four years later, agreed: "Frank Farrell has done much for baseball here, and deserves whatever reward a championship team would bring."[75]

Farrell's partner, William Devery, was a close personal friend dating back to when he had been captain at the Nineteenth Precinct, a half-block from Farrell's old poolroom. Farrell so appreciated Devery's protection that he let him live rent free in a house he owned in the heart of the Tenderloin. Originally a bartender, Devery joined the police force in 1878 and advanced rapidly, aided by his patrons, Richard Croker and Tim Sullivan. Devery had a turbulent career and while serving as a captain in the Tenderloin and Hell's Kitchen neighborhoods was frequently accused of permitting gambling and disorderly houses. Testimony given at the legislature's 1894 Lexow Committee Hearings investigating police corruption led to his indictment on criminal charges and dismissal from the force. However, when he appealed, Devery was acquitted on a technicality and reinstated.[76]

In 1898 Devery was promoted to inspector, and six months later, chief of police. According to the muckraker Lincoln Steffens, "He was no more fit to be a chief of police than the fish man was to be director of the Aquarium, but as a character, as a work of art, he was a masterpiece." During his flamboyant and crooked tenure Devery could usually be found meeting with bail bonds agents, dive owners, and poolroom operators in the heart of the Tenderloin. His regime was so blatantly corrupt that by 1901, when the legislature abolished his position and replaced it with a commission system, he owned $640,000 worth of real estate. The Democratic bosses circumvented the reform by getting the new commissioner to appoint Devery as his deputy and then left him in charge. Shortly thereafter, Devery was again arrested and charged with neglect of duty, but was found not guilty. A few days later, Seth Low became mayor, and one of his first actions was to fire Devery.[77]

In 1914 Farrell and Devery decided to sell their franchise since they were going broke. They had become estranged from each other because of the club's disappointing performance on the field and at the box office. The Highlanders peaked in 1904, led by spitballer Jack Chesbro, who won 41 games (the modern-day record for victories), losing the pennant on a wild pitch on the final day of the season. Thereafter they rarely finished in the first division. Their poor showing was underlined by the expertise of the far more popular Giants. Furthermore, the Highlanders (renamed the Yankees in 1913) made a substantial profit only in 1910, when the club came in second and netted $80,000. In January 1915, following a seventh place finish, the team was sold for $460,000 to Jacob Ruppert Jr., owner of the Ruppert Breweries and an ardent fan who had long coveted the Giants franchise, and his partner C. Tillinghast Huston, a civil engineer who had made a fortune in Cuba after the Spanish-American War.[78]

Ruppert briefly attended Columbia College but left to learn brewing from the bottom up. He joined Tammany in 1888 at the age of twenty-one, seeking prestige, power, and protection for the family business, which became the leading brewery in the state after he took over. The family contributed heavily to Tammany, and Ruppert became influential in party affairs, serving on the powerful Finance Committee alongside Andrew Freedman. In 1897 Croker personally selected him to run for the city council presidency to balance the slate with a German-American candidate. But his nomination was withdrawn after it failed to placate disappointed German Americans, who had hoped for a mayoralty nomination for a compatriot, and because it aroused the jealousy of other New York brewers. One year later, in recognition of his party loyalty, Ruppert was nominated for Congress from the heavily Republican Fifteenth District and won the election in a big upset. He represented the district for four terms, compiling an undistinguished record.[79]

Ruppert was prepared to go to any length to produce a winning team. In 1918 he and Huston hired the experienced Miller Huggins to manage the club and thereafter spent freely to bring in top talent. The key transactions were with Harry Frazee, a theatrical impresario who had purchased the Boston Red Sox, a top AL team, in 1917. Frazee soon sold off many of his best players because he was often in debt and needed new money for future Broadway shows, including *No, No, Nanette*. Following the 1918 season, when the Sox won the World Series, Frazee sold three of his top players, outfielder Duffy Lewis and pitchers Ernie Shore and Dutch Leonard, to the Yankees for $50,000. Then in mid-1919 the Sox sold one of their top pitchers, the troubled spitballer Carl Mays, to the Yankees for $40,000. The Yankees finished in third that season.

In December 1919, the Yankees startled the baseball world with the announcement of the purchase of Babe Ruth from the Red Sox for the unprecedented price of $125,000 plus a $350,000 loan. But the Yankees were not done raiding the Red Sox. At the end of the 1920 season they hired Red Sox manager Edward G. Barrow as business manager, who promptly negotiated a trade that brought them Red Sox pitcher Waite Hoyt, a future Hall of Famer. The Yankees dynasty of the 1920s was largely built off the once-great Red Sox.

Ruth's performance with the Yankees in 1920 proved he was worth whatever the price. Besides a record 54 home runs, he set an all-time slugging percentage record of .847. He packed the stands with fans eager to see a new style of baseball that emphasized power over science. Ruth eventually hit 714 home runs, batted .342, and led the Yankees to seven pennants and four world championships.[80]

The Political Nexus

The political influence of Chicago's and New York's owners helped their teams establish franchises, locate ballpark sites, and protect themselves against interlopers. Clout also hoped with such mundane matters as license fees and police protection. However, it had less impact on gambling, a menace that threatened the integrity of the game.

Like other commercialized amusements, baseball teams were required to obtain municipal licenses that established criteria to promote order and public safety. The fees provided a means for the municipality to obtain badly needed revenue and also provided city leaders with political leverage over weak owners who lacked political clout, such as Abner Powell in Atlanta. Chicago teams could not get licenses until certain stipulations were met: the names of incorporators had to be filed with the mayor; new ballparks required frontage consents from surrounding property owners; fields were barred near churches, hospitals, and schools, where they would be nuisances; the grounds had to be inspected for safety; and special permits were required before intoxicating beverages could be sold.[81]

License fees varied from city to city, depending in part on a team's political clout. New York baseball teams paid the city's standard $500

amusement fee, while in Cincinnati, where the local Republican machine ran the Reds, the club paid only $100 until 1912, when reform
mayor Henry Hunt raised the levy to $750. Chicago's license fees were on
a sliding scale depending on the ballpark's seating capacity. Until 1909,
when the fee structure was substantially altered by the revised municipal codes, its major league teams were assessed just $300. After that the
Cubs were reassessed at $1,000, since West Side Park seated over 15,000,
while the White Sox were charged only $700, since their park seated
fewer than 15,000. Semiprofessional fees were reduced from $100 to
$75.[82]

Political connections helped Chicago owners keep assessments to
manageable levels. After World War I, when the municipality nearly
went bankrupt and desperately needed additional sources of revenue, one
popular remedy was raising license fees. A bill was submitted to the city
council that set the maximum fee for a ballpark at $3,000, but it was
revised down to $2,000. The Sox were assessed the maximum rate since
Comiskey Park seated over 40,000, while the Cubs were charged $1,500
since their North Side field seated fewer than 20,000.[83] This was merely
the first round of increases. In 1921, Alderman Anton Cermak (a future
Chicago mayor and founder of the modern Cook County Democratic
machine) proposed extending the license system on a voluntary basis to
certain uncovered professions while simultaneously raising established
fees. He submitted a bill calling for a 5 percent tax on the gross receipts of
local ball clubs. The club owners estimated that if this levy had been in
effect a year earlier it would have cost the Sox $30,000 and the Cubs
$20,000. Alfred Austrian, the attorney for both teams and a prominent
figure in Chicago politics, met with the council's Revenue Subcommittee and argued the folly of Cermak's proposal. Austrian urged reconsideration, citing court decisions that had forbidden municipal taxes on a
percentage basis, and warned that ticket prices would have to be raised to
meet the proposed assessment. He knew this argument would have a
telling impact on the ambitious Cermak, who was set to run for the Cook
County Board presidency and was fighting to keep the cost of popular
amusements within the budget of his ethnic working-class constituents.
Austrian outlined a compromise, subsequently enacted, doubling the
license fee for major league teams.[84]

Police protection was the major service teams expected from the municipality. The need to maintain order at the ballpark dated back to the
original NL constitution of 1876, which required teams to provide police
protection. In the 1880s the White Stockings, for example, employed six
guards for home games and brought in additional officers whenever large

crowds were anticipated, but security generally remained inadequate. In 1899 a city council member, apparently concerned about the safety and welfare of baseball fans, introduced an ordinance requiring the police department to detail officers to the ball games at the expense of the baseball team, but his proposal died in committee.[85]

The police maintained order outside the parks, and for many years even patrolled inside Chicago and New York ballparks. Chicago's patrol officers worked inside and outside its ball fields at no charge to the local teams. As many as two hundred mounted and foot officers were detailed to protect fans at the World Series and other major dates. The sportswriter Ring Lardner estimated that since an average team spent from twenty to fifty dollars a day for security, the Chicago clubs were saved several thousand dollars each season. During the 1920s, an average of thirty-one officers a day worked inside Wrigley Field and Comiskey Park at no charge to the teams. Legislation was introduced in the 1920s to tax the Cubs and Sox for security work, but the bills never reached the floor. A 1931 blue-ribbon Chicago Police Committee report castigated this situation and urged that officers be assigned to duty only when "it is deemed absolutely essential," that they be off duty, and that the city be reimbursed for their salaries. However, nothing came of this suggestion, and Chicago's police continued to work inside the ballparks for decades.[86]

New York City police also gave favored treatment to the baseball teams until 1907. Police Commissioner General Thomas A. Bingham, a mainstay in the administration of Tammany-backed reform mayor George McClellan Jr., decided to enforce the law prohibiting the use of municipal police within a private place of business unless there was a clear and present danger. This made New York the only city where regular police officers were not on duty in the ballparks. The Giants tested the commissioner, announcing they would not engage any private police officers for opening day and warning Bingham he would be held responsible for the consequences. A riot occurred when many of the seventeen thousand spectators swarmed over the field at the beginning of the ninth inning. After fifteen minutes of chaos, the Giants appealed to police officers stationed outside for assistance, but they refused to help out.[87]

The *New York Times* supported Bingham's actions since the law was quite clear. Bingham had previously complained that his staff was often weakened when officers were detailed to perform work that should have been done by private security. He felt entrepreneurs who assembled crowds for their own profit should consider the cost of security as a necessary expense.[88]

Following their confrontation with Bingham, the Giants decided to hire uniformed Pinkertons for security, while the Highlanders employed retired police officers. These operatives were adequate as long as fans remained calm. But when fans got out of control, the special police were virtually useless because spectators refused to listen to them since they had no legitimate authority or any real power. Indeed, the guards were probably more frightened of the multitude than the fans of them, and they tried to avoid antagonizing spectators. In 1913 the Giants tried to improve security by replacing the Pinkertons with a specially trained corps under former Pinkerton agent Harry V. Dougherty, who operated his own detective bureau and was well connected through his brother, the city's chief of detectives. Dougherty selected only husky men who were trained in military drill and outfitted them in drab gray uniforms to give them the appearance of authority.[89]

After 1907 the police rarely worked inside New York ballparks unless huge crowds were expected, and then special details were assigned. For example, the city assigned police to the Polo Grounds late in 1908 when the Cubs came into town for a crucial weekend series and again for the pennant-deciding final game of the season. Baseball magnates, like other entertainment entrepreneurs, tried to circumvent Bingham's orders, with little success. They urged, to no avail, that officers be assigned when needed, rather than waste time enforcing dated Sunday blue laws.[90]

One main duty of officers at the ballparks was dealing with ticket scalping. Scalping was especially notorious at New York baseball fields and theaters. Ticket scalping was so widespread before the 1911 series between the Giants and Athletics that several state legislators who were unable to get tickets considered submitting bills to put professional baseball under the newly established state athletic commission. Extensive preparations were announced the following year to eliminate scalping at the series that matched the Giants and the Red Sox. Plainclothes and uniformed officers were detailed to keep known speculators from obtaining extra tickets at the public sale. An area was cordoned off for fans waiting in line for tickets, but all plans went awry because the police cooperated with scalpers, who secured a large cache of tickets. The first one hundred people in line were recognized as either officers or scalpers. People with pull were seen going through the ticket office several times. Instead of going to the end of the queue, these repeaters returned right to the front, where police officers helped them get back into line. Scalpers got additional tickets by buying them from other people who had waited in line and by putting boys and women in line to purchase tickets for them. One journalist estimated that a quarter of the reserved seats were sold to speculators.[91]

The principal job of police officers assigned to ballparks was crowd control. The threat of a riot or some lesser disturbance always existed whenever thousands of people gathered in a limited space, and baseball crowds tended to be particularly unruly. Sometimes after making controversial decisions, umpires had to be escorted to safety through an enraged mob.[92]

Security problems were frequently aggravated by the proximity of fans to the ballplayers. The stands in the old wooden parks were located close to the diamonds, so athletes could clearly hear the derogatory comments bellowed at them. Young, hot-tempered ballplayers were quick to take offense and sometimes climbed into the stands to retaliate. In 1904 Cincinnati assigned a security guard near the visitors' bench to protect players from abusive fans and to protect spectators from aggressive players. Spectators who stood on the field when seating capacities were exhausted were restrained only by ropes and security. They could swarm the field to protest an umpire's decision or halt play by taking a shortcut across the field to beat the rush home. Security forces were in a difficult situation and had to use their best judgment when restraining crowds. They risked fomenting a riot if their actions were too aggressive in certain cases or too weak in others. Nonetheless, games were rarely halted because of uncooperative fans.[93]

One of the most notable episodes of disorder occurred on opening day at Brooklyn's Washington Park on 12 April 1912. Fans standing on the field obstructed the view of Mayor William Gaynor and other patrons and hindered play. After the Dodgers' private security guards failed to clear the field, Ebbets requested assistance from the municipal police detailed outside the park. The deputy commissioner in charge refused to allow his officers inside the park because it was private property, but when the mayor saw the event getting out of hand, he ordered the police to intervene. When the officers entered the field the crowd panicked and tried to run away, but there was no room to move. The playing area could not be cleared, and the game was called at the end of the sixth inning.[94]

Gambling, Politics, and Professional Baseball

Baseball's rhetoric asserted that it was an uplifting, clean, and honest sport, but the game was actually strongly tainted by gambling. Professional baseball was an important nexus between urban machine politics and organized crime, albeit a lesser one than prize fighting or horse racing. Several big league owners had close identifications with gambling, most notably Farrell, a professional gambler, while Stoneham was closely tied to Arnold Rothstein, and Charles Weeghman was a personal friend of Mont Tennes, head of organized gambling in Chicago and operator of the infamous racing wire. In addition, Ruppert, Stoneham, and Fleischmann all owned racing stables. In 1919 Stoneham and his minor partners McGraw and McQuade purchased a Havana sporting complex comprised of the Oriental Park racetrack and the Casino National. However, two years later the new commissioner of baseball, Judge Kenesaw Mountain Landis, forced them to sell.[95]

Baseball's main attraction was the action and drama of the game and did not require gambling to maintain interest. Nonetheless, professional baseball's nature made it conducive to wagering since people could bet on many segments of the game. Fans wagered on the outcome, the total number of hits and runs, the call of a pitch, and even if a batted ball would be caught. Men and women bet on baseball, especially in cities like Boston and Pittsburgh, which had no thoroughbred racing to interest the gambling crowd. After 1910 betting on baseball became increasingly attractive for those Chicagoans who had given up trying to evade Mont Tennes's monopoly on racetrack news. Baseball gamblers could get quick information about the result of games by subscribing individually to ticker services like Western Union or by frequenting bars or other hangouts that had the service.[96]

The pool, which dated back to around 1871, was the most popular system of wagering on baseball. The first form was an auction pool, in which the pool maker would "auction" to the highest bidder the choice of teams to win a championship. After the highest bidder made a selection, the next highest bidder would choose a team, and so on down the line. An auction could also be arranged for such statistical accomplishments as hits or runs. The money wagered was combined to form a stake, less the pool maker's 10 percent commission. The auction pool system died out in the 1880s and was replaced by bookmaking, in which a professional gambler established odds on the likelihood of certain teams winning or losing or certain quantifiable feats being achieved. Consequently, more people could bet on a favorite under the new system than could in the auction pool system. However, pools did continue to be a popular form of baseball gambling. In the new style of pools, the initiator would give each bettor combinations of clubs or players. In another version of the pool, wagerers could select their own combinations. The bettor whose team achieved the most (or, in another variant, the fewest) hits or runs during the week won the pool. Baseball pools were widespread and were found at the workplace and at such centers of the male bachelor subculture as barber shops, billiard parlors, and tobacconists.[97]

Baseball magnates wanted to curtail public gambling on baseball to safeguard its prestige and honest reputation. They were afraid betting would destroy baseball's appeal by encouraging fans to believe that gamblers were fixing games, as occurred in boxing and horse racing. Owners wanted to differentiate baseball from those sports and maintain its self-proclaimed higher moral stature that helped make it a popular middle-class sport. Concerns about fixes were no idle fear, and when the NL was established in 1876, a primary goal was to put the sport on a superior ethical plateau. However, just one year later a bookmaker bribed four players on the league-leading Louisville Grays to cost the club the pennant. They were summarily expelled. In 1881 the integrity of the sport was further damaged when umpire Richard Higham was dismissed for betting on games he worked.[98]

Persistent rumors about fixes persisted into the twentieth century, including attempts to bribe players in the first two World Series. The most notorious suspected fixer was Hal Chase, an outstanding ballplayer, who had begun his major league career in 1905 with the Highlanders and was regarded as the finest defensive first baseman in the game, despite his unusually large number of errors. He revolutionized the position by playing off the base and was unmatched in defending against bunts and initiating double plays. "Unfortunately," as Harold Seymour pointed out, "his defects of character more than matched his playing skill," and he was the archetype of all crooked ballplayers. His heart and his integrity were always suspect, and Chase undermined several managers and teams. His teammates knew him as a pool shark, a sharp (if not always honest) poker player, and a heavy bettor on ball games. "My limit was $100 per game and I never bet against my own team," asserted Chase. "I had to have a bet on the side and we used to bet with the other team and the gamblers who sat in the boxes."[99]

Chase first disrupted his team in 1908 when he left the Highlanders in August for an outlaw club in California after a journalist had written that the manager had questioned his integrity. Chase returned in 1909 and one year later was accused by manager George Stallings of fixing games to make Stallings look bad so he could replace him. Chase went to President Farrell and told him he would leave unless Stallings, who had guided the club to a second place finish, left first. Farrell fired Stallings and replaced him with Chase as player-manager for six thousand dollars. The Highlanders fell to sixth place, with a record of 76-76. Harry Wolverton directed the Highlanders to a last place finish in 1912, and he was replaced by the veteran manager France Chance, formerly of the Cubs, and the squad was renamed the Yankees. Chance was chagrined with

Chase's play and told sportswriters one afternoon: "Did you notice some of the balls that got away from Chase today? They weren't wild throws; they were only made to look that way. He's been doing that right along. He's throwing games on me!" Chance had noticed what Chase's teammates, discerning fans, and sportswriters had not: that Chase frequently got to first base just late enough to miss an accurately thrown ball and turn it into an error. Two days later Chase was traded to the White Sox for two lesser players. Chase jumped to the Federal League in June 1914 after giving the White Sox ten days' written notice, testing the option clause in his contract. He batted .347 for Buffalo in 1914 and led the Federal League in homers the following season.[100]

In 1916 he joined the Cincinnati Reds and led the NL in batting with a .339 average. He was by then a full-fledged fixer and gambler, actively recruiting other players to join his fixes and collecting commissions on bets he arranged. His teammates complained about him to Manager Christy Mathewson, who suspended Chase on 9 August 1918 for "indifferent playing," which Mathewson later explained meant fixing games. Chase denied that he had tried to get Giants pitcher Pol Perritt to throw a game, but admitted having twice bet on ball games in which he had not played.

Early in 1919 the NL held a secret hearing about various allegations stemming from three teammates who claimed Chase had offered them bribes. Pitcher Jimmy Ring testified that one afternoon in 1917 when he was brought in to relieve, Chase told him, "I've got some money bet on this game kid. There's something in it for you if you lose." Ring lost the game, inadvertently, and Chase give him fifty dollars the next morning. Despite a preponderance of evidence, the NL exonerated Chase, probably to protect the good name of baseball and avoid a lawsuit. Chase was then traded to the Giants even though McGraw had testified against him in the hearings. But then McGraw always had room for another .300 hitter. The historian Eugene Murdock argues that "the Chase whitewash was practically an open invitation for players to throw games with little fear of retribution." Yet Chase did not get off. Later in the season, McGraw quietly suspended Chase "indefinitely" after NL president John Heydler gave Stoneham an affidavit from a Boston gambler and a copy of a five-hundred-dollar check made out to Chase to fix a game in 1918. Chase had offered bribes to five different major leaguers in 1918 and 1919.[101]

Chase's malfeasance became public in June 1920 during a failed lawsuit by outfielder Lee Magee against the Cubs, who had fired him. In the course of the trial it was revealed that on 25 July 1918 when Magee and

Chase were both with the Reds, they had each bet five hundred dollars against their team. A few months later, Chase was indicted in connection with the Black Sox scandal, but never stood trial.[102]

Organized baseball could do little about the widespread poolroom betting or other wagering outside the parks, despite the raised fears for the integrity of the game. One outfit in Pittsburgh, where baseball betting occurred mostly in cafes and poolrooms, ran a national pool with prizes of one thousand dollars a week. Another pool reportedly made thirty to fifty thousand dollars a week. A 1911 study of the gambling problem in New Haven estimated that forty thousand factory workers and boys held pool tickets costing ten thousand dollars.[103]

Organized baseball did little to curb gambling inside ballparks, which was particularly heavy in Boston, Pittsburgh, Chicago, St. Louis, and Cincinnati. Ban Johnson tried to keep his league clean, twice hiring private detectives to investigate particularly flagrant ballparks, but got little support from his colleagues. In 1917 Johnson urged Harry Frazee to clean up rampant open betting at Fenway Park, but was told to mind his own business. Johnson was warned later on by Allan Pinkerton that "if you do not make some move very soon you may be sure they [the gamblers] will corrupt your game." Johnson tried to interest NL owners in working together with the Pinkerton Agency to fight the gambling menace, but got no cooperation. They did little more than keep lists of known gamblers and refuse to sell them tickets or post signs inside their parks declaring that betting was forbidden and that violators would be removed from the premises. Those warnings were rarely followed by action since club owners feared interrupting friendly wagering would create ill will. As a result, bookmakers were seldom apprehended and rarely convicted. It was difficult to make an arrest stick unless the accused operated out of a regular place of business, plus gamblers often had political protection. Many professional gamblers in Pittsburgh even attended games free on passes obtained from council members and other municipal leaders. Besides, there was little public demand for strict enforcement of the proscriptive laws because gambling was considered a widespread but victimless crime, and the average baseball fan was worried that he might get arrested while making a friendly wager.[104]

Public opinion encouraged ball clubs to clean up their parks only when gambling became too obvious to be ignored. In 1912 the *Atlanta Constitution* urged the Crackers to hire special police or get the city police to prevent the open gambling going on behind home plate. The usual response to public pressure was to post detectives to watch for known gamblers and frighten them off. However, this did not scare off the gamblers, who knew they might, at worst, be ejected from the grounds. A 1906 local court had ruled that bookmakers were guilty only if operating out of a regular place of business, but walking about and taking private bets was allowed.[105]

After World War I baseball management made its strongest effort to fight gambling in the parks. The Cleveland Indians hired about thirty detectives supervised by H. Clay Folger to spot known gamblers, remove them from the field, and turn them over to plainclothes police for arrest. But elsewhere the attempt to control gambling was halfhearted. In New York the Yankees kept a list of about one hundred undesirables they wanted kept out. Detectives circulated in the Polo Grounds to gather evidence of wrongdoing, apprehending people seen moving from seat to seat who they suspected were searching for potential bettors. However, even if bettors were arrested and convicted, they usually received a token fine. In 1920, for instance, forty-seven spectators were seized for wagering at Comiskey Park, tried, found guilty, and fined all of one dollar. On the rare occasion when professional bookmakers were brought to justice, they were typically indicted on a lesser charge of disorderly conduct for which they might be fined five or ten dollars, hardly a forceful deterrent.[106]

The gambling menace climaxed when it was revealed in September 1920 that the previous year's World Series in which the heavily underdog Cincinnati Reds had upset the White Sox, five games to three, had been fixed. The scheme was initiated by first baseman Chick Gandil and shortstop Swede Risberg and reputedly financed by the organized crime kingpin Arnold Rothstein, who supposedly won $350,000 betting on the series. The alleged co-conspirators included pitchers Eddie Cicotte and Lefty Williams, utility player Fred McMullin, and outfielders Happy Felsch and Shoeless Joe Jackson, a former South Carolina millhand who was among the greatest players of all time. Third baseman Bucky Weaver knew about the plot, but did not participate in its execution.[107]

The 1919 White Sox were considered the finest team in baseball. They had won the World Series two years earlier over the Giants, but except for Eddie Collins, perhaps the most outstanding second baseman ever, the ballplayers were generally underpaid by the stingy Comiskey. Collins was a college graduate who had been a member of Connie Mack's "$100,000 infield" until 1915, when Mack dismantled his star-laden team. During his twenty-five-year career he batted .333 and had 744 stolen bases. He was the highest paid man on the Sox, earning $14,500 (the salary he had brought with him from the Athletics), plus a $500 bonus as captain. He did not get along well with his less-educated teammates, who resented him. First baseman Gandil did not speak to him for two years; and in 1919 during infield practice, none of the other infielders would throw him any balls.[108]

Prior to the scandal, Comiskey had an excellent public image and a great relationship with the press. He was known for his resourceful operation of the White Sox, his beautiful and expensive ballpark, and his lavish parties. The "Old Roman" wined and dined the press with extravagant meals and spirits at the ballpark press room and paid for their first-class travel while on the road. He had spent freely to get top players; in 1915 he bought Collins's contract for $50,000 and obtained Jackson from Cleveland for $30,000 and two minor leaguers. However, the public was not aware of how he squeezed his players. They received $3 a day for meal money while other teams budgeted $4, and he even tried to charge them for laundering uniforms. Comiskey changed his mind only after the players boycotted the laundromat for several weeks.[109]

Of course, what irked the players the most was how badly they were paid. In 1919 the eight Black Sox averaged $4,300 in salary, with Weaver's the highest at $7,200. The eight were relatively uneducated and less urbane than their teammates and had not negotiated effectively with Comiskey. Joe Jackson, who batted .356 over his thirteen-year career, third highest in major league history to that point, was making just $6,000. Fourteen-year veteran Eddie Cicotte, the ace of the pitching staff, earned $5,712 plus a $3,000 bonus.[110]

The players sought to renegotiate their salaries in midseason since their team was on a pennant-winning pace and had record gate receipts. When Comiskey refused to consider their proposal, the players threatened to strike, but Manager "Kid" Gleason talked them out of it. This only added to their resentment of Comiskey. The player who was most aggrieved against management was Eddie Cicotte, who had been promised a $10,000 bonus if he won thirty games, but felt Comiskey had benched him to prevent him from reaching that goal. Cicotte won his twenty-eighth game on 5 September and did not pitch again until two weeks later, when he won his twenty-ninth. He pitched five days later when the team had a chance to clinch the pennant, but gave up five runs in seven innings and was taken out for a pinch hitter. This was his last regular season appearance. The New York Times thought that resting the veteran was a wise managerial decision because starter Red Faber was out with a sore arm, leaving the Sox with just two experienced starters for the nine-game World Series.[111]

Shortly before the series, first baseman Chick Gandil allegedly got seven teammates to agree to fix the series for $100,000. The key were starting pitchers Cicotte and Williams because of their central position in the game. Cicotte, who was renowned for his control, hit the first batter he faced, a signal to the gamblers that the fix was in. He lost the first and fourth games, exhibiting unusually poor control and terrible fielding. Williams was particularly ineffective, especially in the deciding eighth game after his family had been threatened by a gangster in Chicago, lasting just one-third of an inning, giving up three runs. Weaver and Jackson, in contrast, played well. Weaver batted .324 with eleven hits, and Jackson had twelve hits and led the team with a .375 average, although he fielded lackadaisically. The seven collaborators supposedly divided up $80,000 for their efforts, Gandil getting $35,000, Cicotte, $10,000, and Jackson, who had been promised $20,000, got just $5,000.[112]

Gleason and some of the players, especially catcher Ray Schalk, suspected something was amiss, but could not put their fingers on it, and certain keen observers, particularly the sportswriters Hugh Fullerton and Ring Lardner, were also suspicious. Fullerton sent a telegram to the papers carrying his syndicated column: "ADVISE ALL NOT TO BET ON THIS SERIES. UGLY RUMORS AFLOAT." His suspicions were reinforced right from the start of the first game, when Cicotte hit the Reds' lead-off man. Lardner composed a song for his friends in the press box to the tune of "I'm Forever Blowing Bubbles": "I'm forever blowing ball games,/Pretty ball games in the air. I come from Chi/I hardly try/Just go to bat and fade and die;/Fortune's coming my way,/That's why I don't care./I'm forever blowing ball games/And the gamblers treat us fair."[113]

After the series Fullerton insinuated that it had been fixed and recommended halting future interleague competition. Rumors of skullduggery abounded for a while, but except for Fullerton, few sportswriters tried to follow up on the story. The *Sporting News* argued that rumors of foul play were undoubtedly false despite the large presence of gamblers. Comiskey was skeptical about the series, but kept most of his concerns to himself out of fear of hurting him or his team. After the series he publicly avowed his confidence in his players and offered a $20,000 reward to anyone providing contrary information, but he was sufficiently suspicious to hold up the World Series checks of eight players. Comiskey explained his predicament to his friend State's Attorney MacClay Hoyne, indicating that if the suspected scandal was made public, it would ruin him and organized baseball. Hoyne promised to keep the matter out of the courts while Comiskey hired a private detective to investigate the lifestyles of his suspects to see if they were making suspiciously large purchases.[114]

The miserly Comiskey opened his purse a bit before the next season. Cicotte was paid $10,000 plus a $3,000 bonus; Williams's salary was doubled to $6,000; Jackson's was raised to $8,000; Felsch went from $3,000 to $7,000, plus a $3,000 bonus. The 1920 White Sox squad was pretty much the same team except for Gandil, who never reported. They played well, despite strong animosity between the "Clean Sox" and the "Black Sox" and were in the thick of the pennant race all season long, even though some players were still throwing games. Cicotte won twenty-one games and Lefty Williams won twenty-two; Joe Jackson, who hit .382, was among the leading batsmen. The Sox ended up in third place with 96 victories, just two games behind the pennant-winning Indians, and one behind the Yankees.[115]

Late in the season, on 24 September, Fullerton's *Chicago Herald-Examiner* broke a shocking story alleging that a recent Cubs game had been fixed. Cubs president William Veeck Sr. admitted that he had received several phone calls and telegrams warning him that the game scheduled for 31 August had been fixed and that he had accordingly ordered Manager Fred Mitchell to pitch Grover Cleveland Alexander instead of the scheduled Claude Hendrix.[116]

Three days later State's Attorney MacClay Hoyne announced impanelment of a special grand jury to investigate baseball gambling, including the rumored chicanery during the 1919 World Series. Hoyne called the grand jury in response to growing public demands for a full inquiry into baseball corruption as well as his personal need for a campaign issue for the forthcoming Democratic primary election. The grand jury uncovered a great deal of evidence that the series had been fixed. Cicotte, Jackson, and Williams all confessed, based on the advice of Alfred Austrian, Comiskey's attorney, without getting any grants of immunity. In the meanwhile, Happy Felsch admitted his complicity to a journalist. Americans were shocked by the revelations that the national pastime had been tainted.[117]

The Black Sox scandal was an important symbolic event, coming at a time when many old stock Americans were worried about the future of their country. Although the Allies had won World War I, it seemed they were losing the peace. The country appeared in danger of being drawn into foreign entanglements through the League of Nations. Growing fears of Bolshevik successes in Europe and radicalism at home led to the Red Scare and the suppression of civil liberties. The postwar economic depression led to strikes in such major industries as steel and railroads; there was even a strike by Boston police officers. The country was coming apart at the seams. Paranoia and anti-Semitism led some Americans to believe that baseball, the great American institution that was supposed to epitomize the country's traditional values, had been done in by a Jewish criminal (Arnold Rothstein), who had masterminded and bankrolled the plot.[118] If baseball was no good, what hope was there for the rest of our culture and society?

In 1921 seven of the alleged Black Sox went on trial for conspiracy to defraud the public, committing a confidence game, and harming the property rights of Comiskey and the AL. There was no indictment for fixing games because Illinois had no laws forbidding the corrupting of sporting events. Of the eight suspected players, only utilityman McMullin, who had appeared twice as a pinch hitter, was not tried. Ten gamblers were also indicted, but just two went to trial. The prosecutor's case was severely hampered because State's Attorney Hoyne stole the Cicotte, Jackson, and Williams confessions, along with their waivers of immunity. Hoyne took the documents when he cleaned out his office after failing to get renominated in the recent primary. The people behind the theft were Alfred Austrian and William Fallon, a prominent New York attorney who represented Rothstein and was a personal friend of Charles Stoneham and John J. McGraw. The defendants were found not guilty and the ballplayers were carried out of the courtroom on the shoulders of the jurors, who were proud of having vindicated the tarnished name of the national pastime.[119]

Despite the verdict, the new baseball commissioner, Judge Kenesaw Mountain Landis, immediately blacklisted all eight of the players. The former federal judge, just beginning his two-decade iron-fisted rule of baseball, chose to set a higher standard for baseball law, which he alone adjudicated, than was required for civil law. In 1924 Shoeless Joe Jackson challenged Landis's decision, suing the White Sox for back pay. Jackson lost his suit, however, because his missing confession was conveniently produced by defense attorney Alfred Austrian, who could not explain how he had obtained the purloined papers.[120]

The close ties that existed between local politicians and professional baseball in Atlanta, Chicago, and New York were typical of the relationship that existed between most franchises and urban politicians. During the Progressive Era, every single major league team had political connections of some sort, and it was not much different in the minor leagues. Major league owners were attracted by potentially high profits. Back in the early 1890s the majors struggled, but in 1894, for example, only two of twelve teams lost money, one or two broke even, and the rest made from $5,000 to $40,000, led by the Giants and the Orioles. Overall, this was quite good considering that the nation was in the midst of the worst depression up to that time, epitomized by the Pullman strike that year. The majors fared even better in 1895. The economic historian Robert Burk argues that the cartel's earnings were due to the reserve clause, its ability to impose wage scales and limit individual salaries, and rule changes that promoted offense.[121]

It became harder to make money in the late 1890s. In 1898 only half of the teams made money, and most lost some in 1899. Boston and Philadelphia each made about $50,000 in 1899, while New York and the hapless Cleveland team suffered big losses. Cleveland that year had a budget of merely $45,000, or half that of Boston, which spent $95,000 (42 percent of which was for salaries). The sharp decline in 1899 reflected a 500,000 drop in attendance caused mainly by poor competition, but also, according to Robert Burk, the belated impact of the 1893 depression. The majors responded by dropping the four weakest teams for the 1900 season.[122]

The baseball boom of the early 1900s dramatically turned around the business of major league baseball. Franchises in the early 1900s quickly developed into excellent investments, especially for those with influential political ties. By 1906 for instance, the Cleveland Indians, originally purchased for $10,000, were worth $100,000, well below the major league average. Two years later the *New York Times* estimated that a pennant-winning Giants club would earn $240,000, which turned out to be not much of an exaggeration. While we have limited data on profits, a 1912 study of the baseball business in *McClure's*, the noted muckraking periodical, reported that in 1908 the St. Louis Browns reputedly had earned $168,000 on a capital investment of $80,000, while the Cardinals of the NL were said to annually net $100,000. The Detroit Tigers reportedly lost about $105,000 from 1901 to 1906, but then turned the corner with an outstanding team led by Ty Cobb and earned $343,000 over the next five years. Then from 1914 to 1918 the club made an average of $48,000 each year. The Cleveland Indians, which had been one of the worst franchises in the late nineteenth century, earned about $500,000 between 1904 and 1912. A 1913 article in the prestigious *Independent* noted, "The profits of baseball investment have proven so dazzling in the last ten years that many prominent businessmen, politicians, and capitalists have gone into the business with every promise of success."[123]

In 1910 the *Sporting News* published a hypothetical accounting for a "typical" major league franchise that made $200,000 (a high estimate) on a net income of $382,000. The biggest expense was players' sala-

ries, $75,000 (41.2 percent), followed by the team president's salary of
$25,000, which in accounting terms is an expense but was part of the
owner's overall compensation and should really be considered profit.[124]

The middle of the decade was more difficult for organized baseball
since profits evaporated because of competition from the Federal League
and then the war-abbreviated 1918 season. However, prosperity returned
to baseball after the war. During the 1920s, the "Golden Age of Sport,"
profit margins averaged 18.3 percent on annual gross incomes in excess
of $10 million.[125]

Most entrepreneurs attracted to baseball at this time were not the
fabulously wealthy sports enthusiasts like the Belmonts or Vanderbilts,
who dominated expensive elite sports such as horse racing and yachting
and shunned more plebeian recreations like baseball. Professional baseball was for the new urban folk. Major league club owners were primarily
men of new affluence, often Irish Catholics or German Jews. Irish magnates included Frank Farrell, Charles Comiskey, Connie Mack, and Tammanyite James Gaffney of the Boston Braves. Entrepreneurs of Jewish
origin included Andrew Freedman, Julius Fleischmann, Barney Dreyfuss
of the Pittsburgh Pirates, and the Frank brothers, who ran the Baltimore
Orioles of the AL (1901–2). Their baseball team was a means of making
money and gaining acceptance, status, and respectability. In many ways
their experience was similar to the Jewish artisans and nickelodeon operators who built up the motion picture industry, also originally a low-
status business avoided by those who preferred more conservative and
prestigious investments.[126]

These owners had important political connections that helped their
sporting businesses succeed. The political domination of professional
baseball reflected the influence of urban politicians in many aspects of
city life. This created a fascinating paradox since WASPs and other acculturated Americans regarded baseball as the institution that best epitomized the finest American beliefs, traditions, and values. Yet the baseball
magnates were urban politicians, often machine politicians, who symbolized all that progressives and small-town Americans believed was
wrong with and destructive to American society. These owners were in
an excellent position to run their teams efficiently and effectively by employing their clout to get inside information and preferential treatment
from the municipality.[127] This is perhaps best illustrated by the relationship of professional teams to their urban environment, particularly their
efforts to build baseball parks at the most productive locations.

Lake Front Park, popularly known as the "Palace of the Fans," was built by Albert G. Spalding in 1883 for the Chicago White Stockings on the city's lakefront. It was supposedly the most modern ballpark of the day. Note the "luxury suites" on top of the grandstand. (*Harper's Weekly*, 14 May 1883, 292)

This view of the second Polo Grounds' double-decked grandstand, circa 1900, is from Eighth Avenue between 157th and 159th Streets. Horse-drawn carriages are parked in the distant outfield. (Neg. no. 45794; courtesy of the New-York Historical Society, New York City)

The last wooden ballpark constructed in either the National or the American League, Hilltop Park was a modest one-story edifice in Upper Manhattan that seated sixteen thousand. It was constructed in a developing section of multistory apartment buildings, where the land was too valuable for a baseball field. (Courtesy of the National Baseball Library, Cooperstown, N.Y.)

West Side Park, shown here in 1904, was the home of the Cubs from 1893 until 1916, when they moved to the new Weeghman Field, later known as Wrigley Field. Note the small number of bleacher seats and how the surrounding neighborhood was extensively built up. (CHi-03976; courtesy of the Chicago Historical Society)

An overflow crowd at West Side Park for a game against the New York Giants during the exciting 1908 season. A large number of fans are sitting on the field quite close to the playing area. This predominantly male audience is very well dressed, wearing suits, vests, ties, and hats. People then dressed very formally when they went out, not even taking off their ties or rolling up their sleeves on this hot afternoon. (SDN 54.405, ICHi-29205; courtesy of the Chicago Historical Society)

The Leland Giants, shown here in 1909, was the outstanding independent team in Chicago and probably the finest African-American team in the United States. Manager Frank Leland is in the middle of the front row in his business suit. His star player, Rube Foster, stands at the extreme right of the second row. (BL-1045–86; courtesy of the National Baseball Library, Cooperstown, N.Y.)

Completed in 1910, Comiskey Park was the oldest in use when it was torn down in 1990. This view of the double-decked stand is from the left field bleachers. Note the prominence of straw hats among the bleacher fans. Also note along the third base line the prominent sign: No Betting Allowed in This Ballpark. (Barnes-Crosby, photographer, ICHi-19088; courtesy of the Chicago Historical Society)

Charles Ebbets opened his modern ballpark in 1913, and it quickly became a Brooklyn landmark. The site was within a forty-five-minute subway, trolley, or El ride for four million New Yorkers. The photograph, taken in 1914, depicts the impressive entrance into a flamboyant ticket lobby. (Courtesy of the National Baseball Library, Cooperstown, N.Y.)

Ponce de Leon Park was the field of the Atlanta Crackers from 1907 to 1923, when it burned down. The design of the field was similar to those of the premodern major league parks, only smaller. It was located in a white residential neighborhood of single-family homes, with an amusement park to the south and vacant lots to the north. The cheap cost of land and a siding of the Southern Railroad to the east attracted factories by 1915. (GPC-7-29; courtesy of the Atlanta History Center)

Weeghman Park, the modern ballpark of the Chicago Whales of the Federal League modeled after the Polo Grounds, became in 1916 the home of the Chicago Cubs (later renamed Wrigley Field). The view presented is westward along Addison Avenue. (Chicago Daily News photograph, ICHi-24343; courtesy of the Chicago Historical Society)

The 1919 champion Chicago White Sox. Front row, left to right: Eddie Collins, Nemo Leibold, Eddie Cicotte, Erskine Mayer, Lefty Williams, Byrd Lynn. Second row: Ray Schalk, Shano Collins, Harvey McClellan, Dickie Kerr, Happy Felsch, Chick Gandil, Buck Weaver. Third row: Kid Gleason (mgr.), John Sullivan, Roy Wilkinson, Grover Lowdermilk, Swede Risberg, Fred McMullin, Bill James, Eddie Murphy, Joe Jackson, Joe Jenkins. (Courtesy of the National Baseball Library, Cooperstown, N.Y.)

Yankee Stadium was an imposing edifice when it opened in 1923 with the largest capacity of any baseball park. The first triple-decked ballpark and the first to be named a "stadium," it represented a significant improvement over the prior fireproof structures and ended the era of the first modern ballparks. (Courtesy of the National Baseball Library, Cooperstown, N.Y.)

Politics, Ballparks, and the Neighborhoods

I've made more money than I ever expected to, but I am putting all of it, and more, too, into the new plant for the Brooklyn fans. Of course it's one thing to have a fine ball club and win a pennant, but to my mind there is something more important than that about a ball club. I believe the fan should be taken care of. A club should provide a suitable home for its patrons. This home should be in a location that is healthy, it should be safe, and it should be convenient.

—Charles Ebbets, 1912

An accessible, safe ballpark with sufficient seating capacity for its fans was a basic requirement for any successful baseball team. These semipublic structures were privately owned, but open to the fee-paying public. The early ballparks were cheaply constructed and teams moved fairly often, seeking superior locations, which were determined by access to cheap rapid transit, rent, and the neighborhood's social character. Franchise mobility halted once major league ballparks were built with expensive fire-resistant materials and thus, unlike their predecessors, could not be easily dismantled and moved elsewhere if the neighborhood declined or the lease was lost. The great cost and permanence of these grounds required careful planning. Owners needed access to the best available information about all factors that affected potential sites, such as the character of the neighborhood, real estate prices, anticipated transportation developments, and future land uses. Once the ballpark was completed, protection for the big investment was needed against any municipal interference, such as cutting streets through the playing field. Team owners secured the necessary assistance and security from their political associates.[1]

The Era of the Wooden Ballparks

Chicago Ballparks, 1870–1909

Chicago's early baseball history was characterized by a great deal of geographic mobility. The White Stockings moved six times between 1870 and 1893, playing their first season just south of the city at twelve-thousand-seat Dexter Park Racetrack, which had a special grandstand for women. The six-mile trip there from downtown took an hour by horsecar, thirty minutes by the railroad. When the White Stockings joined the NA in 1871, the team moved to a municipally owned central location next to Lake Michigan, in walking distance of present-day Grant Park. The federal government had previously granted the site to the city with the stipulations it not be sold, used for profit, or house any permanent structures. Nonetheless, the baseball club constructed a park there. Rectangularly shaped Lake Park (also known as the Union Base-Ball Grounds) had seven thousand seats and was surrounded by a six-foot-high wall to discourage nonpaying spectators. Season tickets cost fifteen dollars and there were special sections for women and government officials. Lake Park lasted only one season because on 9 October, while the White Stockings were on a season-ending road trip, the Great Chicago Fire destroyed the grounds along with fifteen thousand other buildings.[2]

When the White Stockings rejoined the NA in 1874, they played on the South Side at the Twenty-third Street Park. The field was accessible by slow horsecars, replaced three years later by steam-powered trains that cut traveling time in half. However, in 1878 the club was able to move back to its original lakefront location in walking distance from many fans' workplaces. Yet as the rebuilt city emerged from the ashes of the Great Fire, more spectators moved further away from the old urban core and relied increasingly on public transportation to get them to and from work. Consequently, Spalding wrote to the superintendent of the West Division Rail Company to request more service and longer trains on game days, which meant greater transportation profits.[3]

The White Stockings were an excellent draw at Lake Front Park. In the pennant-winning season of 1882, for instance, attendance averaged nearly twenty-nine hundred per game, the best in the NL. Spalding spent ten thousand dollars remodeling the grounds one year later, making it the finest in the United States. The refurbished park had a two-thousand-seat grandstand, a six-thousand-seat bleacher section, and standing room for two thousand. The grandstand was shaped in a half hexagon that extended parallel to the foul lines and near the playing field. There were eighteen private boxes above the grandstand by third base that had armchairs and curtains to protect against the wind, the sun, and fulsome fans. Forty-one people were employed at the park, including a band, ushers, ticket sellers, refreshment sellers, cushion renters, and six police officers. The playing field was the smallest in major league history (right field was 196 feet, center field, 300 feet, and left field, 180 feet) to conform to the shape of the lot. Balls hit over the fence were ground rule doubles in 1883, but homers in 1884, when the club hit a record 142 homers compared with only 13 the year before. Five Chicagoans hit 20 or more homers (no other major leaguer exceeded 14), led by Ned Williamson's 27, a record until 1919. The NL thereafter passed a rule requiring outfields to be at least 210 feet. The White Stockings' use of refurbished Lake Front Park was brief because the federal government secured an injunction barring professional baseball at the site as a violation of the original grant, which had forbidden commercialization.[4]

In 1885 the White Stockings moved to the West Side, the city's most heavily populated section. The team played at the new thirty-thousand-dollar six-thousand-seat Congress Street Park, just fifteen minutes from downtown. But the city had so "many baseball-maniacs" that the capacity was immediately tested by a four-game series with the Giants that drew forty thousand fans. Congress Street Park was at Congress Street and Loomis Avenue in a middle-class neighborhood that strongly opposed the ballpark as a threat to its tranquility and future. Residents' fears of declining property values were misplaced because land values continued to escalate and new homes were constructed. The new field had a smaller seating capacity than Lake Front Park, but had an aura of permanence because it was surrounded by a twelve-foot brick wall rather than a wooden fence. The field was encircled by a banked cycling track and electric lights used in 1886 for a combined skating rink and amusement park.[5]

In 1891 Albert Spalding scheduled half of his home games at the South Side Park (at Wentworth Avenue and Thirty-fifth Street), previously used by the Chicago Pirates of the PL, and in 1892 played all

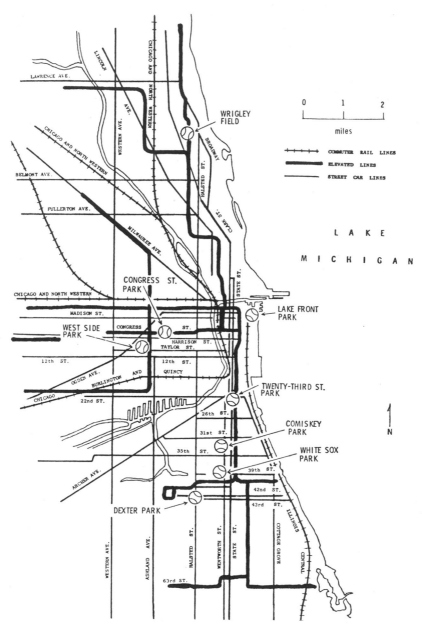

Map 1. Chicago Baseball Parks, 1870–1916, and Mass Transit Lines, c. 1915.

home games there. This newer, more modern park rented for fifteen hundred dollars, one-fifth the cost of Congress Street Park, which was located in a more populated neighborhood. Spalding saw a great potential for the South Side becoming a hotbed of baseball interest because of its good mass transit (cable cars went nine-twelve miles per hour, and the new steam-powered el went fifteen miles per hour) and the coming world's fair in nearby Hyde Park, which was expected to make the South Side a choice residential area. Spalding made a lot of money at the new field by renting it out for other entertainments. In just 1893 Spalding made twenty-nine thousand dollars from rentals. Most fees ranged from two hundred to five hundred dollars, with twenty-seven hundred dollars for the lucrative Thanksgiving Day football game. However, Spalding's lease with the Wentworth family that owned the lot prohibited Sunday games, which was a major drawback.[6]

Spalding did not abandon the West Side, and in 1893 built a new park on property he owned at Polk and Lincoln Streets (now Walcott), a site used for baseball five years earlier by a Western Association team. The field, which Spalding's real estate company rented to the ball club for six thousand dollars, was across the street from Cook County Hospital in an almost exclusively white native-born middle-class residential ward. An elevated electric streetcar line under construction promised to cut traveling time from downtown to the park site to just seven minutes. The new thirty-thousand-dollar West Side Park was used in 1893 just on Sundays, but in 1894 most games were played there and all were in 1895. West Side Park had a large symmetrical playing area (left field was 340 feet, center field, 560 feet, and right field, 340 feet). A string of barbed wire divided the twenty-five-cent bleachers from the fifty-cent pavilion, and wire was also strung in front of the bleachers to prevent spectators from interfering with games.[7]

West Side Park was the scene of a frightening fire on 5 August 1894 in the midst of a game attended by ten thousand fans. During the seventh inning fans noticed a yellow flame in the bleachers. Panic set in as some five thousand spectators scrambled for exits. Over five hundred were injured in the crush, many pushed into the barbed wire fence as the crowd rushed for safety. The fire destroyed or badly damaged nearly one-half of the stands and forced the club to temporarily play at the Thirty-fifth Street Grounds.[8]

Chicago's last wooden major league park, the seventy-five-hundred-seat White Stockings Park (Thirty-ninth between Princeton and Wentworth) was constructed in 1900 by Charles Comiskey for his new American League club. The site rented for one thousand dollars a year and was a half mile south of where Spalding's team had played and where Comiskey had managed in the PL in 1890. In 1884 the park had been the home of the Chicago Unions of the short-lived Union League, and more recently (1893 to about 1898), the grounds of the Wanderers Cricket Club. It was located in the ethnic working-class neighborhood of Armour Square, and Comiskey's cheap admissions policy catered to its residents. The Sox outdrew the Cubs that year by 150,000. The field, renamed White Sox Park in 1904, was readily accessible to downtown and South Side patrons, but remote for North and West Siders, who had to travel downtown and then transfer to southbound streetcars. Nevertheless, the White Sox were popular right from the start and drew the largest average attendance in the AL. White Sox Park was a notorious pitcher's park. The Sox hit no home runs at home in 1904 and 1907, while their pitchers gave up only two in 1904 and three in 1906.[9]

New York Ballparks, 1876–1911

New York City's teams were geographically mobile in the late nineteenth century, although not as much as the White Stockings. In 1876 the Mutuals played at Brooklyn's Union Grounds before they were thrown out of the NL for failing to finish their western road trip. Four years later, on 29 September 1880, the Polo Grounds began to be used for baseball by the independent Metropolitans, an independent professional nine. The site at the northern edge of Central Park was owned by James Gordon Bennett Jr., publisher of the *New York Herald* and one of the greatest sports enthusiasts of the day, who had originally used it in 1876 for the Westchester Polo Association, the first in the United States. The Polo Grounds was accessible by carriage via Central Park or by the Harlem Railroad, which had a station two blocks away. In 1883 when the Gothams and Metropolitans joined the majors, they both played at the Polo Grounds, the former on the east diamond and the latter on the western field. The site was so large that there was no fence between the two fields.[10]

Visiting AA teams were unhappy with the arrangement, and in 1885 the Mets built their own grounds at 107th and First Avenue. Double-decked Metropolitan Park seated eight thousand and was structurally fine but had been built on a garbage dump, and the uneven and rocky playing surface was of poor quality. Pitcher Jack Lynch warned, "a player . . . may go down for a grounder, and come up with six months of malaria." Consequently, the field was seldom used by the Mets, who still played mostly at the Polo Grounds.[11] In 1886, following the sale of the Mets to Erastus Wiman, the club moved to Staten Island, where they played at the St. George's Cricket Grounds. Admission tickets included a round-trip twenty-minute ferry ride from Manhattan. The St. George Grounds seated forty-one hundred in a racetrack-styled rectangular grandstand.[12]

Certain New York city council members at this time were putting a lot of political pressure on the Giants, formerly the Gothams, because they were disappointed with the allotment of passes. They initiated eviction proceedings in a plan to cut a street through the Polo Grounds at 111th Street, ostensibly to improve property values. The generous distribution of tickets, bribes, and help from Tammany associates protected the field for a number of years, but an adverse court decision forced the Giants to move before the start of the 1889 season.[13]

The Giants considered moving out of New York to a local suburb because of their problems with city hall. The *New York Times* urged city leaders to help the club find a new field because baseball was wholesome entertainment and instilled civic pride and relocating to an undeveloped neighborhood could promote progress there. The owners chose to remain in New York, with the nation's largest potential market, and moved to a site called Manhattan Field in the suburban-like Washington Heights community at 155th and Eighth Avenue. It was two miles north of the old Polo Grounds and accessible by the Sixth Avenue el, commuter trains, streetcars, and Harlem River boats. In 1890 the PL club built Brotherhood Park (157th and Eighth Avenue) separated by just a canvas fence from Manhattan Field. On 12 May Mike Tiernan of the Giants hit a home run out of Manhattan Field that landed inside Brotherhood Park while a game there was also underway. The new park was originally symmetrical (335 feet for left field, 500 feet for center field, 335 feet for right field), but was redesigned in July and ended up with unusual dimensions (277 for left field, 500 for center field [433 feet in 1909], and 258 feet for right field). The new park had a larger playing area, a greater seating capacity, and less visibility for fans watching from Coogan's Bluff, which overlooked both fields. When the two teams were consolidated after the collapse of the PL, the improved Giants team moved to the PL site, thereafter known as the new Polo Grounds. The combined rent for the two fields was about ten thousand dollars. The park had a bar below the grandstand that sold beer, whiskey, wine, and cigars. The new Polo Grounds was the largest wooden ballpark, with a second deck added in the mid-1890s. By 1908 it had thirty thousand seats, surpassed only by Harvard Stadium and a number of racetracks.[14]

While New York's Polo Grounds may have been the most famous

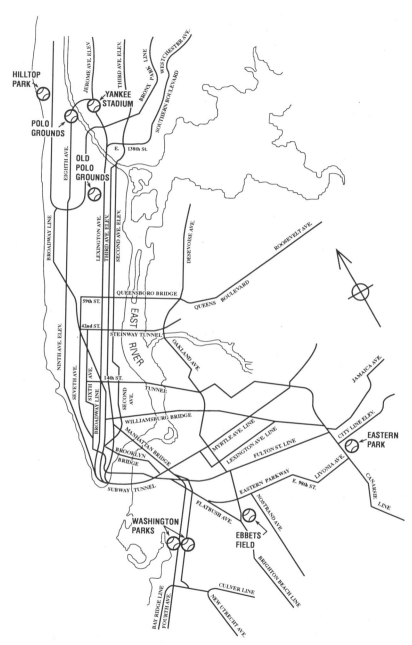

Map 2. New York Baseball Parks, 1883–1923, and Mass Transit Lines, c. 1923.

name in nineteenth-century ballparks, the first enclosed fields constructed specifically for baseball were built in Brooklyn. In 1862 William Cammeyer built his fifteen-hundred-seat Union Grounds in Williamsburg, and later that year Reuben S. Decker opened the Capitoline
Grounds on a skating rink on his family's farm in Brownsville in the
western part of Kings County. It had sheds and stables, lockers for players, a restaurant, a bandstand, and a second-floor sitting room for women.
After the NA was established, the Union Grounds was used by the Eckfords (1871–72), the Mutuals (1871–75), and the Atlantics (1873–75),
who had played in 1872 at the five-thousand-seat Capitoline Grounds.
When the NL was established in 1876, the Mutuals played at the Union
Grounds, and the field was used one year later by the Hartfords, who had
moved to Brooklyn after the first game of their second season in Hartford,
Connecticut.[15]

Brooklyn's next major league park was the thirty-thousand-dollar
twenty-five-hundred-seat Washington Park, originally built in 1883 for
the city's Interstate League team and used by the Brooklyn AA team one
year later. It was located near the Gowanus Canal in the Red Hook section of South Brooklyn, a heavily industrialized area inhabited by Irish
tenement dwellers. The field burned down on 23 May 1889, and the
Bridegrooms replaced it with a new grandstand. One year later when the
club jumped to the NL, their AA successors, the Gladiators, played at
Ridgewood Park, which had been previously used (1886–89) for Sunday
games. It was just across the Brooklyn-Queens border, a twenty-minute
el ride from the Brooklyn Bridge. In 1890, the city's third major league
club, the Wonders of the PL, played at the hundred-thousand-dollar
double-decked Eastern Park in Brownsville, a rapidly growing residential
community of first- and second-generation immigrants. After the season
the NL and PL clubs merged, and the consolidated team played at Eastern
Park, which turned out to be a big mistake. The seventy-five-hundred-
dollar rent was steep, the site was far from centers of population, transportation was inadequate, the streetcar tracks were dangerous to walk
across to get to the field, most local residents were not baseball fans (by
1900 one-fifth of Brownsville residents were Russian Jews), and winds
coming off Jamaica Bay made sitting in the stands unpleasant.[16]

The Brownsville lease expired after the 1897 season, and the Trolley
Dodgers returned to the friendlier confines of Red Hook, where the club
would be closer to the fans. The move was applauded by South Brooklyn
merchants, who estimated a ballpark in their neighborhood was worth
$250,000 in added business. Construction of the new $60,000 Washing-

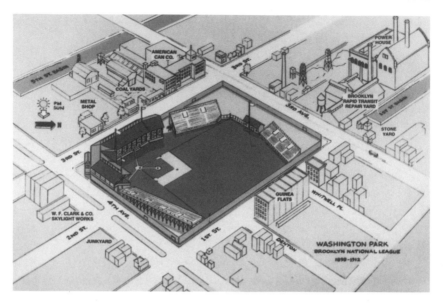

Map 3. Brooklyn's Washington Park, 1898–1912, and Environs. (From Okkonen, *Baseball Memories*, 37. Reprinted by the permission of the author.)

ton Park, located directly across the street from the original Washington
Park (Third Street and Fourth Avenue), was subsidized by two streetcar
lines whose routes passed within a block of the field. The lot was com-
pact, so box seats were only fifteen feet from home plate. In 1908, when
the park was refurbished at a cost of $22,000, there were about 15,200
seats, one-tenth in the quarter bleachers. However, the capacity was
seldom taxed since Brooklyn finished in the second division every year
from 1902 to 1915.[17]

The importance of political connections in helping teams secure a
suitable ballpark site was exemplified by the AL's struggle to establish a
New York franchise. The junior circuit badly wanted a team in the city,
but Andrew Freedman's opposition was a formidable obstacle. After
Freedman had sold his controlling interest in the Giants in 1902, the AL's
path seemed open, and the league signed up players for the new team
even before owners had been selected. However, Freedman promised
John T. Brush that he would continue using his political connections and
his influence in the real estate market to protect the Giants against competitors. Freedman already had leases on virtually all ballpark sites, and
after making a complete survey of Manhattan, he and his associates secured options on vacant lots that might be used for parks; they dismissed

Manhattan north of 155th Street as too rocky for a field. Initially it seemed that the AL was not going to find a decent site, but in December 1902 a satisfactory location was found at 142d and Lenox Avenue that Freedman did not control and that would be serviced by the new subway. The proposed site was extremely expensive, however, and the AL sought financial assistance from the subway line. League representatives urged John B. McDonald of the Interborough Rapid Transit Construction Company to purchase the site and lease it to the ball club. McDonald was impressed by their evidence that a baseball field would stimulate traffic and took the proposal to August Belmont II, the principal financier of the underground, and convinced him to support the plan. However, when the matter was brought up before the company's board of directors, Freedman, a director of the firm, blocked the proposal, which forced the AL to give up its plans for the East Side site.[18] AL president Ban Johnson became discouraged and was convinced he could not get a field in time for the upcoming season without the support of powerful politicians with sufficient influence to counter Freedman. Johnson was approached in March 1903 by Joseph Gordon, who was fronting for Frank Farrell and former police chief William Devery. Gordon told Johnson that he had lined up lots at 165th and Broadway, where his backers would build a ballpark if awarded an AL franchise. With the season a month away, Johnson sold the old Baltimore franchise to Gordon's syndicate for eighteen thousand dollars.[19]

The site belonged to the New York Institute for the Blind, which leased it to the Highlanders for ten years at ten thousand dollars per annum. The property was in an elevated and underdeveloped part of Manhattan, had a wild appearance, and was essentially a rock pile that needed an enormous amount of expensive excavation before it could be ready for baseball. The lucrative two hundred thousand dollars excavating and seventy-five thousand dollars building contracts were given to Thomas McAvoy, the local Tammany district leader. Another serious drawback was the site's accessibility. In 1903 it was serviced by a single mass transit line that took fifty minutes from city hall. With the construction of the West Side subway, scheduled for operation in time for the 1904 season, more fans could more quickly reach the park. Completion took two years longer than anticipated, however, but thereafter traveling time from downtown was cut in half.[20]

Considerable community opposition emerged when the ballpark project was announced. Petitions were circulated, allegedly at Freedman's behest, requesting the city to open streets through the site to promote neighborhood development, which would ruin the area for base-ball. Local property owners claimed that a ballpark's presence would encourage the establishment of saloons, disorderly conduct, and the de-moralization of the community. However, their appeal was denied by a three-to-two vote of the Washington Heights Board of Improvements. Neighborhood hostility continued even after the park was constructed. Property owners sought redress from the Board of Estimate, but the High-landers had enough friends at city hall to protect their investment. The community got its revenge in the November elections, when anti-park candidates defeated two local aldermen who had originally supported the Highlanders.[21]

The Hilltop Park grandstand, the last wooden major league park, was a flimsy, simple edifice, free of ornamentation. It had a seating capacity of sixteen thousand, including fifteen hundred quarter seats. Parking lots for carriages and automobiles were located inside the grounds. The man-agement originally announced that the fences would not be covered by unsightly advertisements, but this policy was short-lived, since no later than 1907 ads appeared on the outfield walls. Two years later a Durham Bull sign advertising tobacco, twice as tall as the rest of the fence, was put up in right center field. These billboards were nearly ubiquitous in major league ballparks; anyone hitting the sign got fifty dollars.[22]

Minor League Ballparks in Atlanta, 1885–1924

As frequently as major league teams moved from field to field, minor league teams probably changed even more often. Atlanta teams played at five different sites between 1885 and 1907 because of unstable local fran-chises and leagues, ownership changes, community opposition, and the financial influence of transportation interests. In 1885, when Atlanta established its first professional nine in the Southern League, the club played on the North Side of town at Athletic Park (on North between Williams and Lovjoy). Atlanta had no professional team in 1887. One year later, it was represented by one of the four teams in the obscure Interstate Amateur League, whose players (despite the organization's title) were all first-year professionals. In 1889 Atlanta rejoined the South-ern League with the intent of moving from Athletic Park a few blocks eastward to Peters Park (at North and West Peachtree), a popular recre-ational area. The new baseball field was to be subsidized by the Atlanta Street Railway line that ran right past the grounds. The site was named for Ed Peters, a prominent streetcar executive who had been instrumen-tal in developing North Avenue as an access route. Construction began at

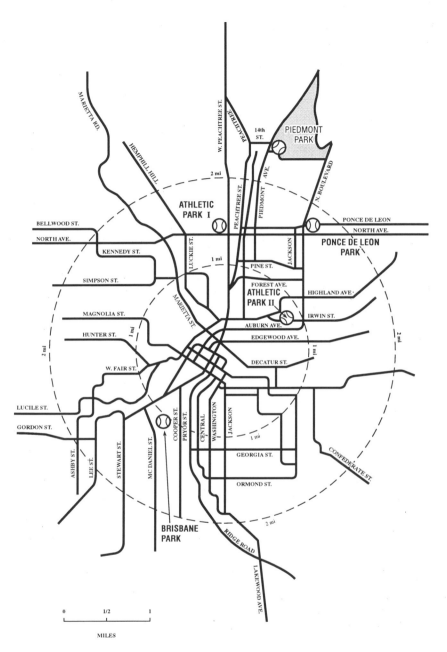

Map 4. Atlanta Baseball Parks, 1885–1923, and Mass Transit Lines.

the beginning of the season in June, and the Crackers played all their early season games on the road. But the Southern League folded at the start of July before the Crackers ever made it home. Atlanta had no professional ball club until 1892, when the Southern League Crackers played at the thousand-seat Brisbine Park (at Ira and Crumley), one mile from the city center in the fashionable southern part of town. Two years later the Crackers broke their lease to move to the second Athletic Park (at Jackson and Irwin), the second-largest baseball field in the South. The shift was financed by transit magnate Joel Hurt's Atlanta Consolidate Railway (ACR), which promised to get fans to the park from downtown in just five minutes. In 1896, after the ACR refused to provide additional support, the rival Atlanta Traction Company provided financial backing and the club returned to an enlarged Brisbine Park, which got a new grandstand roof. After the Southern League collapsed in the spring of 1898, the city had no pro team for four years.[23]

In 1902 the Selma franchise of the year-old Southern Association moved to the Gate City. The Crackers played two miles north of downtown at Piedmont Park, an athletic field built for college sports in 1896 at the old Exposition Grounds just outside the city limits. A fence was built around the field, the diamond was rearranged, and the grandstand capacity was increased to twelve hundred seats, including a separate smoking section. The new park's major advantages were its cheap six hundred dollars a year rent, its sod field (earlier Atlanta fields had dirt surfaces), and excellent transportation. Fans could reach the grounds by three streetcar lines in as little as eight minutes from the center of town. In 1903 further improvements increased the grandstand capacity to twenty-two hundred seats, set aside a section for women and their escorts, and provided female fans with a fully furnished and carpeted bathroom with an attendant.[24]

Despite these advantages, Piedmont soon proved unsatisfactory because its seating capacity was inadequate for holiday games or crucial contests. After the Georgia Railway and Electric Company purchased the Crackers in 1906, it moved the team to a new site across the street from the transit line's amusement park, three miles from downtown, just inside the city limits. The park was in a mixed-use neighborhood, surrounded by the amusement park on one side and single-family middle-class white homes, factories, and vacant lots on the other three sides. The $60,000 Ponce de Leon Park was a wooden structure with 6,800 seats (later enlarged to 8,000) that was expected to lessen the overcrowding problems at Piedmont Park. However, there were 8,426 spectators at the first game on 23 May 1907. The new fields, like other wooden minor league parks, were intimate structures, with seats as close as thirty feet from home plate, which enabled fans to see the players' faces and hear what they were saying. Atlanta's ballparks were segregated, with a separate entrance and seating area for African Americans. Most fans traveled to Ponce Park by streetcar or jitney, but a parking lot was set up behind the stands for car drivers. When the field was destroyed in a 1923 fire, it was soon replaced by 14,000-seat Spiller Park, a fire-resistant edifice that cost $250,000.[25]

The location of Piedmont and Ponce de Leon Parks on the city's outskirts was typical of minor league cities. These towns were not very large, and the city limits, where land was cheapest, were just a couple of miles from the center of town. More importantly, minor league teams were often financed by local transportation interests who wanted their ballparks located beyond walking distance but close to their transit routes. St. Paul was a rare exception. Its ballpark was purposely located in the central business district to cater to white-collar fans. In 1901 St. Paul's president George Lennon decried the practice of locating minor league parks in the suburbs "so that the transit companies will subscribe liberally towards starting the club."[26]

The Era of the Fireproof Parks

New major league parks built after Hilltop Park were constructed with fire-resistant materials costing hundreds of thousands of dollars. These modern facilities were enormous investments that could not be readily dismantled and rebuilt elsewhere like the old wooden parks, making it essential that teams purchase their own sites or else secure long-term leases to protect their investments. The new structures symbolized and acclaimed the maturity, stability, permanence, and legitimacy of the professional baseball business and gave shrewd owners an opportunity to increase the number of seats and raise admission prices. The technology to build safer buildings with reinforced concrete was developed by engineers in the late nineteenth century. This material was cheaper and stronger than stone (which was more attractive, but cracked easily), reduced the amount of steel needed for construction, and fireproofed the steel. Noncombustible materials had been utilized for ballpark construction as early as 1894 in Cincinnati and 1895 in Philadelphia and Baltimore. The Philadelphia Phillies' ballpark was rebuilt after a fire in 1894 had destroyed the park. The Huntingdon Grounds (later known as Baker Bowl), had a steel grandstand designed to look like a medieval castle and was baseball's first cantilevered structure, which eliminated supports that obstructed many seats. However, the enormous expense of fire-proofing discouraged teams from constructing completely fire-resistant facilities. A substantial portion of Cincinnati's "Palace of the Fans," constructed in 1902 to replace stands that had burned in 1900, used incombustible materials. It was an extremely attractive structure designed in the beaux arts style. The ballpark historian Michael Gershman considers it the first major league ballpark built with a distinctive architectural style and thinks it looked more like a Greek temple or a bank than a ballpark. The structure's physical highlight was its semicircular concrete opera boxes secured by hard-carved Corinthian columns to a frieze behind the plate that had "Cincinnati" carved on it. However, it was not well built—by 1907 girders were cracking and supports were decaying—and a fire in 1911 destroyed much of it.[27]

The great breakthrough in ballpark construction occurred in 1909 when Philadelphia's Shibe Park and Pittsburgh's Forbes Field were built using primarily structural steel and concrete. The three-hundred-thousand-dollar Shibe Park had a beautiful exterior designed in the French Renaissance style and seated twenty-three thousand. Triple-tiered twenty-five-thousand-seat Forbes Field, a ten-minute trolley ride from downtown in the Schenley Park neighborhood, was designed by Charles W. Leavitt Jr., who had previously designed several New York racetracks, including Belmont Park in 1905. It had such innovations as elevators for the third-tier luxury boxes and a spacious promenade under the grandstands, where fans could escape heavy rains. Owner Barney Dreyfuss barred signs to maintain the purity of the architecture. The Athletics and Pirates started quite a trend, for within six years seven more fireproof major league parks were constructed, and other grounds were remodeled with fire-resistant materials. By 1915 the only unimproved field was the Philadelphia Phillies' Baker Bowl. In addition, several Federal League teams built fireproof edifices, as did minor league teams in larger cities such as Newark, San Francisco, and Toledo.[28]

The fireproof ballpark era resulted from management wisely taking advantage of favorable social and economic conditions. Baseball was in the midst of an unprecedented boom in the late 1900s that encouraged owners to construct bigger parks with greater seating capacities at a moment when labor and material costs had become relatively cheap. Journalists had recommended that owners keep up with the times and learn from Australia and England, which had immense outdoor fields with imposing grandstands largely built on stone foundations.[29]

Magnates also felt under pressure to improve their grounds' beauty and comfort because of competition for the public's recreational dollars from magnificent amusement parks like Coney Island and Chicago's White City; from vaudeville, whose better theaters had lavish interiors, comfortable seats, and wide aisles; and by the early 1910s, from downtown movie theaters that had glittering foyers, plush seats, and well-mannered ushers. Fans were no longer satisfied with uncomfortable benches in ramshackle grandstands and bleachers surrounded by unsightly wooden fences. Owners believed they needed their own comfortable, stylishly designed buildings to compete for the consumer's fifty cents. As the historian Bruce Kuklick points out, classically designed Shibe Park "was 'a lasting monument,' built to endure, with a grandiose beauty that should express continuing prosperity and assured advance." Albert G. Spalding described the new Polo Grounds built in 1911 as "more fitting of an outdoor opera house than a ball park, showing that Base Ball promoters have progressed." Baseball was in its own way contributing to the City Beautiful movement.[30]

The new parks offered greater seating capacities, potentially higher profits, and also improved safety. It was dangerous to play games in the fire traps that had previously served as ballparks. During the 1890s about twenty-five baseball fields caught on fire, including St. Louis's Sportsman's Park, which had five fires in the 1890s. In 1894 alone, four of the twelve major league parks caught on fire, including Chicago's West Side Park.[31]

Between 1900 and 1911 at least six conflagrations erupted in major league parks (including White Sox Park in 1910 and the Polo Grounds in 1911), plus several others broke out at minor league fields. Furthermore, cheap construction caused injuries. Flimsy wooden structures were vulnerable to strong winds and to overcrowding, which weakened already feeble grandstands. Late in the 1897 season a platform connecting the Polo Grounds bleachers to the grandstand gave way under the weight of fans rushing for cover from a rainstorm. Six years later a wooden railing broke at the Phillies' grandstand, resulting in twelve deaths and injuries to hundreds.[32]

Progressive Era urbanites were extremely conscious of the need for safe buildings because of events like the Great Chicago Fire of 1871 that killed about 300 people and left 100,000 homeless, as well as more recent disasters at semipublic places. In 1903, for instance, 602 people lost their lives in Chicago's Iroquois Theater fire, and a year later a blaze aboard the excursion steamer *General Slocum* in New York waters caused the death of 1,030.

Municipalities were beginning to give greater attention to safety conditions at public and semipublic places. They rewrote building codes to promote public safety and cut soaring insurance rates by tightening regulations regarding the construction materials, establishing standards for safety, and expanding fire limits. Ballparks were subject to the same regulations that affected all other semipublic buildings. Chicago had specific articles in its revised building code of 1910, drafted shortly after the 1909 fire at White Sox Park, that proscribed the construction of combustible grandstands seating over five thousand spectators within the city's fire limits. It also required that wooden parts of fields be annually treated with a fire-retarding solution and set a maximum number of seats between aisles.[33]

Reformers and safety experts were also concerned about roofstands, seating areas constructed on top of buildings overlooking ballparks in Atlanta, Chicago, Detroit, and Philadelphia, whose owners charged five or ten cents to watch the ball game. This cheap competition vexed Chicago owners, who as early as 1885 sought injunctions against landlords with roofstands. In 1907 the Cubs tried to use their political clout with the city's building commissioner to remove the two 125-seat roofstands overlooking West Side Park as dangerous hazards, less out of an interest in safety than in eliminating cheap competition. One year later a youngster fell off a roofstand to his death when he got too excited at Joe Tinker's homer off Christy Mathewson. This unfortunate event assured that the city's amended building code of 1910 would regulate roofstands, permitting them only if solidly constructed on fire-resistant buildings with adequate fire escapes.[34]

Municipal ballpark regulations usually required annual inspections and the assignment of fire marshals at games to make sure aisles were kept clear. During the wooden park era, owners occasionally sold more tickets than they had seats, which created a potentially dangerous situation, but were almost never punished.[35] Government inspectors checked out the ballparks before each season to uncover structural defects and make sure they were repaired. Inspections were not intended to be punitive, but to prevent unnecessary accidents due to vandalism, normal wear and tear, and negligence resulting from poor planning, cheap or shoddy construction, and lax enforcement of building codes during construction. The owner or contractor, who wanted to keep costs low by

rushing the work and using second-rate materials, sometimes used political ties to influence building inspectors. For example, Chicago's West
Side Park, built in 1893, had been inadequately inspected because its
contractor, Michael F. Powers, was a business partner of Buildings Commissioner Joseph Downey.[36]

The city's authority to inspect and close structures with code violations made teams vulnerable to political pressure. Club owners tried to
protect themselves by keeping on friendly terms with local politicians,
liberally distributing passes, donating fields for political functions, and
making politicos their partners. In 1909 Charles W. Murphy foolishly in-
curred the wrath of County Treasurer John R. Thompson when he doubled the rent at Thompson's downtown restaurant in a building Murphy
had recently purchased. Thompson retaliated by sending a note to the
building commissioner detailing violations at West Side Park. A team of
inspectors sent to check out the complaint found many infractions, leading to a heavy fine for Murphy.[37]

The Modern Chicago Ballparks

Chicago's first fireproof field was built in 1910 by Charles Comiskey
following the example set by the Athletics and the Pirates. Comiskey
had sought a new location as early as 1903, securing an option on a West
Side lot (Harrison and Throop), but did not exercise the option because of
its proximity to the Cubs' West Side Park and because it was in an area
largely inhabited by new immigrants from eastern Europe who mostly
were not baseball fans. Comiskey's lease was expiring after the 1909
season, and the landlord wanted a huge increase. Comiskey decided to
purchase a lot one half-mile south owned by Roxanna A. Bowen, daughter of former mayor John Wentworth, long utilized as a community garbage dump, for $100,000 plus back taxes. Comiskey used his political
clout to get the city council to close off a key avenue to street traffic. The
new site was still in the Armour Square area and on the edge of Bridgeport, both working-class white ethnic neighborhoods that provided a
core of Sox fans.[38]

Zachary Taylor Davis, an MIT-trained architect, was hired to design
a huge new fireproof park that could accommodate overflow crowds.
Comiskey wanted a spacious field that would favor pitchers and thus
benefit his weak-hitting defensive team and that had a lot of cheap seats
working-class fans could afford. His original plan called for an ornate
facade in the beaux arts style similar to Shibe Park and in line with
Daniel Burnham's Chicago Plan of 1909, a fountain, and a cantilevered

grandstand to limit obstructed seating. This design was estimated to cost $900,000 to construct, but Comiskey felt that was too much. Instead the park was constructed for $550,000. According to the historian Robin Bachin, "the grand Romanesque arches dominating the facade recalled the visual imagery of community churches . . . as well as the commercial architecture of neighboring warehouse buildings. The red-brick building material . . . further integrated the ballpark into the fabric of the urban streetscape. Comiskey Park became an emblem of local ethnic pride, and of South Side community identity." The money saved meant the park was built without embellished ornamentation or cantilevers, resulting in many seats with sight lines blocked by the vertical posts that held up the roof. A green cornerstone was laid on 17 March, St. Patrick's Day, a gesture to reflect Comiskey's Irish heritage and attract the substantial Irish population in the surrounding neighborhood.[39]

When White Sox Park opened on 1 July, nearly filled to capacity, it had thirty-two thousand seats, including seven thousand in two twenty-five-cent bleachers separated by an electric scoreboard in center field. Renamed Comiskey Park in 1913, it drew the largest yearly audiences in the AL and was the site of three consecutive World Series beginning in 1917, including its stint in 1918 as the Cubs home field because of its much greater seating capacity.

The field was laid out symmetrically, the foul poles 363 feet from home plate, and center field 420 feet. Since the lot was large, the grounds did not have the irregular shape of other contemporary ballparks. The steel and concrete park included many novel safety features introduced at Shibe Park and Pittsburgh's Forbes Field, such as gradually sloped runways in place of stairways, enabling spectators to leave much quicker than before. Drainage got a lot of attention because Chicago was exceptionally flat, and the ungraded old grounds had drained poorly. Comiskey installed a system of gravel subsoil and tile conduits under the playing field and raised the ground level to improve its run-off capabilities.[40] One innovation that was tried and quickly forgotten was the use of electric lights for night baseball. On 27 August 1910 over twenty thousand attended a night game between Rogers Park and Logan Square, two leading semipro teams. This was the second artificially lit game at a major league park (the first was in Cincinnati in 1909), but it would be twenty years before professional baseball at night would gain acceptance.[41]

Although the new park moved the Sox only a half-mile north, the team was quickly affected by important changes in nearby areas. The Douglas community east of Wentworth Avenue between Twelfth and

Thirty-Ninth Streets had become an African-American neighborhood that was expanding thanks to the influx of black southerners during the Great Migration of 1916–19, which doubled Chicago's African-American population. The presence of a large black community so close to the park may have frightened off white fans, especially following the 1919 race riot, when thirty-eight people were killed. Some whites traveling to Comiskey Park probably felt trepidation getting off the el or the Wentworth Avenue streetcar in the vicinity of a black community. Only a small part of this loss in attendance was offset by the black fans who attended Sox games on Sundays when off from work.[42]

African-American fans generally preferred Chicago American Giants games held at nearby Schorling Park. John Schorling purchased the old Sox grounds in 1911 and renamed it Schorling Field. He and his partner, Rube Foster, purchased the park to take advantage of the growing concentration of blacks in the vicinity.[43]

The new Sox park had only a slight impact on property values but had a direct influence on local land use by attracting businesses that catered to Sox fans. New stores included a Greek ice cream parlor and several bars, most notably McCuddy's, which remained in business through 1990, the final season of the original Comiskey Park. Johnny McCuddy had received inside information from Comiskey about the ballpark before it became public knowledge and built his bar across the street from the main entrance before the field was constructed. After the ballpark was built, some vacant parcels were turned into parking lots.[44]

The ballpark's impact on local property values was limited, in part because it bordered on the Illinois Central Railroad tracks and warehouses to the west and the Wentworth streetcar tracks to the east. Chicago was in the midst of a real estate boom that lasted from 1900 to the late 1920s. Typical city lots doubled in value between 1900 and 1916 and increased by 150 percent between 1918 and 1926. However, Bridgeport and Armour Square were modest neighborhoods that did not participate in this boom, and their property values did not rise significantly in the early 1900s. The site of the park fared better, rising in value by 40 percent from 1909 to 1916, while lots adjacent to the field and the Illinois Central tracks tripled. From 1918 to 1926 the value of the park and most fronting real estate increased by only one-third to one-half, which was typical of the neighborhood. Comiskey Park's principal impact on land values was at the corner of Thirty-fifth and Wentworth, just east of the main entrance, which nearly tripled in five years because of anticipated development there to take advantage of baseball fan traffic.[45]

Chicago's North Side was the last section of the city to develop, getting adequate transportation only in 1893 when the el was built, but quickly became one of the city's most desirable residential areas. The el made travel to the Loop easy, although North Siders still found it difficult and time-consuming to travel to the West or South Sides. North Side baseball fans seldom bothered going to either West Side Park or White Sox Park, and instead patronized local semiprofessionals who played in the excellent City League. After the 1906 World Series the Logan Squares, who had their own North Side field at Diversey and Milwaukee, played exhibitions against barnstorming teams comprised of Cubs and Sox stars and won both games.[46]

The absence of professional baseball on the North Side prompted the minor league American Association to seriously consider establishing a franchise there. In 1909 a syndicate led by the Cantillon brothers purchased a Lakeview lot at Clark and Addison for a ballpark, but failed to build one. Lakeview was a middle-class residential area inhabited by native-born white American families who lived in single-unit homes, two-family dwellings, or apartments. In 1913 the new Federal League organized a team on the North Side, three miles north of the central business district at DePaul University Field. One year later, when the teams in the Federal League proclaimed themselves a new major league, the Chicago ChiFeds built a new ballpark on the Cantillon's grounds to take advantage of the area's middle-class residential character and fine public transit facilities. The team's thirty-year lease called for an average rental of eighteen thousand dollars per year.[47]

The announcement caused a great stir in Lakeview. Support for the new team came from local merchants, including seven hundred Sheridan Park business owners who signed a resolution indicating their approval. However, residential property owners near the proposed field vehemently opposed the project, informing Mayor Carter H. Harrison II that the crowds would "disturb the peace and quiet of the neighborhood and destroy the district as residential property." The petition fell on deaf ears. The protesters failed to block issuance of a building permit because they lacked the necessary support of a majority of frontage owners. The ChiFeds controlled half of the frontage and were backed by two other landlords who planned a bar and a cafe on their sites.[48]

The new $250,000, twenty-thousand-seat Weeghman Park, completed in six weeks, was completely fireproof, as required by the city's building codes. It was designed by Zachary Davis, the architect of Comiskey Park, who modeled the new structure after the Polo Grounds but ended up with a single deck that did not extend far down left field and no detailed ornamentation on the inner facade. There were only two thousand quarter seats in the bleachers. Weeghman installed the first permanent concession stands so fans would not have their view obstructed by vendors and let them keep balls batted into the stands. The new grounds would go down in baseball lore as one of the most beautiful parks. In the 1920s it was surrounded by trees, and in 1927 a second deck was constructed. Ten years later Bill Veeck, son of the team president, installed its famous ivy vines after former owner Philip Wrigley's plans for planting trees in the bleachers and on the scoreboard steps had failed. The park, now called Wrigley Field, remains in use today by the Chicago Cubs and is second in age only to Boston's Fenway Park and Detroit's Navin Field (Tiger Stadium), both of which date to 1912.[49]

Several other Federal League teams, including Brooklyn's, were similarly compelled by law to build incombustible fields, an expensive burden that the AL teams had been spared. Owners had supported strict new building codes to keep out competition, just as other business leaders had supported certain progressive reforms (like meat packers who supported the Meat Inspection Act of 1906), because doing so was in their own financial interests. These teams already had ballparks they could replace or rehabilitate as they chose, but the revised building codes required potential competitors to meet such rigorous safety and construction standards that they had to build new fireproof parks. Such an expensive initial outlay would deter most potential investors and would make success difficult for those not daunted by that barrier.[50]

After the Cubs and ChiFeds merged in December 1915, the owners consulted with real estate brokers and transit executives and opted to abandon the dilapidated West Side Park to play at the new North Side field. The neighborhood on the West Side had deteriorated into a slum inhabited by poor first-generation Italians and Russian Jewish immigrants who seldom attended ball games. West Side fans, however, attacked the move, claiming they had been loyal for thirty years and were now suddenly abandoned, since the new Cubs Park was too far away.[51]

Land uses near the new Cubs home were only slightly affected by the park, principally near the Clark and Addison entrance, where vacant lots were replaced with cheap shops catering to the fans. The streets behind the park, however, retained their residential character. Land values in the immediate vicinity doubled between 1918 and 1926, but Cubs Park had no noticeable impact since property values throughout Lakeview also doubled despite the city average gain of 150 percent. At abandoned

West Side Park the situation was quite different. Property values did not change from 1909 through 1916 (although the field's value rose by nearly 50 percent), but from 1918 to 1926, following the move by the Cubs, the value of land around the former ballpark appreciated almost threefold because the state in 1921 built the Illinois State Hospital and the University of Illinois Medical School there. The impact of these institutions on property values, not to mention land uses, was direct and much more important than that of any ballpark.[52]

The Modern New York Ballparks

On 14 April 1911, just days after the start of the baseball season, the thirty-thousand-seat Polo Grounds burned down, leaving only the left center and center field bleachers standing. The homeless Giants played the next month and a half at the much smaller Hilltop Park. John T. Brush decided to rebuild at the same location because fans were accustomed to traveling there by either a special elevated express from Wall Street or by the cheaper eight-cent ride on an East Side el to 125th Street and a transfer to the Eighth Avenue trolley, which ran right to the park. Wealthier patrons came in carriages or automobiles. Some downtown businessmen would split the expensive carriage fare, which was a dollar for the first mile plus forty cents for each additional mile. Carriage owners parked their vehicles behind a rope that stretched across the field and often sat in their vehicles to watch the game.[53]

Brush was exhorted by the press to replace his old grounds with a concrete and steel park, which city building superintendent Robert Miller insisted upon, even though the building codes did not require it. Brush intended to build a large modern park to increase seating capacity for his popular team. Before construction began, he negotiated a thirty-five-year lease at an annual rent of seventy thousand dollars to protect his investment. The Giants were in a rush to get the new grounds fabricated and did not seek competitive construction bids, making an unusual decision to hire a contractor on a cost-plus-profit basis. The new park was completed in just a few months by eight hundred laborers working on three shifts around the clock.[54]

The fireproof new Polo Grounds seated 31,316 spectators in two horseshoe-shaped decks, yet 38,281 squeezed their way in for first game of the World Series in October. It had about the same capacity as Comiskey Park, but underwent several enhancements in seating. In the 1910s the only ballpark with a larger seating area was Braves' Field in Boston, built in 1915 with about 40,000 seats. By 1923 the capacity of the Polo

Grounds reached 55,000, surpassed only by the new Yankee Stadium, located across the Harlem River in the Bronx. The grandstand was topped with NL teams' coats of arms, and the facade of the concrete decks was originally decorated with Roman Colosseum frescoes (removed in 1922–23 when the decks were extended to the new concrete center field bleachers). The top of the upper deck was highlighted by open winged eagles. The playing field had similar dimensions as the old Polo Grounds (left field was 277 feet, center field was 433 feet [483 feet in 1923], and right field was 256 feet). The second deck in the outfield had a unique 23-foot overhang, which made possible a 250-foot home run. Brush drastically cut the number of cheap seats, claiming that fans preferred to sit in more expensive seats. The new grandstand destroyed the free view from the promontory of Coogan's Bluff, although fans could still see a part of the field from the nearby viaduct and el platform. But henceforth, whoever wanted a good view of the game would have to pay for it.[55]

The new modern grounds that Brush and his fellow magnates were building carried enormous overhead expenses that teams reduced by increasing ticket prices, which generated 80 percent of their gross income. Proceeds from general admission tickets were equally divided with the visiting team, while additional fees for higher-priced seats were kept by the home club. Other revenue came from selling concession privileges and advertising space in scorecards and on outfield walls, which could bring in another ten thousand dollars. Only a few owners, such as William Wrigley and his son Philip K. Wrigley, refused to place posters on their fences because they felt these advertisements would detract from the beauty and rustic imagery of their fields.[56]

Another profitable use of a ballpark was to lease it out during the off-season and on days when the home team was out of town. Clubs rented their fields to promoters of other sporting events, including cycling races, boxing matches, and college football games, and to popular amusements like vaudeville and the circus. Comiskey Park's greatest promotion of the period was the 1911 world championship wrestling match between Frank Gotch and Gene Hackenschmidt, while in New York Marcus Loew promoted a combined vaudeville and motion picture show at Ebbets Field in 1914 that attracted twenty-one thousand. One year later the park was used for boxing matches, the first outdoor matches in New York City since 1899. However, the primary tenants were mainly other baseball clubs. The Reds, for example, got 20 percent of the net when they rented out their field for Sunday semipro games, but their profits paled in comparison with those of the Giants, who rented out the Polo Grounds to the

Yankees from 1913 through 1922 for as much as sixty-five thousand dollars a year.[57]

By 1920 the neighborhood surrounding the Polo Grounds had significantly changed from 1889, when the Giants had first moved there. Washington Heights was no longer a suburban community but had become an integral part of the city with excellent mass transit. The Heights had become a popular residential area filled with multistory apartment buildings whose inhabitants were mainly middle-class, native-born Americans, although increasingly upwardly mobile Irish and Jewish tenants were moving in. The presence of the ballpark did not have a direct impact on the community except just south of 155th Street, where a casino and dance halls were frequented by the "smart set" after ball games. Other nearby neighbors were even less affected by the park because of its natural boundaries: the Harlem River to the east, railroad repair sheds to the north, and Coogan's Bluff, the Aqueduct, and the Speedway to the west.[58]

The Polo Grounds had even less of an impact on property values than on land uses. Manhattan real estate was the most valuable in the United States, with prices continuously escalating, doubling between 1905 and 1929. Property to the northwest of the Polo Grounds nearly quadrupled in value in this period, while land to the more built-up south increased by just 50 percent, an appreciation typical of real estate all along the Upper East Side from the northern end of Central Park to 155th Street.[59]

At the same time that the Giants were building their modern new Polo Grounds, their Brooklyn rivals were covertly planning their own fire-resistant ballpark. Washington Park was a dangerous fire hazard in a heavily industrialized area near the docks of the Gowanus Canal. The stench of black fumes emanating from factory smokestacks and river craft and the absence of cooling breezes made the stands hot and uncomfortable. In addition, Washington Park's principal advantage of central location was rapidly dissolving as people moved to the more outlying sections of the borough and as improvements in mass transit made other locations equally accessible.[60]

President Charles Ebbets of the Dodgers formed the Pylon Construction Company, a dummy corporation, to secretly purchase parcels for a ballpark in an underdeveloped section of Flatbush east of Prospect Park, derogatorily known as "Pigtown." Ebbets surreptitiously purchased 4.5 acres from over fifteen different owners for two hundred thousand dollars so they could not take advantage of the project and drive up prices. In early 1912 when Ebbets announced his acquisitions and plans to build a modern fireproof park, his proposal was widely derided because the site seemed to be in the middle of nowhere and inaccessible. Ebbets, how-ever, was optimistic since the location was just four miles from the Brooklyn Bridge and could be reached by transfer on fifteen different transit lines. He explained to NL president August Herrmann: "The new site is midway between the fashionable Bedford and Flatbush sections of Brooklyn, twenty minutes by subway and 'l' road from Wall Street and City Hall." Ebbets was gambling that these attractive residential sec-tions would continue to expand toward each other in the direction of the proposed field.[61]

The construction of the new ballpark was an important project for Brooklyn, and city officials gave Ebbets considerable assistance in plan-ning and implementing his venture. It did not hurt that Ebbets and one of his prime contractors, Steve McKeever, were both well-connected for-mer politicians (McKeever had been on the city council from 1898 to 1901). Buildings Superintendent John Thatcher assisted in the matter of digging sewers, and Park Commissioner M. J. Kennedy advised on land-scaping. Construction costs drove the project up to $750,000, which left Ebbets bankrupt. He was forced to take in his contractors, Steve and Ed McKeever, as half partners for the bargain price of $100,000.[62]

Ebbets Field was unveiled for public inspection on 16 March 1913 to an estimated crowd of 12,000. It had 18,000 seats, all located close to the diamond, and standing room for 3,000. The playing field was highly asymmetrical (a left field of 419 feet, 450 feet for center field, and 301 feet for right field), which reflected the odd dimensions of the property. The exhibition game that inaugurated Ebbets Field on 5 April drew a crowd estimated by the *New York Times* at 30,000 and by other sources at 20,000 to 25,000 fans. This far surpassed the park's capacity and thou-sands had to be turned away. Perhaps an omen of the times ahead was that the designers had not built a press box, and no one remembered on opening day to bring the keys to open up the bleachers. Seating was increased to 21,000 after the 1916 World Series and eventually reached 31,497, limited only by the size of the lot.[63]

Ebbets tried to make his field as aesthetically pleasing as possible, a civic gesture toward beautifying the neighborhood that was mainly mo-tivated by competition with Coney Island's amusement parks and the new movie palaces. The brick wall surrounding the field was painted a dark olive green, and ivy seeds were planted at the base of the wall so vines would grow up the fence. This provided a good background for batters as well as a rustic atmosphere. The ticket lobby was covered with an ornate stucco and marble rotunda. The foyer held a massive chandelier with twelve arms shaped like bats with suspended globes designed to look like baseballs. The ballpark had several features aimed at improving fan comfort as well, such as opera chairs with curved backs made two inches roomier than standard seats because they had just one armrest and a parking lot across the street from the main entrance.[64]

Land uses in the vicinity of Ebbets Field were not much affected by the park's presence, although one realtor took advantage of the opening day excitement to put an ad in the *Brooklyn Eagle* encouraging fans unfamiliar with the neighborhood to consider becoming homeowners there. As Ebbets had anticipated, the neighborhood rapidly became a popular residential area of apartments and private homes. People were willing to live within walking distance of the ballpark, although not directly across the street. Local residents developed a keen sense of attachment and identification with the Dodgers, the most famous institution in the entire borough. The players were part of the community, and like the Philadelphia Athletics, many owned homes in the area or lived in nearby boarding houses. The abandoned Washington Field was soon revived for baseball when it became the home of the bakery magnate Robert B. Ward's TipTops of the Federal League in 1914. Ward originally planned to expand the old Washington Park, but municipal building codes required him to tear down the building and put up a new edifice, with wood on a concrete base, that cost at least two hundred thousand dollars.[65]

Property values around the Flatbush ballpark increased enormously with the advent of the Dodgers, higher than the average for King's County, which was enjoying an enormous boom in the early 1900s. Brooklyn values doubled from 1905 to 1911 and registered a small gain over the next eight years at a time when overall city rates actually declined. The county's real estate boom resumed after World War I, with values doubling in the 1920s. By comparison, property values at the ballpark tripled from 1910 to 1920 and rose by at least that much in the 1920s. The field's presence was a factor because it publicized the area and gave residents and business owners confidence in its future prosperity. But while Ebbets Field may have precipitated the boom, there were more fundamental reasons for it. In 1910 land values in the vicinity were lower than they should have been considering the area's future potential. Improved rapid transit enabled residents to easily commute to work, making the area increasingly desirable as a residential location. As the bedroom communities of Bedford and Flatbush expanded toward each other, speculators anticipated a significant demand for property. Once that demand began to be felt, latecomers started purchasing land in the hopes of making a quick profit, substantially driving up market prices. Ebbets saw that the neighborhood had all the necessary preconditions for a great real estate boom and an attendant population explosion, which is why he moved quickly while the real estate was still cheap.[66]

The same season that Brooklyn moved into its new ballpark, the Yankees moved to the Polo Grounds. The American Leaguers needed a new place to play because their Hilltop Park lease had expired. The neighborhood was rapidly becoming a desirable residential area, and a line of flats was pushing northward toward the park. Consequently, the team's landlord, the New York Institute for the Blind, decided the property was too valuable for a baseball field when it could obtain far greater profits by subdividing the land for eight- to twelve-story apartment buildings.[67]

The Yankees had hoped for some time to build their own fireproof structure. Back in 1909 Frank Farrell had secretly purchased lots in the Spuyten Duyvil section of north Manhattan around 225th Street. However, the project never came off because of legal problems in filling in the creek that ran past the site, community opposition, and rising costs. The Giants offered the homeless American Leaguers use of the Polo Grounds to reciprocate for the Yankees' hospitality in 1911 when the old Polo Grounds had burned down. This was expected to be a temporary arrangement, but the Yankees stayed for ten years. The arrangement was mutually beneficial since the Giants got a substantial portion of their rent paid by their tenant, and the Yankees got to play at a huge new fireproof structure.[68]

When Jacob Ruppert and his partner, C. Tillinghast Huston, purchased the Yankees in January 1915, they intended to build their own facility as soon as possible. The Yankees were a distant second to the Giants in the affections of New Yorkers, and the AL wanted a new park where the club could develop its own identity. There was also a lot of pressure on the Yankees to build because of rumors that the Federal League was moving into the city. Organized baseball believed the New York market would be best protected against the invaders if the Yankees got their own centrally located field, since this might discourage the Federal League teams and would at least put the Yankees in a much stronger position to successfully compete against interlopers.[69]

Ruppert and Huston abandoned Farrell's Spuyten Duyvil project, where so much time and money had been wasted. They wanted to remain in Manhattan, the center of New York's commerce, transportation, and population. Consideration was given to several locations, including the East Side site at 142d and Lenox, where the Highlanders had originally expected to play back in 1903. However, the property owners demanded eight hundred thousand dollars for the land, considerably more than the Yankees were prepared to pay. The Yankees then contemplated moving to one of the cheaper outlying boroughs. They considered Queens, whose population was rapidly growing and offered a great deal of underdeveloped, low-price land. Its inaccessibility had previously deterred the Yankees, but recent transportation innovations made it easier to get to Queens from the more densely populated boroughs.[70]

Ruppert and Huston also carefully considered the Bronx, which in the past had suffered from the same disadvantages as Queens. By 1915, however, transit facilities were much improved, and approximately five hundred thousand people lived there, considerably more than in Cincinnati or Washington, which both had major league franchises. Bronx business owners appealed to the Yankees to move there, anticipating that a ballpark would attract commerce and introduce Manhattan baseball fans to the advantages of living in the Bronx.[71]

As Ruppert and Huston continued their quest for a suitable site, they were shocked by an announcement late in 1915 that the Feds had taken an option on the 142d Street locale. FL president James Gilmore released a detailed, ambitious plan indicating how the Feds would profitably exploit the plot by subdividing and then developing the area, using a portion for a modern fireproof ballpark and the rest for apartment houses and businesses. The Feds actually had no intention of invading New York. Gilmore's report was a bluff because the Feds lacked the financial resources for the proposed undertaking. They were trying to pressure the major leagues into negotiating a deal, which they succeeded in getting, to terminate the costly competition.[72]

The demise of the Federal League made a ballpark less essential for the Yankees. AL president Ban Johnson still wanted them to build their own field and escape the shadow of the Giants, but Ruppert and Huston were cautious about leaving the excellent facilities of the Polo Grounds. The substantial annual rent of sixty-five thousand dollars was still only a fraction of the cost of a fireproof field. After the United States entered World War I, the ballpark question receded further into the background. The major league season was cut short by about a month, and attendance and profits fell off sharply. The war also had an unsettling effect on the construction industry, which made it a bad time to build a new ballpark.[73]

Interest in all sports boomed after World War I, and baseball in New York became more popular than ever, especially after the legalization of

Sunday baseball. Ruppert and Huston were prepared to remain at the Polo Grounds if they could secure a long-term lease instead of the usual one-year contract, but Charles Stoneham refused. In 1920 the Giants' owner told the Yankees that they were no longer welcome as tenants. He wanted to keep the lucrative Sunday dates for himself and was afraid that his club would become second-class citizens at its own park since the Yankees had acquired an outstanding gate attraction in Babe Ruth, who would help his new club set a major league attendance record in 1920.[74]

Stoneham was working in collusion with AL president Ban Johnson, who was engaged in a major confrontation with the Yankees over their acquisition of Boston hurler Carl Mays. Mays quit the Red Sox in 1920 with no explanation and was traded a few weeks later to the Yankees. Johnson suspended Mays in an attempt to break the contract, but the Yankees went to court for a restraining order enabling Mays to pitch for them. Johnson was irate over this unprecedented test of his authority and tried to obtain the Yankees' lease so he could gain control of the franchise and oust the owners. He coaxed Stoneham into canceling the lease by promising him that the Giants would select the future owners and also pick the third member of a new national baseball commission. However, Johnson's many enemies placed sufficient pressure on Stoneham, who relented. The Giants agreed to allow the Yankees to play at the Polo Grounds for $100,000 a year until they could obtain their own playing field.[75]

The resumption of the Yankees' drive to build their own facility was decried by fans and by such influential journalists as John Sheridan and Frederick C. Lane. Sheridan argued that it was inefficient for teams located in the same city to play at different ballparks. Boston, Philadelphia, and Chicago teams each had their own fields, but in 1920 the St. Louis Cardinals moved into the Browns' more accessible Sportsman's Park. The *Sporting News*, the leading baseball periodical, agreed with Sheridan, adding that the severe housing shortage in New York was far more pressing than the needs of any business or popular amusement and urged New York to use its valuable space for housing.[76]

Notwithstanding these judicious opinions, the Yankees went ahead with plans to build their own park because they needed to prepare for the long-term. Beginning in the fall of 1920, various Manhattan sites were considered, ranging from expensive downtown sites in Greenwich Village and midtown, where a field was proposed to be built on piers over the Pennsylvania Railroad tracks, to cheaper uptown sites. Manhattan was ultimately ruled out despite its excellent transportation and prestige because of prohibitive real estate costs and the impracticality of excavating the solid granite bed that ran under the borough. On 6 February 1921 Ruppert and Huston announced that they had secured a good site by their purchase for $675,000 of the Astor estate in the West Bronx at 161st Street near the Harlem River. The property had been considered for a baseball field in 1890 by the Brotherhood of Professional Base Ball Players and in 1903 by the American League, but was rejected as too remote. However, in 1921 the site was merely sixteen minutes from downtown Manhattan via the four-year-old Jerome Avenue Line, a Bronx extension of the Lexington Avenue subway, and also could be reached by the Sixth and Ninth Avenue els. The area was accessible for Bronxites by crosstown surface routes. The press unanimously lauded the decision, which symbolized strong faith in the future of baseball and of New York City.[77]

Construction did not begin immediately because local property owners opposed to the ballpark tried to get Mayor John Hylan to open streets through the site, and it took a year before the zoning board approved the closing of several streets. Furthermore the Yankees chose not to break ground until 1922, when high labor and material costs dropped to a more reasonable level. It took nine months to build the huge triple-deck structure that cost nearly $1.8 million. "The House That Ruth Built" (or, more accurately, "the House That Sunday Baseball Built") was easily the most expensive and imposing baseball field of the day. Its capacity was originally fifty-eight thousand, but a reported seventy-four thousand fans were at opening day on 18 April 1923. By comparison, the average major league ballpark then seated only twenty-five thousand. The stadium was cavernous, with the center field bleachers originally 490 feet from home plate. Foul lines were only 295 feet in right and 281 in left, but the distance to the fences increased quickly from there to the power alleys. Such innovations as a mezzanine level that used the steel support beams to support seating in space unused in other parks and a partly cantilevered upper deck provided more seats close to the diamond than in any prior ballpark. Attention was given to fans' needs with the inclusion of ample telephone booths, sixteen toilets, and refreshment counters at all seating levels. Planners expected virtually all spectators to arrive by public transit, so they devoted little consideration to parking.[78]

The new structure was called Yankee Stadium, the first playing area not referred to by such rural names as "park," "field," or "grounds." The "Stadium" represented baseball's prominence in American culture and, in time, the Yankees' eminence in baseball.[79] The change in nomenclature was significant because it symbolized a shift in the relationship between the national pastime and urban society. The rustic titles and the layouts of earlier parks were rural metaphors that reinforced the agrarian ideology of baseball. The change in terminology indicted that the sport was beginning to identify more with its urban milieu, particularly appropriate since the 1920 census had reported that the majority of Americans were living in cities. The term *stadium* emphasized the massive size of the ballpark and the sophisticated technology utilized to build it, themes generally associated with complex urban societies. The next generation of ballparks adopted the same terminology, such as Cleveland's Municipal Stadium (1932) and New York's Shea Stadium (1964). Indoor fields built since 1965 have been called domes, such as the (Houston) Astrodome (1965), the (Seattle) Kingdome (1977), and the (Minneapolis) Hubert H. Humphrey Metrodome (1982). The latest retrograde structures built in the 1990s have gone back to older style nomenclature with Jacobs' Field (Cleveland) and Camden Yards (Baltimore).

Yankee Stadium was built during an enormous construction boom in its neighborhood. The *Sporting News* asserted that many new residents were attracted to the area so they could watch games from nearby rooftops or walk to the grounds and purchase tickets. However, the area's development as a residential community was independent of the park's presence, which may have actually discouraged many people from moving in. The neighborhood grew mainly as a consequence of the new rapid transit facilities that served the west Bronx and made it easy for people working in Manhattan to commute home. A heavy demand for decent housing after World War I spurred developers to construct apartment buildings in the west Bronx because of cheap real estate prices and the completion of the Jerome Avenue elevated line. Builders knew that cheap rapid transit was a vital concern of apartment hunters. The new well-built six-story apartments along tree-lined Grand Concourse quickly attracted thousands of upwardly mobile New Yorkers to the Bronx.[80]

The construction of Yankee Stadium had a significant impact on land uses in its immediate vicinity, giving business owners confidence in the locality's future and generating many new enterprises that catered to baseball patrons. The valuable blocks east of the park were crowded with small restaurants, bars, garages, and a theater. Nearby drug stores added lunch counters to feed the hungry fans. The Concourse Plaza Hotel, a short walk from the stadium, was completed late in 1923 in the hope of providing lodgings for the Yankees and visiting teams.[81]

Contemporaries believed the park's presence had a beneficial impact on the neighborhood's land values, which sharply increased between

1920 and 1930. The west Bronx in the vicinity of 161st and Jerome enjoyed a real estate boom prior to the coming of the ballpark. Property values doubled from 1910 to 1919, even though values for the entire borough increased by only 5 percent. In the 1920s the price of land near the stadium tripled while average Bronx valuations rose by 87.2 percent. The sharp appreciation of property near the ballpark was typical of real estate along the entire course of the Jerome Avenue el, even though it passed through many different kinds of neighborhoods. It was the proximity of a cheap, accessible route to Manhattan that accounted for most of the appreciation, rather than the coming of Yankee Stadium.[82]

The presence of Yankee Stadium did contribute to the boom in its immediate vicinity by creating an anticipated source of revenue for local merchants, advertisement for the area, and psychological support for investors. The value of the park site and commercial lots immediately to the east nearly quadrupled, an increase slightly greater than the community's rate of growth. The values at 161st Street, a very important thoroughfare just north of the stadium, increased by 8.5- to 10-fold, a startling increase, due less to the ballpark than to its proximity to a subway station, which made it prime commercial property.[83] The stores and public institutions on this street were the real lifeblood of the community, not Yankee Stadium. The courthouse and county offices a few blocks east on 161st Street made it the center of borough politics as well as a thriving commercial area. While the presence of Yankee Stadium might have symbolized the vitality of the locality, this section of the west Bronx was already becoming a thriving new neighborhood.

◇

The location of the original professional baseball parks constructed with cheap flammable materials changed quite often. Their sites were chosen according to the availability of cheap mass transit, rent prices, the social character of the neighborhood, and financial support from local transit interests. Beginning in 1909 expensive fireproof structures were built in major league and larger minor league cities to increase seating capacities and to replace dangerous wooden stands with safer facilities. The expense and immutability of such ventures compelled owners to either buy their own sites or secure long-term leases for their own security and to establish excellent connections with local political leaders. Powerful political allies helped professional clubs by supplying inside information on land prices and transit lines, both crucial in selecting the best potential location for future ballparks. Furthermore, political friends protected investments against competitors and community opposition, provided friendly enforcement of the municipal codes, and secured essential services and preferential treatment from municipalities.

Major league ballparks were usually constructed in middle-class residential neighborhoods easily accessible to fans. The exceptions were Comiskey Park and Washington's National Park (later Griffith Stadium), both originally built in working-class communities on or near sites where professional baseball had long been played.[84] The coming of a ballpark was usually not welcomed by residents in built-up areas because they were worried that the large noisy crowds and the businesses that sprang up to cater to spectators would have a deleterious impact on their neighborhoods. On the other hand, owners of underdeveloped sites hailed the coming of a ballpark because of anticipated new opportunities in commerce and housing. However, a ballpark's main impact on an area's future was psychological, since its influence on land uses and property values seldom extended more than a couple of blocks from its entrance. Major civic additions, such as hospitals and universities, had far greater fiscal and psychological impacts on local neighborhoods.[85]

FOUR

Professional Sunday Baseball and Social Reform

It is irrational, woefully short-sighted and a matter of censure for us to expect in this day of mental freedom and advanced thought, for healthy-bodied healthy-minded persons to give the whole of Sunday either to churchly visitation or mere abstinence from toil. . . .

    Artisans, clerks, factory employees, are ground to the grind six days in the week, with never a chance to witness the game on which their hearts are set. . . . Six days a week they toil over littered desks or over heartless machines, dreaming of the game, longing for an opportunity to witness one, and then when the day of freedom comes the game is closed through mere narrow prejudice.

    —Rabbi Charles Fleischer, 1911

Professional baseball on Sundays was restricted at the turn of the century because of blue laws that regulated public behavior on the Christian sabbath. These laws significantly influenced the composition of crowds because they barred games when most blue-collar workers had leisure time. Sabbatarians were pietistic, native-born Protestants who regarded the sabbath as a day intended solely for religious functions. Pietistic denominations included Baptists, Congregationalists, Lutherans (Missouri Synod), Methodists, and Presbyterians, all revivalist sects that professed Arminianism, or the belief that godly behavior was required as ongoing proof of a person's conversion and salvation. Pietists believed that it was their responsibility to regulate the entire community's moral conduct by any means necessary, ranging from social pressure to legal sanctions. Their sabbath views directly conflicted with the attitudes of most Catholic and German Lutheran immigrants, who were accustomed to a Continental sabbath of rest and recreation after church, and Jewish newcomers, who celebrated the sabbath on Saturday.[1] Social reformers found it difficult to get these blue laws liberalized in the face of strong conservative resistance that was based on religious, cultural, and social concerns about defending the traditional WASP way of life. The issue of Sunday baseball exemplified the problems that advocates of a pluralistic, secular modern society faced at the end of the nineteenth century.

Sunday Baseball in Chicago

In the early 1870s professional baseball teams often played on Sundays. However, when the NL was founded, it opposed Sunday ballplaying and originally allowed only exhibition games on that day. After the 1877 season the NL banned all Sunday games as part of its campaign to secure the patronage of the middle class, who were believed to be unalterably opposed to Sunday baseball and other alleged sabbath desecrations. The prohibition was strictly enforced, and in 1880 the league expelled Cincinnati, a heavily Germanic city where a Continental sabbath was observed, for scheduling Sunday games. However, the public, especially the working class, strongly demanded Sunday ball, which contributed to the formation of the American Association in 1882. AA teams scheduled Sunday games where permitted, mainly in western cities such as Cincinnati, Louisville, and St. Louis and, temporarily, even in Brooklyn (1886–89), where the games were played across the county line in Queens. AA teams in cities without Sunday ball, like Pittsburgh and Cleveland, sometimes arranged weekend schedules to play away on Sunday in a western city following a Saturday home date. Several early minor league franchises were established with the expectation that their Sunday crowds would provide a profit margin, anticipating audiences up to five times as large as on weekdays. In 1886 the *Palladium of Labor* pointed out, "The clubs can always depend upon a large turnout to Sunday games, as they are patronized by the working class who find it impossible to get off during the week." The NL experimented with Sunday ball that year at the insistence of fans in Kansas City and St. Louis, before and after the season, but chose not to change its policy. Consequently, the St. Louis club dropped out of the league.[2]

The NL's policy meant that the White Stockings could not play on Sundays even though many other amusements operated unmolested on the sabbath. Working-class Chicagoans vigorously opposed the state's blue laws and other morals regulations, and city officials, who exercised considerable home rule, did not enforce the detested restrictions. German, Irish, and other foreign-born residents who comprised 77.9 percent of Chicago's population in 1890 had traditionally enjoyed drinking, athletic activities, and outings on Sundays. Thy had considerable political clout, exemplified by the election of German-born John Peter Altgeld as governor in 1892.[3]

During the 1880s the authorities did not interfere with the popular amateur and semiprofessional Sunday baseball games. Downstate legislators decried this lack of respect for the sabbath and repeatedly introduced bills to proscribe baseball and other Sunday amusements. White Stockings owner Albert G. Spalding defended Sunday sports against one such measure in 1887 and called for home rule:

> It will be hard on the young fellows who compose our amateur clubs. . . . And I feel sorry for the boys, for I think baseball is the best exercise in the world for a youth and there are many young workmen, clerks, and cashboys in Chicago who can find no time save Sunday to indulge in such pastime. It seems to me that such questions as Sunday problems in a city so large as Chicago should rest with the municipal and not the state authorities. The City Council, it seems to me, could regulate such matters to a far better advantage and doubtless in a manner more satisfactory to our people.[4]

The absence of Sunday professional ball in Chicago encouraged a minor league to place a franchise on the South Side in 1888, and its first Sunday game set a city attendance mark. Fred Lange, a star with the White Stockings in the 1890s, claimed it was the largest crowd he had ever seen.[5]

When the AA and the NL merged after the 1891 season, each team determined its own Sunday policy. Clubs in Cincinnati, Louisville, and St. Louis scheduled Sunday home games, but Chicago did not. Spalding's South Side lease prohibited Sunday amusements, and the West Side middle-class community surrounding Congress Street Park strongly opposed Sunday ball, afraid it would harm their rest and repose. Spalding himself thought that Sunday ball would be bad business because it would cut into weekday patronage, plus he expected disapproving middle-class fans would boycott future games.[6]

On 23 December 1892 president James Hart of the White Stockings announced a new policy of Sunday games for the forthcoming season. Hart claimed the new attitude reflected changing public opinion toward sabbath entertainments. He was also afraid that unless he took such action, new teams might invade Chicago and play on Sundays. Hart justified his decision by referring to the ongoing debate over the Sunday opening of the Columbian Exposition. He pointed out that if the world's fair was open on Sunday, then baseball should be played. On the other hand, if the exposition was closed on the sabbath, then tourists and working-class Chicagoans would need an alternate healthy amusement, like professional baseball. This decision committed the club to move to a new park where it could stage Sunday games.[7]

Chicago ballplayers were not enthusiastic about Hart's announcement because they feared losing an off day, having salaries cut, and suffering a decline in their occupational prestige. They disagreed with the *Sporting News*, which anticipated that the number of spectators lost by introducing Sunday ball would be more than offset by new fans.[8]

Chicago's first professional Sunday game was played on 14 May 1893 at the new Polk Street Grounds. The crowd of 13,500 made Sunday ball an immediate success. Little organized agitation emerged against Sunday baseball because Sabbatarians were devoting their full attention to fighting the proposed Sunday opening of the world's fair on 28 May. The fair was opened on Sundays because of pressure from several newspapers and labor unions like the Knights of Labor, as well as concessionaires and fair administrators concerned about profits. However, Sunday crowds were smaller than those on other days, largely because the high cost of attending the fair reduced working-class interest. In 1894 W. W. Clark's interdenominational International Sunday Observance League initiated organized opposition to Sunday baseball. Clark and some associates met in March with Democratic mayor John P. Hopkins, a staunch supporter of a liberalized Sunday, who refused to move against the baseball team. The league then secured an injunction against the ball club claiming that Sunday games were a public nuisance that had caused a sharp decline in property values and encouraged the establishment of disorderly saloons near the ballpark. However, Hart found a sympathetic judge who dissolved the injunction on a legal technicality, and Sunday ball continued. These games were so popular in 1894 that sabbath crowds reportedly averaged 10,000 spectators, over four times the typical weekday attendance.[9]

Sabbatarians were disappointed with these results but did not give up. They tried to stop Sunday games the following season by instigating a test case to determine the legality of Sunday baseball. On Sunday,

23 June, complaints were sworn out against the entire White Stockings squad, resulting in the arrest of several players in the third inning. Bonds were quickly posted, and the game resumed to the delight of thirteen thousand fans. In September the defendants were convicted of sabbath desecration and fined four dollars apiece. The verdict was appealed and overturned four months later. This judgment effectively legitimized Sunday baseball in Chicago, although council members and state legislators tried to blackmail the club, threatening to introduce bills to stop professional Sunday ball unless granted more passes or such favors as the use of the park for certain functions.[10]

The relative ease by which Chicago secured Sunday baseball was typical of most midwestern and western cities. By the 1890s nearly every western professional team played in a city with Sunday ball. The most important exceptions were Cleveland and Detroit, both with large immigrant populations. The Tigers did play on Sunday from 1900 to 1909 at suburban Burns Park, where the authorities did not interfere, but were prevented from playing in Detroit until 1910 because of the influence of Good Government groups that favored the ban.[11] Cleveland did not succeed until a year later because of a bizarre alliance between powerful pietist societies and saloon keepers afraid of losing about three-quarters of their patronage to the Indians on their busiest day.[12]

Midwestern Sabbatarians mainly focused their unsuccessful fight against Sunday baseball in the courts. Western jurists consistently ruled against Sunday blue laws, basing their decisions on sociological evidence that reflected popular tastes and demands, rather than legal precedents. One of the earliest cases occurred in 1887 when a St. Louis judge ruled that Sunday baseball was not a public nuisance but a source of good clean fun for thousands of people.[13] Thirteen years later the Missouri Appellate Court ruled that baseball was not subject to Sunday blue laws that had been enacted years before the invention of the game. The jurists reasoned that the lawmakers could not possibly have intended to deprive the masses of this healthy outdoor sport that was in no way comparable to such "vile" amusements as horse racing and cock fighting, which the edicts had originally banned.[14]

Sunday Baseball in New York

While western towns were enjoying a Continental sabbath, eastern cities observed an American sabbath. Local blue laws dating from colonial times or the early national period were ardently supported by small-town native-born white Americans who dominated their state legislatures and feared the immigrant-congested cities they perceived as centers of vice, crime, and corruption. Pietists believed that a crusade was necessary to protect their Protestant heritage and traditional way of life, part of which entailed Sabbatarianism and the support of blue laws. Sabbatarians hoped that Sunday blue laws would serve the dual purposes of providing social control over city folk by curtailing their opportunities for immoral activities and acculturating them to traditional patterns of behavior.[15]

Eastern Sabbatarians were led by voluntary interdenominational groups such as the New York Sabbath Committee, which since the 1850s had fought Sunday mail delivery, newspaper printing, and the opening of museums and libraries. New York was their principal target because it was the nation's largest city and was seen as a center of sin and paganism. In 1900 76.9 percent of its population was of foreign origin, mainly Jews and Catholics who opposed a strict sabbath. Sabbatarians believed it was important to maintain an American sabbath in New York to secure order and sustain their values there as well as to set an example for colleagues elsewhere to emulate. If they could defeat the "ungodly" in this un-American metropolis, then they could succeed elsewhere.[16]

The fight over Sunday baseball in New York dated back to the late 1880s. The first battle occurred over the Brooklyn AA team, who had first played on Sundays at Ridgewood Park on 25 April 1886. In 1889 blue law advocates mobilized community opposition to noisy ball games and secured indictments and a conviction against the field's owner, who was fined five hundred dollars for violating the Sunday codes. This effectively halted professional Sunday ball in the metropolitan area.[17]

A counterattack by Sunday baseball advocates was initiated in the state legislature in 1897 under the leadership of New York City Republican Jerry Sullivan, a former umpire who had successfully campaigned for his seat by advocating Sunday ball. Several bills were introduced seeking blue law relief; the one given the best chance to pass circumvented the intent of the penal codes by punishing baseball promoters with just a token fine. However, none of the reform proposals passed.[18]

Tammany Hall strongly supported blue law reform on behalf of their immigrant constituents, who resented the restrictions the state placed on their leisure and business options. Sunday baseball was of particular concern to a machine closely tied to New York's major league teams as well as to the city's semiprofessional clubs that regularly played on Sundays despite the proscriptive laws. As boss Richard Croker told reporters:

I do not know of any sound reason why baseball playing should not be allowed on Sundays as well as any other day. I am in favor of it. Ministers ride their bicycles on Sunday and find enjoyment in it and there are thousands of citizens who would find good, honest enjoyment in a game of baseball, and it does not make any difference whether it is played on Sundays or weekdays, as there is nothing demoralizing in it.

. . . Why tie up people so they cannot enjoy themselves in a harmless and healthful way on Sunday? The rich and the well-to-do enjoy themselves every day in the week when the masses of people are at work. Now I say that those who work six days in the week ought to have the opportunity of seeing a ball game on Sunday if they want it. You can trust that the people will not desecrate the Sabbath. It would simply furnish rational enjoyment. If golf is allowed . . . on Sunday, should not baseball?[19]

Amateur Sunday baseball was supported by a broad coalition of New York reformers, including labor leaders, progressives such as Paul Reynolds of the Social Reform Club and Felix Adler of Ethical Culture, settlement house workers such as Lillian Wald, and Social Gospelers such as Rev. W. B. Rainsford of Trinity Church and Lyman Abbott of *Outlook*. They believed that young men needed exercise and relaxation on Sundays since these youths had no opportunity during the week for such exhilarating activities.[20]

Social Gospelers were particularly vocal because they wanted to make the church more relevant to the needs of urbanites and felt that Sabbatarianism was driving working-class men away from God. They pointed out that Sunday baseball in the West had not destroyed that region's moral fiber. Liberal clerics preferred that young workers get their recreation from sports rather than from drinking or gambling.[21] Rainsford described the dilemma of his working-class parishioners:

I am in favor of young men playing baseball on Sunday for their own amusement. I believe that young men should have some recreation on Sunday. There are many of them in my church who work diligently all the week up to late Saturday night and who come to me and ask what they can do in order to get more recreation. I tell them to come to morning service, then go out on their bicycles, or go out and play baseball or golf or some form of beautiful sport. Such sports improve the body and make those who participate all the better for it.[22]

Social Gospelers drew the line with professional baseball because it was a commercial venture and work for the players. They feared that professional games would attract large noisy crowds and disrupt the peace and calm of the surrounding neighborhood. These views were typical of other conservative progressives, such as Governor Charles Evans Hughes.[23]

Although professional Sunday baseball was not played in the state's three largest cities, New York, Buffalo, and Rochester, semiprofessional ball was played on the sabbath in New York City, and professional Sunday baseball was permitted by local consent in such smaller cities as Albany, Schenectady, Syracuse, and Utica. Judges rarely convicted amateur or semiprofessional violators, sympathizing with public opinion that it was unfair to enforce the penal codes against working-class youths who had no other recreational outlets, while the middle and upper classes could amuse themselves during the week as well as on the sabbath, when many of them went off to their country clubs for golf and tennis.[24]

The police rarely interrupted semiprofessional games because there was little public pressure to enforce the law, and club owners were often protected by their political influence. Promoters were punished for violating Sunday codes only if they charged admission fees. Consequently, semipro owners in the early 1900s employed imaginative means to circumvent the law. They would sell programs, scorecards, or magazines in lieu of tickets or assess "donations" from patrons.[25]

The success of certain upstate franchises and the semiprofessionals encouraged major league teams to consider staging Sunday games. New York clubs also played regularly on Sundays during western road trips and played exhibitions and even some regularly scheduled Sunday games at the West New York Field Club Grounds in Weehawken, New Jersey, without interference. The field was first used for Sunday games by the New York Mets in the summer of 1887. The Giants used it twice in 1898 against Brooklyn and twice again in 1899 against Louisville. In 1903 John T. Brush scheduled a postseason Sunday game with a semiprofessional team at Harlem's Olympic Field, a popular semiprofessional park, ostensibly as a philanthropic endeavor to entertain people employed six days a week who had never seen a professional game. Brush actually staged the game to encourage public interest in professional Sunday baseball and test the authorities' response. Seven thousand fans paid twenty-five cents each for a scorecard entitling them to a seat, and the game was played to its conclusion without interruption.[26]

Brush's successful experiment, the continuing popularity of semiprofessional games, and Tammany's victory in the 1903 elections encouraged New York magnates to test the blue laws in 1904 by staging regular season games on Sundays. The owners hoped that their political influence would save them from Sabbatarian harassment and lead to the general acceptance of commercialized Sunday baseball.[27]

The first regular season Sunday game played in greater New York was at Brooklyn's Washington Park on 17 April 1904 before twelve thousand spectators. These fans had been admitted to the park after purchasing a scorecard for fifty or seventy-five cents, depending on their seat location. Members of law and order associations, ministerial groups, and Sabbatarian leagues immediately complained to Police Commissioner William G. McAdoo, who had attended the contest but had not seen any violations. He agreed to give the matter serious consideration. The commissioner decided to permit games in isolated neighborhoods like Ridgewood or the industrial section of Red Hook, from where he had not received any complaints about Sunday games, but ruled out play in densely populated Manhattan since he felt matches there would create a public disturbance. His decision prevented the Giants from playing Sunday baseball at the Polo Grounds—a clause in the Highlanders' lease already had prevented them from scheduling Sunday games at their field. President Farrell hoped to hold Sunday events at Ridgewood Park, where he was guaranteed political protection, but that field was within the five-mile territorial limits of the Dodgers, which gave them exclusive rights there, and Ebbets refused to grant the Highlanders permission to use Ridgewood Park.[28]

McAdoo's pronouncement did not satisfy Brooklyn Sabbatarians, who warned him that he was legally required to enforce the penal codes. They pointed out that in 1899 the courts had censured a Buffalo sheriff for not preventing the local minor league club from playing on the sabbath. McAdoo bowed before their pressure and agreed to prepare a test case. He forewarned Ebbets that arrests were going to be made at his next Sunday game but that it would be permitted to continue. On Sunday, 24 April, the Dodgers' battery, the opposing batter, and three ticket sellers were arrested at the start of the game. The contest then went on, and the arrested ballplayers were replaced by the men originally slated to start.[29]

The case was tried before Justice William Gaynor, a longtime friend of Sunday baseball. He released the defendants, ruling that the peaceful repose and religious liberty of the community had not been disturbed and criticizing the police for reviving obsolete laws. He made a special plea for harmless Sunday amusements, noting that while rural residents had suitable entertainment available during the week, city folk were more restricted in their opportunities.[30]

Brooklyn Sabbatarians were disappointed with this ruling and prepared another test case with the cooperation of District Attorney John Clarke, who provided legal advice and assigned police officers to Washington Park to observe and gather evidence about the Sunday, 29 May game. Indictments were drawn up on the basis that programs had been sold at the park in lieu of tickets to evade the law. Justice Gaynor tried the case of *People v. Poole*, ruling on 18 June that Sunday games to which the public had been invited were ipso facto a violation of the penal codes. This decision ended professional Sunday ball for the 1904 season. The indicted ballplayers were ultimately acquitted in September, too late to reschedule any Sunday games, but that ruling encouraged the Dodgers to reintroduce Sunday games the following season.[31]

After Brooklyn had played several Sunday games at the start of the 1905 season, the Sabbatarians vehemently protested the lack of action by the city. Commissioner McAdoo told the pietists that he was perplexed by the seemingly contradictory court rulings in 1904. Corporation Counsel James Delany counseled him that Gaynor's ruling in *People v. Poole* was the correct one, and that publicly advertised Sunday games that charged admission were patently illegal. Based on Delany's opinion, McAdoo ordered the police to stop all further Sunday games. The Dodgers had no choice but to cancel their game scheduled for 28 May. Ebbets sought an injunction to prevent future police interference, but Supreme Court Judge James Kelley ruled against him, reaffirming Delany's opinion:

> I agree that there is no prohibition against the man who is forced to labor during the weekday preventing him from enjoying himself in an orderly and decent manner on Sunday so long as the repose of the community is not interrupted. But the prohibition is clear against Sunday games which are advertised, to which the general public are invited, which they attend in great numbers and to witness which no money is charged directly or indirectly or which are conducted for financial profit. This is not the wholesome recreation of the individual which the law will not permit. *It may be sport*, but it is public sport and a *quasi-business* undertaking.[32]

In 1906 the New York magnates again scheduled Sunday games. The first regular season game ever held in Manhattan was played on 29 April with the approval of the city administrators as a benefit for survivors of the San Francisco earthquake. Sunday games were resumed at Washington Park, where spectators got in by placing money in a "donation" box.

It looked as if Sunday baseball was finally going to become a reality because Brooklyn police officers made no effort to stop them. However, in June the new police commissioner, William Bingham, ordered an end to Sunday games. Bingham believed in enforcing the letter of the law, evidenced by his decision to keep police officers out of ballparks and other private property. In addition, he was under strong pressure from Sabbatarians and those politicians who owned Brooklyn semipro teams that were being hurt by the Dodgers' competition on Sundays. These sports enthusiasts expected that the semipro games would not be halted because of their popularity in the community and officers' fears of displeasing the local Tammany bosses and getting transferred to undesirable assignments. Commissioner Bingham's firm stance was supported in court by Justice John A. Blanchard, who ruled that the donations were merely a ploy to circumvent the intent of the law and that Sunday ball was still illegal. Consequently, the Dodgers stopped holding Sunday games.[33]

In 1907 the locus of sabbath reform shifted away from the playing field and the courts and back to the state legislature, where bills to legalize Sunday sports had been annually introduced since 1897. The Sunday baseball issue was heavily partisan, with Democrats favoring reform and Republicans opposing change. It was an ethnocultural issue that symbolized two distinctly different ways of life and worldviews. The Democrats primarily represented urban ethnic groups who sought social freedom while the Republicans represented small-town pietistic WASPs who wanted to protect their way of life by exerting social control over urban newcomers. The legislature was controlled by upstate Republicans, who usually outnumbered the Democrats (almost exclusively from New York City) by a two-to-one margin in the Assembly and by three-to-two in the Senate. The Republicans usually killed reform measures in committee before they could even get to the floor for debate.[34]

Several bills were introduced in 1907 to legalize amateur and semiprofessional Sunday baseball, including one by an assemblyman who owned a semiprofessional team and another by an assembly member who was a former pugilist. These proposals were strongly backed by Charles Ebbets, who lobbied on their behalf and sought support and cooperation from Brooklyn semiprofessional teams by promising to rent them his park when the Dodgers were out of town.[35]

The Assembly's Codes Committee held a three-hour hearing on the Sunday baseball issue. The Sabbatarian viewpoint was represented by several pietistic clergymen who claimed that Sunday laws were necessary to protect public morals, safeguard the beliefs of the religiously inclined, and defend the citizenry in the enjoyment of their day of rest. Conservative ministers claimed that Sunday baseball had a deleterious influence on youths because it lured them away from home and Sunday school. They castigated it as an entering wedge for more harmful activities. They employed sociological evidence rather than theological arguments to show that the American sabbath was necessary for the welfare of working-class people and thus merited state support. Tammany Assemblyman Alfred E. Smith and other proponents of Sunday reform countered these arguments, asserting that the majority, particularly in New York City, wanted Sunday baseball and that a small minority should not determine public standards of behavior. They argued that baseball was a positive force that contributed to law and order by providing a healthful and moral diversion for young men who might otherwise spend their time at dance halls, saloons, or other vile resorts, where they would be subject to temptation.[36]

None of the Sunday reform bills introduced in 1907 were passed, and only one even got out of committee. The debate had no impact on the legislators, whose minds were already made up and whose attitudes accurately reflected their constituents' opinions. For more than a decade, Sunday relief measures continued to be introduced in the state legislature, but upstate Republicans defeated every proposed change until after World War I.[37]

In the early 1910s the painstaking task of securing Sunday baseball began gathering support from smaller cities that had Sunday ball. Club owners in the New York State and the International Leagues believed they needed Sunday ball to make a profit or at least break even. Authorities in Albany, Elmira, and Utica rarely interfered with Sunday ball games, but local club owners worried that the blue laws could be enforced in the future, which might force them out of business. Consequently, team owners wanted the blue laws rewritten.[38]

Sabbath reformers promoted home rule so that each town could decide this issue for itself. As the *Buffalo Express* argued, "The country legislature should have nothing to say regarding questions of this nature so far as municipalities are concerned. They should give the cities an opportunity to decide, because such questions are of more importance to cities than the rural districts." Smaller cities' aspirations were reflected by a 1913 resolution of the New York Mayors' Conference that supported local choice on Sunday ball. The mayors also petitioned Governor William Sulzer, a Democrat, to support home rule and local option, asserting that their working-class constituents should be able to enjoy their limited leisure time. They further noted that even factory owners favored Sunday baseball as a safety valve to keep their workers happy and prevent labor unrest.[39]

In the early 1900s Sunday baseball in Binghamton divided people along class and ethnic lines. In 1912 the local franchise in the New York State League was purchased by the shoe manufacturer George F. Johnson, a renowned welfare capitalist who supported sport and other recreations to bolster employee loyalty. Johnson was such an ardent advocate of Sunday baseball that he staged some Sunday games for free just to demonstrate its popularity and donated profits from other Sunday games to local charities. As a prominent figure in Broome County Republican circles, Johnson secured in 1913 the nomination and election of a proponent of Sunday amusements to the Assembly in place of the ardent Sabbatarian incumbent.[40]

In the meantime, except for an exhibition for ten thousand newspaper carriers in 1909 and a benefit for Titanic survivors in 1912, no more professional Sunday games were played in New York City until 1917, when several eastern major league teams tried to take advantage of the wartime situation. Ostensibly charitable measures to raise money for war relief, these games were actually an attempt to institutionalize Sunday baseball in their respective cities. Boston, Philadelphia, and Pittsburgh officials prevented this scheme, but it was approved in New York and Washington.[41]

The first Sunday game in New York during the war was on 17 June 1917 at the Polo Grounds, where the Yankees played the St. Louis Browns before 21,795 paying spectators and another 8,000 guests. Ten thousand dollars from ticket sales was donated to a reserve regiment about to go overseas. However, when the Dodgers held a benefit game on 1 July, their management was arrested on warrants secured by Sabbatarians. Three months later a three-judge panel found Ebbets and Manager Wilbert Robinson guilty of sabbath desecration, pointing out that the charitable use of the profits did not absolve their guilt.[42]

The next Sunday game was played at the Polo Grounds on 19 August between the Giants and the Reds. John McGraw and Cincinnati manager Christy Mathewson received summonses the next day because of their participation. Their prominence brought the Sunday issue national attention. McGraw was the most famous manager of the era and Mathewson, who had never played on Sundays, was the idol of many American youths. They were tried by Magistrate Francis X. McQuade, a longtime friend of Sunday entertainments, who dismissed the charges. McQuade castigated the Sabbatarians and commended the managers for donating their services to the patriotic cause of war relief.[43]

This incident created favorable publicity for the Sunday baseball movement, which became a prominent issue second only to patriotism in the fall off-year election. Charles Ebbets was assisted by Jacob Ruppert in canvassing local candidates for state office on their attitudes about Sunday baseball, and they reported that 90 percent of the nominees favored it. Supporters included such prominent progressives as Mayor John Purroy Mitchell and Al Smith, a candidate for the presidency of the Board of Aldermen. This marked the first time that Ebbets had been assisted by another New York City owner in his quest for legislation to permit Sunday baseball. The owners had previously stayed out of the fight because it would have generated negative publicity and they did not want to lend credence to the Sabbatarian claim that the true purpose of Sunday reform was to commercialize the sabbath.[44]

When the legislature convened in 1918, a bill to legalize professional Sunday baseball on a local option seemed likely to pass. A broad-based, statewide, urban coalition had been formed that included baseball club owners, motion picture moguls seeking the same privilege for their enterprise, most newspapers in the state, organized labor, progressives, and veterans' organizations and women's groups concerned with providing wholesome entertainment for returning soldiers. The backing by women's organizations was an important development since they had previously been outspoken in support of the American sabbath.[45]

In March Brooklyn Republican senator Robert Lawson's bill to permit professional Sunday baseball between the hours of 2:00 and 6:00 P.M. on a local option basis was favorably reported out of committee, the first time any legislation calling for commercialized sabbath amusements had proceeded that far. Lawson's measure passed the Senate by a vote of 26-20 and seemed headed for passage in the Assembly until Republican leaders responded to their rural constituents' demands to kill the bill. Republican governor Charles S. Whitman had endorsed Sunday baseball during 1917, but was facing a tough reelection fight in 1918 and needed to indulge conservative upstate voters. On his orders, the Assembly's speaker buried the Lawson bill in the Rules Committee.[46]

Whitman was defeated for reelection by Al Smith, an early and consistent supporter of Sunday baseball. Smith failed to bring in a Democratic legislature with him, but a survey of new legislators found that many upstate members were less opposed to legalizing Sunday baseball than in the past because of its adoption that summer in Washington, D.C., and the influence of the war. Many Americans did not feel that soldiers who had fought for freedom overseas should come home to find their own liberty diminished by Prohibition and strict blue laws. Upstate politicos also realized the need to cater to the large bloc of returning veteran voters.[47]

Early in the 1919 session, a bill to permit professional Sunday baseball between 2:00 and 6:00 P.M. on a local option basis was introduced in the Senate by Democrat James J. Walker, the future mayor of New York. Despite the steadfast opposition of Sabbatarians like the renowned Rev. Henry Ward Beecher, who attacked the Walker bill as an entering wedge for bolshevism, and Republican control of the legislature, the measure passed both houses. The Senate approved 29-22, and the Assembly concurred 82-60. Democrats supported the bill nearly unanimously, and sufficient backing from urban Republicans defeated rural opponents.[48] Governor Smith promptly signed this measure along with another bill permitting theaters to show movies on Sundays, explaining:

> I am of the firm opinion that those members of a community who oppose all recreation on Sunday . . . have no right when they constitute a minority to impose their views upon the majority who disagree with them and to prohibit the latter from exercising rights and privileges to which they deem themselves entitled, the exercise of which will in no wise interfere with the orderly and proper observance of the day of rest by those desiring to refrain from attending amusements.
>
> The witnessing of a baseball game . . . either with or without the payment of an admission fee, is a most harmless diversion. It is in no sense deteriorating to the moral fiber of the witnesses. . . .
>
> Some such form of relaxation on Sunday is almost imperative and certainly most beneficial in the cases of the great masses of our people who during the six weekdays are employed in confining occupations, having during those days no opportunity for recreation of any sort.[49]

The passage of Sunday baseball provisions in most cities was perfunctory. New York City's Board of Aldermen quickly passed a bill, and the major league clubs immediately scheduled Sunday games. These games attracted enormous crowds, with one at the Polo Grounds drawing about twenty-five thousand. Over twenty thousand fans crowded into either the Polo Grounds or Ebbets Field on succeeding Sundays that season.[50] As one reporter noted, this innovation substantially altered the complexion of the spectatorship: "Up to yesterday, baseball in Greater New York was for the semi-idle, the floating population of New York City. Yesterday these bleachers teemed with life. The men from the docks and the factories came and they brought their wives and children. These dark benches hold thousands of fans who never in their lives had been to a big league game."[51]

The successful effort to secure commercialized Sunday baseball for New York took over twenty years, indicating the difficulty of altering behavioral norms by legislation even when a majority favored such changes. Although the ball clubs had substantial backing from Tammany Hall, Sunday games were not permitted until the social conditions fostered by World War I encouraged the formation of a broad-based coalition seeking blue law reform. The political machine was never omnipotent, despite myths to the contrary. In spite of Tammany's control over the police and magistrates, Sabbatarians had previously always been able to appeal successfully to higher authorities to stop professional Sunday baseball. Furthermore, in a state where there was little home rule and the legislature was very powerful, the Democrats were nearly always the minority party in Albany and needed Republican support to pass their measures.[52]

The situation in New York was typical of eastern states, where sabbath reform encountered such vigorous opposition that it took about thirty years longer to achieve than in the Midwest. New Jersey was probably the most lenient eastern state in its enforcement of Sunday blue laws. Major league teams in the 1890s took advantage of its lax implementation to stage Sunday exhibitions in Bayonne, Hoboken, and Weehawken, where they were viewed by thousands of New Yorkers. The only penalty was token fines. Newark's team in the Atlantic League played on Sundays because of its owners' political protection. Nonetheless, the New York teams did not arrange regular season games in nearby New Jersey, although other professionals, like the Detroit Tigers, did play away from their regular fields on Sundays.[53]

The last major league cities to secure Sunday baseball were Boston (1929), Philadelphia (1933), and Pittsburgh (1934). While Massachusetts had a progressive political tradition, it also had, like Pennsylvania, a history of strict sabbath observance dating back to colonial times. Rural pietists dominated both state legislatures, and in cooperation with representatives from the richer districts, exercised substantial political and social control over urban immigrants and workers.[54]

At the turn of the century Boston NL owners were convinced that local middle-class opinion was so utterly opposed to Sunday amusements that they even refused to schedule away games on the sabbath until 1903 rather than antagonize their fans. The city's population in 1900 was largely of foreign origin (72.2 percent), of which a large segment was conservative Irish immigrants, who were less outspoken than German immigrants in their support of sabbath reform. Early in the century several reform bills were introduced in the state legislature, but not until 1920 was a measure passed permitting even amateur Sunday baseball. Eight years later a referendum was held on the question of allowing professional Sunday ball on a local option basis. President Emil Fuchs of the Braves spent two hundred thousand dollars on booklets, placards, pamphlets, four million sample ballots, and bribes for city council members to promote Sunday ball. Voters in large cities and 80 percent of smaller communities approved the proposal, and in 1929 Boston's major league teams began playing on Sundays.[55]

In the commonwealth of Pennsylvania, foreign-born Americans and their children were a minority in the state and in eleven of the eighteen largest cities. This was in sharp contrast with Massachusetts, New Jersey, and New York, where at least two-thirds of most big-city inhabitants were of foreign origin. The only Sunday games played in Pennsylvania before 1920 were in the mill towns of Reading, Scranton, and Wilkes-Barre, where industrialists supported baseball as a means of attracting new workers and as a source of social control.[56]

The Philadelphia Athletics began trying to secure Sunday baseball in 1911, but it was not until 1926 that Connie Mack scheduled a Sunday game as a test case. The courts upheld the constitutionality of the blue laws, however, and Sunday ball was still banned. Mack's partner, Jack Shibe, was a prominent Democrat, and he went to work in Harrisburg to secure a local option law and put additional pressure on the legislature by threatening to move the team to Camden, New Jersey. Mack helped by fielding an outstanding team (from 1929 to 1931 the Athletics was one of the best squads in baseball history). The depression forced him to start breaking up the team, but he avowed that Sunday baseball would enable him to meet his payroll and keep the team together. In 1933 voters approved a statewide referendum on Sunday baseball, and the legislature responded by passing an enabling act to permit Sunday baseball. The old progressive governor, Gifford Pinchot, was personally opposed to the bill but acceded to popular will, recognizing that the blue laws were "unfair discrimination of the rich against the poor."[57]

Sunday Baseball in Atlanta

The last section of the country to secure Sunday baseball was the Old South, where the sabbath was generally observed as a day of rest and religious contemplation with only the most essential services in operation. Stores were closed and public amusements were shut down. Local blue laws dated from colonial times, but there was little need to enforce them since most social pressure was usually sufficient to maintain the spiritual quality of the day.[58]

The rapidly growing commercial center of Atlanta epitomized the new progressive urban South. Its population more than tripled from 1900 to 1930, when it reached 270,366. Like other landlocked cities in the heart of the South, the Gate City's inhabitants in 1900 were principally pietistic, native-born white Americans, along with a substantial fundamentalist black community (39.8 percent) and a small immigrant (7.9 percent) population. Atlantans were progressive when it came to commerce but conservative in social conduct. Atlanta observed a strict American sabbath that in 1927 helped it earn Billy Sunday's description of it as "the most religious city in the country." Atlanta's experience with Sunday baseball was typical of most Old South cities, where there was virtually no agitation for sabbath reform before the 1920s.[59]

Sunday baseball was played in Atlanta in the early 1900s by soldiers at the local army camp. Military installations were not subject to local ordinances, and the federal government had no restrictions on Sunday activities on its property. Fort McPherson's commander encouraged Sunday sports to help him keep an eye on his enlisted men and be certain they were engaging in good clean fun. Local Baptist and Methodist ministers, through the Sabbatarian Evangelical Ministers Association, opposed the games because many civilians attended. The army sought to assuage their antipathy by allowing civilians to play only if they had at least two soldiers on their teams. This deterred professional nines from using the grounds for league games, although the Crackers did play Sunday exhibition games at Camp Jessup after World War I to entertain the troops and raise money for recuperating soldiers.[60]

During the 1920s Atlantans were permitted by tacit consent to use certain public facilities on Sundays, such as swimming pools and tennis courts, and they attended semiprofessional ball games at Spiller Park. Commercialized amusements, however, were still forbidden. Some talk about opening movie theaters on the sabbath began in 1929, and an alderman suggested allowing the Crackers to play on Sundays.[61]

In 1933 Mayor James Key decided that the time had finally come for Atlanta to permit popular Sunday amusements for the benefit of the working classes. Key had a long and distinguished career in public service and was in his second term as mayor. A devout churchgoer and Sunday school teacher, he was becoming increasingly liberal in matters of social conduct, having just returned from Paris, where he had spoken out in favor of repealing Prohibition. Key held a meeting with the Crackers early in the summer of 1933 and gave them permission to hold a Sunday game in August. He believed that the crowds attending semiprofessional games had amply demonstrated the public thirst for Sunday sports and preferred to see the masses enjoy an organized amusement like professional baseball rather than makeshift recreation.[62]

Key's announcement shocked many Atlantans, and Sabbatarians mobilized to fight back. The Evangelical Ministers Association and the Christian Council obtained an injunction preventing the game as a public nuisance and a violation of state law. Key was disappointed by that impediment and decided to demonstrate public support for Sunday baseball through a referendum. He hoped that a large plurality would encourage the city council to pass an act permitting Sunday amusements.[63]

Atlanta's progressive clergy, led by Rev. Witherspoon Dodge, pastor of the Radio Church, supported Key. Dodge attacked the injunction, claiming that the Sunday blue laws were too broad and dated. He believed that since sabbath amusements like tennis and swimming were already tolerated, then "there is no reason why baseball should be excluded."[64] The opposition was led by Dr. Louie D. Newton, paster of the Druid Hills Baptist Church. Newton attacked his old friend the mayor for a lawless attitude, stating, "I do not believe that any public servant, however benevolent may be his personal intentions . . . can set aside the law and instruct other public servants to support him in this stand. It involves the principle of orderly society against anarchy."[65]

The Sunday baseball issue was tested in the September Democratic primary. Party leaders hoped that the Sunday issue would generate some interest in the election, but there was a meager turnout. The baseball question carried by a vote of 7,495 to 5,111, and a similar proposal regarding movie theaters also passed by a narrower margin. It was expected that this victory would encourage the city council to pass a measure legalizing Sunday amusements. However, the council members balked, claiming that the proposal was unconstitutional since state law forbade Sunday amusements and also that the vote was not representative, for only 12,606 ballots were cast out of a total population of 270,000.[66]

Key persisted despite this setback and in October convinced the council to pass a bill repealing the city ordinance on Sunday behavior, leaving the state statutes as the only sabbath codes applicable in Atlanta. This was important because a new state edict permitted Sunday amusements when operated by charitable organizations. Key called on local theater owners and told them they could keep their businesses open on Sundays if a benevolent society took them over for the day. Key's suggestion was adopted, and Atlanta had Sunday movies in the late fall. The Sabbatarians fought back, but were stymied by Key's evasive tactics and disheartened by growing public sympathy for Sunday amusements. Professional Sunday baseball was subsequently introduced in the spring of 1934, when the Junior Chamber of Commerce agreed to operate the Crackers on Sundays and distribute a share of the profits to charity. The success of this innovation plus the initiation of night games a year later encouraged the management to add a new section to the grandstand in 1936 to accommodate increased patronage.[67]

Atlanta's struggle with Sunday baseball was similar to those in such Old South cities as Charleston, Norfolk, and Richmond, where social beliefs and values changed slowly. However, it was quite different from those of several port cities and southwestern towns that had Sunday baseball in the nineteenth century or the early 1900s. There were three distinctive southern urban responses to Sunday baseball, with some cities more western than southern in their social policies or in their response to this particular problem. Texas cities, such as Dallas, Fort Worth, Galveston, Houston, and San Antonio, were in many respects more western than southern in their attitudes about social control and public regulation of individual behavior. Texas still retained some of its frontier heritage of political and social democracy. Its cities had a much more heterogeneous population than the Old South cities, mainly of German and Mexican ancestry, whose traditions included a Continental sabbath. The foreign-born population ranged from 18.3 percent in Fort Worth to over 46.0 percent in Galveston and San Antonio.[68]

The Delta city of New Orleans, with a foreign-born population in 1900 of 37.6 percent, was completely dominated by its Continental heritage. Sunday amusements had been a popular local tradition ever since the antebellum period, when the sporting set held boxing matches and horse races on the sabbath. Working-class folk there had ample opportunities to enjoy themselves as they pleased on their day off. When professional baseball was brought to New Orleans in the 1880s, Sunday games were naturally scheduled.[69]

Two other prominent port cities that enjoyed Sunday games were Memphis and Mobile. Sunday baseball was a popular diversion in Memphis, a river town noted for its resorts and lawlessness. Memphis had a fairly large foreign-born population (15.5 percent) for a city in the heart of the South. Considerable public support for a liberal sabbath was supported by the municipal government controlled by Boss Edward Crump, a leading Southern progressive.[70] Mobile, situated on the Gulf of Mexico, was similar to Memphis in its tolerance, but had a much larger foreign-born population (20.9 percent) and a remarkably high proportion of Catholics for a southern city (35.4 percent). Townsfolk supported Sunday games, and the minor league team began playing on Sundays in 1908.[71]

Sunday observance patterns indicate that this area was not uniformly opposed to social change. Although city dwellers in the Deep South were vigorously opposed to alterations in public mores, even such an apparently innocuous innovation as Sunday baseball, some areas permitted sabbath games at a time when major eastern cities did not. The more liberal southern towns were located at the region's western boundaries or on major waterways, where they had greater accessibility to new ideas and varied patterns of social behavior. Their inhabitants were not as homogeneous as the white populations in such Old South cities as Richmond, Jackson, and Atlanta, and their cosmopolitan character made them more receptive to different modes of social conduct.[72]

◇

The development of Sunday baseball typified the route that social change followed as the United States modernized. Commercialized Sunday ball was first legitimized in the Midwest and West, the regions that were often in the forefront of social reform, particularly in matters of personal freedom. Progressives in California, Oregon, and Wisconsin pioneered in such political reforms as home rule, direct primaries, referendums, woman's suffrage, and regulation of working conditions. Reformers in Cleveland, Denver, and Detroit promoted social justice, economic opportunity, and political democracy through such innovations as municipal ownership, regulation of public utilities, the juvenile justice system, and structural reform of city government.

The conservative force of tradition was weaker there than in either the East or the South. Many westerners and midwesterners were recent immigrants from abroad or the East and had relatively few vested interests to protect. Social behavior was less restricted, and there was less effort to impose traditional, middle-class WASP values from above. The

West's democratic political and social climate encouraged tolerance for new ideas and different ways of doing things, partly due to the absence of any single group powerful enough to impose its culture upon others. The outcome was that blue laws restricting Sunday ballplaying were never implemented in many communities and in others were easily evaded.

The East was the next region to secure blue law reform, and doing so took a long arduous fight. As usual, New York City was in the forefront of reform among the big cities, although smaller cities usually got Sunday baseball first. Pietistic Easterners had a vested interest in maintaining the traditional American sabbath because it affirmed their social status, sustained their cultural heritage, and helped them control the dangerous newcomers living in urban areas. Rural WASPs wielded enormous influence in state legislatures and higher courts, which enabled Sabbatarians to consistently defeat the efforts of team owners and their political allies to secure Sunday baseball. This fight against Sunday ball was critically important to native-born Americans, who were waging a desperate fight to preserve their culture and society.

The conservative South was the last section to adopt social changes and, with exceptions in Texas and certain river towns, the last region to allow Sunday baseball. The South was the most homogeneous part of the country, and new attitudes and modes of behavior had a difficult time diffusing through it. Southerners seemed frightened of the unfamiliar, and the region did not provide a hospitable environment for groups that behaved or thought differently from the norm.

Sabbatarians fought a long, hard, but ultimately unsuccessful fight to impose their definition of the American core culture upon urban newcomers, a value system they felt was deeply rooted in their religious beliefs. Ironically, one of the latent functions of the movement to secure professional Sunday baseball was to provide an opportunity for working-class people to conveniently attend ball games, where they could internalize a great deal of the American value system inherent in the game. Baseball, America's secular religion, would eventually succeed where the voluntary, nondenominational pietistic organizations had failed.

Professional Baseball as a Source of Social Mobility

In Me younger days, 'twas not considhered rayspictable f'r to be an athlete. An athlete was always a man that was not sthrong enough f'r wurruk. Fractions druv him fr'm school, an' th' vagrancy laws druv him to baseball.

—Finley Peter Dunne, *Mr. Dooley at His Best*

Along with church, crime, entertainment, and politics, sports like baseball were regarded as valuable alternative avenues of vertical mobility for ambitious, hardworking, and talented young men who were poor, uneducated, and lacked useful social contacts to help them get ahead. Professional baseball was thought to be open to anyone regardless of ethnic or class origin, and candidates would succeed or fail on their own. Unfortunately, little empirical research has been done to test whether or not sport has actually been an important source of social mobility.[1] In this chapter I will examine the class backgrounds, careers, income, and subsequent occupational history to determine if the game was a valuable source of vertical mobility for those young men who needed an alternate route to success.

The Professional Ballplayer in the Nineteenth Century

To understand the occupational role of the professional baseball player in the early 1900s, it is useful to first look at the development of the occupation. In 1860 James Creighton became the first professional ballplayer when he was secretly paid by the Brooklyn Excelsiors. Al Reach and other players soon received under-the-table compensation that included gifts, direst payments, phony jobs, and profits from benefit contests.[2]

Professionalization began in earnest after the Civil War in response to the strong demand by amateur clubs for winning teams. Using gifts, jobs, and shares of the gate money, they recruited good ballplayers regardless of social status. Young Albert G. Spalding left his Rockford home in 1867 to play for the Chicago Excelsiors because a wholesale grocer promised him forty dollars a week and a schedule that would not conflict with baseball. In Washington, D.C., the Nationals were virtually all government clerks. The Brooklyn Atlantics, Morrisania Unions, Philadelphia Athletics, Troy Haymakers, and New York Mutuals offered patronage or jobs in local industries to recruit players. In 1868 Henry Chadwick reported that "clerkships in tax offices, inspectorships of streets, sewers, docks, and other city places have been at the disposal of Directors and Managers of the leading professional organizations." The Mutuals were subsidized by Tammany Hall and on the city payroll. The team's president was city coroner, who hired several players to work in his office, and their teammates got sinecures at city hall. The team used its political connections to recruit top players, like the third baseman of the New Jersey Irvingtons, who got a twelve-hundred-dollar job as a city clerk.[3]

Professionalization was originally opposed for fear the richest clubs would monopolize the best talent, that gambling and corruption would seep in, and that the sport would become commercialized, curtailing opportunities for club members to play and creating disharmony between rival nines. Winning would become overemphasized and play would become work, requiring extensive practice, discipline, and science.[4]

Many ostensibly amateur teams of the late 1860s had professional ballplayers on their squads who jumped from team to team, depending on the best offer. The historian George Kirsch found that by the spring of 1869 at least twelve clubs were compensating some or all of their starting teams in some fashion with payments ranging from six hundred to fifteen hundred dollars. The first all-salaried baseball nine was the great Cincinnati Red Stockings of 1869, organized by civic-minded businessman Aaron Champion, who wanted to bring national recognition to his community. The players were paid from six hundred to two thousand dollars for the season, having originally worked at either low white-collar or skilled occupations. The Red Stockings included two men in insurance, two hatters, a jeweler, an engraver, a bookkeeper, and a marble cutter.[5]

The Red Stockings went on a national tour in 1869, winning fifty-seven, losing none, and tying one. The successful tour demonstrated the advantages of hiring full-time professional ballplayers. Several other teams promptly adopted this practice, most notably the Chicago White Stockings, which signed William Craver, captain of the Troy Haymakers, for two thousand dollars. The other players, also drawn from top eastern teams, were paid about fifteen hundred dollars. The White Stockings were one of the highest paying clubs and became known as the "$15,000 club" because of their high wages.[6]

Growing professionalism led to rumors that matches were prearranged so that a series would go the limit to increase gate receipts and betting as well as to assure insiders which side to bet on. The 30 November 1870 convention of the National Association of Base Ball Players was dominated by professional teams, and the amateurs left to form their own organization. In March 1871 ten fully professional teams met in New York and formed the National Association of Professional Base Ball Players (NA), adopting the rules of the earlier association while working to make baseball a commercial success.[7]

The NA was primarily a player-oriented league. Clubs were sponsored by sports enthusiasts who did not expect to make big profits. Several teams, including the Mutuals, were cooperatives. The NA lasted for five shaky seasons in which twenty-three different teams were fielded. Problems began with the cheap ten-dollar franchise fee that let in weak, undercapitalized teams in small cities that drew smaller crowds and could not compete for top players. The *New York Times* questioned whether NA squads were superior to the finest contemporary amateur clubs, whose free games "will afford more genuine sport."[8]

NA teams had unstable eleven-man rosters because players jumped from club to club for higher salaries. The pros were well compensated; most got thirteen hundred to sixteen hundred dollars, and stars received up to twenty-five hundred dollars. The average ballplayer earned twice what an artisan made and four times as much as non-farm employees. Undercapitalized teams could not compete with clubs like the Chicago White Stockings or the Boston Red Stockings, which led to insufficient competition. Nearly all the best men played for the Boston Red Stockings, superbly managed by Harry Wright, a baseball genius who had previously managed the Cincinnati Red Stockings. Boston's team was second in 1871 and then won the next four pennants, going 71-8 in 1875.[9]

The early professionals were mostly of English stock, although there were also many German and Irish Americans. A handful of other ethnicities were represented, including Lip Pike and Nate Berkenstock, who were Jewish, and Esteban Bellán, who was Cuban. Pike was a star player who averaged over .300 in ten seasons. A five-year veteran of the NA, he went on to lead the NL in home runs in 1877 and managed three seasons. At least 74.9 percent of the 311 men in the NA were native-born; 6.4 percent were foreign-born, and 18.7 percent were of unknown origins. Immigrants fared well in this cohort, especially the English-speaking newcomers, who could assimilate most easily. Furthermore, several of them were former cricket players who adapted their bat and ball skills to baseball. In addition, since baseball was still a relatively new sport, the native-born players were barely more familiar with it than the immigrants were.[10]

Eighty-three percent of the professionals known to have been American-born came from cities. These men were mainly from the Northeast, the alleged origin of baseball, particularly Philadelphia (39), Brooklyn (38), Baltimore (27), and New York (20), which collectively comprised the birthplace of two-fifths (39.9 percent) of all the professionals who ever played in the NA. Eight of the twenty-three teams in the NA represented one of these four cities, and their recruiting began at home with the best amateur players. Baseball was just beginning to spread in popularity to the Midwest and beyond, partly as a result of the socializing influence of the Civil War but mainly because of advancements in communication and transportation.[11]

Little is known about the former professions of NA players. The historian Melvin L. Adelman found in his masterful study of midnineteenth-century New York sport that 61.8 percent of the New Yorkers and Brooklynites active in the NA were skilled workers and the rest were white-collar workers, backgrounds nearly identical to those of the best local amateurs in 1866–70. A job in the NA paid well, but lacked prestige and security. In particular, players with white-collar jobs were reticent to become professional athletes, especially if it meant moving to a new city.[12]

The NA was superseded in 1876 by the NL, which promised to put baseball on a sound financial footing. The NL put players in a distinctly subordinate role to management by creating the reserve clause in 1879 to curtail a player from jumping from the team that owned his contract. The team, however, was free to sell, trade, or release him whenever it chose. Owners hoped that the reserve clause would halt the upward spiral of wages, which averaged over fifteen hundred dollars in the early 1880s. In 1878 wages comprised 68 percent of team expenses, but dropped to 54.0 percent in 1880 and continued to dwindle for the next one hundred years. The reserve clause prevented better players from testing the open market for their services. Magnates justified the reserve clause as necessary to sustain competition, claiming that without it the wealthiest teams would acquire all the best players.[13]

Another ploy for keeping down wages was the maximum salary level. The salaries of the stars determined the wage scale for all players, and owners figured that if they could keep a ceiling on the top wages, they could pay rookies and fringe players that much less. A costly competition for players ensued in 1884 because of competition from the short-lived Union Association (UA). For instance, the average $3,000 salary of the St. Louis Browns (AA) was directly attributable to competition with the local UA team. During the following season, the NL and the AA established a $2,000 maximum salary, significantly lower than the Browns' high average. Most minor league teams adhered to this guideline, but the big league owners did not, fearing their stars would jump to a team evading the agreement. Detroit's salaries in 1885 averaged $2,795, which included three men at $4,000. The eighteen men on the Giants' salary list in 1888 and 1889 averaged $2,792. Clubs still compensated their better players well, either paying them under the table or by some other circumvention. In 1887, for instance, after Mike "King" Kelly, a future Hall of Famer, was sold by the Chicago White Stockings to the Boston Red Stockings for $10,000, he signed a contract for $2,000 but got another $3,000 for selling a photograph of himself to his employer. Charles Comiskey, player-manager of the St. Louis Browns, reputedly earned $6,000 in 1889, making him one of the highest paid players of his era.[14]

Despite the good salaries, professional baseball players did not have much status and were generally regarded by the middle class in the same unfavorable light as actors and boxers.[15] This attitude was epitomized by an 1872 *New York Times* editorial that blamed the coming of the professionals for having "a healthy amusement degenerate . . . into an 'event' for the benefit of the betting fraternity":

> There has grown up within the past two or three years a class of men who make their livelihood wholly by playing base-ball matches. The professional player, aside from his private character, is not precisely a majestic object. It may not be incumbent upon any man to lead a life

of really productive industry, but it certainly seems as though one might find some other occupation than hiring oneself to win matches for the Black Stockings and White, Blue Stockings and Gray, who claim to be the exponents of the national game. Evidently the professional player himself sympathizes with this view, for except when compelled to play during the Summer season, he keeps himself out of sight in those quiet retreats connected with bars and not free from a suspicion of rat-pits where the sporting men of the Metropolis meet for social improvement and unpremeditated pugilism. . . . The professional player . . . is usually a worthless, dissipated gladiator, not much above the professional pugilist in morality and respectability. Not only does the employment of these men in a match game render the result simply a question of money, for the club which can afford to hire the best players is of course the winner, but it opens the way to dishonorable and fraudulent practices. The professional player can, if he chooses, insure the defeat of the side on which he plays. It is only necessary for the gambler who has large sums at stake to buy him, in order to make certain of winning his bets. That this is frequently done, any one who reads the report of the quarrels which usually follow an important match game, will find abundant reason to believe. The professional player thus makes the game an instrument in the hands of gamblers and so brings it into deserved disrepute. . . .

In every point of view he is an eminently undesirable person and he ought to be peremptorily and completely suppressed. Let our young men meet and play base-ball if they choose. They will thus improve their physical well-being without detriment to their morals. To employ professional players to perspire in public for the benefit of gamblers, is, however, a benefit to no one, and furnishes to dyspeptic moralists a strong argument against any form of muscular Christianity.[16]

The main reason for the big leaguers' low prestige was their poor moral conduct and ill-mannered behavior both on and off the field. The first known scandal occurred in 1865, when three New York Mutuals conspired to lose to the Brooklyn Eckfords. Rumors of fixed games swirled around the NA, particularly about the Mutuals, the White Stockings, and the Red Stockings. According to *Beadle's Dime Base Ball Player* in 1875, "Any professional base ball club will 'throw' a game if there is money in it. A horse race is a pretty safe thing to speculate on in comparison with the average ball match." Then in 1877 four players on the league-leading Louisville club fixed a number of late season games in the interests of a pool operator named McCloud, which cost them the championship and their careers as professionals.[17]

Some professionals tried to win at all costs and by any means, including cheating, deception, and fraud. Typifying these methods borrowed from contemporary business practices was Mike "King" Kelly, a superstar of the 1880s famous for his innovations, like the hook slide. He won two NL batting championships, was a fine fielder, and was renowned for his baserunning, with a high of eighty-four stolen bases in 1887. Kelly was the most colorful and popular player of the day and was reportedly one of the first celebrities hounded by autograph seekers. When he was sold to Boston in 1887, fans gave him a house and a carriage to get him to the ballpark. Kelly inspired Frank O. Small's 1887 painting *Slide, Kelly, Slide* and one of the first popular baseball songs, John W. Kelly's "Slide, Kelly, Slide" two years later. King Kelly manipulated the rules of the game whenever possible. As the *New York Journal* pointed out, "Mike Kelly was the trickiest player who ever handled a baseball. . . . There was nothing he would not attempt. . . . Baseball rules were never made for Kel." As a baserunner, Kelly exploited the single umpire system. If the arbiter was busy watching a ball hit to the outfield, Kelly sometimes took a short cut from first base to third by running across the pitcher's mound. He was also the first player to "cut" third base on his way home from second. Unfortunately his fast living eventually caught up with him, and he died at the age of thirty-six in 1894.[18]

According to folklore, Kelly took advantage of substitution rules, which required the replacement to notify the umpire by merely leaping off the bench and announcing "Kelly now catching," to catch a foul ball and make a put out. He was allegedly the first catcher to drop his mask along the third base line to hamper runners coming home. The folklorist Tristram Coffin claimed Kelly's greatest stunt occurred while playing right field in the twelfth inning of a game when it was getting very dark. There were two outs, the bases were loaded, and a shot was hit over Kelly's head. He raced back, far out of the vision of the umpire, leaped up, shook his glove in satisfaction, and jogged in to the bench. The batter was called out and the game was suspended because of darkness. His teammates slapped his back and said, "Nice catch, Kell." "Not at all," responded their hero, "'Twent a mile above my head."[19]

Major leaguers were decried for their disorderly conduct on the diamond, where they constantly bickered with umpires, cursed and jeered the opposition, and brawled with umpires, fans, and other players. They behaved just as badly off the field, drinking, gambling, and associating with gamblers and prostitutes. They adjusted poorly to their new-found wealth and acclaim, recklessly spending their wages and rarely saving any money. Many were broke before the start of the next season and were constantly requesting salary advances.[20]

Owners were concerned that the poor conduct of their free-spirited players would undermine their control and that bad publicity would hurt at the box office. An article in *Spalding's Official Base Ball Guide* (1885) entitled "Drunkenness in the Ranks" reported that "the hundreds of thousands of dollars invested in base ball stock companies can no longer be placed in jeopardy by this growing evil."[21]

Albert G. Spalding employed Pinkertons to spy on his players. The agents gave him negative reports on seven of fifteen players, particularly Kelly and James McCormick, who were followed "all over the tenderloin districts, through the whole roster of saloons and 'speak-easy' resorts." A detective reported that Kelly was seen at a bar after midnight drinking lemonade, an accusation Kelly angrily denied: "In that place where the detective reports me as taking a lemonade at 3 A.M., he's off. It was straight whiskey; I never drank a lemonade at the hour in my life." The seven errant players were each fined twenty-five dollars, which covered the cost of the investigation. A few days later Kelly and McCormick encountered the Pinkerton agent at the train station and badly beat him up before joining their teammates on the Detroit-bound train.[22]

Team presidents tried to force miscreant players to improve their conduct by imposing curfews and putting clauses into their contracts requiring them to moderate their drinking habits and abstain from other vices. Players who complied received bonuses; disobedience brought fines. In 1886 Spalding held back $250 of Kelly's and McCormick's salaries of $2,000 as an incentive to get them to cut back their drinking, but this brought no results. Despite their carousing the White Stockings won the pennant in 1886, and Kelly led the NL in batting with .388, his second title in three years. Nonetheless, Spalding sold both players after the season, Kelly going to the Boston Red Stockings for the astonishing price of $10,000. The Chicago press and local fans were aghast at the sale of their hero. The *Chicago Evening Journal* offered a strong pro-labor perspective, applauding Kelly and McCormick for "the pluck to stand out against the petty tyrant managers . . . and resisting the Russian methods of the Chicago Club directors." "It is time," the paper suggested, "that other players vindicated their privileges as American citizens."[23]

Many middle-class parents discouraged their sons from entering professional baseball, even if it was relatively well-paying, because they did not want them associating with such immoral, low-class men. Few collegiate ballplayers became professionals because of the stigma attached to pro sports. Parents vigorously disapproved of their daughters socializing with or marrying ballplayers. When Robert Todd Lincoln's daughter married White Stockings pitcher Warren Beckwith, he reproved his son-in-law as a "baseball buffoon" and did not rest until he had destroyed their marriage. Bill Lange, an 1890s star Chicago center fielder, quit baseball prematurely because his sweetheart's father disapproved of ballplayers.[24]

The class origins of late nineteenth century professional ballplayers were probably not much different from those of the pioneer major leaguers. A sample of fifty-two star players born between 1860 and 1879 revealed that the majority (53.3 percent) had blue-collar backgrounds and only one-third had white-collar backgrounds. One-fourth (26.7 percent) came from agricultural families, a big increase compared with an earlier cohort who overwhelmingly had urban backgrounds.[25]

Players and their families were dissatisfied with their low social status. As one wife noted, it was distasteful to have her husband's job classified with prizefighting. Players did not appreciate being forced into third-rate hotels, but quality inns would not book them because of their well-earned disorderly reputations and the proprietors' fears that their presence would offend other guests. In 1885 members of the Giants led by their captain John Montgomery Ward, a practicing attorney, organized the Brotherhood of Professional Base Ball Players. The union's goals were to improve wages by fighting the maximum salary level, promote a higher level of moral conduct, ameliorate their job's status, and encourage the overall development of baseball. Membership joined with management to fight the worst excesses of their badly behaved colleagues. The brotherhood called for strict discipline, hundred-dollar fines for miscreants, and the automatic blacklisting of any individual with four violations.[26]

Believing they were making no progress against management, the brotherhood's members organized the Players' League (PL) in 1890. This cooperative association of capitalists and players barred reserve clauses, income limitations, blacklisting, and firing of players during the season. The new major league's presence created a seller's market that led to a bidding war for the best players and created more jobs for new players. The NL's payroll for 1890 reportedly was $311,964, including $70,500 in signing bonuses. Many players got substantial raises to prevent them from jumping, such as Giants star Jack Glasscock, who was paid $5,000 in 1890 plus a $4,000 bonus. Pitcher John Clarkson reportedly received $10,000 to defect from the PL, and Spalding offered King Kelly a blank check to follow. Kelly turned it down, reportedly saying, "My mother and father would never look at me again if I could prove a traitor to the boys."[27]

The PL collapsed after only one season when its financial backers were co-opted and given the opportunity to buy into the NL. Salaries in 1891 remained extremely high. Giants hurler Amos Rusie was paid $6,200 and star catcher Buck Ewing returned after a year in the PL for $7,000, a 40 percent raise over his 1889 salary, probably the highest salary paid any player in the nineteenth century. After the 1891 season, the AA and NL merged to form a new twelve-team league, which created a glut of experienced ballplayers. Then in June 1892 rosters were cut from sixteen to thirteen. Owners took further advantage of the players' tenuous position to reintroduce a strictly enforced salary limit of $2,400. Players had little recourse but to accept. Nine Philadelphia players had their salaries slashed to $1,800 in 1893 from an average of about $3,100 in 1892. Most men resigned themselves to their situation, but Amos Rusie fought the system by sitting out the entire 1896 season rather than accept a pay cut. His team's owners thereafter reimbursed him $3,000 for his lost wages to prevent any legal action, but this was less than one-half of what Rusie had earned back in 1891.[28]

Deflated salaries were the norm for the rest of the 1890s. The most expensive team was the Boston Red Sox, whose manager, Frank Selee, was paid $4,000 in 1898, and his players averaged $2,200, probably the highest in the league. Two superstars were paid slightly more than the limit, eight got a little less than $2,400, and the rest got considerably less. The high-powered Baltimore Orioles of 1899 did not fare as well. Manager and co-owner Ed Hanlon got $10,000 but the players got $29,000 total, or an average of $1,933 each. Four superstars received slightly more than the maximum and eleven got less than the limit, seven of them earning well below $1,500. Certain players on other teams made as little as $600 a season. The players' weak bargaining position was further damaged after the 1899 season when four clubs were dropped from the circuit. One-third of the major leaguers were suddenly out in the cold, and the remaining men were in a perilous situation.[29]

Most observers believed that once the nineteenth-century ballplayers left the playing field, they ended up about where they had started out, in the lower class. At best they became bar owners. The journalist Henry Chadwick, for example, estimated that 80 percent of the retired athletes who had become business owners purchased saloons.[30] Early pro ballplayers did have limited success in securing good jobs after retirement (see table 2), but they ended up in better social standing than the conven-

Table 2. Occupations of Former Major Leaguers, Active 1871–82

Occupational Category	Number	Percentage
High white-collar		
Professionals	4	1.8
Managers, high officials, and major proprietors	28	12.8
Low white-collar		
Clerks, sales, and kindred workers	40	18.3
Semiprofessionals	29	13.2
Petty proprietors, managers, and low officials	37	16.9
Total white-collar	138	63.0
Farmers	3	1.4
Blue-collar		
Skilled	26	11.9
Semiskilled and service	46	21.0
Unskilled	6	2.7
Total blue-collar	78	35.6
Grand total	219	100.0

Sources: Compiled from Allen, Notebooks; *Sporting News,* 4 Oct. 1996, 2 Feb. 1895; *Boston Evening Transcript,* 19 Oct. 1889; *Atlanta Constitution,* 2 Sept. 1907.

tional wisdom believed. One-third (35.6 percent) of men active in the NA, the NL, and the AA between 1871 and 1882 did slide down into the blue-collar class, a substantially higher decline rate than the 12 percent reported by Stephan Thernstrom for contemporary Boston's white-collar workers.[31] Nearly two-thirds had white-collar jobs (63.0 percent), mainly in lower-status occupations, and virtually none became farmers (1.4 percent). Former players did not get many good job offers because they had no readily marketable skills, were not well educated, and were poorly regarded by the middle classes.

Retirees who secured high-status white-collar jobs (14.6 percent) mainly became businessmen. The most common business ventures were sports related. Six former players, including Charles Comiskey, Albert Reach, and Albert G. Spalding, eventually owned major league franchises, while Reach, Spalding, and Harry Wright manufactured and distributed sporting goods. Spalding outstripped his rivals to establish the dominant position in the industry. Former players also had some success securing high-ranking government positions (2.7 percent), like Cap Anson, a twenty-two-year veteran White Stocking, who used his fame to get elected city clerk in 1905 but quickly resigned because he could not handle the responsibilities of the job.[32]

Most retired ballplayers who managed to retain their class position worked at low-status white-collar jobs as clerks, salesmen, shopkeepers, or baseball managers (48.4 percent). They had some success getting jobs that required direct contact with customers, such as salesmen and real estate agents (5.0 percent), because employers hoped their fame might attract clients. The principal job of just 11.0 percent was coach or manager, in which they could utilize their expertise gained from years of playing professional ball.[33]

Nearly one out of every eight retirees was involved in such low-status enterprises as bars (5.9 percent), billiard parlors (2.7 percent), or bookmaking (3.2 percent), which reflected their social backgrounds and personal experiences with their own leisure time. Men who became bar owners were usually closely tied to local politicians, who helped them get the necessary licenses. Some retirees who became tavern owners, like Dickey Pearce and George Zettlein, were themselves actively involved in politics.

Major leaguers who entered the blue-collar category were primarily involved in such service occupations as security guards or police officers (10.0 percent), fire fighters (2.7 percent), and bartenders (2.7 percent) and collectively surpassed the proportion of skilled workers (11.9 percent). Weak or nonexistent civil service regulations enabled friendly public officials to help many ballplayers get secure jobs with the city. Politicians probably also assisted players in obtaining work as bartenders. Henry Chadwick claimed that each winter about one-fifth of the total number of big leaguers spent their off-season working in saloons.[34]

The retired ballplayer's primary job did not necessarily reflect his fame, which usually correlated better with tenure. Some successful entrepreneurs like Charles Comiskey had long careers in the majors, yet ten-year veterans could still end up as freight handlers or milkmen. Most players eventually faded into oblivion, including Amos Rusie, who won 245 games but ended up working with the grounds crew at the Polo Grounds, the scene of his greatest triumphs.[35]

The Professional Baseball Player, 1900–1920

The status of the professional ballplayer in 1900 was not high, yet the prestige of the sport had never been higher, with middle-class men and women attending games in growing numbers. Many magazine articles lauded the sport as a moral, exciting, and socially useful game. All professional athletes were still viewed disdainfully because of the middle- and upper-class emphasis on amateurism that glorified athletes who played for fun instead of profit, did not devote themselves full-time to sports, and supposedly would not do anything necessary to win. Pro ballplayers were slighted because of their bad reputations, generally modest social origins, and low salaries. Future prospects looked dim with just a single eight-team major league and continuing misconduct on and off the field. Reprobates in the early 1900s included Mike Donlin of the New York Giants, Bugs Raymond of the Giants, star hurler Rube Waddell of the Athletics, and the Detroit Tigers' Ty Cobb, the greatest player of the era. Donlin was jailed in 1902 for striking an actress and was arrested again four years later for attacking a railroad conductor. Cobb was unsurpassed in his violent behavior on and off the field. He slid into bases with flying spikes, fought with other players, and climbed into the stands to attack detractors.[36]

. Despite the behavior of these individuals, the status of ballplayers improved markedly in the early 1900s, partly due to independent efforts by players and management. Players organized two short-lived unions, the Protective Association of Professional Base Ball Players (1900) and the Base Ball Players' Fraternity (1912) to ameliorate their professional image by encouraging members to behave properly. Of course, they also sought traditional union goals, such as higher wages, limitations on the reserve clause, and revisions in player transfers.[37]

Management tried to raise the social status of both the sport and their players so as to increase middle-class interest, and thereby profits, and to raise their own status. Managers Connie Mack and John J. McGraw required their men to wear business suits on road trips, instead of the customary sweaters, to symbolize the desire for middle-class respectability. Paradoxically, no manager had encouraged as much rowdiness on the field as McGraw. They also tried to book their squads into the finest hotels, where ballplayers were previously unwelcome. Mack never forgot how early in his playing career he and his teammates were unable to rent a room in a third-rate Washington hotel until they promised to stay out of the dining room and "not mingle with the other guests." "There is room for gentlemen in any profession," noted Mack. "I will not tolerate profanity, obscene language or personal insults from my bench. I will always insist as long as I am manager . . . that my boys be gentlemen."[38]

Another important move by Mack to better his athletes' status was to vigorously recruit college players. He felt they were excellent athletes who learned quickly and responded well to orders. Mack believed their presence would help set a model of proper conduct for his less sophisticated players and improve the status of professional baseball. Relatively few college players had entered organized baseball in the 1890s because of the pay scale and the brutish reputation of major leaguers, but Mack astutely believed that college stars would be attracted to professional baseball if they could be shown that their future colleagues were respectable and that a baseball career promised high wages, fame, and a suitable lifestyle.[39]

Major league owners and opinion makers in the early 1900s began indicating a growing satisfaction with the class of men entering professional baseball. More married men began joining teams and were said to bring a sobering tone to the locker room. Men with families supposedly saved their money instead of wasting it and thus were regarded as a positive influence on the wild young bachelors who had given baseball its bad reputation.[40] Owners also attributed the growing temperance in drinking and social habits to veteran players learning from "clean-living collegians the need to conserve their physical health for their professional success."[41] Management undoubtedly exaggerated the degree in improved behavior, however. Nineteenth-century players were probably less degenerate than popularly pictured and married players and former collegians were not as upright as depicted.

In contrast to dissipated athletes like Bugs Raymond and Rube Waddell, the God-fearing college man Christy Mathewson was held up as a paragon of virtue (his card playing and gambling were conveniently forgotten about) and a proper role model for children. While there certainly were many hard-living ballplayers, a lot of bad behavior could be simply attributed to the boisterousness of extended adolescence in the male bachelor subculture of team sports. One player who had originally studied for the ministry discovered much to his joy and amazement that he was not out of place in his chosen field. His colleagues did not drink heavily, did not speak profanely, and even offered him assistance.[42]

The sportswriter Ring Lardner caricatured the less urbane players in such popular tales as You Know Me Al, but his characters were atypical. Casey Stengel, believed to have been the model for one of Lardner's more ingenuous characters, had attended dental school and married an accountant who was the daughter of a prominent contractor. Stengel gained his unsophisticated reputation as a result of such antics as hiding a bird under his cap and then releasing it at an opportune moment.[43]

The main requirement for attracting players from the middle classes was an improved salary scale. The rise of the AL doubled the number of positions and precipitated a bidding war for established players as the junior circuit tried to establish its claim to major league status. In 1901 111 of 182 AL players had prior major league experience, and by the 1902 season, 74 men had jumped to the AL for higher salaries. The average jumper got a $500 raise. The historian Robert Burk claims that the average salary reached $3,000 in 1902 compared with under $2,000 in 1899, and then dropped back to under $2,500 in 1903 when the leagues signed the National Agreement, which capped salaries. At a time when clerks made $14 a week and skilled mechanics only $15 to $17, major league wages were excellent. Baseball players earned considerably more than school teachers or professors, and veterans had incomes comparable to those of some doctors and lawyers.[44]

By 1904 stars such as Jack Chesbro of the Highlanders and Ironman McGinnity and Mathewson of the Giants were paid over $5,000. Salaries continued to rise to about $3,000 on average by 1900. Fringe players were said to earn upwards of $2,000, regulars $5,000, and stars over $10,000. The highest paid team was the Chicago Cubs, with a $90,000 payroll divided among its twenty-three-man roster. Player-manager Frank Chance got $7,500, and his five best men each got over $5,000. The highest paid manager was John McGraw, who got $10,000, and the top player, Pittsburgh superstar shortstop Honus Wagner, got $18,000.[45]

Unproven rookies were more modestly compensated. A typical first-year player got $1,200, but as late as 1912 some were getting only $900. There were exceptions, notably star Harvard pitcher Walter Clarkson, the highest paid rookie of the era, who signed with the Highlanders during his senior year in 1904 for $4,000. Young players who started out with low salaries could expect periodic increments if they performed satisfactorily. Catcher Ed Sweeney signed with the Highlanders in 1908 for $1,500, a $300 raise over his minor league salary with the Atlanta Crackers. By 1913 his sixth year in the majors, he was earning $5,300, although he never hit above .270.[46]

Salaries continued to rise during the decade, the big impetus coming from the Federal League. The teams in the new league tried to copy the early AL by seeking immediate recognition as a major league through the recruitment of stars and other experienced players. The competition provided 264 men with major league jobs and drove up wages for all players. Eighty-one major leaguers (including 18 contract jumpers) and 140 minor leaguers joined the new league.[47]

National and American League owners remembered the large number of players who had jumped to the AL in 1901 and wanted to prevent that from happening again by keeping their employees under contract and quashing competitors even if it meant making substantial concessions to the players. Major leaguers took advantage of their strong bargaining position to press for large raises and long-term contracts. The Boston Red Sox payroll, for instance, increased by 25 percent for the 1914 season. The most heated bidding was for stars such as Ty Cobb, who secured a $20,000 contract for the 1915 season. He was one of twenty notable major leaguers whose salaries increased by 92 percent from 1913 to 1915. High quality players who were not stars also benefited from the bidding. Yankees shortstop Roger Peckinpaugh was paid $2,400 in 1913, but a year later he signed a contract for $3,600 plus a $1,000 bonus as team captain. Then in 1915 he negotiated a new three-year pact at $6,000 per annum. Jumpers were also well compensated, like four aged Cubs heroes whose new teams paid them an average of $6,500.[48]

Complete data are available on the salaries of the Philadelphia Phillies, who earned $3,400 on average in 1914 and $4,300 in 1916. Their raises reflected the interleague competition for players as well as the players' skills, having won the NL championship in 1915. By comparison, the majors as a whole averaged salaries of about $3,500 in 1916 and $3,900 in 1917. The lowest salaried club by far was the Athletics, whose entire payroll in 1917 was merely $40,000, $30,000 less than the second lowest, the Cincinnati Reds. The *New York Times* estimated the highest payrolls belonged to the Cubs ($140,000), the White Sox ($130,000), and the Giants ($120,000). By 1920, when the Phillies were in last place and most of their stars either had been traded or had retired, their average salary had dropped to $3,300.[49]

Salaries continued to rise at a rapid rate in the 1920s, and experts estimate that by 1923 the typical major leaguer earned $5,000. Salaries averaged about $7,500 in 1929, with superstars getting three and four times as much, topped by Babe Ruth's $80,000. The depression forced down wages considerably to an average of about $4,500 in 1936, still outstanding when 12 million Americans were out of work.[50]

A player's salary varied from his peers because of individual achievement, team performance, ticket sales, ability to negotiate, and the miserliness of individual owners. The wealthy beer baron Jacob Ruppert and his partner C. Tillinghast Huston were generous to their outstanding Yankees, a great gate attraction in the 1920s, and paid them the highest salaries in baseball. On the other side of the coin were proprietors like Charles Comiskey and Connie Mack, who had no outside income and earned their living exclusively from baseball. They were much tighter with their money. The main cause of the Black Sox scandal was the resentment by some of the fixers at their average salary of $4,300, which was relatively low considering their accomplishments.[51]

Minor league salaries were naturally substantially lower than those paid to big leaguers. In the early 1900s the average minor leaguer earned about $571, or about one-fourth the income of major leaguers. Most minor leaguers, especially in the lowest classifications, were apprentices, learning and improving their skills, though there were some in the twilight of their careers, hanging on for one last try at the majors—or at least a paycheck and an enjoyable lifestyle. A player fresh off the sandlots, starting in Class D, the lowest level of organized baseball, was paid $50 to $100 a month.[52] Beginning in 1904 Atlanta's nine was in the Class A Southern League, whose good pitchers then made from $200 to $300 a month. However, in 1904 Atlanta's two best hurlers received $400. A salary limit of $200 a month was established in 1912 and was raised in 1921 to $244. An average Atlanta player earned considerably more in six months than local blue-collar workers and many white-collar workers earned in an entire year.[53]

The pay scale in the highest minors, Class AA (which comprised the International League, the American Association, and the Pacific Coast League), was quite good, and some minor leaguers earned more than major league rookies. Class AA had no salary limits, and veterans could get as much as $300 to $400 a month. Furthermore, a major leaguer optioned out to Class AA teams often still received his prior salary, even if the old club had to subsidize him. The Pacific Coast League took advantage of the mild California weather to play up to 225 games, the longest season of any professional league, which also enabled players to earn more. In 1915 Harry Heilmann decided not to return to the Detroit Tigers because his hometown San Francisco team promised him $5,600, much more than Detroit wanted to pay.[54]

Off-Season Occupations

Ballplayers had many opportunities to supplement their wages during their long off-season if they chose to work. A number would have a chance to play postseason ball games. In the 1909 Chicago intracity series the Cubs received $717 each for beating the White Sox; the Pirates earned only $746 each for their win in the World Series. In 1910 a six-game series between the Giants and the Highlanders drew over 100,000 fans and netted $85,000. Each victorious Giant got $1,110, the losers,

$706. Atlanta and other smaller communities often staged benefit games to supplement their heroes' incomes.[55]

Professionals also supplemented their incomes by playing after the season for weekend semiprofessional clubs until the weather got too cold, in California winter leagues, and in barnstorming tours that gave small-town fans and local stalwarts a chance to test themselves against big league competition. The magnates detested these trips, believing they were entitled to the exclusive use of their employees' athletic talents. Greedy owners like Charles Ebbets often staged exhibition games during the regular season on days when no league game was scheduled, requiring their players to participate for no extra pay. Yet they tried to prevent players from doing the same thing for their own benefit. Owners especially opposed to postseason tours by World Series teams were afraid they might embarrass the league by losing to a semiprofessional outfit.[56]

Noted players gladly cashed in on numerous off-season opportunities resulting from their fame. Some worked as part-time college coaches. Star players were vigorously recruited by business owners expecting the players' notoriety would bring in business. Honus Wagner was in great demand to appear in vaudeville shows, endorse products, and sign ghostwritten newspaper articles. But when Wagner's picture appeared on baseball cards manufactured by a tobacco company without his permission, he forced the company to halt production. In the 1890s Cap Anson became the first ballplayer to appear on stage, performing a routine based on his diamond exploits. Theatrical promoters sought idols like McGraw, Mathewson, and Ruth for vaudeville. In 1912 McGraw earned $45,000 in fifteen weeks on the B. F. Keith circuit. Fans were anxious to see these players in the flesh and put up with amateurish performances.[57]

The most controversial use of players was crediting them as authors of ghostwritten articles that they might not have even read. In 1913 the Baseball Writers Association was formed to try to halt player bylines, especially during the World Series. Sportswriters received a lot of support from Ban Johnson, himself a former journalist, who was upset that ghostwritten commentaries frequently belittled organized baseball's leadership.[58]

Christy Mathewson was the most important "author," although essays ascribed to him were actually written by John W. Wheeler, a nationally renowned syndicated columnist. Matty's columns were printed in sports pages across the country, and the public had total confidence in him. Mathewson reportedly did not even inspire the articles and was paid fifteen thousand dollars just for his name. Despite those revelations, fans supported him and other baseball "authors." The *Chicago Daily News*, which published Mathewson's syndicated column, surveyed its readers, who voted overwhelmingly to keep printing the interesting and informative articles. Besides, the readers responded, Mathewson was intelligent enough to have written them had he wished. Mathewson did collaborate with Wheeler in *Pitching in a Pinch* (1912), one of the first manuals to teach the art of pitching, and on a series of children's books, beginning with *Pitcher Pollock* (1914) and *Catcher Sloan* (1915).[59]

As the prestige of their occupation rose, ballplayers were increasingly successful in getting off-season work as salesmen, real estate agents, and other white-collar jobs involving direct public contact. Sporting goods shops, car dealerships, clothing stores, and insurance agencies hired well-known players, expecting their presence would attract customers.[60]

Most big leaguers were probably satisfied with their wages and did little in the off-season except hunt and fish. Players did not train in the off-season, instead waiting until spring training to get into shape. A minority prepared for the future by learning a trade, attending college, or opening a business.[61] Estimates of the proportion of major leaguers who worked at blue-collar jobs in the off-season ranged from one-tenth to one-fourth. Certainly when blue-collar workers like barber Sam Crawford made the majors, they often stopped working at their trade. Yet, at least 32 percent of the 1908 Pittsburgh Pirates, a highly successful veteran team, held manual jobs that winter, mainly working at trades they had learned before going into baseball.[62] Scanty evidence exists about the off-season activities of minor league players, but given their low salaries, they were probably much more likely to hold second jobs than major leaguers were. Contemporary observers suspected that the urban-reared players usually worked as bartenders, drivers, or police officers and that rural ballplayers worked at agricultural jobs.[63]

Surveys of off-season plans of the Atlanta Crackers in 1914 and 1917 suggest that players were more successful in the off-season than their contemporaries realized. In 1914 most of the fourteen players intended to work, but just three expected to take on blue-collar jobs, and in 1917 most of the players who were not bound for the service or the majors expected to get white-collar jobs. Cracker players during this period increasingly chose to remain in the Gate City after the season, hoping to utilize their fame to secure suitable jobs. The *Atlanta Constitution* encouraged local business owners to hire them because their presence would improve business and demonstrate civic-mindedness. Athletes who found the most lucrative jobs, such as car salesman, were generally native Atlantans who had previously starred at local colleges and had already built up an excellent reputation in the community.[64]

Social Status of Major Leaguers

Because of the enhanced status of the occupation, improved salaries, and new opportunities to take advantage of fame, more middle-class men were drawn to professional baseball in the early 1900s. Results from a questionnaire sent in 1971 to athletes who played in the majors between 1900 and 1919 indicate that 44.6 percent had white-collar fathers, 20.9 percent had farming fathers, and 34.4 percent had fathers who were manual laborers.[65] These proportions are much more strongly weighted toward the middle classes than is the occupational distribution of all American males in 1910 (see table 3). The percentage of players' fathers who were nonmanual workers was more than double the percentage of all male Americans who were, and they were concentrated in the higher white-collar occupations. The percentage of players whose fathers owned farms was almost equal to the percentage of farm owners among all American males. Players' fathers were half as likely to be from the working classes compared with all men, but much more likely to be artisans.

Ballplayers in the 1920s and 1930s continued to come primarily from middle-class backgrounds. Nearly half (48 percent) of a sample of 100 ballplayers active in the 1920s and 1930s came from white-collar families, with just three-tenths (30 percent) from blue-collar and one-fifth (22 percent) from farming households. However, by the 1940s recruitment patterns changed dramatically because there were more players from blue-collar backgrounds (38.9 percent) than from white-collar ones (35.5 percent). In addition, the star players came overwhelmingly from the blue-collar ranks. This reflected the great numbers of second-generation immigrants who had started making their way into the major leagues in the mid- and late 1930s.[66]

The social status of women whom ballplayers married also indicated baseball's increased approval from Americans. The public image, popularized in sports columns and Ring Lardner's short stories, was that players married entertainers, like Mike Donlin and Babe Ruth's wives, or women from lower-class occupations. However, more than three-tenths of players' wives had continued their education past high school: 20.3 percent of those without college experience and 68.3 percent of the college-educated men had college-educated wives. The data demonstrate that professional ballplayers were certainly regarded as much better po-

Table 3. Occupations of Fathers of Major Leaguers Active 1900–1919, Compared to All U.S. Males, 1910 (Percentage)

Occupation	U.S. Males, 1910	Players' Fathers
Professionals	3.1	10.2
Proprietary		
Farm	19.9	20.9
Others	7.9	27.0
Clerks	9.2	7.4
Skilled	14.5	23.7
Semiskilled	11.2	7.4
Unskilled		
Farm	14.0	0.0
Others	20.2	3.3
	100.0	99.9

Sources: Edwards, *Comparative Occupational Statistics,* 187. The 1910 statistics include semi-professionals as professionals and foremen as skilled workers whereas my categorization of players follows that employed by Thernstrom in *Other Bostonians,* 290–92, in which both categories are considered low white-collar.

Note: Percentages for players' fathers computed from weighted sample of 117 respondents to my questionnaire. This column does not total 100.0 due to rounding.

tential spouses than they had been in the past. Comparing major leaguers to their wives by fathers' occupations, three-fourths of the ballplayers married within their social class and were more likely to marry up the social ladder than down it.[67]

Finally, the major leaguers' higher social status was reflected by their own education. At least three-fourths had attended high school, which was then largely a middle-class institution. As late as 1920 only one-third of elementary school students went on to high school. In addition, a remarkable one-fourth of players (25.8 percent) had attended college, while less than 5 percent of the male 1910 college-age population of the United States had done so. Although most college attendees never would complete their studies, a surprising number did graduate. In 1901, for instance, 35.3 percent of major league rookies who had attended college finished their degrees; 41.7 percent did so in 1910; and 35.9 percent did in 1920. Even for nongraduates, the time spent on campus probably helped them develop new skills.[68]

The large proportion of college-trained major league baseball players reflected the higher social standing of the new recruits. College students then were drawn primarily from the higher socioeconomic groups. Only 20.6 percent of the college-trained big leaguers came from working-class backgrounds, but 37.3 percent of less-educated players did. Colleges demanded winning teams, so coaches recruited outstanding ballplayers because of their athletic talent and not their academic abilities. Their ballplayers saw professional baseball as a good outlet for their abilities.[69]

College baseball in 1900 had already been a major sport for over a generation, and leading newspapers and magazines devoted considerable attention to it. Experts acknowledged that the leading schools—Brown, Georgetown, Harvard, Princeton, and Yale in the East, Michigan and Illinois in the Midwest, and St. Mary's in the Far West—fielded excellent teams, and their best players were regarded as proven performers. Their publicity gave collegians a big advantage over sandlot heroes, who were harder to discover. Fred Beebe of the University of Illinois, for example, had planned to become an engineer after graduation, but discovered that engineers were not in demand. However, he had acquired considerable fame as a varsity pitcher and, when approached by professional scouts, decided to try baseball rather than face a possible dismal future in his chosen profession.[70]

The typical aspiring professional ballplayers, particularly those from working-class families who were not college bound, developed their reputations by participating in amateur city leagues or village teams. Playing provided an opportunity to relax, make a few dollars, possibly advance in their jobs, and perhaps even be discovered by professional scouts. The early baseball experiences of Johnny Kling, the great Cubs catcher, was typical of other sandlot stars: "I discovered when I went to work that baseball helped me a lot. I got a job and was advanced faster and given better chances than the fellows who did not play, so I realized baseball was valuable as a side-line. At that time I had little idea of devoting all my time to it. I managed and pitched for the Schmeltzers, a Kansas City sporting goods house, and worked in the store when not playing."[71]

In cities like Chicago amateur baseball was taken particularly seriously, and neighborhood, ethnic, and semiprofessional teams were important community institutions. The level of competition was very high, and several graduates of its amateur leagues became major leaguers. Promising young Chicagoans were recruited by amateur teams sponsored by churches, ethnic societies, fraternal orders, politicians, and businesses to play on weekends. Amateur and semipro baseball was so popular that in 1906 a *Spalding's Guide* devoted just to Chicago was published. Amateur players were paid ten to twenty dollars per game plus expenses. In 1907 the best players in Chicago's prestigious semiprofessional City League, which included former big leaguers James Callahan,

Mike Donlin, and Jake Stahl, who all eventually returned to the majors, earned several hundred dollars each season plus whatever they made from side bets.[72]

Sandlot players entering professional baseball usually began in Class D. The career pattern for college attendees was different since they were generally older and had already proven themselves. Marginal college players usually opted for other careers rather than begin in the low minors, which offered poor wages. Good college players usually started in Class A or higher. Davy Jones planned on a legal career after college but also wanted to marry his sweetheart. Jones found he could make more money playing in the minors than as a law clerk, and so he opted for baseball. Other athletes, like Harry Hooper of St. Mary's, went into baseball because they hoped it would lead to good business contacts. Hooper agreed to sign with the Sacramento minor league team only after management promised to get him an engineering job in the city. A few collegians, like pitcher George A. Davis Jr., son of a New York state senator, went right from the campus to the major leagues. He signed with the Highlanders in 1912 for five thousand dollars and made his major league debut four days later. Davis was only 7-10 in his four-year career, but he attended Harvard Law in the off-season and became an attorney.[73]

Only 3.2 percent of the 1,557 men who played in the major leagues between 1871 and 1890 had attended college. The most notable was Lee Richmond, who in 1880 tossed a perfect game in his major league debut for Worcester against the Chicago White Stockings, a few days before leading Brown to the college baseball championship. The NL started to actively recruit college athletes in the late 1890s to make the sport more respectable and thus bolster attendance. The proportion of college players in the 1890s increased to 8.1 percent, nearly triple that of the prior decade. Most collegians up to then had refused professional offers because of the poor pay and low prestige.[74]

After 1900 the proportion of college players seeking baseball careers rose substantially. By 1904 one-fourth of all rookies had college experience. The *New York Times* noted the growing influx of collegians into the majors and indicated that such a goal would have horrified college graduates just a few years earlier. Professional baseball was now seen as a fine profession with excellent pay, clean-cut and intelligent colleagues, and a suitable lifestyle.[75]

Baseball managers were at first reticent about hiring collegians, deeming college boys inexperienced, unaware of the trickery and subtleties involved in the sport, and unable to carry their load. However, Connie

Mack believed that collegians could readily adapt and hired several for his Athletics, including Jack Barry of Holy Cross, Jack Coombs of Colby, Eddie Plank of Gettysburg, and Eddie Collins of Columbia. His 1906 team had ten former collegians. Mack was successful with them, winning six pennants between 1902 and 1913, a record that encouraged other managers to recruit college stars. The competition for college players became so heated that big league clubs sought close ties with leading college coaches in hopes they would send their best players to them. The fierce struggle for these athletes enabled men like Walter Clarkson to negotiate lucrative contracts.[76]

College players entering professional baseball encountered a great deal of antipathy from veterans, typical when workers of different backgrounds entered an established occupation. Older players were afraid of losing their high-paying jobs and were jealous of players who entered the big leagues directly from college or after a brief minor league apprenticeship. Veterans were cruel and nasty to the new recruits, but the collegians, often former football stars, did not let their new colleagues abuse them.[77]

The best college players were effectively already professionals, often with few scholarly pretensions. They generally played for whichever institution promised them the greatest rewards, which could go beyond room, board, and tuition. A Cubs player revealed that during his two years at college he had studied penmanship and accumulated five hundred dollars in his bank account. Furthermore, leading collegians frequently played baseball for financial compensation in the summer without losing their amateur status.[78]

Educators were apprehensive about the growing trend of college-trained professional athletes. They felt it was not what their schools had been established for and generally agreed that a college athlete who became a professional wasted years at school. Joseph E. Raycroft, head of physical education at Princeton and president of the Intercollegiate Basketball Association, argued, "It seems to me that a college graduate should fulfill a greater position in life than that which is open to him as a professional athlete. However, I do not hold that there is anything dishonorable about professional athletics, but this field does not afford the college man a broad enough scope for the full use of the advantages which his college training has given him."[79] Antipathy toward college attendees becoming professional athletes was further reflected by Fielding Yost's decision to rescind the varsity letters of those Michigan players who became professionals.[80]

Colleges were more worried about the impact of professionalism on their institutions than its influence on individual athletes. The root of the problem was the eligibility rules. Judson P. Welch of Penn State noted, "Everybody knows that nearly all the college teams have been padded with professional players. . . . These men have no class standing, prepare no lessons, go to no recitations."[81]

The amateur standing of college ballplayers was jeopardized by summer baseball. College athletes from the finest baseball programs secretly played for pay during summer recess and then returned to play for their varsity teams. They played for hotels, semiprofessional clubs, and professional leagues outside the jurisdiction of organized baseball, earning up to two hundred dollars a month. These men protected their eligibility by playing under pseudonyms or by indirectly receiving compensation for playing baseball. For example, a ballplayer might make an outlandish wager with his boss, such as betting fifty dollars that he could jump over a baseball bat. The player would, of course, win the wager and thus maintain his amateur status. When college athletes played for a hotel team, they were ostensibly paid for other duties, like waiting on tables, rather than for playing baseball and socializing with guests. The summer baseball situation was well publicized in popular magazines like *McClure's* and *Outlook*. It made headlines in 1913 with the disclosure that Jim Thorpe, the pentathlon and decathlon champion at the 1912 Olympics, had played ball in 1909 for a minor league team in Rocky Mount, North Carolina. Unlike most players, Thorpe had played under his real name. He was forced to return his gold medals. Thorpe subsequently played major league baseball for the New York Giants.[82]

There were strong differences of opinion among university officials on the summer baseball question. Opponents, like Captain Frank Pierce of West Point, the president of the National Collegiate Athletics Association, castigated summer baseball since it encouraged cheating and lying by players to maintain their amateur status. Furthermore, the experience gave summer ballplayers an unfair advantage over those who did not have the same opportunity to better their skills. During their stints on other teams, these semiprofessionals supposedly forgot about fair play while learning to manipulate rules, jeer the opposition, and use foul language. Pierce and other critics did not decry professional baseball as such, but claimed it was immoral for professional players to continue proclaiming their amateur standing and then deriving the benefits of that status.[83]

President Nicholas Murray Butler of Columbia University and other proponents argued that an athlete playing summer ball was like a superior student earning money by tutoring or a member of the glee club getting paid for singing in a church choir. They claimed that all students, including athletes, should be allowed to utilize their best talents to obtain money for educational expenses and that academic standing should be the only determinant of eligibility for intercollegiate sports. They pointed out the difficulty of enforcing any proscriptions against summer ball and that any radical change in the amateur codes would only encourage players to falsify affidavits affirming their amateur status.[84]

Summer baseball regulations varied enormously throughout the country. Some schools, like Brown, had no sanctions against varsity athletes earning money by playing baseball in the summer. Brown's representatives noted that almost every school it played had athletes on the field who had competed for compensation during the summer. These permissive schools recognized the realities of the situation and did not penalize their athletes.[85]

Colleges rarely took strong action to prevent summer ball or discipline guilty student-athletes. Opposition was mainly centered in the Midwest, where moralists like Amos Alonzo Stagg of the University of Chicago tried to get the Western Athletic Conference to drop intercollegiate baseball rather than permit continuing transgressions. However, most coaches and athletic directors found it easier to overlook the violations than drastically alter the status quo. They knew that if one school decided to protest the eligibility of its opponents, then its own roster would be equally scrutinized. Before 1920 colleges in leagues like the Southern Conference and the Missouri Valley Conference allowed their players to compete for compensation on hometown clubs not recognized by organized baseball.[86]

Geographic Origins of Major Leaguers

The conventional wisdom about professional baseball players not only asserted that they were poor ignorant men but also that they were primarily from rural regions. In reality, by 1900 professional players were still mainly from urban origins, although fewer were than had been in the past. I compiled a sample of 593 men who had played at least one year in either Chicago or New York. Nearly three-fifths (58.4 percent) of the American-born players with known birthplaces were from cities (defined as having a population over 2,500), even though just 35.4 percent of the national population in 1890 and 51.2 percent in 1920 lived in cities (see table 4). Two-fifths (41.6 percent) came from rural areas, but the biogra-

Table 4. Known Birthplaces of Native-Born Major Leaguers, Active 1900–1919

Size	Number	Percentage
Under 1,000	173	30.4
1,000–2,500	64	11.2
2,500–8,000	66	11.6
8,000–10,000	13	2.3
10,000–20,000	34	5.9
20,000–50,000	42	7.4
50,000–100,000	39	6.8
Over 100,000	139	24.4
	570	100.0

Source: *Baseball Encyclopedia.*

phies of many rural-born players indicated that they had been raised in cities. The overrepresentation of urbanites directly contradicted the sport's rural mythology. In the period 1920–39, however, the proportion of urban players declined slightly to 53.7 percent, about equal to the urban share of the national population in 1920.[87]

The largest American communities were well represented in the majors: one-fourth (24.4 percent) of the players came from cities with over 100,000 inhabitants. In 1890, when these players were children or not yet born, the ten largest cities were home to 11.7 percent of the white American population, yet contributed 16.8 percent of the major leaguers active from 1900 to 1919. These cities produced over 40 percent more ballplayers than would be expected considering their share of the national population. The overrepresentation was unevenly distributed. Boston contributed less than one-half its expected share while Cincinnati, Cleveland, and St. Louis all contributed more than three times their expected proportion. San Francisco was also a fertile recruitment area, producing nearly three times its expected proportion. Chicago overproduced by a factor of 1.5 (see table 5). All the most productive cities except San Francisco had long major league traditions that promoted interest in the sport. San Francisco did have a strong minor league heritage and also benefited from a mild climate, where baseball could be played year round. New York and Boston's underrepresentation was largely because of their limited space available for baseball diamonds.

Chicago was an excellent producer of baseball talent, but in the eyes of the *St. Louis Post-Dispatch* was less productive at the turn of the century than before because of the declining space available for diamonds: "The passing of Chicago from recruiting fields was due wholly to the activity of the builders. Only a few years ago great spaces, even in the

Table 5. Ten Leading Cities as Birthplaces of Major League Ballplayers, Active 1900–1919 (Percentage)

City	U.S. White Population in 1890	Native-Born Players
New York	2.7	1.4
Chicago	2.0	3.0
Philadelphia	1.8	1.9
Brooklyn	1.4	1.2
St. Louis	0.8	2.8
Boston	0.8	0.3
Baltimore	0.7	1.4
San Francisco	0.5	1.4
Cincinnati	0.5	1.7
Cleveland	0.5	1.7
	11.7	16.8

Sources: Computed from data in *Eleventh Census, 1890,* xciii, clxii–clxiii, 452, 454, 460, 470–71, 473–74, 478; *Baseball Encyclopedia.*

thickest settled parts of Chicago, lay vacant, and on these lots myriads of youngsters pitched, caught and batted. As the city grew, these lots were covered one by one. Today [1905] the boy who would play ball in Chicago has to travel long distances to find a diamond, and the ambitions of the Chicago juveniles seem to have shrunk in inverse ratio to the length of these journeys."[88]

Besides playing space another major determinant for a city's representation was the quality of local amateur and semiprofessional baseball, leagues that provided the training essential to develop future professional ballplayers. Keen competition in high school leagues or associations sponsored by religious and fraternal societies enabled young players to improve their skills. Sportswriters who accepted the rural myths of baseball wrongly argued that farm boys were better prepared to become professionals because they had lots of space for baseball fields. Without competition and superior coaching, however, players could not improve their skills to the degree necessary to become major leaguers. While most small towns had at least one amateur ball club, those teams played only other small-town teams that probably had just a few outstanding players. Competition to make the team was much fiercer in metropolitan areas, where gifted youngsters progressed to higher quality leagues and consistently played against other superior athletes and so were forced to continue refining their skills. At the apex of sandlot ball, particularly in Chicago, Cleveland, and St. Louis, semiprofessional baseball was enormously popular and well supported by local fans. Their leagues provided a strong inducement to excellent athletes to continue in the sport by rewarding them with money, adulation, and fame.[89]

The most productive sources of players in the early 1900s were Pennsylvania (14.0 percent), Ohio (10.6 percent), Illinois (8.5 percent), and New York (7.6 percent). The Northeast still produced a large share of major leaguers (32.4 percent), but was supplanted as the leading region by the Midwest (41.8 percent). The South was represented by 16.5 percent, the Far West by 5.4 percent, and 3.4 percent were born abroad (about half the percentage of the earlier cohort), mostly in Canada and Cuba. The foreign-born presence had declined by nearly half since the previous century, reflecting the head start native-born youths had over immigrants. There were no data for 0.5 percent.[90]

The broadening scope of players' geographic origins reflected the national expansion of baseball. Most late nineteenth-century minor leagues were in the Northwest and Midwest, but there were also a few in the South and Far West, most notably the Southern League (1885), a Texas association (1888), and two leagues in California (1885, 1886). These leagues encouraged local interest in baseball and helped motivate youngsters to become professional ballplayers. California and Texas were by far the most successful warm weather states in the early 1900s, producing 6.1 percent of the major leaguers. By the 1920s and 1930s California was second only to Pennsylvania in producing major leaguers at a rate 3.4 times greater than its share of the white population. Cities in the West continued to be major producers of ballplayers, led by Oakland, San Francisco, and Los Angeles, sending, respectively, 6.2, 4.5, and 3.9 times their expected number of players based on their populations. St. Louis produced the most players (28), ranking sixth by its ratio (3.4), and was the highest rated city with a major league team, followed by Cincinnati and Pittsburgh, which produced more than twice their expected ratios. The 52 largest cities contributed 19 percent more than their share of the national population. New York was third in the number of players produced (21), but had a low ratio (.433), which reflected both its excellent semipro leagues and especially its lack of playing fields.[91]

Ethnic Backgrounds

Fans believed that professional baseball was a democratic sport that recruited its players from all white ethnic groups. The reality was that nearly all professionals in the nineteenth century were native-born Americans or Irish or German immigrants, and over 90 percent of the professionals in the early 1900s were drawn from these three groups. The main change was the increased proportion of WASPs attracted by the higher salaries and improved status of major league baseball. Just a handful of immigrants succeeded in baseball, although they were beginning to achieve notoriety in boxing, basketball, and other sports that did not require much space to play.[92]

Baseball was probably more valuable as a source of vertical social mobility for the Irish than for any other ethnic group. In the late nineteenth century the Irish worked primarily at the lowest-paying city jobs that required sheer brute strength. The historian Stephan Thernstrom found that in 1890 merely 10 percent of first-generation Irish Bostonians had white-collar jobs, and while second-generation Irish Bostonians (born 1860–79) did much better than their parents, with 38 percent ending up in white-collar jobs, that was significantly less than the 52–53 percent of second-generation western Europeans and 73 percent of all native-born white Americans who had white-collar occupations. Their relative lack of success was further illustrated by their high concentrations in unskilled and semiskilled jobs (36 percent). Opportunities for the second-generation Irish were limited by their social origins, discrimination, absence of an entrepreneurial tradition, and limited education.[93]

Ambitious but deprived Irish immigrants primarily sought alternate avenues of advancement in areas such as construction, politics, religion, and athletics. Irish migrants came to the United States with a manly athletic tradition and quickly became avid sports fans and athletes in their new country. Irish immigrants and Irish Americans were especially successful in boxing, which drew its participants primarily from the lowest classes, and outstanding Irish pugilists like John L. Sullivan completely dominated the ring in the nineteenth century. Even by 1918 they still comprised 40 percent of contenders. These successful pugilists were well paid, celebrated among Irish Americans, and lionized by sports enthusiasts.[94]

Because it was popular in northeastern and midwestern cities, where numerous Irish immigrants had settled, virtually all second-generation Irish boys played baseball, often for politically sponsored social and athletic clubs. The ablest Irish ballplayers were recruited to play pro ball, inspired by such Irish stars as King Kelly and John McGraw. In general, Irish parents encouraged their sons' athletic interests, welcoming the opportunity to add well-paid breadwinners to their families. This attitude differed markedly from the perspective of most nineteenth-century middle-class parents, who abhorred the idea of their sons becoming professional players.[95]

Because they thought many players had Irish-sounding names, the public saw baseball as an Irish-dominated occupation. One expert estimated that about one-third of the major leaguers in the early 1890s were of Irish descent. Irish prominence in baseball continued well into the twentieth century, including a substantial presence in executive positions on the playing field. In 1915, for instance, eleven of the sixteen major league managerial posts were held by those of Irish descent.[96]

Germans comprised the largest immigrant group in the United States and adjusted to their new country more successfully than most newcomers, typically owning farms and working as urban artisans. Compared with the Irish, they were more geographically dispersed, less concentrated in cities, and more likely to end up in rural areas. German newcomers clustered in rural communities like New Ulm, Minnesota, and New Braunfels, Texas, and in ethnic communities in cities such as Cincinnati, Chicago, Milwaukee, and St. Louis, where they maintained their traditional culture and institutions, including beer gardens, music, theater, and turner halls. Their athletic experience did not include team sports, but the second generation readily took to American sports, which were much more fun than gymnastic drills.[97]

According to one expert German-American players in the early days of professional baseball were somewhat outnumbered by the Irish until the 1890s. German Americans attracted to baseball as a career were more likely to see it as a way of maintaining their lower middle-class status than as a way of moving up the social ladder.[98]

The first relatively successful new immigrant group in baseball was the Czechs. They came to the United States in the late nineteenth century from a part of east central Europe where physical culture was supported by the sokol movement of the 1860s. This nationalistic movement sponsored calisthenics and gymnastics to build up the Czech people for the future revolution. Czech immigrants in Chicago and the industrial towns of Pennsylvania and Ohio founded athletic clubs in the late nineteenth century to promote physical culture and ethnic pride. Sokols began to sponsor baseball leagues around the turn of the century because the national pastime was popular with the second generation and because members saw baseball as a way to attract Czech boys into the sokol movement. Sunday games in Chicago's Czech leagues drew large crowds, and the results were reported in Czech papers and occasionally even in the English dailies. The quality of play was high, and by 1910 Chicago's Czech teams had produced several big leaguers. Unlike other eastern Europeans, who usually criticized their ballplaying sons, most Czech Americans were proud of their young men who became major leaguers. The Czech paper *Denni Hlasatel* looked forward to the day when every major league team would have at least one Czech on its roster.[99]

Baseball was not a valuable source of vertical mobility for the newer ethnic groups at the bottom of the social ladder. Between 1901 and 1906 there were a total of 5 Czech, 2 Jewish, and 0 Italian rookies. There were no first-year men from any of these groups in 1910, and in 1920 there was just 1 Czech and 2 Italians out of 133 rookies. Those second-generation newcomers who made the majors were badly treated by veterans, who worried that the new players might take their jobs, destroy the game's prestige, and force down salary levels. Most fans also wanted the sport to remain distinctly "American" and jeered and belittled players they viewed as sons of new immigrants. Explanations for the absence of players from the new ethnic groups occasionally had racist overtones, such as the *New York Tribune*'s suggestion that they lacked the courage necessary to stand firmly in the batter's box and take a strong swing at the ball.[100]

Players of Jewish heritage were conspicuously absent from baseball. Although they comprised a considerable percentage of the population in New York and Chicago and almost since the inception of professional play had been involved in management, few Jews played in the majors. German Jews were successful in the front offices of baseball teams, particularly in Cincinnati, where the attorney Louis Kramer was a founder, secretary-treasurer, and last president of the American Association. In 1882 Nathan Menderson was president of the Cincinnati Reds and was later succeeded by Aaron S. Stern. Then in 1902 Mayor Julius Fleischmann was a principal in the political syndicate that bought the Reds from John Brush.[101]

Over 2 million eastern European Jews migrated to America between the 1880s and 1920, including 254,000 in 1908 alone. They mainly came from the segregated cities, towns, and villages in Russia's Pale of Settlement. These impoverished newcomers had been severely restricted by law in occupational options in their former countries. They brought with them some job skills, particularly in the garment trades, a tradition of entrepreneurship, and a profound respect for education. They were far better prepared for city life in the United States than contemporary Catholic newcomers from Italy and Poland, who were the other major new immigrants of the period. The Jewish immigrant generation did well compared with other first-generation immigrants. By 1910 one-fourth of

Boston's Jewish newcomers had white-collar jobs, a success story like that of earlier British immigrants, who spoke English. Even though most Jewish nonmanual laborers were peddlers earning very small incomes, these jobs required risk taking and developed business skills important for the future of these entrepreneurs and their ethnic group.[102]

The success of second-generation Jews was a product of strong personal motivation, their parents' talent for commerce, and the historic Jewish respect for religious education. The stress on religious education paved the way for a positive attitude toward secular education, which provided a basic foundation in skills that would be useful for the kinds of jobs available in a modern urban economy. Jewish parents in the United States sacrificed to educate their sons and encouraged them to stay in school as long as possible, unlike Irish or Italian parents, who wanted their boys to leave school at an early age to get jobs. Consequently, three-fourths of second-generation Boston Jews secured white-collar jobs, primarily in business, a record unmatched by any other ethnic group.[103]

Ambitious second-generation Jews who lacked the capital or initiative to start small businesses, were poorly educated, or had no valuable contacts often sought alternative avenues of social mobility in entertainment or professional sports, particularly boxing. The manly art was a useful skill for lower-class youths to master because they needed to defend themselves from Irish, Italian, or Polish street toughs. Good street fighters often grew up to become criminals, police officers, or boxers. They could learn the rudiments of boxing at local settlement houses or neighborhood boxing gymnasiums. Those who showed promise fought in the amateurs, and the best of them often turned pro.[104]

Jewish pugilists had a rich heritage dating back to England's Daniel Mendoza, the champion from 1791 to 1795, and the Anglo-Jewish boxing tradition was brought to the United States in the mid-1850s by several pugilists, including "Young" Barney Aaron, who became the American lightweight champion in 1857. The first celebrated Jewish-American boxer was Joe Choynski, a heavyweight contender in the 1890s, an anomaly because he came from a prominent San Francisco family. Nearly all the rest were sons of poor Russian immigrants who lived in urban ethnic communities. The first Jewish world champion was bantamweight Harry Harris of Chicago (1901), followed by the far better known Abe Attell, world featherweight champion (1904–12). Jewish prize fighters achieved widespread fame and success, became role models for youngsters to emulate and idolize, and were regarded as heroes who defended the honor of the Jewish people and destroyed negative stereotypes of their physical abilities. Between 1910 and 1919 there were four Jewish champions; only the Irish and Germans had more. In the 1920s only the Italians and Irish had more, and by 1928 Jews had more contenders than any other ethnic group.[105]

Contemporary sportswriters were puzzled by the dearth of Jews in professional baseball since they were so visible in boxing. In 1903 Barry McCormick noted in the *St. Louis Republic*, "He [the Jew] is athletic enough and the great number of Jewish boxers show that he is adept at one kind of sport at least." However, McCormick could identify only two Jewish major leaguers, Barney Pelty and Harry Kane. There were just five Jews in the majors in 1900–1909 and eleven in 1910–19.[106]

One answer for this absence is that baseball did not fit into the new immigrant experience as well as boxing did. Jews living in the crowded Lower East Side of New York or the Near West Side of Chicago had little opportunity to play baseball and develop the necessary expertise. There were no readily accessible lots to play ball, and Jewish young men had little leisure time because of school or jobs. Their spare time came mostly in the evening, too late for baseball, although they could still go to a settlement house to play basketball or learn the fundamentals of pugilism.[107]

Russian Jewish boys in crowded cities who hoped to become professional baseball players did not get parental support. They had no sporting heritage in their culture and parents generally saw baseball as a silly, dangerous, overly exertive children's game played by men in short pants. It was a waste of time, lacked purpose, threatened their authority, introduced their sons to some of the worst features of the host society, and provided an entering wedge for total assimilation. As the comedian Eddie Cantor recalled, "To the pious people of the ghetto a baseball player was the king of loafers." The worst thing his grandmother could call him was "you baseball player you." A disturbed father wrote to the Yiddish-language *Jewish Daily Forward* in 1903, "What is the point of this crazy game? It makes sense to teach a child to play dominoes or chess [but not baseball]. . . . I want my boy to grow up to be a *mensch*, not a wild American runner." Editor Abraham Cahan recommended in response, "Let your boys play baseball and play it well, as long as it does not interfere with their education or get them into bad company. . . . Let us not so raise the children that they should grow up foreigners in their own birthplace." In his magisterial study of New York Jews, *World of Our Fathers*, Irving Howe related one boy's experience: "I couldn't tell my father I played ball, so my mother would sneak out my baseball gear and put it in the candy store downstairs."[108] He wanted to be a "real" American, not a greenhorn like his father.

Gifted Jewish ballplayers considered baseball a meritocratic and democratic institution and expected their achievements to gain them personal acceptance and respect for their ethnic group from the broader society. However, the rare Jewish major leaguer encountered a great deal of discrimination. As major leaguers William E. Stahl and Jack Regan noted in 1910, "In looking over the list of names comprising the American and National Leaguers we fail to discover any of those well worn Semitic cognomens such as Moses, Abraham, Ikey, Solomon, Aaron, etc., or the tribe of numerous 'skys.' Something wrong. Is the work too arduous?"[109] Several Jewish ballplayers altered their names to hide their ethnic backgrounds and thus avoid prejudice. Five players with the names Bohne, Cooney, Corey, Ewing, and Kane had originally been named Cohen but had changed their names in an attempt to avoid prejudice. German players who were thought to be Jewish, like Johnny Kling and Jacob Atz, received considerable abuse from anti-Semitic colleagues.[110]

Certain baseball owners in cities with large Jewish populations wanted to hire Jewish ballplayers to attract local Jews to the ballparks to root for their heroes. The Giants made special efforts between 1910 and 1930 to recruit a Jewish star since the surrounding neighborhood was rapidly becoming a Jewish area. Manager John McGraw reportedly believed that a star Jewish player in New York would be worth his weight in gold. After the Federal League folded following the 1915 season, the Giants signed up some of their best players, including star outfielder Benny Kauff, who was believed to be Jewish, but was actually Slavic. In 1923 Mose Solomon, nicknamed the "Rabbi of Swat," having batted .429 with forty-nine homers for Hutchinson, Kansas, in the Southwestern League, put in a brief appearance with the Giants. He was "just the sort of hero McGraw has wished for . . . [with] verdicts in several fist fights . . . because of reflections on his ancestry as a Jew." However, Solomon played just two games, with three hits in eight plate appearances.[111]

Three years later it appeared the Giants had found their Jewish star in Andy Cohen, who played thirty-five games for the Giants before he was sent back to the minors for more seasoning. He hit .353 with Buffalo of the International League in 1927 and was brought back to New York the following year amidst great fanfare as the "Great Jewish Hope" to replace superstar Rogers Hornsby, who had been traded to Boston because of his unpopularity with teammates and his gambling problem. Cohen was publicized as an inner-city youth making good but was actually born in Baltimore to immigrant parents and raised in El Paso, Texas, where the Jewish community was small, and educated at the University of Alabama. Cohen brought out Jewish fans, became a huge ethnic hero, paved a path for other Jewish players (whose numbers peaked in the 1930s and 1940s), but never fulfilled his potential. As Hornsby had promised on his departure, he outhit his successor, who batted .274, by about one hundred points. Cohen lasted just one more season, hitting a respectable .294 in 1929, with a lifetime .281 batting average.[112]

Other teams were less interested in recruiting Jews. According to Bob Berman, who briefly played for the Washington Senators, he was scouted in 1918 by Branch Rickey of the St. Louis Cardinals, who wanted to sign the DeWitt Clinton High School star until he found out Berman's religion. The Yankees were notorious for avoiding Jewish players. Except for Phil Cooney, who played one game in 1905, the Yankees did not have a Jewish player until Jimmy Reese joined the team in 1930.[113]

Most Jewish ballplayers did not come from New York, home in 1920 to one-half of the Jews residing in the United States, and those who did, like Al Schacht, lived in the outlying boroughs, where they could play in the sprawling schoolyards, city streets, and empty lots. In any given decade only about one-third of the Jewish major leaguers came from New York. Some players came from major cities such as Atlanta, Chicago, and San Francisco, while Harry Kane was born in Hamburg, Arkansas, Barney Pelty in Farmington, Missouri, and Moxey Manuel in Pascagoula, Mississippi. Far removed from inner-city Jewish influences, these young men assimilated into the mainstream American culture that approved of and supported baseball much faster than Jews raised in Brownsville or the Lower East Side.[114]

Italian and Polish immigrants were also slow to break into the major leagues. Many Italian and Polish immigrants arrived without white-collar skills, capital, or experience in urban living. They emphasized traditional rather than modern values such as education and social mobility, which did not prepare them well for their new country. Not surprisingly, just 12 percent of their first generations in Boston obtained white-collar jobs. These newcomers typically took their children out of school at early ages before they could learn new ideas, such as putting individual success ahead of the family, and were sent to work. Consequently, among the second generation, only 42 percent of Italians and 36 percent of Poles ended up in white-collar jobs, compared with 75 percent of the Jews.[115]

Poor, uneducated Italian and Polish youngsters needed alternate opportunities if they wished to get ahead. Like Jewish youths in similar circumstances, many Polish and Italian young men became boxers. Second-generation Italians and Poles became successful in boxing well before they made an impact in baseball. The first Polish world champion was middleweight Stanley Ketchell in 1907, and the first Italian was lightweight Pete Herman in 1917. Italians were particularly prominent in professional boxing—in 1912 an Italian, Fireman Jim Flynn, fought Jack Johnson for the heavyweight championship. By the late 1910s Italians ranked third in their number of prime contenders, and from 1920 to 1955 Italians had more world champions than any other ethnic group.[116]

Despite their boxing successes, few Italians or Poles entered professional baseball. In 1925, for instance, there was just 1 Pole and 0 Italians out of 116 rookies. The first Polish batting champion was Al Simmons in 1930, and the first Italian, Ernie Lombardi in 1938, a generation after both groups had already produced boxing champions. Unlike boxing, which drew men primarily from the lowest social classes, baseball attracted men from all social classes because of its intrinsic and extrinsic rewards. Furthermore, like their Jewish contemporaries, many Italian and Polish newcomers lived in crowded tenement communities where there was limited space to play baseball, could not play interscholastic ball because they had dropped out of school, and had little leisure time during daylight hours because they worked. Family pressure to avoid becoming too Americanized probably discouraged some of these boys from playing as much baseball as they would have liked.[117]

The underrepresentation of Italians and Poles on major league rosters continued until the mid-1930s. In 1929, for example, only four regulars among the five major league teams in Chicago and New York were of recent immigrant stock, and two of them were Jewish. In the early 1930s the numbers of Italian and Polish rookies began to become more noticeable, and by 1935 there were 9 Italian rookies out of 115. Many second- and third-generation Italians (most notably the three DiMaggios) and Polish minor leaguers were beginning to reach the majors. By 1941 about 8 percent of the big leaguers were Italian and 9.3 percent were Polish, more than double each group's share of the total white population in the country.[118]

The Racial Question

Native Americans were far more prominent and successful in professional baseball at the turn of the century than the new immigrants. The first Indian major leaguer was Lou Sockalexis, a man of outstanding talent who played for Cleveland from 1897 to 1899 (in 1915 the team was named the Indians in his honor), and he was followed by about thirty other Indians over the next twenty years. Native Americans were then eminent in sports, as exemplified by the success of the Carlisle Indian School in football and Jim Thorpe's triumphs at the 1912 Olympics. Indian major leaguers got substantial attention in the press because their presence seemed so remarkable given that the Indian wars and Wounded Knee were not that far in the past. In addition, a number of Native Americans, notably pitcher Albert "Chief" Bender of the Philadelphia Athletics and catcher John "Chief" Meyers of the New York Giants, were outstanding performers. Baseball's propagandists effectively publicized the backgrounds of these big leaguers as proof of the sport's democratic recruitment policies.[119] Thanks in part to this advertising, Native Americans were attracted to baseball as a career because they believed the sport was free of racial prejudice. As Bender noted, "The reason I went into baseball as a profession was that when I left school [Dartmouth], baseball offered me the best opportunity both for money and advancement. . . . I adopted it because I played baseball better than I could do anything else, because the life and the game appealed to me and because there was so little of racial prejudice in the game. . . . There has been scarcely a trace of sentiment against me on account of birth. I have been treated the same as the other men."[120]

Cubans were another nationality identified on major league rosters. Cubans had a long history of familiarity with the sport, which during the late nineteenth century was identified with the freedom and liberty of the United States, in contrast to bull fighting, the national pastime of the imperialist Spaniards. The first Cuban major leaguer had been Esteban Bellán, who played three years in the National Association. By the 1890s professional teams were visiting the island in the winter and encountering increasingly stiff competition. In 1908, for instance, the Cincinnati Reds lost seven of eleven games to Cuban nines. Visiting players and managers were impressed by the quality of Cuban ballplayers, and soon organized baseball began to recruit there. In 1911 Cincinnati Reds manager Clark Griffith initiated the signing of Cubans to major league contracts when he purchased the minor league contracts of Armando Marsans and Rafael Almeida. Four years later there were at least five Cubans in the majors and eleven in the minors.[121]

Race was a big concern in recruiting Cubans. There was less racism on the island, and all races played professional baseball together. Although there were many black stars, most notably José Méndez, known as "the Black Matty" for his dazzling pitching against big league clubs in spring exhibition games, they could not be signed to American major league teams because of prejudice. Baseball magnates claimed that the

Cubans they signed were white Spaniards ("Castilians"), well-to-do, and from superior family backgrounds. However, outfielder Jacinto Calvo, who played for Cal Griffith's Washington Senators in 1913 and 1920, and pitcher José Acosta, who played for the Senators and the White Sox between 1920 and 1922, also played for black clubs. Veteran ballplayers were not happy with the presence of Cubans, afraid that they would take away jobs and cause an overall drop in salaries by accepting lower wages. However, the veterans did not have much to fear from the Cubans, or even from Native Americans, since just a handful became professional ballplayers and fewer still made the majors. Cubans and Indians together comprised well under 2 percent of all the major leaguers in the Progressive Era.[122]

Asians and African Americans were completely excluded from organized baseball because of racism, even though players were supposedly selected solely on the basis of merit. Few Asians other than Hawaiians played baseball during this period, and, compared with blacks, their omission received little attention. In 1915, however, two crises erupted when Pacific Coast League managers tried to hire Asians. Early in the season Walter McCredie of Portland tried to put a Chinese Hawaiian player on his roster, but the other players objected and he was released. After the end of the season Frank Chance, former manager of the Cubs and the Yankees and then owner and manager of the Los Angeles club, discovered an Asian player of great promise. But, fearing the wrath of his players and West Coast fans, he decided not to challenge local prejudices. One year later Jimmy Claxton, who had played with black teams, was signed by the Oakland Oaks of the Pacific Coast League after he was introduced by a part-Indian friend as Native American. He pitched on 28 May but was released six days later after another individual informed management that Claxton was of white, Native American, and African-American ancestry.[123]

The exclusion of blacks was especially significant since at least seventy-three players of African descent competed in organized baseball before the racial barriers were raised in 1898. The first African American to play for a white professional team was John W. "Bud" Fowler, who played for New Castle, Pennsylvania, in 1872. Twelve years later Moses Fleetwood Walker, a preacher's son who had studied at Oberlin and Michigan, became the first African-American major leaguer when his Toledo team of the Northwestern League joined the American Association in 1884. He was the starting catcher and batted .251. His younger brother Welday also played a few games for Toledo.[124]

These pioneer black players were poorly treated by teammates, opponents, and fans. In 1889 the *Sporting News* reported that "race prejudice exists in professional baseball to a marked degree, and the unfortunate son of Africa who makes his living as a member of a team of white professionals has a rocky road to travel." White players not only refused to socialize with black teammates or sit with them for group portraits but also tried to force them out of the sport. African Americans were given poor coaching, pitchers tried to bean them, and sliding runners tried to spike them. Fowler and second baseman Frank Grant, the best African-American ballplayer of the late nineteenth century, were forced to wear shinguards for protection.[125]

Spectators were equally ill-disposed toward black athletes, insulting them and threatening their lives. Late in the 1884 season Toledo's manager received a letter from Richmond a few weeks before a scheduled series there: "We the undersigned do hereby warn you not to put up Walker the negro catcher the evening that you play in Richmond, as we could mention the names of 75 determined men who have sworn to mob Walker if he comes on the grounds in a suit. We hope you will listen to our words of warning so that there will be no trouble; but if you do not there certainly will be. We only write this to prevent bloodshed, as you alone can prevent."[126] Fortunately for Walker, he was injured and did not play.

Certain white players, most notably Cap Anson, refused to play against blacks. On 11 August 1883 the White Stockings had an exhibition game scheduled against Walker's Toledo nine. Cap Anson refused to play ball "with no d——d nigger," implying that the African American's presence would "contaminate" his club. Walker had a sore hand and was not expected to play, but Manager Charley Morton put him in the lineup in right field. The game took place despite Anson's diatribe because Spalding wanted to collect on the guaranteed purse. The NL champion White Stockings won, 7-6 in ten innings.[127]

One year later the White Stockings scheduled another exhibition game against Toledo, now in the AA, after being promised by Morton that Walker would be kept out of the game. Spalding's secretary claimed that while "the management of the Chicago Ball Club have no personal feeling about the matter . . . the players do most decisively object," and Spalding wanted harmony in his clubhouse. Anson again refused to play if Walker participated. But the game went on with Walker catching for the home club. Three years later Anson again drew the color line when the White Stockings were scheduled to play an exhibition against Newark of the International League, whose star hurler, black lefthander George Stovey, was 34-14 that season. He was kept out of the game ostensibly because of illness, but actually to appease Anson. On the same day the International League directors decided by a vote of 6-4 (the minority was the four teams that still had blacks) to exclude African Americans from the league.[128]

The *Newark Call* sympathized with the black players:

If anywhere in this world the social barriers are broken down it is on the ball field. There many men of low birth and poor breeding are the idols of the rich and cultured; the best man is he who plays best. Even men of churlish dispositions and coarse hues are tolerated on the field. In view of these facts the objection to colored men is ridiculous. If social distinctions are to be made, half the players in the country will be shut out. Better make character and personal habits the test. Weed out the toughs and intemperate men first, and then it may be in order to draw the color line.[129]

Quotas soon emerged and owners agreed to stop signing new black players. Year by year there were fewer African Americans in organized baseball. After 1890 only three blacks played for predominantly white teams, but some primarily black teams continued to play in the low majors. In 1891 the Cuban Giants, a six-year-old professional African-American team, represented Ansonia of the Connecticut League, and in 1895 five or six men from the Page Fence Giants, also an African-American team, joined Adrian in the Michigan State League for a late season pennant drive. In 1898 the Acme Colored Giants represented Celoron, New York, in the Iron and Oil League. However, the team was mired in last place, and the players were released midseason. Thereafter African Americans were excluded from organized baseball except for one man who played in the Canadian League in 1899. The principal challenge to the color line during this period occurred during spring training of 1901 when Orioles manager John McGraw tried to pass off Charlie Grant of Chicago's Columbia Giants as Native American Charlie Tockahama. However, Charles Comiskey recognized Grant and ended that charade.[130]

Four years later Fred Tenney, manager of the Boston Nationals, reportedly intended to sign Harvard's star African-American shortstop William C. Matthews, who batted .300 or better for the Crimson in 1904 and 1905. Chicago Cubs president James A. Hart justified racial objections to the collegian: "I do not think it right to inflict him on others who have objections, or forcing white players to sleep in the same car with him and associate as informally as they would have to under such conditions."[131]

A minor challenge to baseball's racism arose in 1910, when the United States League was established outside the jurisdiction of organized baseball. This league promised to hire any able athlete regardless of race, and reportedly three of the first hundred players signed were black. However, this experiment was short-lived, for the league collapsed almost immediately after the start of the season.[132]

Discrimination in baseball matched the prejudice rampant in the broader society. Jim Crow customs were enacted into laws in the South and sanctioned by the inaction of Washington and the Supreme Court's 1896 decision in *Plessy v. Ferguson*. Just as blacks were being forced out of occupations in which they had been successful, like barbering and catering, they were being pushed out of professional cycling and horse racing. Sprint cyclist Major Taylor was barred from the southern racing circuit and white riders frequently ganged him to try to defeat him. Black jockeys had dominated racing for years, winning most runnings of the Kentucky Derby in the nineteenth century. However, the occupation was becoming quite lucrative, and by 1900 top riders earned retainers of over ten thousand dollars. This encouraged more whites to race and force out the black jockeys. African Americans were not pushed out of prizefighting, a sport that drew its participants from the lowest social classes. White fans enjoyed watching black boxers get beaten up, but felt threatened when they became major contenders. Heavyweight champion John L. Sullivan drew the color line against Australian Peter Jackson, but there were a few black champions in lighter weight classifications, most notably George Dixon, bantamweight (1888–91) and featherweight champion (1891–1900), and lightweight Joe Gans (1902–8). In 1908 after the outspoken and fiercely independent Jack Johnson won the heavyweight title and became a symbolic threat to whites, opportunities in boxing for blacks became increasingly limited (New York soon banned interracial bouts), especially shots at world championships.[133]

African Americans had their own professional baseball teams and even a short-lived league prior to their exclusion from organized baseball. The first pro African-American team was probably the Philadelphia Orions, established in 1882, although it was overshadowed by the Cuban Giants, organized in 1885 by Frank Thompson, a hotel worker, in Babylon, Long Island. The club was composed of players drawn from the Orions and two other squads. Thompson nicknamed them "Giants" for

New York's popular major league team and "Cubans" in hopes of avoiding racism. They worked at the Hotel Argyle, played ball to entertain the guests, and competed against black and white clubs, including the Philadelphia Athletics. The following winter they played at a St. Augustine, Florida, hotel. In the spring of 1886 Walter Cook, a businessman, brought the club to his hometown of Trenton, New Jersey, and put the players on salaries that ranged from twelve to eighteen dollars a week. The Cuban Giants were originally regarded as a novelty, but received favorable reviews from sportswriters and white players. They were good enough to play exhibitions against the New York Metropolitans and the Philadelphia Athletics of the American Association in 1885 and subsequently played against several NL teams. The Athletics were so impressed by first baseman Arthur Thomas that they supposedly offered him a major league contract. In 1889, reinforced with the addition of star pitcher George Stovey and star infielder Frank Grant, the Cuban Giants represented Trenton in the white Middle States League.[134]

Top African-American clubs in the early twentieth century played high quality baseball. They were competitive in their occasional games against major league teams, all-star aggregates played on Sundays, and postseason series. Between 1903 and 1906, for instance, Rube Foster and his team, the Philadelphia Giants, reportedly beat the Dodgers, the Giants, and both Philadelphia major league teams. Although white players, managers, and journalists often praised the abilities of black athletes, they were embarrassed to lose to semipros, especially blacks. Ty Cobb, a notorious bigot, refused to play African Americans after his poor showing in Cuba in 1910. In a 1916 attempt to avoid further embarrassment, baseball's national commission began requiring barnstormers to obtain their clubs' written consent before playing during the off-season; fifty-one players were subsequently fined for violations. In 1917 Charles Ebbets fined star pitcher Rube Marquard one hundred dollars after he lost a postseason exhibition game to the Lincoln Giants: "The Brooklyn team is averse to permitting its team, or any of its players, participating in games with Negroes. There are only semi-professional Negro teams, and when there is an outcome like yesterday's game, when Rube was beaten, President Ebbets believes it tends to lower the caliber of ball played by the big league in the eyes of the public, and at the same time make the major league team the subject of ridicule."[135]

A *St. Louis Post-Dispatch* reporter maintained that black ballplayers were actually superior to their white counterparts because of their physiognomy: "It is in baseball that the descendant of Ham is at his athletic best. Less removed from the anthropoid ape, he gets down on ground balls better, springs higher for liners, has a stronger and surer grip, and gets in and out of a base on all fours in a way that makes the higher product of evolution look like a bush leaguer." He predicted that whites would eventually be superseded by blacks in baseball, as they had been in boxing.[136]

Most black semiprofessionals in the early twentieth century were southern railroad porters, waiters, or government employees who played baseball on weekends. The very best made baseball their full-time jobs, working for teams like the Chicago Giants. They were busy twelve months a year, touring the Midwest during the week, playing in the prestigious Chicago City League on weekends, and working in California leagues or for Florida hotels during the winter. Touring teams played up to two hundred games a year, traveled by modest means, stayed at whichever hotel would admit them, and were paid on an irregular basis. Sol White, a former ballplayer and author of the *History of Colored Baseball* (1907), estimated that the average black player at the turn of the century was paid around $466 compared with $571 for minor leaguers and $2,000 for major leaguers. Robert Peterson, the doyen of black baseball historians, found that between 1910 and 1919 typical black ballplayers were paid $40 to $75 a month, while stars received $105. The highest reported salary of $250 a month was paid to the great John Henry Lloyd in 1917. Full-time players earned wages comparable to black letter carriers and school teachers, and some stars were better paid than school principals. Nevertheless, black ballplayers were not highly regarded by the black middle class, who considered them unrespectable and irresponsible and barred them from some neighborhoods.[137]

Most profits from black baseball, however, ended up in white hands. Nearly all the early black clubs were owned by whites, and the traveling teams scheduled their games through Nat Strong, a powerful white booking agent with Tammany connections, who was president of the Intercity Association from 1907 until his death in 1935. He controlled several New York fields and had major interests in five African-American teams. Strong became the leading agent in the East, charging 10 percent to arrange games and forcing the few African-American owners to accept disadvantageous terms, such as one-hundred-dollar guarantees for profitable Sunday doubleheaders in New York. Teams that refused to do business on Strong's terms were often blocked from getting ball games.[138]

In 1905 several eastern club owners formed the National Association of Colored Professional Clubs of the United States and Cuba. It was not actually a league with a championship season, but rather a booking agency for traveling teams and a means to curtail players from jumping teams. Walter Schlichter, a prominent owner of Philadelphia African-American teams and sports editor of the *Philadelphia Item*, was president, and Strong was secretary. They imposed salary limits and impeded bookings for teams that did not cooperate. In 1911 Strong led a fight to oust the politically connected cafe proprietor John W. Connor of the Brooklyn Royal Giants, the only African-American club owner in New York. Connor had refused to accept Strong's stipulations of a fixed guarantee rather than the customary, and more profitable, percentage of the gate. Connor obtained control of the Harlem Oval (142d and Lenox Avenue) and booked his own games against teams outside the National Association. But he had a hard time getting good bookings, and by 1913 Strong took over the Royal Giants.[139]

In 1920 Rube Foster organized the Negro National Baseball League to wrest control of black baseball from white domination. There were eight franchises, all but Kansas City's owned and operated by blacks. Foster served as president and secretary. He was a strong race man who felt that since the players and two-thirds of the spectators at the games were black, the profits should wind up in black hands. Foster promoted competition by sending some of his own players, including star Oscar Charleston, to weaker teams. Foster hoped that this league would not only encourage opportunities for black capitalists but also generate jobs for blacks on and off the diamond, as scouts, umpires, clerks, and secretaries.[140]

African-American ballplayers worked to break the color line, enter the majors, and share the prestige and high salaries of white big leaguers. In the early 1900s they pinned their aspirations on the success of Cubans and Native Americans, hoping their presence indicated a liberalized attitude toward men of color. The advancement of light-skinned Cubans was watched with particular interest by African-American players and journalists such as Lester Walton, sports editor of the *New York Age*, a leading black newspaper. Walton wrote at the end of the 1911 season: "With the admission of Cubans of a darker hue in the two big leagues it would then be easy for colored players who are citizens of this country to get into fast company. Until the public gets accustomed to seeing Negroes on big league teams, the colored players should keep their mouths shut and pass for Cubans."[141] Rumors had circulated for years that certain major leaguers identified as white, Cuban, or Indian were actually black. Catcher Vincent "Sandy" Nava and outfielder George Treadway were suspected of passing for white. Nava played for Providence in 1882–

84 and for Baltimore the next two years, while Treadway played for three NL teams (1893–96).[142]

The experience of blacks in baseball was quite different from that of the new immigrants. White newcomers were poorly represented until the mid-1930s, but at least they were present and theoretically had an equal chance of making the majors once well assimilated. Their disadvantages reflected their class and social environment—lack of places to play, poor coaching, bad equipment, and parental disapproval. But black athletes had no chance at all. Black youths did not have to become acculturated into the American sporting tradition because it was already part of their culture. Although the finest African-American ballplayers were acknowledged by experts as sufficiently skilled to play in the majors, their skin color eliminated them from any possible consideration.

Social Mobility among Retired Professional Ballplayers

The career history of professional athletes has always been quite different from those in other occupations because their tenure is so short. An average major leaguer in the early 1900s lasted about three years. Even if we discount those who lasted just a few weeks or seldom played (while remaining on the roster), then the mean is closer to eight years, which meant retirement at an early age. Ballplayers seldom played past their midthirties, when speed and reflexes slowed down and left them unable to compete with younger, fleeter, and lower-paid players. When dropped from the majors, the typical player usually went down to the minors and eventually drifted out of baseball. Facing retirement could be a severe psychological crisis for players because of their uncertain future and almost certain loss of status and income. Even the most easygoing athletes worried about their futures as they aged, aware of the stories of prior players who ended up indigent. These fears were reflected in the high suicide rate among former professional ballplayers.[143]

Most professional ballplayers never even made the major leagues, but little data about their subsequent occupations exist. Contemporaries believed these men obtained poor-paying, low-prestige jobs such as gas station attendants or bartenders. Such men presumably were not well educated, lacked savings to start businesses, and had little fame, except perhaps in their hometowns or in cities where they had once played. Their athletic experience was probably not useful in helping them obtain good jobs, and compared with major leaguers a higher proportion probably became manual laborers.

Some scanty evidence exists on the jobs of certain Atlanta Crackers who never made the majors. In 1902 Al Weinfeld, Atlanta correspondent for the *Sporting News,* surveyed the whereabouts of the 1895 Crackers. Three were still in baseball, three had manual jobs, and seven held non-manual jobs (two were eastern politicians, two were hotel keepers, one was a railroad clerk, one was a cigar store owner, and one was an Atlanta pool hall proprietor). Later Atlanta players obtained similar jobs as well as positions in baseball as minor league managers, scouts, and college coaches. One player married the owner's daughter and became an executive with the Crackers. Hometown players, especially local collegians who remained in the Gate City, apparently did quite well, securing good paying positions that entailed public contact, such as salesmen and managers or else opening their own businesses. These data suggest that minor leaguers, particularly the better educated, could fare well after baseball.[144]

Most major leaguers were unprepared for any particular occupation when they retired, excluding those related to baseball. The conventional wisdom was that ballplayers fared poorly after leaving the diamond, usually ending up as bartenders or saloon owners. A 1905 report in the *Sporting News* claimed that 80 percent of retirees made under twelve hundred dollars a year, or less than a rookie's annual salary. A press survey in 1911 of thirty-four old-timers who had passed away that year revealed that many had ended up as common laborers and had squandered their baseball earnings.[145]

I accumulated data on the subsequent work histories of 478 men out of a total sample of 593 who played at least one full season in either Chicago or New York between 1900 and 1919 (see table 6). After their typical eight-year major league careers, they retired to jobs that were much better than contemporaries realized. The principal job of four-fifths (82.4 percent) was white collar; 14.1 percent became blue-collar workers; and just 3.6 percent became farmers. The new jobs seldom paid as well as baseball, but were much better then those of the 1871–82 cohort, one-third of whom (35.6 percent) became manual laborers.[146]

Although only a small percentage (5.9 percent) of former ballplayers became professionals, this was twice the percentage of all male Americans in 1910 who did. This number reflects the high percentage of college attendees—one-fourth had attended or completed college. These successful men were mainly engineers, doctors, and lawyers, and others were accountants, dentists, teachers, and pharmacists who later became players. They often found it difficult to sustain their professional careers while

Table 6. Subsequent Jobs of Retired Major League Baseball Players, 1900–1959 (Percentage)

Occupational Category	1900–1919 N = 478	1920–39 N = 321	1940–59 N = 216	1950–59 N = 790
High white-collar				
Professionals	5.9	10.3	7.4	7.8
Managers, high officials, and major proprietors	19.0	10.0	8.8	14.1
	24.9	20.3	16.2	21.9
Low white-collar				
Clerks, sales, and kindred workers	10.0	20.2	28.3	24.5
Semiprofessionals	33.5	24.3	26.9	29.9
Petty proprietors, managers, and low officials	14.0	12.1	11.6	10.9
	57.5	56.6	66.8	65.3
Total white-collar	82.4	76.9	83.0	87.2
Farm	3.6	4.5	1.9	0.9
Blue-collar				
Skilled	3.8	4.7	7.4	4.7
Semiskilled and service	8.8	13.1	6.9	6.5
Unskilled	1.5	0.9	0.9	0.6
	14.1	18.7	15.2	11.8
Grand total	100.1[a]	100.1[a]	100.1[a]	99.9[a]

Sources: Data on men who played at least one year in Chicago or New York between 1900 and 1919 drawn from Allen, *Notebooks;* study data on 321 men active between 1920 and 1939 and study data from a sample of 216 men active between 1940 and 1959 in Chicago or New York collected from Vertical Files, National Baseball Library, Cooperstown, N.Y.; data on players active between 1950 and 1959 drawn from Rich Marazzi and Len Fiorito, *Aaron to Zuverink: A Nostalgic Look at the Baseball Players of the Fifties* (Briarcliff, N.J, 1982).

Note: Occupational categories taken from Thernstrom, *Other Bostonians,* 290–92.

a. Does not total 100.0 due to rounding.

playing baseball and dropped them for good, like licensed dentists Dave Danforth and Doc White, neither of whom returned to their professions after retiring from the diamond. Some highly motivated men studied during the off-season and later practiced their professions; Davy Jones and Doc Casey operated drug stores after retiring.[147]

Retirees who held other high-level, white-collar jobs were primarily either baseball executives or government officials, although there were also bankers, brokers, factory owners, and business managers. Some time after retirement, 5 percent of the former players owned or operated professional or semiprofessional baseball teams. Clark Griffith, the former star Highlanders pitcher, became president and owner of the Washington Senators in 1919. Other former players usually got into the business at a more modest level, since they lacked the requisite capital, but got backing from friends or an old boss. Charles Comiskey helped some former players, including Frank Isbell, purchase minor league teams, and in return expected first choice of any prospects. Certain former players who became baseball executives were mainly figureheads, like the ailing Christy Mathewson, president of the Boston Braves from 1923 to 1925, when he died, or Casey Stengel, manager and president of the Worcester Eastern League nine in 1925.[148]

Retired nineteenth-century players often ended up working for their municipality, mainly in service jobs such as police officer or fire fighter, but the later cohort also held more prominent roles. About one in fourteen (7.1 percent) held an executive-level job in government sometime after retirement. Some worked in big cities where they might utilize a former owner's political clout, while in small towns they were often the most famous resident and used their fame to get elected to public office. Dodgers pitching star Nap Rucker was his community's water commissioner, while Del Howard was mayor of Kearney, Illinois.[149]

Most retirees were concentrated in the lower status, white-collar occupations (57.5 percent), particularly in athletics. Former players often maintained their middle-class status by utilizing their expertise to secure jobs in baseball. The primary jobs of 146 former Chicago and New York major leaguers (30.5 percent) were as managers, coaches, scouts, and umpires. They were nearly three times as likely to remain in baseball than ballplayers active in the period 1871–82, when only about 11 percent secured such occupations. Furthermore, at some time after retirement nearly half (46.4 percent) of my entire sample of 593 worked in some aspect of athletics. The greatly increased opportunities in baseball resulted from its growing popularity in the early 1900s and the accompanying expansion of professional and amateur baseball throughout the United States.

Retired major leaguers had an excellent chance to become minor league managers. At some time after retirement, one-fourth (149) of the entire sample worked as minor league managers, and it was the principal occupation for 10.5 percent. This job required expertise in baseball, which former major leaguers presumably possessed. The typical big leaguer who ended up as a minor league manager had played 9.5 years in the majors, or about 1.5 years more than the average man in my sample. Minor league managing was a popular job among retirees because it enabled them to maintain a close association with baseball, provided training for a possible big league post, and, in the top minors, was well compensated. In 1917, for instance, Harry Wolverton was paid six thousand dollars to manage the Los Angeles Angels.[150]

Major league managers were chosen almost exclusively from the ranks of former stars. Managers comprised 9.8 percent of the entire sample (58), and it was the principal job for 4.7 percent (28). Their median playing tenure was fourteen years, surpassed only by coaches (usually the manager's cronies), who played over fifteen seasons. Virtually no one became a big league manager without major league experience as a player, but big league managers rarely had prior managerial experience. The exceptional managers without playing experience were usually owners or club executives temporarily filling in, like Horace Fogel of the Giants, who managed forty-two games in 1902. The large incidence of stars as managers differs markedly from modern recruitment patterns. Several of the best recent managers, such as Tony LaRussa and Sparky Anderson, were either fringe players or had no major league experience at all. In the past managerial selection was often based on the false premise that outstanding performers would make the best managers because they could readily instruct others, plot strategy, and gain respect from players because of their reputation. Owners slowly realized that just because a talented athlete played baseball well did not necessarily mean he could teach or lead others. Stars like Ty Cobb and Rogers Hornsby did not have the temperament required for leadership or the patience needed to get the best out of their teams.

A big league manager's position was tenuous, rarely lasting more than a few years. Managers were quickly fired if the team did not win since it was easier to fire one man than the whole team. Despite the perils, the job was highly coveted because it was prestigious and well paying. By 1910 the best managers were already earning five-figure salaries. The most prominent manager was John J. McGraw, a public celebrity who in 1917 earned thirty thousand dollars a year. Players saw the job as a fitting climax to an outstanding career. Babe Ruth's biggest disappointment was that he was never hired to manage after he retired. But, of course, he could not even manage himself.[151]

Umpiring was another job in baseball for retirees, although just 3.4 percent (21) of my sample ever worked as arbiters. It was a low-status and dangerous job in the nineteenth century, when there was just one umpire at a game, and these conditions continued into the early 1900s. Umpires were often verbally harassed by fans, players, and owners. In 1901 Giants owner Andrew Freedman was so dissatisfied with Billy Nash's umpiring that he barred him from the Polo Grounds. Far more serious episodes involved players punching umpires and spectators throwing rotten eggs or bottles at them. In 1907 second-year umpire Billy Evans was knocked unconscious by a bottle thrown by a disgruntled teenage fan at a St. Louis Browns game at Sportsmen's Park. The umpire's travail was not helped by the failure of the NL to rotate the arbiters (Tom Lynch in 1897 refereed sixty-three games involving Boston) or stand up for them. Sometimes umpires lost control and responded violently to abuse, fighting with disrespectful players or fans. In 1897 umpire Tim Hurst was jailed after a game in Cincinnati when he was hit on the foot by a heavy beer mug. Hurst threw it back at the crowd and injured a spectator.[152]

Working conditions for umpires improved during the early years of the twentieth century because of the implementation of a two-umpire system by 1909, declining rowdyism, the building of large modern ballparks where fans were farther from the playing field, and the efforts of AL president Ban Johnson to back up his umpires. There was less than half as much turnover among AL umpires compared to those in the NL. In the early 1900s most salaries ranged from $1,500 to $2,000, with a top of $3,000. The best umpires supplemented their income by working the World Series, which paid $400, raised in 1918 to $650. Umpire salaries rose rapidly in the next two decades, reaching a range of $4,000 to $10,000 in 1937.[153]

The growing popularity of baseball and the improving prestige of the profession enabled at least 5.9 percent (35) of the entire cohort to become college coaches. After the turn of the century some colleges began hiring former pros as full-time coaches, although faculties expected this would have a deleterious influence, particularly on recruiting, retention, and fair play, since they assumed these coaches would do whatever was necessary to win.[154]

Major colleges and universities tended to hire former major leaguers, while smaller colleges frequently hired local minor leaguers. Ray Fisher at Michigan and Harry Wolters at Stanford were former Yankees who became successful college coaches, keeping their well-paying, prestigious jobs for over twenty years. Former big leaguers who became college coaches had usually been capable players, lasting about eight years in the majors, and had often attended college, which athletic directors preferred. They believed these men could communicate and relate well to the varsity ballplayers as well as support university ideals and traditions.

There were also opportunities outside baseball for former major leaguers to utilize their fame. Retirees whose primary jobs were as sales-men, clerks, and related occupations comprised 9.6 percent of the sam-ple, and many others held secondary jobs in this category. Sometime after retirement better than one in nine worked in either sales (7.8 per-cent) or real estate (3.8 percent). They were hired by firms that hoped to take advantage of their famous names to lure potential customers. Sales work capitalized on an athlete's reputation because it placed him in di-rect contact with the public. Another 6.4 percent were clerks or inspec-tors, two-fifths of whom were government employees.

Retirees who were either small businessmen or petty officials (13.4 percent) were usually involved in enterprises in their hometowns or cities where they had once played. They operated all sorts of shops, but were mainly concentrated in recreational ventures, such as bowling al-leys, billiard parlors, and sporting goods stores (3.6 percent) and taverns (2.2 percent), the same kinds of businesses the 1870s cohort had oper-ated. The decline in the liquor trade was partly a consequence of Prohibi-tion and the closing of taverns, but mainly a result of ballplayers' im-proved status and the growth of the white-collar job sector.

The proportion of ballplayers who ended up as farmers was small. Although about two out of every five major leaguers came from rural regions, and one out of five had farming fathers, just 7.7 percent of my sample ever worked on farms after retirement, and a mere 3.6 percent made farming their life's work. This is understandable since former play-ers could not use their fame or athletic expertise to any advantage as farmers.[155]

Ballplayers who became manual workers suffered enormous losses in income and prestige. Blue-collar work was the principal job for 14.0 per-cent (another 5.6 percent worked with their hands at some time after leaving baseball). Retirees who became manual laborers were more likely to drop from prominence than their more successful teammates, and thus their numbers may have been underestimated, but certainly no more than one-fifth of the major leaguers in the early 1900s worked at blue-collar jobs.[156] Retirees who became artisans (3.8 percent) generally worked at secure, well-paying trades they had learned before becoming professional ballplayers. Nearly three-fourths of the blue-collar men were semiskilled or service workers, with 8.6 percent working as either police officers, security guards, or fire fighters at some time after baseball. Government work was still popular because of the adequate pay and excellent security.

Blue-collar workers could supplement their wages by playing and coaching weekend semiprofessional baseball teams. By the 1910s industrial leagues were well established in manufacturing centers like Detroit and Cleveland. These leagues had often been established as part of welfare capitalism programs that sought to discourage strikes and encourage employee loyalty. Industrial leagues received a tremendous boost during World War I, when many big leaguers sought essential industrial employment, which exempted them from the draft. Companies readily signed up professional athletes, not for the assembly line, but to play baseball for the company nine. White Sox players Joe Jackson, Lefty Williams, and Byrd Lynn played for Harlan and Hollingsworth in Wilmington, Delaware, in 1918 and won the Delaware River Shipbuilding League. After the war these leagues became even more popular. Companies in these leagues occasionally hired former professional ballplayers at higher wages with the expectation that they would play or manage.[157]

Just a handful of former players (1.5 percent) ended up at the bottom of the social structure as unskilled laborers. These few players included both uneducated fringe players and college-trained stars. Hal Chase and Buck Herzog were college-trained professionals who became major league player-managers, yet they both died indigent.[158]

Chase was the son of a prosperous lumber dealer in Los Gatos, California, and briefly played college ball at St. Mary's. He played in the majors from 1905 to 1919 and was at one time among the highest paid players. However, he left organized baseball in disgrace as a fixer and gambler. Chase became a player and part owner of the San Jose club in the independent semiprofessional Mission League and apparently continued his errant ways. He was accused of trying to fix games in the Mission League, which banned him, and also in the Pacific Coast League, which barred him from its ballparks. Chase ended up as an alcoholic and a drifter. During the depression he washed cars for a Civil Works Administration project.[159]

The new occupation of retired ballplayers active in the early 1900s depended on such factors as fame, length of service, social background, education, and even personality. There was normally a close correlation between tenure and fame, since the more famous players usually had the longer careers. Blue-collar workers had the shortest average major league tenure (7.82 years) compared with farmers (8.12 years) and white-collar workers (9.23 years), who played nearly one and a half years longer than their blue-collar colleagues. They were most likely to utilize their fame to help them get started. Athletic renown was of greatest benefit to men who remained in baseball after retirement. On average they had the longest careers (10.07 years), about a year and a half longer than players who did not stay in baseball (8.62 years). Yet fame, as the sociologist Rudolph Haerle Jr. has pointed out, was crucial only in determining a player's initial occupation. Thereafter other variables, including that first position, became more important in determining the main job.[160]

The most important variables in determining a player's principal occupation were education and social background. Over 93 percent of the college-educated respondents ended up with white-collar jobs, and virtually all the rest became farmers. On the other hand, 67.5 percent of those with no college education got white-collar jobs, one-fourth ended up in manual occupations, and the rest were farmers. Social background was nearly as important in determining a player's future, even though he was in his thirties by the time he left baseball. Eighty-five percent of players with white-collar backgrounds ended up with nonmanual jobs. By comparison, 77 percent of players with fathers who farmed and 58 percent of players with fathers who performed manual labor ended up working in nonmanual occupations. Here is another way of looking at the relationship between a father and his big league son: a farmer's son was four times more likely to become a farmer after retiring from baseball than any other son was. A manual laborer's son was three times as likely to become a blue-collar worker than the son of a skilled worker and six times as likely to do so as the son of a farmer. The typical big leaguer's future class could be better predicted by his education and his social class than by his batting average or his won-loss percentage.[161]

Social background was important for several reasons. Middle-class youngsters usually had a better education, which helped them secure good jobs. They were encouraged by their parents and teachers to have high expectations and were taught certain traditional bourgeois values like thrift and deferral of present gratification for future investment, which better prepared them for retirement. In general, ballplayers from poor families did not get the same kind of encouragement when they were growing up. Their families rarely had much money, so when these players received their lucrative paychecks they were not prepared to save some of the money for the future. Such athletes often spent their wages almost as soon as they were paid, if not before. They often had to seek salary advances before the season started because they were broke.[162] Further, many lower-class players spent money freely to demonstrate their success to themselves, their friends, and their teammates.

The occupations of retired major league baseball players in subsequent decades differed only modestly from those of the men active in

1900–1919. There was a decline in white-collar employment in the 1920–39 cohort to 76.9 percent, probably because many retired during the Depression Era, and this percentage remained about the same in the 1940s (78.5 percent). In the 1950s, however, seven out of eight (87.3 percent) players took white-collar jobs. These variances reflect the changing American economy, the ups and downs of baseball's popularity, the impact of World War II, and the changing social and ethnic backgrounds of players. Major leaguers of the 1920s and 1930s had a rough retirement because of the depression. In the 1940s cohort, more players were from blue-collar origins than white-collar ones for probably the first time in the century. Players in the 1950s, in contrast, had the advantage of middle-class backgrounds, the benefits of televised games, which enhanced their fame, and the ease of retirement during a prosperous era.

◇

The public's conception of the professional baseball player during the Progressive Era was largely inaccurate. Ballplayers were not reared in rural regions, were not poorly educated, and did not come from the bottom of the social ladder. They mostly came from cities, were relatively well educated, and were sons of skilled workers and high-income manual laborers. Retired players suffered a decline in income, but generally managed to obtain respectable white-collar jobs, frequently in baseball. Their rate of falling into the manual class was not much greater than that of contemporary urban white-collar workers.[163]

Professional baseball was vastly overrated as a source of vertical mobility during the early twentieth century. The number of major league positions varied from time to time but never exceeded four hundred (except for the Federal league era), tenure was short compared with that of other occupations, and most players were upper lower-class and middle-class and native-born whites or of old immigrant stock. The high pay and prestige of baseball attracted sons of respectable families. Opportunities were quite limited for lower-class youngsters seeking an alternate route to social advancement. They had to compete for the few major league openings with lower middle-class youths, who had more opportunities to play and practice, superior competition, finer coaching, and better equipment. Virtually none of the major leaguers were children of recent immigrants from eastern or southern Europe, who were in the lowest social classes. Baseball did not fit in well with their cultures and inner-city lifestyles, they had few role models, and parents strongly disapproved of playing sports. If they made it into organized baseball these ballplayers frequently encountered discrimination. Second-generation immigrants from Italy, Poland, and Russia had very little success in competing for highly sought major league jobs until the middle years of the depression, by which time they were well acculturated and better prepared to compete on an equal footing with more established Americans. African Americans, Asians, and women, unfortunately, did not even need to apply.

Conclusion

The Social Functions of Professional Baseball

> These are the saddest of possible words,
>   Tinkers to Evers to Chance;
> Trio of bear cubs and fleeter than birds,
>   Tinkers to Evers to Chance;
> Thoughtlessly pricking our gonfallon bubble
> Making a Giants hit into a double—
> Words that are weighty with nothing but trouble
>   Tinkers to Evers to Chance
>
>   —Franklin P. Adams, 1908

A substantial disparity existed between the ideology of baseball, which presented the sport in its most favorable light, and the realities of the game. The baseball creed constituted a cultural fiction that, though inaccurate, influenced the way people behaved and thought.[1] The truth did not matter since baseball operated as a means of describing and reinforcing the values that regulated behavior and goal achievement as well as determined suitable solutions to specific social problems. The principal values and goals of the core middle-class culture were expressed through the national pastime's history, folklore, and heroes. The values implicit in the rhetoric of baseball were those associated with a traditional, bourgeois, small-town society.

The baseball creed stood for fair play, gentlemanly virtue, self-reliance, middle-class decorum, community pride, and rural traditions. This ideology was an important stage in the development of the broader contemporary American sports ideology, which claims that sports participation improves character development and discipline, promotes physical and mental fitness, encourages competition, advances nationalism, and provides a source of social mobility.[2]

Elements of the baseball creed dated back to the days of amateur baseball in the 1860s, but it was not until the early 1900s, when the game was fully institutionalized, that a systematic mythology was completely developed and gained widespread acceptance. As fully articulated, that social construct touched base with the prevailing broad-based progressive ethos that promoted efficiency, order, traditional values, social control, and acculturation. The ideology differentiated baseball from boxing and horse racing, both commercialized sports that had little in common with conventional middle-class patterns of thought and behavior. At the same time, the increasingly popular upper middle-class game of college football was developing a forward-looking ideology emphasizing industrial, bureaucratic, and democratic values, while baseball's primarily looked back to a glorious past. Football's ideology would have enormous appeal once Americans were comfortable identifying themselves as a modernized nation, but in the early 1900s the notion of mass team play seemed somehow un-American.[3]

The baseball ideology had both instrumental and symbolic functions. Symbolically, baseball represented prevailing American beliefs and values; instrumentally the game purportedly improved its participants and spectators in socially beneficial ways. Baseball was expected to teach its fans the dominant WASP belief system and serve as a bulwark against social developments that challenged or threatened the core culture. From the earliest days of the Massachusetts Bay Colony, "respectable" Americans expected to spend their free time "usefully" and not merely amusing themselves. Puritans and other middle-class colonists stressed that leisure activities needed to be moral, performed in moderation, and socially functional. Rifle-shooting was sanctioned because it prepared for hunting and defense, but shuffleboard and billiards were stopped because they did not improve useful skills and encouraged gambling. This ethic, however, did not apply to the powerful Virginia planters and others with aristocratic pretensions who approved of amusements for the sake of pleasure, especially when they helped promote social differentiation.[4] Nor did it apply to the "boys of pleasure," members of the antebellum male bachelor subculture who enjoyed such amusements as gambling, gouging, boxing, and cockfighting.

The popularity of organized sports in midnineteenth-century America required proof of salutary benefits for participants. Early support for sports came from such Enlightenment thinkers as Benjamin Franklin, Thomas Jefferson, and Dr. Benjamin Rush, who argued on behalf of the Greek ideal of the unity of a sound body and a sound mind, and such noted European educators as Johann Pestalozzi, who asserted that vigorous exercise was important for the mental and physical growth of youngsters. In the 1830s and 1840s social reformers, health professionals and faddists, and evangelical Christians concerned about overcrowded cities, rising rates of crime, public health, debilitating sedentary middle-class lifestyles, materialism, vile amusements, and the loss of pastoral values promoted a variety of reforms, such as temperance, municipal parks, and rational recreation, to improve the lives of city folk. They urged urbanites to participate in gymnastics, swimming, and other physical activities to improve their health, morality, and character, holding up as positive examples contemporary robust Oxbridge athletes and German immigrants who belonged to turner societies. Critics encouraged rowing and yachting to promote international sporting competition and other sports, like cricket and especially baseball, that stood for fair play, rugged individualism, and community pride. After the Civil War, Brahmins like MIT president Francis A. Walker promoted American football as a moral equivalent of war. Furthermore, employers stopped assuming that workers would "waste" free time with escapist amusements and tried to indoctrinate them to "re-create" themselves so they would return to work on Monday ready to do a good job.[5]

According to the conventional wisdom at the turn of the century, baseball was a useful entertainment because of its social functions. Baseball was supposed to promote order and social integration by improving character development and discipline, encouraging community pride, acculturating newcomers, and providing opportunities for social mobility. Opinion makers expected that ballplayers and spectators would cultivate many of the finest American qualities, such as competitiveness, honesty, patience, respect for authority, and rugged individualism, traits that previous Americans had supposedly developed on the frontier. Baseball became for many old stock Americans an extension of the frontier into the depraved cities, where it could indoctrinate the new urban folk into the core society's value system.

Youngsters were expected to learn proper traditional values by playing baseball and by emulating heroes like the great batsman Ty Cobb, who, by practicing hour after hour, demonstrated the importance of hard work for getting ahead. Boys mastered proper moral conduct by copying the behavior of their idols, ballplayers who supposedly abstained from smoking, drinking, and other unseemly behaviors. Young players experienced competition, "valor and endurance . . . , grace under pressure and dignity in defeat." They were taught to be altruistic and cooperative by sacrificing their own at-bat for the good of the team.[6]

The acculturation process for second-generation newcomers was allegedly aided through their participation in the sport's rituals. Spectatorial rites included such patterned behavior as rooting for the home team, booing visiting teams, jeering umpires, and arguing about the game with other fans. Old stock Americans interpreted the simple act of learning to accept the umpire's authority as a valuable civics lesson. The didactic function of baseball was important to frightened native white Americans worried about their country's future as millions of newcomers from eastern and southern Europe flocked into American cities.

Baseball supposedly also helped keep fully assimilated Americans involved in society. These people saw their traditional values and beliefs operating successfully at the ballpark and on the playing field. Their belief system still appeared to be valid and relevant despite great contemporary social changes. Participation in baseball's rituals encouraged community pride among fans who identified with their hometown team and its accomplishments. They were proud of the local club, which they identified as an index of their city's progressivism. Furthermore, since white men intermixed at games, a man from virtually any class or ethnic group could momentarily feel he was just as good as anyone else. For a few hours in the afternoon, he realized a part of the American Dream.

Baseball also theoretically helped integrate urban society by serving as a source of social control. Attending baseball games was seen as a safety valve, a substitute for public dissension. Disgruntled workers could scream and yell all they wanted at the baseball grounds, where such conduct was acceptable and harmless. It was much healthier for society that the alienated and disappointed act out their hostilities at the baseball field than in the streets or at home. Their anger would be left at the ball game, and they would go home exhilarated and sober, prepared to work efficiently the following day.

The sport's final ascribed function was as an avenue of social mobility. Professional baseball supposedly provided jobs for hard-working, ambitious, and talented young men regardless of their social origins. Such opportunities would promote social integration because it gave all young men faith and confidence in America. The range of ethnic groups in the major leagues provided evidence that the sport recruited solely on merit, which indicated to second-generation youths that there was a place for them in the broader society. If talented and hard working, they could achieve their personal goals.

One must be cautious in evaluating the success of baseball's purported latent functions, however. How does one quantify the relationship between pride in the home team and identification with the city? Many fans took great pride in their team's accomplishments as a vicarious means of affirming their own self-worth and merit. But loyalties frequently waned if the club did badly, since the team's performance might reflect poorly upon fans. It has never been proven that identification with a sports team is transferable to other institutions. Sports ideologists have suggested without substantiation that the excitement of late season pennant races in Boston in 1967, Detroit in 1968, and New York in 1969 helped deter riots in those cities. Some journalists even posited that Mayor John Lindsay owed his reelection in 1969 to the Mets' drive to the world championship, which deflected attention from the political campaign.[7]

The assumption that watching a baseball game can be cathartic by enabling fans to relieve their frustrations and aggression through participation in the rituals of spectatorship has not been tested. There have been investigations, however, into the role of other sports as a safety valve for pent-up emotions. The social psychologists Robert Goldstein and Jeffrey Arms studied the impact on male spectators of observing aggressive and nonaggressive sports and found that hostility increased significantly after seeing a football game but not after watching a gymnastics meet. Leonard Berkowitz examined the impact on college students of watching violent boxing scenes from the movie *Champion* and found that his subjects became more instead of less aggressive. Most evidence suggests that viewing aggressive sports will not promote catharsis but will instead produce more aggression.[8] Watching a game, then, probably has little if any cathartic influence and may actually prompt more hostility.

The value of baseball as an educational and socializing institution is appealing and plausible, but not necessarily valid. Crucial to many aspects of the sport's integrative mechanisms was the fundamental assumption that baseball was a democratic participatory and spectator sport. But kids living in inner-city areas had less opportunity to play the game than other youngsters, and not everyone, particularly working-class youths, could attend games in the early 1900s and participate in the rituals of spectatorship. Furthermore, professional baseball's recruitment patterns were not democratic since African Americans were excluded and recent immigrants were few and far between on big league rosters.

One carefully studied aspect of the sports creed has been its character-building component. The psychologists Bruce C. Ogilvie and Thomas A. Tutko examined the character-building capabilities of participatory sports and found little substantiation. They argued that the kinds of people attracted to competitive athletics are those who have already developed emotional stability, self-control, and social responsibility and can accept the consequences of failure. The sociologist Harry Edwards pointed out that coaches do not recruit athletes with "bad character" who need to be molded into responsible young adults. They have no time for troublemakers. Edwards further noted that the great emphasis on winning led to cheating and recruiting violations and a deemphasis on fair play. Ogilvie and Tutko recommended, "If you want to build character, try something else."[9] These conclusions do not support baseball's dubious claims for players' social and personal improvement.

Social mobility was the one measurable latent function of baseball. Baseball provided jobs for lower-class boys, since one-third of the major leaguers came from blue-collar families. But two-thirds came from farming or white-collar families, far more than their share of the overall male population. Furthermore, few jobs were available in the majors (336 to 400 per season depending on the size of team rosters), and only a handful went to the children of new immigrants. Retired ballplayers did better than contemporary observers expected (nearly four-fifths had white-collar jobs), but unless they remained in baseball their success was not a function of fame but rather of social background.

In addition to these ascribed latent instrumental functions, professional baseball also had important symbolic functions. For example, organized baseball's efforts to demonstrate the domestic origins of the national pastime and spread the game and its message around the globe reflected the intense nationalism and incipient imperialism at the turn of the century. The absence of African Americans and women from organized baseball symbolized that the United States was white man's territory, and the acquittal of the Black Sox signified that all was right with the country. One could even point to player and fan interest with statistical accomplishments and setting records as representing the American belief in progress, a novel concept for most new immigrants.[10]

Baseball, in particular, symbolized the dominant myths of turn-of-the-century America, namely the agrarian/rural myth, the myth of social integration, and the myth of social democracy, which all represented some of the core culture's most important principles. These notions represented the prevailing worldview of middle-class WASPs and helped reinforce their basic assumptions about American society.

The rustic connotations of baseball fit in well with America's agrarian mythology. In 1893 the historian Frederick Jackson Turner developed the frontier thesis, arguing that the American character and many of its finest attributes were developed on the frontier by hard-working, self-reliant pioneers. The Turner thesis became a dominant paradigm of American historiography and an accepted social construction of reality among Americans. As the historian George Mowry aptly put it, "By the end of the nineteenth century the agrarian assumption that the countryside in some mysterious way bred character and patriotism while the city fostered opposed vices was entrenched in American social lore, politics and literature." The agrarian myth, noted the historian Richard Hofstadter, gave particular adulation for "the special values of rural life over city life."[11]

The arcadian myth was loosely related to the agrarian and frontier myths. While the agrarian myth focused on quality of life and values and the frontier myth on character building, the arcadian myth was mainly concerned with the peace and tranquility a city person could obtain by turning, or returning, to nature. This would provide a respite and an antidote to the pathological features of urban life. Many urbanites made concerted efforts to return, albeit temporarily or even vicariously, to nature. City dwellers read Jack London novels, backpacked and hiked in national parks, cycled out into the countryside, and even went bird watching. Social reformers encouraged youngsters to join the Boy Scouts, play in parks and playgrounds, and escape boring and unhealthy city summers by going away to fresh air camps where they could improve their health and recapture a simpler and purer life.[12]

Baseball at the amateur level, and at the more visible professional level, fit in well with these perspectives. Professional baseball was associated in every possible way with a romanticized earlier and less complicated era when rugged individuals built up the country. Sportswriters and other commentators viewed baseball as a distinctly rural game that had originated in a rustic setting in upstate New York. The arcadian image was reflected by the location of ballparks in quiet residential areas; their picturesque interiors with grassy green fields, green painted fences, and ivy-lined outfield walls; and their bucolic-sounding names. Fields were semipublic islands of urban greenery, much like municipal parks.

Verdant oases in a largely concrete world, the grounds were places where spectators could readily slip back into an idyllic rural past. The rustic motif was bolstered by the conventional beliefs about the origins and characteristics of professional ballplayers. The pervasive myth of their rural origins was reflected by the popular nickname "Rube" given many players, including Richard Marquard, son of a Cleveland district attorney.

Even though professional baseball was not actually a rural sport in terms of its historical origins, recruitment patterns, the social backgrounds of owners, and the sites of ballparks, sportswriters and other journalists consistently promoted that idea, and it did become the conventional wisdom. Fans saw baseball as an extension of rural America into the cities, where it would help urbanites become good Americans through playing the game and participating in the rituals of spectatorship. The lessons learned in the past by pioneers and yeomen farmers would be taught by baseball. Furthermore, baseball certified for old stock American fans the superiority of rural life over city dwelling and demonstrated the applicability of supposedly rurally developed traits in the modern urban environment. Hard work, honesty, and individualism still counted.

A second element of baseball's ideology that fit in well with dominant themes in Progressive America was the myth of social integration. Robert Wiebe has pointed out that the United States was a distended society in need of mechanisms to help it develop a sense of community and restore social order. Conservative progressives were deeply involved in a search for order, which encompassed rationality in business, politics, and social relations.[13] They recognized that American society needed new links to bind people together in what was an increasingly impersonal and heterogeneous society. Baseball not only symbolized the potential for social integration but also, like the public school system, seemed to provide ways to secure that goal. Paradoxically, while baseball was regarded as one of the finest American institutions and one that would successfully promote certain progressive ideals, the club owners were invariably political bosses or their associates. These politicians were enemies of the progressives, yet they operated the sport that was supposed to promote social order. Cooperative journalists portrayed the national pastime in such a way that it supplied many legends, myths, and symbols useful for social integration. Baseball, in theory, did not merely entertain but also contributed to individual and national development.

If professional baseball was to serve as an important source of discipline and social control, it was essential that the sport have the broadest possible audience. Working-class people who attended ball games had an opportunity to gain familiarity with the traditional American culture and become acculturated, and therefore good, citizens. However, the cost of attendance, the starting time of games, and strict enforcement of Sunday blue laws in the East and South imperiled the goal of social integration by making it inconvenient or difficult for blue-collar fans to get out to the ballpark. The Sabbatarian movement was promoted by pietistic, rural WASPs whose goals were to maintain a strict sabbath and impose their lifestyle upon new immigrants. In many ways baseball epitomized what these native-born Americans were fighting to protect, but was seldom available to those very groups they hoped to influence. The work of the Sabbatarians thus inadvertently interfered with their own goals.

The baseball creed's third parable, the myth of social democracy, was integrally related to the myth of social integration. In theory, everyone could attend a professional ball game, and anyone with talent and perseverance might become a professional ballplayer. Commentators repeatedly affirmed that men from all social classes attended games, where they mingled on equal terms, while ambitious, hard-working young men from all white ethnic groups were on big league rosters. Even Native Americans were on major league teams just a few years after Wounded Knee. Limited education and lack of connections were no barriers to any lad taking advantage of his ballplaying abilities. Unfortunately, these conventional beliefs were wrong. The democratic myth of baseball projected an idealized image of American society that people liked to believe. The national pastime encouraged everyone to think that the United States was a democratic country where all white men were entitled to equal social justice, equal political rights, and equal opportunities for advancement. After all, people from all walks of life played baseball, attended games, ate hot dogs, and cursed the umpire. The absence of African Americans, Asians, and women from the playing fields was conveniently overlooked.

Progressivism was characterized by a strong emphasis on democracy. Many reforms were initiated during the Progressive Era to secure political democracy, including direct election of senators, primaries, referendums, recalls, and woman's suffrage. Economic democracy was an important goal of Wilsonian progressives, who wanted to keep opportunities open for small business owners and also for urban liberals, who sought to protect the weak through labor and welfare legislation. Progressives felt that all people should have a chance to get ahead, although they recognized that all people did not start out with the same life chances. They supported social justice but not social democracy. Except by settlement workers, people from different backgrounds were not expected or encouraged to participate together in activities.

Even at the baseball park, the supposed bastion of American democracy, the more well-to-do fans generally sat in a separate and more expensive section. Furthermore, all people did not attend ball games, either out of choice or because of inconvenient game times, high costs, and Sunday blue laws. They did not have a reasonably fair chance to become professional ballplayers because of such factors as inadequate competition, lack of practice fields, parental opposition, ethnicity, and gender. In Progressive America, certain citizens were more equal than others, just as they had been in the past.

Aspects of the instrumental and symbolic functions of baseball's creed touched base in some way with all the elements of the broad-based progressive coalition, although its members were mainly concerned with the sport as a means of promoting social integration. Business leaders, professionals, and other progressives, who had little direct contact with the working class, appreciated baseball because it provided a means of social control and social integration, which in turn supported their traditional values, beliefs, and way of life against the new forces of change. Their attitudes were similar to those of other WASPs who lived in small-town America and wanted to exercise control over the dangerous cities. The main aspect of baseball that interested progressive educators was how it helped immigrant children acculturate. Progressives such as settlement workers and liberal machine politicians, who had a lot of direct contact with the lower classes, often disagreed with the more conservative progressives on issues of personal conduct and freedom. They did not support baseball because it promoted social control and weakened cultural pluralism, but rather thought of baseball in more democratic terms as a popular entertainment that promoted better health and fitness, encouraged local community ties, provided avenues of vertical mobility, and also helped assimilate interested youth.

During the 1920s the conflicting value systems of the immigrant-heavy cities and the WASP countryside continued to mark a formidable dividing line in America. The 1920 census reported that for the first time there were more Americans living in cities than in rural areas. A bitter struggle was at hand between old stock Americans espousing the traditional mid-Victorian belief system and urbanites of recent immigrant stock supporting more modern beliefs. The small-town folk felt uncomfortable with the transforming effects of population growth, immigration, industrialization, bureaucratization, and urbanization. They feared the loss of national vigor and the individual's role in mass society. Many Americans were disillusioned with their country after World War I, having apparently lost the peace to communists, union leaders, and other radicals. The Black Sox scandal seemed to symbolize the rotting away of their way of life. The old stock response against modernity included anti-intellectualism, privatism, the promotion of greater social control through Prohibition, immigration restriction, and demands for conformity from new immigrants. The most extreme reaction was the use of violence by vigilante groups like the Ku Klux Klan to impose their moral values on blacks, Catholics, and Jews.[14]

Americans in the 1920s relied heavily on heroes to promote old values and prove their continuing relevancy in a rapidly changing world. Rugged individualists like Henry Ford and Thomas A. Edison were the great mass heroes of the 1920s. They were successful entrepreneurs who seemed to prove that hard work and self-reliance still counted and that organization and teamwork were not essential for success. That Ford and Edison were also geniuses of organization was conveniently overlooked. The greatest hero of all was Charles Lindbergh. This fearless aviator brought together the spirit of the pioneer and the technology of a machine that was the product of a sophisticated modern society. Lindbergh combined in his great adventure the best qualities of an older America and contemporary urban society.[15]

Sport in the 1920s played an important role in promoting traditional values through its heroes. During the "Golden Age of Sport," an improved standard of living provided Americans with a lot more discretionary income and leisure time. Participation in sports and watching sporting events became more widespread than ever before. Industrial workers could take advantage of corporate-financed athletic programs designed to keep workers contented, loyal, and out of unions. Company sports included mass participation in bowling, basketball, and softball leagues and spectator-oriented semipro baseball and football teams. In addition, formerly elite sports like golf and tennis were becoming much more available for mass participation because of the construction of public golf courses and tennis courts. Baseball remained the number one spectator sport, but the rise in attendance in the 1920s failed to keep up with the growth in population, and the sport was fast losing its once near monopoly of the public limelight. Boxing and horse racing, which had been widely banned during the Progressive Era, gained new respectability and wide acceptance in the 1920s. The legalization of boxing in New York in 1920 helped pugilism gain respectability and large audiences. Its success was epitomized by the 1927 Tunney-Dempsey championship bout attended by over one hundred thousand fans at Chicago's Soldier Field in which Tunney earned $990,000 in his successful defense of the title. Thoroughbred racing also boomed with its increased legalization. Yearly purses quadrupled between 1918 and 1926, and the number of races in the 1920s rose by 60 percent. In the meantime amateur sports such as college football and high school basketball were becoming national crazes. By the late 1920s massive stadiums such as the seventy-thousand-seat Yale Bowl were filling up for important games. In Indiana, where basketball was the rage, some gymnasiums had seating capacities that surpassed the towns' populations.

Every major sport had at least one great hero who had succeeded through hard work, courage, self-reliance, and determination. Football had Red Grange; golf had Bobby Jones; tennis had Bill Tilden; swimming had Gertrude Ederle; and boxing had Dempsey. But the paramount sports star of the decade was Babe Ruth, a prowess hero who had achieved greatness by the sheer extent of his extraordinary natural ability. As Benjamin G. Rader points out, "the Ruthian image of home-run blasts ran counter to the increasingly dominant world of bureaucratization, scientific management, and 'organization men.'" Ruth was a new kind of baseball hero, unlike the hard-working Ty Cobb or the Christian gentleman Christy Mathewson, who only gently threatened traditional white middle-class norms. Sportswriters then were barkers for organized baseball and conveniently forgot about his rakish behavior, instead mythologizing him as an ingenuous man-child. He was idolized for his excesses— power, strength, appetite, and lust—like the great nineteenth-century boxing hero John L. Sullivan. Ruth's hedonistic behavior reflected the anti-Victorian morality of the 1920s that flaunted Prohibition and the old moral order that small-town Americans were trying to restore. In addition to the legendary Ruth, baseball in the 1920s had a second important hero, commissioner Kenesaw Mountain Landis, an ethical hero who redeemed baseball from the sins of the Black Sox. Under his strict leadership the sport regained its stature as the finest and noblest mass American institution. Fans assumed that as long as Landis was in charge, the game's standards of fair play and competition would not be subverted by un-American miscreants. Landis was a media-created hero who, with his long white mane of hair, looked the part of a wise patriarchal arbiter. Conveniently forgotten, however, was his actual work on the bench, since he had more decisions overturned than any federal judge in history.[16]

In the 1920s baseball was probably more successful in helping socialize and integrate white Americans than it had ever been. Sunday baseball and an improved standard of living made it possible for all fans to participate in the rituals of spectatorship. Baseball also helped integrate a whole new community of fans who, beginning in 1922, heard radio broadcasts of the World Series. The pro game had become the democratic spectator sport its ideology had long proclaimed it to be, at least for white fans. The notable caveat of segregated seating at southern ballparks, including the major league park in St. Louis, remained. Participation in the rituals of baseball promoted social integration in the minds of fans and celebrated the values of small-town society in an urban age. Professional baseball continued to supply some of the heroes mainstream Americans needed to confirm their belief in the applicability of the old traditions and standards to their current situation. A greater proportion of those athletes than ever before were coming from small towns and rural America. Nonetheless, urban second-generation immigrant youths were playing baseball (or at least some version of it) nearly everywhere, and in the next decade, names like DiMaggio, Greenberg, and Simmons became prominent on big league rosters. At the same time, however, African-American ballplayers remained largely invisible to most baseball fans, despite the excellence of the black leagues, because of the color line.

In the 1920s baseball's position as the national pastime was seriously contested by new and improved forms of entertainment. Millions began to enjoy the weekend pleasures of motoring, weekly attendance at luxurious movie palaces, and daily listening to music, drama, and variety shows on their radios. Nonetheless, baseball certainly maintained its status as the national game despite the Black Sox scandal and strong competition from such other sports as horse racing, boxing, and football. As baseball sustained its premier status as the national game, the realities of the professional game began catching up with its myths. But the biggest illusion of all, the democratic myth, was not even broached for another generation. Crossing that line made Jackie Robinson the biggest hero of all.

Appendix

A Note on Methodology

The data on the social origins of major leaguers active between 1900 and 1919 are from a questionnaire I sent in 1971 to the 403 men who had played in the big leagues prior to 1920 and were reportedly still alive.[1] This supplemented my research in Lee Allen's Notebooks at the National Baseball Library on the social origins of 593 men who had played at least one entire season (operationally defined as 100 at-bats or 50 innings pitched) for any team in Chicago or New York in the period 1900–1919. Data on social backgrounds were gathered for just 60 of the 593, of whom 51.7 percent had fathers who were not manual laborers, 16.7 percent were sons of farmers, and 31.7 percent were sons of manual workers.[2] The data were largely drawn from newspaper sources, often in feature stories that I thought might be biased toward the more successful and more rural players.

The questionnaire I sent to the 403 players asked for biographical data about the player, his wife, and their parents. I received 117 usable responses. As I had expected, the better-educated players responded in far greater proportion than their share of the major league population. Fifty-eight college attendees and 59 who did not attend college responded. The college attendees may have been more successful, more self-confident, and less suspicious of the motives of the inquiry than their less-educated peers, which may account for their greater responsiveness. To make the cohort more representative of the actual population of major leaguers in the early 1900s, I then weighted the responses so that the proportion of those who did not attend college to those who did would be 74.2 to 25.8, the ratio derived from my sample of 593 major leaguers. This larger sample is a quite accurate representation of the population of major leaguers, since data drawn from Lee Allen's Notebooks indicate that between 1900 and 1920, 671 of the 2,750 men, or 24.8 percent, attended college.[3] I achieved the required ratio by multiplying the number of respondents who did not attend college by a factor of 2.83. I analyzed the raw data for a variety of social relationships using the Statistical Package for the Social Sciences to test for levels of significance and strength of correlations. The level of significance used throughout was .001.

My job categorizations followed those Stephan Thernstrom used in *The Other Bostonians*.[4] However, the data for all American males in 1910 were organized slightly differently, with semiprofessionals placed in the professional category and foremen in the skilled group.[5] Thernstrom more logically places both occupations in the low white-collar cluster. If we add the semiprofessional fathers of major league ballplayers to the professional category, then the professional fathers would have comprised 11.6 percent of the sample.

Notes

Abbreviations

AC	*Atlanta Constitution*
AJ	*Atlanta Journal*
BE	*Brooklyn Eagle*
BM	*Baseball Magazine*
CDN	*Chicago Daily News*
CT	*Chicago Tribune*
NP	*National Pastime*
NYT	*New York Times*
NYTr	*New York Tribune*
SL	*Sporting Life*
SN	*Sporting News*

Introduction

1. John R. Krout, *Annals of American Sport*, vol. 14 of *The Pageant of America*, ed. Ralph Gabriel (New Haven, 1929); Jennie Holliman, *American Sports, 1785–1835* (Durham, 1931); Foster Rhea Dulles, *America Learns to Play: A History of Popular Recreation, 1607–1940* (New York, 1940). Krout was Holliman's and Dulles's advisor at Columbia University. Among articles in the leading journals, see Frederick L. Paxson, "The Rise of Sport," *Mississippi Valley Historical Review* 4 (Sept. 1917): 143–68; John R. Betts, "The Technological Revolution and the Rise of Sport, 1850–1900," *Mississippi Valley Historical Review* 40 (Sept. 1953): 231–56; John R. Betts, "Mind and Body in Early American Thought," *Journal of American History* 43 (Mar. 1968): 787–805; Louis A. Perez Jr., "Between Baseball and Bullfighting: The Quest for Nationality in Cuba, 1868–1898," *Journal of American History* 81 (Sept. 1994): 493–517; and Elliott J. Gorn, "'Gouge and Bite, Pull Hair, and

Scratch': The Social Significance of Fighting in the Southern Backcountry," *American Historical Review* 90 (Feb. 1985): 18–43.

2. Neil Harris, ed., *The Land of Contrasts, 1880–1901* (New York, 1970), 2.

3. Carl B. Cone, "Sports History with a Kentucky Bouquet," *Register of the Kentucky Historical Society* 77 (Autumn 1979): 276. Marshall Smelser did not dare to write *The Life That Ruth Built* (New York: Quadrangle/*New York Times* Books, 1975) until the end of his career. Jules Tygiel, a younger scholar, chose to write a dissertation about the San Francisco working class rather than the integration of baseball because "baseball is not the stuff upon which successful careers in history are normally made." Only after graduate school and a tenure-track appointment did he have enough confidence to turn to sport history. See *Baseball's Great Experiment: Jackie Robinson and His Legacy* (New York, 1983), vii–viii.

4. Richard E. Sykes, "American Studies and the Concept of Culture: A Theory and Method," in *American Studies: Essays in Theory and Method*, ed. Robert Meridith (Columbus, 1968), 77.

The North American Society for Sport History had its first annual conference in 1973 and one year later commenced publication of the *Journal of Sport History*. There are now several journals that focus on sport history, including the *International Journal of the History of Sport* (Great Britain), the *Canadian Journal of the History of Sport*, and *Sporting Traditions* (Australia).

5. Ken Burns and Lynn Novick, "Preface: Where Memory Gathers," in Geoffrey C. Ward, *Baseball: An Illustrated History* (New York, 1994), xviii.

6. The standard survey of sport history is Benjamin G. Rader, *American Sports: From the Age of Folk Games to the Age of Television*, 3d ed. (Englewood Cliffs, N.J., 1996). For a cultural analysis of American sport history, see Elliott Gorn and Warren Goldstein, *A Brief History of American Sports* (New York, 1993).

Baseball has received the greatest attention of any single sport. For single-volume overviews of baseball, see Benjamin G. Rader, *Baseball: A History of America's Game* (Urbana, Ill., 1992), and Charles Alexander, *Our Game: An American Baseball History* (New York, 1991); for more comprehensive coverage, see Harold Seymour, *Baseball*, 3 vols. (New York, 1960–90), and David Quentin Voigt, *American Baseball*, 3 vols. (Norman, 1966–70; University Park, Pa., 1983). See also Richard C. Crepeau, *Baseball: America's Diamond Mind, 1918–1941* (Orlando, 1980); Ted Vincent, *Mudville's Revenge: The Rise and Fall of American Sport* (New York, 1981); Melvin L. Adelman, *A Sporting Time: New York City and the Rise of Modern Athletics, 1820–1870* (Urbana, Ill., 1986); George B. Kirsch, *The Creation of American Team Sports: Baseball and Cricket, 1838–72* (Urbana, Ill., 1989); Warren Goldstein, *Playing for Keeps: A History of Early Baseball* (Ithaca, 1989); Robert F. Burk, *Never Just a Game: Players, Owners, and American Baseball to 1920* (Chapel Hill, 1994); G. Edward White, *Creating the National Pastime: Baseball Transforms Itself, 1903–1953* (Princeton, 1996).

For biographies, see Joseph Moore, *Pride against Prejudice: The Biography of Larry Doby* (Westport, Conn. 1989); Charles C. Alexander, *John McGraw* (New York, 1988); Charles C. Alexander, *Ty Cobb* (New York, 1984); Peter Levine, *A. G. Spalding and the Promise of American Sport* (New York, 1985); Eugene C. Murdock, *Ban Johnson: Czar of Baseball* (Westport, Conn., 1982).

7. Timothy Breen, "Horses and Gentlemen: The Cultural Significance of Gambling among the Gentry of Virginia," *William and Mary Quarterly* 34 (Apr. 1977): 242n9; Sykes, "American Studies," 77; Clifford Geertz, "Deep Play: Notes on the Balinese Cockfight," in *The Interpretation of Cultures* (New York, 1973), 412–53. See also Victor Turner, *The Ritual Process* (Chicago, 1957).

8. On the early history of baseball to 1860, see Adelman, *Sporting Time*, 121–44; Kirsch, *Creation of American Team Sports*, 50–77; and Goldstein, *Playing for Keeps*, 17–66.

9. Adelman, *Sporting Time*, 173–74; Kirsch, *Creation of American Team Sports*, 93; Goldstein, *Playing for Keeps*, 43–48; Rader, *American Sports*, 35, 64–66. For a discussion of baseball's popularity as played by nineteenth-century youths, see Ronald Story, "In the Country of the Young," in *Cooperstown: Symposium on Baseball and the American Culture (1989)*, ed. Alvin L. Hall (Westport, Conn., 1989), 328–37.

Leonard Ellis and Anthony Rotundo see baseball's cultural appeal as a mirror of the competitive character of nineteenth-century manhood and the organization of male life into sectors of striving and safety. In Ellis's analysis teams take a turn at leaving home and then returning home, mirroring the daily pattern of going to work. This seems a little odd to me since normally we think of recreation as an escape from work. See Leonard Ellis, "Men among Men: An Exploration of All-Male Relationships in Victorian America" (Ph.D. diss., Columbia University, 1982), 540–42, 582–88, as explicated in E. Anthony Rotundo, *American Manhood: Transformations in American Masculinity from the Revolution to the Modern Era* (New York, 1993), 243–44.

10. Philip K. Wrigley, owner of the Chicago Cubs, claimed that it was only in the 1920s that competition from other forms of recreation became an important factor in professional baseball. House Judiciary Committee, *Organized Baseball: Hearings before the Subcommittee on Study of Monopoly Power*, 82d Cong., 1st sess., 1951, serial 1, part 6 (Washington, D.C., 1952), 39.

11. Ibid., 1591, 1616–19; John R. Betts, "Organized Sport in Industrial America" (Ph.D. diss., Columbia University, 1951), 215.

12. My understanding of the Progressive Era has been greatly influenced by John D. Buenker, *Urban Liberalism and Progressive Reform* (New York, 1973); Samuel P. Hays, *The Response to Industrialism, 1885–1914* (Chicago, 1957); Richard Hofstadter, *The Age of Reform: From Bryan to FDR* (New York, 1955); Gabriel Kolko, *The Triumph of Conservatism: A Reinterpreta-*

tion of American History, 1900–1914 (New York, 1963); Arthur S. Link and Richard L. McCormick, *Progressivism* (Wheeling, Ill., 1983); and Robert Wiebe, *The Search for Order, 1877–1920* (New York, 1967).

13. Ralph Andreano, *No Joy in Mudville: The Dilemma of Major League Baseball* (Cambridge, Mass., 1965), 6, 11, 13–14; Seymour, *Baseball,* 2:62–64. For an example of the conventional wisdom, see Jim Nasium, "'Hick' Baseball as the Basis of the Game," *Literary Digest* 77 (19 May 1923): 64–66. For a discussion of earlier implications of baseball and middle-class ideology, see Stephen Freedman, "The Baseball Fad in Chicago, 1865–1870: An Exploration of the Role of Sport in the Nineteenth-Century City," *Journal of Sport History* 5 (Summer 1978): 43–48, 50–53.

14. On the interactions among perceptions of reality, see Peter L. Berger and Thomas Luckmann, *The Social Construction of Reality: A Treatise in the Sociology of Knowledge* (Garden City, N.Y., 1966), and Harry Edwards, *Sociology of Sport* (Homewood, Ill., 1973), 269–70.

Chapter 1: "Take Me Out to the Ball Game"

1. Voigt, *American Baseball,* 1:4; Story, "In the Country of the Young," 328–37.

On the congruence between American sport and antimodernizing values, see T. J. Jackson Lears, *No Place of Grace: Antimodernism and the Transformation of American Culture, 1880–1920* (New York, 1981), 108, 109, 301; and Donald Mrozek, *Sport and American Mentality, 1880–1910* (Knoxville, 1983).

2. Betts, "Mind and Body in Early American Thought"; Adelman, *Sporting Time,* 269–86; Steven A. Riess, *City Games: The Evolution of American Urban Society and the Rise of Sports* (Urbana, Ill., 1989), 3–5, 7, 26–30, 34, 46, 253–54.

3. Robert Obojski, *Bush League: A History of Minor League Baseball* (New York, 1975), 11, 217; House Judiciary Committee, *Organized Baseball,* 1394; John R. Betts, *America's Sporting Heritage, 1850–1950* (Reading, Mass. 1974), 118–19; Francis C. Richter, *Richter's History and Records of Baseball: The American Nation's Chief Sport* (Philadelphia, 1914), 155; Neil Sullivan, *The Minors: The Struggles and the Triumph of Baseball's Poor Relations from 1876 to the Present* (New York, 1990); Robin J. Anderson, "On the Edge of the Baseball Map with the 1908 Vancouver Beavers," *Canadian Historical Review* (Dec. 1996): 538–74; James Warnock, "Entrepreneurs and Progressives: Baseball in the Northwest, 1900–1901," *Pacific Northwest Quarterly* 82 (July 1991): 92–100; Bill O'Neal, *The Pacific Coast League, 1903–1988* (Austin, 1990).

4. For early attendance statistics, see *NYT,* 21 Dec. 1882; House Judiciary Committee, *Organized Baseball,* 1394, 1436–37, 1591; Betts, "Organized

Sport in Industrial America," 215; and Voigt, *American Baseball*, 1:117, 181. Major league attendance figures before 1910, and those for the minors before 1920, are unreliable estimates, usually published to hype the sport. For example, the *Cincinnati Enquirer* estimated the local club's attendance in 1886–88 at 3,264, 45 percent higher than the official average of 2,251. See Dean A. Sullivan, "Faces in the Crowd: A Statistical Portrait of Baseball Spectators in Cincinnati, 1886–1888," *Journal of Sport History* 17 (Winter 1990): 356n12, and for price elasticity and crowd size in the American Association, see 364–65; for the Pacific Coast League, see *AC*, 3 May 1908.

5. House Judiciary Committee, *Organized Baseball*, 1394, 1436–37, 1591; Glenn Moore, "The Great Baseball Tour of 1888–89," *International Journal of the History of Sport* 11 (Dec. 1994): 451; *SN*, 28 Jan. 1899; Sullivan, "Faces in the Crowd," 356–57. The Misfits played no home games from July 3 until August 24, played six home games, and then finished on the road, going 1-40 in its last 41 games. J. Thomas Hetrick, *MISFITS! The Cleveland Spiders in 1899: A Day-by-Day Narrative of Baseball Futility* (Jefferson, N.C., 1991); Voigt, *American Baseball*, 1:268–69.

6. House Judiciary Committee, *Organized Baseball*, 1436–37; Voigt, *American Baseball*, 1:181; *Chicago Times*, 5 July 1895.

7. House Judiciary Committee, *Organized Baseball*, 1591; *NYT*, 6 Oct. 1906; Paul Adomites, "The Fans," in *Total Baseball*, ed. John Thorn and Pete Palmer (New York, 1989), 668. Overestimates of daily crowds created problems with visiting teams, who thought they were being shortchanged out of their share of the gate receipts. See Charles W. Murphy to A. Herrmann, 1 June 1912, August Herrmann Papers, National Baseball Library, Baseball Hall of Fame, Cooperstown, N.Y.

The Boston NL club, known as the Beans and the Pilgrims, became the Braves in 1912 after James Gaffney became president. He was a former New York Tammany alderman and partner of Boss Charles F. Murphy. Tammanyites had long been known as the "Braves," followers of higher-ranking sachems.

8. House Judiciary Committee, *Organized Baseball*, 1437–38, 1591, 1593, 1616–19, 1636; Betts, "Organized Sport in Industrial America," 215.

9. *Spalding's Official Base Ball Guide, 1904* (New York, 1904), 269; *Spalding's Official Base Ball Guide, 1905* (New York, 1905), 165; *Spalding's Official Base Ball Guide, 1907* (New York, 1907), 206; *Spalding's Official Base Ball Guide, 1909* (New York, 1909), 105; Betts, "Organized Sport in Industrial America," 160, 256; *SN*, 20 Dec. 1902; *AJ*, 21 Jan. 1905; *AC*, 21 Apr. 1895, 23 Mar. 1898, 23 Oct. 1910, 14 Apr. 1914; House Judiciary Committee, *Organized Baseball*, 1622–24.

10. Smelser, *The Life That Ruth Built*, 58.

11. *Dictionary of American Biography*, s.v., "Chadwick, Henry"; John B. Foster, "Henry Chadwick: The Father of Baseball," in *Spalding's Official*

Baseball Guide, 1909, 7–13; Stephen Hardy, "Entrepreneurs, Structures, and the Sportgeist: Old Tensions in a Modern Industry," in *Essays on Sport History and Sport Mythology,* ed. Donald G. Kyle and Gary D. Stark (College Station, Tex., 1991), 54–59. Chadwick's diaries (1873–1907) and scrapbooks in the Albert G. Spalding Collection, New York Public Library, are an essential source for nineteenth-century baseball.

12. Hugh Fullerton, "The Fellows Who Made the Game," *Saturday Evening Post,* 21 Apr. 1928, 18–19; Tom Nawrocki, "The Chicago School of Baseball Writing," *NP* 13 (1993): 84–86; Fred Lieb, *Baseball as I Have Known It* (New York, 1977), 19–41; Voigt, *American Baseball,* 2:94–101, 232–40; David Quentin Voigt, "From Chadwick to Chipmunks," *Journal of American Culture* 7 (Fall 1984): 31–37; Ralph S. Graber, "Baseball in American Fiction," *English Journal* 56 (Nov. 1967): 1107–14; Donald Elder, *Ring Lardner: A Biography* (Garden City, N.Y., 1956), 302; Jonathan Yardley, *Ring: A Biography of Ring Lardner* (New York, 1977), 4–24; Walton R. Patrick, *Ring Lardner* (New York, 1963), 23–64; Elmer Ellis, *Mr. Dooley's America: A Life of Finley Peter Dunne* (New York, 1941), 24–27; Tom Clark, *The World of Damon Runyon* (New York, 1978), chap. 3.

13. Seymour, *Baseball,* 2:92–93; Frank L. Mott, *A History of American Magazines,* vol. 4, *1895–1905* (Cambridge, Mass., 1957), 374; *Bookman* 31 (10 Dec. 1910): 335, quoted in Betts, "Organized Sport in Industrial America," 404.

14. Albert G. Spalding, *America's National Game* (New York, 1911), 4 (quote); Richter, *Richter's History and Records of Base Ball;* Graber, "Baseball in American Fiction," 1107–14; Walter Evans, "The All-American Boys: A Study of Boys' Sport Fiction," *Journal of Popular Culture* 6 (Summer 1972): 104–19. For an analysis of *America's National Game,* see Levine, *Spalding,* 115–21.

15. *Chicago Times,* 29 May 1887; Allen Sangree, "Fans and Their Frenzies," *Everybody's Magazine,* Sept. 1907, 378–87; Rollin Lynde Hartt, "The National Game," *Atlantic Monthly,* Aug. 1908, 221–32; McCready Sykes, "The Most Perfect Thing in America," *Everybody's Magazine,* Oct. 1911, 435–46; Harvey Lambe, "The Game of Games," *World Today* 20 (May 1911): 541–50; Edwin Davies Schoonmaker, "Baseball and the Theater," *Harper's Weekly,* 17 Jan. 1914, 31–32.

16. Seymour, *Baseball,* 1:3–12. On the origins of baseball, see Robert W. Henderson, *Ball, Bat, and Bishop* (New York, 1947). On the Baseball Hall of Fame, see James A. Vlasich, *A Legend for the Legendary: The Origins of the Baseball Hall of Fame* (Bowling Green, Ohio, 1990).

17. Edward B. Bloss, "The Making of a Baseball Nine," *Outing* 42 (July 1903): 454.

18. Goldstein, *Playing for Keeps,* 2–3, 70; Bruce Kuklick, *To Every Thing a Season: Shibe Park and Urban Philadelphia, 1909–1976* (Princeton, 1991), 191.

19. *The Chicago Amateur Baseball Annual and Inter-City Baseball Association Yearbook* (Chicago, 1904), 7, 13; *Spalding's Official Baseball Guide, 1906* (New York, 1906), 1006, 1011, 1017; Ray Schmitt, "The Semipro Team that Beat the Champs," in *Baseball in Chicago: A Celebration of the Eightieth Anniversary of the 1906 World Series*, ed. Emil H. Rothe (Cooperstown, N.Y., 1986), 22; John J. Evers and Hugh Fullerton, *Touching Second: The Science of Baseball* (Chicago, 1910), 15; Robert Peterson, *Only the Ball Was White* (Englewood Cliffs, N.J., 1974), 64.

20. *NYT*, 1 May 1886; *Chicago Times*, 29 May 1887; "American Games," *Living Age* 281 (18 Apr. 1914): 185–87. On American cricket, see Adelman, *Sporting Time*, and Kirsch, *The Creation of American Team Sports*.

21. *NYTr*, 26 Sept. 1896, 5 May 1910; Charles Murphy, "Taft, the Fan," *BM*, Mar. 1912, 3–4.

22. Charles Fleischer, "A Bit of Baseball Biography," *BM*, June 1908, 34–35.

23. *NYT*, 2 Sept. 1887, 25 Aug. 1904; Hartt, "The National Game," 221; Porter E. Browne, "The Great American Game," *Cosmopolitan*, June 1907, 228. On the Interstate League, see Vincent, *Mudville's Revenge*, 140–51.

24. *NYT*, 3 Oct. 1897. See also *NYT*, 4 Oct. 1891, 21 Sept. 1895, 18 Sept. 1906, 26 Sept. 1906, 12 Apr. 1907. For an opposing viewpoint, see *Chicago Record-Herald*, 1 Sept. 1908. On boosterism, see Daniel Boorstin, *The National Experience*, vol. 2 of *The Americans* (New York, 1965), 113–68.

25. *NYT*, 23 Sept. 1887.

26. *NYT*, 25 Aug. 1904.

27. *San Antonio News* quoted in Seymour, *Baseball*, 1:355–56. The keynote address at a 1902 Little Rock Board of Trade smoker was entitled "Baseball as a City Advertisement." *AC*, 22 Sept. 1902. On baseball and boosterism in the West, see Anderson, "On the Edge," 540–49, 560; and Warnock, "Entrepreneurs and Progressives," 97.

28. Raymond B. Nixon, *Henry Grady: Spokesman for the New South* (New York, 1943), 229; *AJ*, 27 May 1904; *AC*, 23 Jan. 1905. On the "Atlanta spirit," see Don H. Doyle, *New Men, New Cities, New South: Atlanta, Nashville, Charleston, Mobile, 1860–1910* (Chapel Hill, 1990), chap. 6; Blaine A. Brownell, *The Urban Ethos in the South, 1920–1930* (Baton Rouge, 1975), 137–38. On southern boosterism, see David Goldfield, *Cotton Fields and Skyscrapers: Southern City and Region, 1607–1980* (Baton Rouge, 1982), 118–31.

29. *AC*, 14 Apr. 1913, 12 Apr. 1916, 13 Apr. 1916, 14 Apr. 1916, 15 Apr. 1916, 7 Apr. 1917, 8 Apr. 1917. Opening day in Atlanta remained a major affair for decades. *Atlanta Georgian*, 14 Apr. 1935. On boosterism and opening day in western cities, see Warnock, "Entrepreneurs and Progressives, 94–95.

30. *AC*, 28 Apr. 1895, 14 Oct. 1907.

31. *AC*, 7 July 1911. On pennant fever and the advertising value of the Crackers, see *AC*, 5 Sept. 1913.

32. Frederick Lieb, *Detroit Tigers* (New York, 1946), v; Hugh C. Weir, "Baseball: The Men and the Dollars behind It," *World Today* 17 (July 1909):

757. Baltimore, Buffalo, and Milwaukee all surpassed the population of Cincinnati and Washington, D.C., which had big league clubs.

By the time of the 1906 El Series between the Cubs and the Sox, Chicago did not need baseball to prove itself as a world-class city as it had back in 1876, when the White Stockings won their first championship. Then "Chicago bragged a good deal, possibly because Chicago had not yet then so much else to brag of as she does now. Apart from grain handling and output of hog products, Chicago was then very short of municipal distinctions." *NYT,* 5 Oct. 1906. On the 1907 world champion Cubs as an excellent advertisement for Chicago, see *CDN,* 18 Oct. 1907.

33. Sangree, "Fans and Their Frenzies," 387. See also *AC,* 14 Apr. 1913, quoting an editorial in the *Philadelphia Public Ledger.* No one promoted the ideology as unquestioningly as Spalding, who also had the most to gain financially and psychically. See Spalding, *America's National Game,* 4; Levine, *Spalding,* 112, 118–19.

34. "In the Interpreter's House," *American Magazine,* Sept. 1913, 96. See also Bertrand Brown, "Forward with the Old Back Lot," *Outing* 77 (Oct. 1920): 18.

35. *Free Press,* cited in Seymour, *Baseball,* 3:6. On the sports ideology, see Betts, "Mind and Body in Early American Thought"; Adelman, *Sporting Time,* 106, 121–37, 173–74, 279–84, 286; and Robert M. Lewis, "Cricket and the Beginnings of Organized Baseball in New York City," *International Journal of the History of Sport* 4 (Dec. 1987): 316–21. Baseball was identified with muscular Christianity in a 1 August 1875 *Chicago Tribune* article entitled "Baseball and the Churches." It was building up the strength of young members of the Moody Plymouth Congregational Church to help them wrestle with Satan.

36. On the nineteenth-century middle class, see Stuart M. Blumin, *The Emergence of the Middle Class: Social Experience in the American City, 1760–1900* (Cambridge, Mass., 1989); Cindy S. Aron, *Ladies and Gentlemen of the Civil Service: Middle-Class Workers in Victorian America* (New York, 1987), esp. 1–5; John S. Gilkeson Jr., *Middle-Class Providence, 1820–1940* (Princeton, 1986); and Burton J. Bledstein, *The Culture of Professionalism: The Middle Class and the Development of Higher Eduction in America* (New York, 1976). On middle-class manliness and sport, see Joe L. Dubbert, *A Man's Place: Masculinity in Transition* (Englewood Cliffs, N.J., 1979); Roberta J. Park, "Biological Thought, Athletic Attitudes on Sport and Manliness, and the Formation of a 'Man of Character': 1830–1900," in *Manliness and Morality: Middle Class Masculinity in Britain and America, 1800–1940,* ed. J. A. Mangan and James Walvin (Manchester, UK, 1987), 15–42; Steven A. Riess, "Sport and the Redefinition of American Middle-Class Masculinity," *International Journal of the History of Sport* 8 (May 1991): 3–25; and Gerald Roberts, "The Strenuous Life: The Cult of Manliness in the

Era of Theodore Roosevelt" (Ph.D. diss., Michigan State University, 1970). On baseball and the middle classes, see Adelman, *Sporting Time*, 129–31; Seymour, *Baseball*, 1:chaps. 1–3; Irving Leitner, *Baseball: Diamond in the Rough* (New York, 1972); Kirsch, *Creation of American Team Sports*, 84–85; Riess, *City Games*, 34–36, 65–68; and Michael S. Kimmel, "Baseball and the Reconstruction of American Masculinity, 1880–1920," in *Baseball History 3: An Annual of Original Baseball Research*, ed. Peter Levine (Westport, Conn., 1990), 98–112. On baseball and militarism, see David Lamoreaux, "Baseball in the Late Nineteenth Century: The Sources of Its Appeal," *Journal of Popular Culture* 11 (Winter 1977): 597–613. On football, see William James, *The Moral Equivalent of War and Other Essays* (New York, 1971), 6–7, 12; Eugene L. Richards Jr., "Football in America," *Outing* 6 (1885): 62–66; and Walter Camp and Lorin Deland, *Football* (Boston, 1896), 193–204.

37. H. Addington Bruce, "Baseball and the National Life," *Outlook*, May 1913, 103–7. On earlier comments about baseball as a safety valve, see *NYT*, 23 Sept. 1887. Thirty years earlier an essay on West Coast cricket identified sports in general as "the greatest safety valve of Society." *Clipper* 7 (29 Aug. 1857): 42, in Kirsch, *Creation of American Team Sports*, 148.

38. Bruce, "Baseball and the National Life," 107. See also Sangree, "Fans and Their Frenzies," 385.

39. Bruce, "Baseball and the National Life," 107; Seymour, *Baseball*, 2:246–47; William Lyon Phelps, *Autobiography with Letters* (New York, 1939), 356. President Woodrow Wilson was cited as a supporter of baseball who wanted to keep the sport going during the war to relieve mental strain. *AC*, 7 June 1917.

40. Bruce, "Baseball and the National Life," 105–6; Henry S. Curtis, "Baseball," *Journal of Education* 83 (27 Jan. 1916): 466–67; *CT*, 7 Nov. 1920; *NYT*, 3 Sept. 1920.

41. Bruce, "Baseball and the National Life," 105–6; Sykes, "Most Perfect Thing in America," 441, 446; Charles D. Stewart, "The U.S. of Base-ball," *Century Magazine*, June 1907, 314; Hugh Fullerton, "Baseball, the Business and the Sport," *Review of Reviews* 63 (Apr. 1921): 420; Neil Harris, ed., *The Land of Contrasts, 1880–1901* (New York, 1970), 25.

42. Seymour, *Baseball*, 3:29–38; Christian Messenger, *Sport and the Spirit of Play in American Fiction: Hawthorne to Faulkner* (New York, 1981), 165–72; Dubbert, *A Man's Place*, 34–39.

The historian James Warnock argues that at the turn of the century with the United States moving on to the world stage, many people called for the country to use its superior moral influence to promote world peace. It was thought that baseball, by teaching fair play and other virtues, could help prepare Americans to take a more prominent role in the twentieth century. Warnock, "Entrepreneurs and Progressives," 100.

43. Seymour, *Baseball*, 3:120; Bruce, "Baseball and the National Life,"

105–6; Sykes, "Most Perfect Thing in America," 441, 446; Seymour, *Baseball*, 2:102–6, 114; Voigt, *American Baseball*, 2:66, 70; *AC*, 23 Mar. 1913; William McKeever, *Training the Boy* (New York, 1913). On Cobb's cruel behavior, see Alexander, *Ty Cobb*.

44. Mark Inabinett, *Grantland Rice and His Heroes: The Sportswriter as Mythmaker in the 1920s* (Knoxville, 1995), 40; Robert Creamer, *Babe: The Legend Comes to Life* (New York, 1974); Smelser, *The Life That Ruth Built*.

45. Ray Robinson, *Matty, an American Hero: Christy Mathewson of the New York Giants* (New York, 1993); Seymour, *Baseball*, 2:115–16; Ward, *Baseball*, 70–71; *Dictionary of American Biography*, s.v. "Mathewson, Christy."

46. Lawrence Ritter, ed., *The Glory of Their Times* (New York, 1966), 167 (quote); Seymour, *Baseball*, 2:115–16; Douglas Wallop, *Baseball: An Informal History* (New York, 1969), 115–16, 121–23, 167; Lieb, *Baseball as I Have Known It*, 139. *Dictionary of American Biography*, s.v. "Mathewson, Christy."

47. "Editorial," *Commonweal* 2 (21 Oct. 1925): 579.

48. Critics discussed in Seymour, *Baseball*, 3:123–26 (quote on 124).

49. Bruce, "Baseball and the National Life," 107. See also Lambe, "Game of Games," 542; Sangree, "Fans and Their Frenzies," 387; Hartt, "The National Game," 228, 231.

50. Edward B. Moss, "The Fan and His Way," *Harper's Weekly*, 11 June 1910, 13; Hugh Fullerton, "Fans," *American Magazine*, Aug. 1912, 46.

51. Jane Addams, *The Spirit of Youth and the City Streets* (New York, 1909), 96.

52. Theodore Roosevelt, *The Strenuous Life and Other Essays* (New York, 1900); John Higham, "The Reorientation of American Culture in the 1890s," *Writing American History: Essays on Modern Scholarship* (Bloomington, 1970), 73–102; Dubbert, *A Man's Place*, 175–82; Roberts, "Strenuous Life," 84–144; Riess, "Sport and the Redefinition of American Middle-Class Masculinity," 16–21; Donald Mrozek, *Sport and American Mentality, 1880–1910* (Knoxville, 1983), 14–15, 46–47, 63–64. On the park movement, see Lawrence A. Finfer, "Leisure as Social Work in the Urban Community: The Progressive Recreation Movement, 1890–1920" (Ph.D. diss., Michigan State University, 1974), esp. 153–91; Stephen Boyer, *Urban Masses and Moral Order in America, 1820–1920* (Cambridge, Mass., 1978), 33–51; Cary Goodman, *Choosing Sides: Playground and Street Life on the Lower East Side* (New York, 1979); Dominick Cavallo, *Muscles and Morals: Organized Playgrounds and Urban Reform* (Philadelphia, 1981); Stephen Hardy, *How Boston Played: Sport, Recreation, and Community, 1865–1915* (Boston, 1981), chaps. 4, 5; Roy Rosenzweig, *Eight Hours for What We Will: Workers and Leisure in an Industrial City, 1870–1920* (Cambridge, Mass., 1983), chap. 5; and Riess, *City Games*, 128–40, 164–68.

53. *NYT,* 9 Oct. 1912; "Is Professional Baseball Wholesome?" *Outlook,* 19 Oct. 1912, 330.

54. Bruce, "Baseball and the National Life," 106.

55. "On the Bleachers," *New York Medical Journal* 100 (17 Oct. 1914): 778.

56. *AC,* 18 July 1919. See also "Baseball Field": The Real Melting Pot," *New York Morning Telegraph,* n.d., quoted in *SN,* 26 Apr. 1917; Lambe, "Game of Games," 550. Bridgeport, Connecticut's mayor reported that the sport helped assimilate foreign-born workers. "Editorial," *BM,* June 1920, 314.

57. *AC,* 18 July 1909; Seymour, *Baseball,* 3:chaps. 3, 4; *CT,* 14 May 1905.

58. *Dziennik Chicagoski,* 27 June 1919, Works Progress Administration, Federal Writers Project, Illinois, Chicago Foreign Language Press Survey (Chicago, 1942), typescript, Special Collections, University of Chicago Library; Richard Sorrell, "Sports and Franco-Americans in Woonsocket, 1870–1930," *Rhode Island History* 31 (Fall 1972): 117–26. See also Gary Mormino, "The Playing Fields of St. Louis: Italian Immigrants and Sport, 1925–1941," *Journal of Sport History* 9 (Summer 1982): 5–16.

59. Kuklick, *To Every Thing a Season,* 192.

60. *St. Louis Post-Dispatch,* 19 May 1883. See also *St. Louis Post-Dispatch,* cited in *NYT,* 16 June 1884. On the debate of historians on the social composition of baseball crowds, see Steven A. Riess, "From Pitch to Putt: Sport and Class in Anglo-American Sport," *Journal of Sport History* 21 (Summer 1994): 178–79.

61. Hartt, "The National Game," 228, 231; Seymour, *Baseball,* 1:327–28. For a view that 80 percent of fans in the 1920s were middle class, see Edward F. Wolfe, "The Benevolent Brotherhood of Baseball Bugs," *Literary Digest* 78 (7 July 1923): 64–70.

62. New York reporter quoted in *Boston Evening Transcript,* 22 Sept. 1887.

63. *NYT,* 31 May 1890; *Boston Evening Transcript,* 22 Sept. 1887.

64. Adelman, *Sporting Time,* 121–23; Seymour, *Baseball,* 1:15–23; Leitner, *Baseball,* 31–32; Harold Peterson, *The Man Who Invented Baseball* (New York, 1969), 76–77. On the social origins of early amateur players, see Adelman, *Sporting Time,* 125–26, 138–42; Kirsch, *Creation of American Team Sports,* 124, 131, 146–57; and Freedman, "The Baseball Fad in Chicago," 56. On the ballplayers' fraternity, see Goldstein, *Playing for Keeps,* chap. 1; and Benjamin G. Rader, *American Sports: From the Age of Folk Games to the Age of Televised Sports,* 3d ed. (Englewood Cliffs, N.J., 1996), 50.

65. Seymour, *Baseball,* 1:25, 48–49; Adelman, *Sporting Time,* 132–34, 148–51, 159–60, 328n45; George B. Kirsch, "Baseball Spectators, 1855–1870," *Baseball History* 3 (Fall 1987): 4–7, 9–10, 12–18; Michael Gershman, *Diamonds: The Evolution of the Ballpark* (Boston, 1993), 12, 16.

66. For a fictional account of an umpire's trials and tribulations, see *SL,*

13 Nov. 1897; see also Lawrence W. Levine, *Highbrow/Lowbrow: The Emergence of Cultural Hierarchy in America* (Cambridge, Mass., 1988); and John F. Kasson, *Rudeness and Civility: Manners in Nineteenth Century Urban America* (New York, 1990), chap. 7.

67. Seymour, *Baseball*, 1:90; Melvin L. Adelman, "The Development of Modern Athletics in New York City, 1820–1870" (Ph.D. diss., University of Illinois, 1980), 324 (quote); A. G. Spalding to Henry Graham, 26 Dec. 1883, Chicago Baseball Club, Chicago Historical Society, cited in Levine, *Spalding*, 42.

68. Seymour, *Baseball*, 1:328–29, 2:65; Sullivan, "Faces in the Crowd," 361, 362; *AC*, 10 Apr. 1897; *NYTr*, 1 Apr. 1914; Weir, "Baseball," 756.

69. *St. Louis Post-Dispatch*, 19 May 1883; *New York Sun*, n.d., cited in *St. Louis Post-Dispatch*, 16 June 1884; Seymour, *Baseball*, 1:328–29; Harold Seymour, "The Rise of Major League Baseball to 1891" (Ph.D. diss., Cornell University, 1956), 30, 431–32; Charles Brian Goslow, "Fairground Days: When Worcester Was a National League City (1880–82)," *Historical Journal of Massachusetts* 19 (Summer 1991): 140. On attitudes toward women fans, see Anderson, "On the Edge," 564–65.

70. Seymour, *Baseball*, 1:328–29; Seymour, "Rise of Major League Baseball," 189, 431; Goslow, "Fairground Days," 137; John Bowman and Joel Zoss, *Diamonds in the Rough: The Untold History of Baseball* (New York, 1989), 200; *St. Louis Post-Dispatch*, 19 May 1883; Dean Alan Sullivan, "The Growth of Sport in a Southern City: A Study of the Organizational Evolution of Baseball in Louisville, Kentucky, as an Urban Phenomenon, 1860–1900" (M.A. thesis, George Mason University, 1989), 107, 118nn27, 31; David Q. Voigt, "Out with the Crowds: Counting, Courting, and Controlling Ball Park Fans," in *Baseball History 2: An Annual of Original Baseball Research*, ed. Peter Levine (Westport, Conn., 1989), 110.

71. *AC*, 21 Apr. 1895, 23 Mar. 1898, 6 Apr. 1909, 15 Apr. 1916. In the early 1900s Little Rock, Memphis, and New Orleans admitted women free at all times. *AC*, 18 June 1905, 3 May 1908, 6 Apr. 1909. For Vancouver, see Anderson, "On the Edge," 564.

72. See, e.g., *AC*, 1 June 1895; *NYT*, 17 Apr. 1896; *NYTr*, 13 Apr. 1916. In Little Rock, female interest in the sport was so great that the city's largest department store installed a ticker tape machine in the women's restroom so they could get results. *SN*, 30 Mar. 1916.

Women are almost never seen in photographs of bleacher crowds, although they can often be seen in shots of the grandstand or in scenes of the crowd waiting outside for a game. See Spalding, *America's National Game*, 502–3, for a panoramic view of a bleacher section without any women at all, and compare it to other crowd photographs. Those photographs show many women seated in the grandstands and box seats, wearing the fashionable dresses and bonnets of the day. See, e.g., Bill Shannon and George Kaminsky, *The Ballparks* (New York, 1975), 32–36, 44, 182.

73. For an excellent collection of baseball sheet music, consult the New-berry Library in Chicago.

74. Seymour, *Baseball*, 2:65; Voigt, "Out with the Crowds," 110–12; Michael Benson, *Ballparks of North America: A Comprehensive Historical Reference to Baseball Grounds, Yards, and Stadiums, 1845 to the Present* (Jefferson, N.C., 1989), 407–8. Women in Cleveland were estimated to comprise 15 percent of the annual attendance. Survey Committee of the Cleveland Foundation, *Commercial Recreation*, vol. 5 of *Cleveland Recreation Survey* (Cleveland, 1920), 125. Hugh Fullerton claimed that women comprised one-fourth of the total attendance in 1919. *AC*, 8 Dec. 1919.

75. *NYTr*, 29 Apr. 1915, 17 Sept. 1915, 4 June 1916; *AC*, 24 June 1916. Harry Hempstead to A. Herrmann, 26 May 1915, Herrmann Papers. The Reds held a game sponsored by those against suffrage. Seymour, *Baseball*, 2:62.
At the 1913 Derby Emily Davison ran onto the course and grabbed the reins of Anmer, George V's horse, and knocked him down. Neither the horse nor his jockey was seriously injured, but Davison fractured her skull and died. Wray Vamplew, *The Turf: A Social and Economic History of Horse Racing* (London, 1976), 128.

76. Charles W. Murphy to A. Herrmann, 13 Feb. 1913, Herrmann Papers; *AJ*, 22 Apr. 1896; *BE*, 18 Apr. 1895, 3 Apr. 1912; *NYT*, 27 Apr. 1912; newspaper article dated 7 Mar. 1912, John T. Brush File, National Baseball Library, Baseball Hall of Fame, Cooperstown, N.Y.; Ritter, *The Glory of Their Times*, 168; *NYTr*, 12 Oct. 1904; *CDN*, 5 June 1901; Richard Moss, *Tiger Stadium* (East Lansing, 1976), 12–13.

77. Since photographs were often taken at special occasions like opening day and the World Series, which attracted a different audience than was present during most of the season, photographs must be used cautiously. Photographs of crowds abound in contemporary periodicals, baseball guides, books, and historical societies. Excellent crowd photographs can be found in Bloss, "Making of a Baseball Nine," 455; Voigt, *American Baseball*, 2:36; Seymour, *Baseball*, vol. 2, photo pages following 152; David R. Phillips, ed., *That Old Ball Game* (Chicago, 1975), 46, 84–85, 154; and esp. Spalding, *America's National Game*, photo pages following 492, photo pages following 502. Drawings are far more subjective than the relatively neutral camera. See a sketch in Louis Graves, "Fair Weather Hits," *American Magazine*, June 1913, 57, which suggests the presence of a broad-based spectatorship at a ball game.

78. James T. Farrell, *My Baseball Diary* (New York, 1957), 40–41. On clothing and class, see John F. Kasson, *Amusing the Million: Coney Island at the Turn of the Century* (New York, 1978), 38–49.

79. Seymour, *Baseball*, 2:65; Joseph Durso, *The Days of Mr. McGraw* (Englewood Cliffs, N.J., 1969), 97; *NYTr*, 19 Apr. 1895, 22 Apr. 1896; *CDN*, 24 Apr. 1901, 22 Apr. 1915, 18 Apr. 1916; *AC*, 14 Apr. 1912. On elite season box holders at the Polo Grounds, see John T. Brush to A. Herrmann, 18 Nov.

1910, Herrmann Papers. On the prominence of middle-class businessmen and professionals at Vancouver ball games, see Anderson, "On the Edge," 559–63.

80. Durso, *Days of Mr. McGraw*, 81.

81. M. L. Ryan, "The Wonderful Growth of Baseball in Manhattan," *BM*, Apr. 1912, 35; *Palladium of Labor*, 10 Apr. 1886; *Trenton Daily True American*, 24 June 1890. On sport and working-class manliness, see Elliott Gorn, *The Manly Art: Bare-Knuckles Prize Fighting in Nineteenth Century America* (Ithaca, 1986), 140–47.

82. Herbert Gutman, "Work, Culture, and Society," *Power and Culture: Essays on the American Working Class* (New York, 1987), 3–78.

83. Paul Douglas, *Real Wages in the United States, 1890–1926* (Boston, 1930), 112, 114, 208; Sullivan, "Growth of Sport in a Southern City," 106.

84. Sullivan, "Faces in the Crowd," 359; *NYT*, 14 Oct. 1906; *NYTr*, 5 May 1919; *Trenton Daily True American*, 13 May 1891.

85. Sullivan, "Growth of Sport in a Southern City," 101–2; Sullivan, "Faces in the Crowd," 359–62.

86. Douglas, *Real Wages*, 208.

87. *Clipper* 25 (5 May 1877): 42; Harry Wright to Norman (Nick) Young, 12 May 1873, quoted in Voigt, *American Baseball*, 1:42.

88. Seymour, *Baseball*, 1:91; *New York Mercury*, 2 Sept. 1876, cited in Seymour, "Rise of Major League Baseball," 189; *Chicago Times*, 14 May 1888. On the interest of fans despite their inability to attend games, see Jacob C. Morse, *Sphere and Ash: A History of Baseball* (Boston, 1888), cited in David Quentin Voigt, "Cash and Glory: The Commercialization of Major League Baseball as a Sports Spectacle, 1865–1892" (Ph.D. diss., Syracuse University, 1963), 505. On income and standard of living, see Louise Bolard More, *Wage-Earners' Budgets: A Study of Standards and Cost of Living in New York City* (New York, 1907); Robert Coit Chapin, *The Standard of Living among Workingmen's Families in New York City* (New York, 1909), esp. 210–11; Frank Hatch Streightoff, *The Standard of Living among the Industrial People of America* (Boston, 1911); Clarence D. Long, *Wages and Earnings in the United States, 1860–1890* (Princeton, 1960), 4; Albert Rees, *Real Wages in Manufacturing, 1890–1914* (Princeton, 1961), chap. 3; Steven J. Ross, *Workers on the Edge: Work, Leisure, and Politics in Industrializing Cincinnati, 1788–1890* (New York, 1985), 243–45; Alan Trachtenberg, *The Incorporation of America: Culture and Society in the Gilded Age* (New York, 1982), 90–91; Peter Shergold, *Working-Class Life: The "American Standard" in Comparative Perspective, 1889–1913* (Pittsburgh, 1982), 49 (quote), 225.

89. Seymour, *Baseball*, 1:138–47; Voigt, *American Baseball*, 1:123–25.

90. Sullivan, "Faces in the Crowd," 364–65; House Judiciary Committee, *Organized Baseball*, 1437; *CT*, 20 Mar. 1892; *SN*, 30 Jan. 1897, 9 Apr. 1897,

25 Sept. 1897, 17 Mar. 1900; Voigt, *American Baseball*, 1:145, 232. The Polo Grounds in 1900 had twelve hundred quarter seats, and Chicago's West Side Park had twenty-five hundred in 1906. *SL*, 3 Jan. 1903, 14 Apr. 1906.

91. *BE*, 23 Jan. 1897. On other working-class entertainments, see Perry Duis, *The Saloon: Public Drinking in Chicago and Boston, 1890–1920* (Urbana, Ill., 1983); Lary May, *Screening Out the Past: The Birth of Mass Culture and the Motion Picture Industry* (Chicago, 1980); Kasson, *Amusing the Million*; Robert Snyder, *The Voice of the City: Vaudeville and Popular Culture in New York* (New York, 1989); David Nasaw, *Going Out: The Rise and Fall of Public Amusements* (New York, 1993).

92. Survey Committee of the Cleveland Foundation, *Commercial Recreation*, 125–29; *Cleveland Plain-Dealer*, 20 Sept. 1914, 21 Sept. 1914.

93. *CDN*, 3 Mar. 1902.

94. *SN*, 16 Sept. 1909, 30 June 1910, 13 June 1912; House Judiciary Committee, *Organized Baseball*, 1616; Seymour, *Baseball*, 2:68; Nasaw, *Going Out*, 97–99; Kuklick, *To Everything a Season*, 26 (quote).

95. *CDN*, 31 Jan. 1910; *NYT*, 17 Mar. 1913; Seymour, *Baseball*, 2:50; *SN*, 29 June 1916.

96. *NYT*, 25 Jan. 1918, 22 Feb. 1920; *CDN*, 31 Jan. 1920; Seymour, *Baseball*, 2:247–48.

97. Durso, *Days of Mr. McGraw*, 66, 97; *CT*, 9 Oct. 1905, 3 Oct. 1906; *NYT*, 16 Oct. 1913, 22 Sept. 1920; Joseph J. Krueger, *Baseball's Greatest Drama* (Milwaukee, 1943), 3–7, 163; *NYTr*, 26 Sept. 1913.

98. Kirsch, *Creation of American Team Sports*, 180, 189, 193–95; *CT*, 28 Aug. 1904 (quote).

99. Voigt, *American Baseball*, 1:29–30.

100. Voigt, *American Baseball*, 1:64–65, 286–88, 295–96; Seymour, *Baseball*, 1:340–41; *NYT*, 9 Aug. 1894; Voigt, *American Baseball*, 2:101; Riess, *City Games*, 225; Voigt, "Out with the Crowds," 118–19; Adomites, "Fans," 666; poem cited in Ward, *Baseball*, 51.

101. Sullivan, "Faces in the Crowd," 361–62; Sullivan, "Growth of Sport in a Southern City," 112, 120n52.

102. Riess, *City Games*, 225; Voigt, "Out with the Crowds," 119–21; George J. Nathan, "Baiting the Umpire," *Harper's Weekly*, 10 Sept. 1910, 13; Murdock, *Ban Johnson*, 25–27, 55, 98–107; Moss, *Tiger Stadium*, 4; Adomites, "Fans," 666.

103. Riess, *City Games*, 226. On the values and behavior of soccer crowds, see Allen Guttmann, *Sports Spectators* (New York, 1986), 106–8; Tony Mason, *Association Football and English Society, 1863–1915* (Atlantic Highlands, N.J., 1980); and Bill Murray, *The Old Firm: Sectarianism, Sport, and Society in Scotland* (Edinburgh, 1984).

104. Riess, *City Games*, 226–27; Voigt, "Out with the Crowds," 118; *NYT*, 23 Apr. 1905; *Chicago Record-Herald*, 15 Oct. 1906. For opening day riots,

see *NYT,* 13 Apr. 1907; and *BE,* 13 Apr. 1912. In 1910 the intercity series between the Giants and the Highlanders drew overflow crowds and not enough police officers were present. Hundreds scaled the outer walls and had to be driven off by high-pressure hoses. *NYTr,* 12 Oct. 1911. `

105. On orderly and disorderly New York crowds, see *NYT,* 15 Oct. 1911, 16 Aug. 1919. An unusual riot occurred at Ebbets Field on 7 September 1924 when the Dodgers played the Giants. There were only forty police officers present, although fifty thousand fans were expected, far in excess of Ebbets Field's capacity. Early comers included fans with crowbars to unhinge the gates. Lee Allen, *The Giants and Dodgers: The Fabulous Story of Baseball's Fiercest Feud* (New York, 1964), 125.

106. Seymour, *Baseball,* 1:327–28; Voigt, *American Baseball,* 1:178. Fans sitting in the Rooters' Row section of the Cincinnati ballpark could buy twelve glasses of beer for one dollar. Seymour, *Baseball,* 1:198.

107. Farrell, *My Baseball Diary,* 86–88.

108. Abraham Cahan, *Yekl: A Tale of the New York Ghetto* (New York, 1896). The best survey of American ethnic history is John Bodner, *The Transplanted: A History of Immigrants in Urban America* (Bloomington, Ind., 1985). On ethnic sport, see Rader, *American Sports,* chap. 4; Riess, *City Games,* chap. 3; Hardy, *How Boston Played,* 28–32, 137–38, 174–79; and Gary Ross Mormino, *Immigrants on the Hill: Italian-Americans in St. Louis, 1882–1982* (Urbana, Ill., 1986).

109. On Czech ethnic pride, see *Svornost,* 8 Apr. 1890, and *Denni Hlasatel,* 16 Sept. 1911, both in Chicago Foreign Language Press Survey. For an early positive evaluation of the merits of sport for Polish Americans, see "Sports and the Benefits Derived There-From," *Dziennik Zwaizkowy-Zgoda,* 8 Apr. 1904, Chicago Foreign Language Press Survey. Some years later foreign-language papers began printing sports pages in English to attract the interest of the American-born.

110. For the article, see Ande Manners, *Poor Cousins* (New York, 1972), 278, reprinted with a transliteration in Gunther Barth, *City People: The Rise of Modern City Culture in Nineteenth Century America* (New York, 1980), 150–51.

111. Seymour, *Baseball,* 2:83; Harry Golden, *For Two Cents Plain* (Cleveland, 1959), 227–29.

112. George Burns, *The Third Time Around* (New York, 1980), 9–10.

113. *AC,* 15 Apr. 1916; Seymour, *Baseball,* 2:60–61; *CDN,* 26 Aug. 1900, 27 Aug. 1900; Morris Raphael Cohen, *A Dreamer's Journey: The Autobiography of Morris Raphael Cohen* (Boston, 1949), 80–81; Rick Marazzi, "Al Schacht: 'The Clown Prince of Baseball,'" *Baseball History: An Annual of Original Baseball Research,* premier ed., ed. Peter Levine (Westport, Conn., 1989), 34–35; Harry Golden, *The Right Time: An Autobiography* (New York, 1969). See also Irving L. Howe, *World of Our Fathers* (New York, 1975), 182–83, 259, 161.

114. The term *semiprofessional* is actually a misnomer when describing African-American ballplayers, since the top black players made baseball a full-time job even before the emergence of the Negro National League in 1920. On semiprofessional black baseball, see Peterson, *Only the Ball Was White*; Neil Lanctot, *Fair Dealing and Clean Playing: The Hilldale Club and the Development of Black Professional Baseball, 1910–1932* (Jefferson, N.C., 1994); and Michael E. Lomax, "Black Baseball, Black Entrepreneurs, Black Community" (Ph.D. diss., Ohio State University, 1996).

115. *SN*, 26 Jan. 1895; Sol White, *Sol White's History of Colored Baseball with Other Documents on the Early Black Game 1886–1936*, comp. Jerry Malloy (1907; repr., Lincoln, 1995), 26, 28; Jerry Malloy, "Introduction: Sol White and the Origins of African American Baseball," in *Sol White's History of Colored Baseball*, xxxvii; Peterson, *Only the Ball Was White*, 59; Lanctot, *Fair Dealing and Clean Playing*, 31–32; Lomax, "Black Baseball," 188–96; Phil Dixon, with Patrick J. Hannigan, *The Negro Baseball Leagues, 1867–1955: A Photographic History* (Mattituck, N.Y., 1992), 96–97.

116. *CT*, 2 Apr. 1905; Peterson, *Only the Ball Was White*, 62–66; Allan Spear, *Black Chicago: The Making of a Negro Ghetto, 1890–1920* (Chicago, 1967), 79, 117–18; Lanctot, *Fair Dealing and Clean Playing*, 32; "Diamond Jubilee Dinner Program," back page, Old Timers' Baseball Association of Chicago, Morrison Hotel, 1944, Chicago Historical Society; Lomax, "Black Baseball," 253–62. In 1907 and 1910, respectively, Leland and Moseley unsuccessfully tried to organize a national baseball league for blacks. Lomax, "Black Baseball," 253–60; Spear, *Black Chicago*, 118.

117. Spear, *Black Chicago*, 117–18; *Spalding's Official Baseball Guide of Chicago, 1909* (New York, 1909), 7; *CDN*, 26 Sept. 1908; *Chicago Defender*, 12 Dec. 1908; Bruce Chadwick, *When the Game Was Black and White: The Illustrated History of the Negro Leagues* (New York, 1992), 31–33; Peterson, *Only the Ball Was White*, 66 (quote). On Foster, see Charles E. Whitehead, *A Man and His Diamonds* (New York, 1980); and John Holway, "Rube Foster: The Father of Black Baseball," *Blackball Stars: Negro League Pioneers* (Westport, Conn., 1988), 8–35.

118. *Chicago Broad Ax*, 30 Apr. 1910, 14 May 1910; *Chicago Defender*, 4 Mar. 1910, 12 Mar. 1910, 23 Apr. 1910, 11 June 1910, 25 June 1910, 23 July 1910, 20 Feb. 1915; *CDN*, 10 Jan. 1910; *New York Age*, 14 Apr. 1910, 5 May 1910, 21 July 1910, 5 Jan. 1911; Dixon, *Negro Leagues*, 102–3.

119. Spear, *Black Chicago*, 118; Lanctot, *Fair Dealing and Clean Playing*, 37–38; Chadwick, *When the Game Was Black and White*, 31–33; Whitehead, *A Man and His Diamonds*; Holway, *Blackball Stars*, 16–17; Holway, "Rube Foster"; Lomax, "Black Baseball," 269–76. Chicago had four black semipro teams in 1911, the American Giants, the Leland Giants, the Chicago Giants, and the Union Giants, which saturated the market.

120. On black fans, see *New York Age*, 28 May 1908, 17 June 1909, 29 June 1911, 20 July 1911, 7 Sept. 1911, 31 Oct. 1912, 28 Aug. 1913, 7 Sept. 1913,

2 Oct. 1913. On segregated seating in the South, see *AC,* 23 July 1902, 15 July 1919. On drinking and disorderly crowd behavior at black games in Chicago and New York, see Lanctot, *Fair Dealing and Clean Playing,* 17–18, 23–25.

121. Peterson, *Only the Ball Was White,* 62–66; Spear, *Black Chicago,* 117–18; Lanctot, *Fair Dealing and Clean Playing,* 175; Malloy, "Introduction," xli; *Spalding's Official Baseball Guide of Chicago, 1906* (New York, 1906); *Spalding's Official Baseball Guide of Chicago, 1907* (New York, 1907); *Spalding's Official Baseball Guide of Chicago, 1908* (New York, 1908); *Spalding's Official Baseball Guide of Chicago, 1909* (New York, 1909); *Spalding's Official Baseball Guide of Chicago, 1910* (New York, 1910); *Chicago Defender,* 12 Dec. 1908, 23 Apr. 1910, 20 Feb. 1915; *CDN,* 10 Jan. 1910, 25 Jan. 1911; *New York Age,* 12 Apr. 1910, 5 May 1910, 21 July 1910, 5 Jan. 1911, 29 July 1911, 7 Sept. 1911. For advertisements of forthcoming games with ticket prices, see, e.g., *Chicago Broad Ax,* 15 Apr. 1911.

122. *CDN,* 25 Jan. 1911; *New York Age,* 29 July 1911, 7 Sept. 1911; *Chicago Broad Ax,* 12 May 1912; Peterson, *Only the Ball Was White,* 66, 70, 108.

123. Abbott quoted in Peterson, *Only the Ball Was White,* 66. I examined issues of the *Chicago Broad Ax,* the *Chicago Defender,* and the *New York Age* from their inception until the 1920s or their demise, whichever came first. *Chicago Defender,* 12 Apr. 1919. See *New York Age,* 28 Sept. 1911, as an example of blacks following the progress of Cubans and Native Americans in the majors.

124. James Youtsler, *Labor's Wage Policies in the Twentieth Century* (New York, 1956), 38–39; Frederick Lewis Allen, *The Big Change* (New York, 1952), 47, 49; Peter d'A. Jones, *The Consumer Society* (Baltimore, 1965), 299.

125. Sinclair Lewis, *Babbitt* (New York, 1922), 153; Morris Raphael Cohen, "Baseball," *Dial* 47 (26 July 1919): 57–58.

Chapter 2: Professional Baseball and Urban Politics

1. "The Business Side of Baseball," *Current Literature* 53 (Aug. 1912): 169. For rare exposés of professional baseball, see Weir, "Baseball," 752; and Edward Mott Woolley, "The Business of Baseball," *McClure's,* July 1912, 241–45. Contemporary college sports were critically examined by Henry B. Needham in "The College Athlete: How Commercialism Is Making Him a Professional," *McClure's,* June 1905, 115–28, and "The College Athlete: His Amateur Code: Its Evasion and Administration," *McClure's,* July 1905, 260–73. On Johnson, see Murdock, *Ban Johnson.*

2. Vincent, *Mudville's Revenge,* 98–110, 125–28, 173–74, 176–77, 206–7. Vincent also found that one-tenth (13 out of 129) known International Association owners were blue-collar workers (see 142–43). See also Stephen Hardy, "Entrepreneurs, Organizations, and the Sport Marketplace: Subjects in Search of Historians," *Journal of Sport History* 13 (Spring 1986): 23.

3. *AC*, 3 Mar. 1894, 3 Apr. 1894, 19 Mar. 1895, 10 Mar. 1896, 13 July 1896; Atlanta, Minutes of the Atlanta City Council, 27 July 1894, 29 Mar. 1895, and 18 Mar. 1895, typescript, 265, Office of the City Clerk, Atlanta City Hall. As late as 1886 a New York judge had ruled that a baseball club did not need a license to operate. *NYT*, 2 July 1886.

4. *AC*, 19 Mar. 1895; *AJ*, 19 Mar. 1895.

5. *AC*, 20 Mar. 1895; *AJ*, 2 Mar. 1895, 9 Apr. 1896, 11 Apr. 1896; *SN*, 29 Dec. 1894; *SL*, 4 May 1895.

6. *AC*, 13 July 1896, 23 Jan. 1898; *AJ*, 20 Jan. 1898; *SL*, 5 Mar. 1898.

7. W. E. Harrington, "Report of the Committee on Promotion of Traffic," *Street Railway Journal* 30 (26 Oct. 1907): 864; Vincent, *Mudville's Revenge,* 175–79, 206–7; Seymour, *Baseball,* 1:203; *NYT,* 30 Dec. 1906.

8. "Bruffey Tells of Teams that Started in 1886," undated *Atlanta Constitution* article, Baseball Files, Atlanta Public Library; *AJ,* 3 Feb. 1897; *AC,* 31 Jan. 1898, 6 Sept. 1898, 30 Jan. 1903, 2 Mar. 1904, 11 Apr. 1919.

9. *AC*, 23 Jan. 1898, 16 Feb. 1898; *SL*, 5 Mar. 1898.

10. On the history of the Southern League and the Southern Association, see Robert Obojski, *Bush League: A History of Minor League Baseball* (New York, 1975), chap. 11.

11. *AC*, 23 Dec. 1902, 23 Jan. 1905, 28 Jan. 1906; *AJ*, 24 Jan. 1905, 28 Jan. 1905; *SN*, 20 Dec. 1902, 26 Sept. 1903; Obojski, *Bush League,* 217–18. On Powell, see Edward Hoag, "Baseball's Great Innovator," *Sports Illustrated,* 19 Mar. 1973, M6–M8. The New Orleans police commissioner claimed the Pelicans earned sixty thousand dollars in 1901 and 1902, but gave him only six hundred dollars to work on their behalf. *AJ,* 3 Dec. 1902.

12. *AJ*, 27 Mar. 1904, 4 June 1904, 10 June 1904, 27 Jan. 1905; *AC*, 8 May 1904, 4 June 1904; Atlanta, *Tax Ordinance for 1904–1905* (Atlanta, 1905), 17. An attempt in 1900 to tax Pittsburgh's club for twenty-five dollars a game, widely interpreted as a shakedown, did not pass. *Chicago Times-Herald,* 9 Jan. 1900.

13. *AC*, 27 Jan. 1905, 10 Apr. 1910. Other politically connected executives included the city recorder's brother and a solicitor of the criminal court. *AJ,* 27 Jan. 1905; Atlanta Fire Department, *Prompt to Action—The Atlanta Fire Department, 1860–1960: One Hundred Years of Organized Fire Protection* (Atlanta, 1961), 42–44; Thomas M. Deaton, "Atlanta during the Progressive Era" (Ph.D. diss., University of Georgia, 1969), chap. 9. On Southern League profits, see *Spalding's Official Base Ball Guide, 1906,* 191. The Western League, which was similar to the Southern Association, averaged four thousand dollars in profit per team, led by Des Moines with fourteen thousand dollars. *Spalding's Official Base Ball Guide, 1906,* 187.

14. *AJ*, 21 Oct. 1908; Wade Wright, *History of the Georgia Power Company, 1855–1956* (Atlanta, 1957), 88–89; Ralph McGill, *Story of the Trust Company of Georgia on Its Sixtieth Anniversary* (Atlanta, 1951), vii.

15. *Atlanta Georgian,* 16 Sept. 1911, 19 Sept. 1911, 20 Sept. 1911, 3 Nov. 1915; *AC,* 20 Sept. 1911, 3 Nov. 1915; Ed Danforth, "The Crackers Are Ready," *Atlanta City Builder* 7 (Apr. 1921): 13, 38–39; Franklin N. Garrett, *Atlanta and Environs: A Chronicle of Its People and Events* (Athens, Ga., 1969), 2:817.

16. Federal Writers Project, Illinois, *Baseball in Old Chicago* (Chicago, 1939), 7, 9, 13; Vincent, *Mudville's Revenge,* 107, 127–29; John W. Leonard, ed., *The Book of Chicagoans,* vol. 1 (Chicago, 1905), 44, 267, 525; Bessie Louise Pierce, *A History of Chicago,* vol. 3, *1871–1893* (New York, 1957), 478; *CT,* 13 Apr. 1889, 2 Nov. 1905; Frederick F. Cook, *Bygone Days in Chicago: Recollections of the "Garden City" of the Sixties* (Chicago, 1910), 302; Robert K. Barney and Frank Dallier, "'I'd Rather Be a Lamp Post in Chicago than a Millionaire in Any Other City': William A. Hulbert, Civic Pride, and the Birth of the National League," *Nine* 2 (Fall 1993): 42.

The Chicago team eventually became known as the Cubs. Before that the White Stockings were briefly known as the Black Stockings (1888–89), when they wore black socks; as Anson's Colts (1890–97) because of their youth; as the Orphans (1898–1901) after Anson was fired as manager; as Selee's Colts (1902–4) because they were young and in honor of their new manager; as the Nationals or the Cubs (1905–6); and as the Cubs beginning in 1907. See Arthur A. Ahrens, "How the Cubs Got Their Name," *Chicago History* 5 (Spring 1976): 39–44.

17. Barney and Dallier, "'I'd Rather Be a Lamp Post,'" 42.

18. *NYT,* 5 Oct. 1906; *Chicago Times,* 9 Aug. 1887, 18 Dec. 1892; *SN,* 24 Dec. 1892; *CT,* 2 Nov. 1905; Pierce, *A History of Chicago,* 3:478; Levine, *Spalding,* chap. 3, 71–94; Stephen Hardy, "'Adopted by All the Leading Clubs': Sporting Goods and the Shaping of Leisure, 1800–1900," in *For Fun and Profit: The Transformation of Leisure into Consumption,* ed Richard Butsch (Philadelphia, 1990), 81–91; Joel A. Tarr, "J. R. Walsh of Chicago: A Case Study in Banking and Politics, 1881–1905," *Business History Review* 40 (Winter 1966): 451–66.

19. Levine, *Spalding,* xi, 42–48 (quote on 48).

20. Pierce, *A History of Chicago,* 3:478; Levine, *Spalding,* 36–37, 64; Seymour, *Baseball,* 1:119; Voigt, *American Baseball,* 2:232; Voigt, "Cash and Glory," 525. Incomplete records suggest that gate receipts for 1878, 1879, and 1881 ranged from twenty-three thousand dollars to thirty-two thousand dollars. Levine, *Spalding,* 36. For scattered data on early major league profits and losses, see *SL,* 8 Oct. 1883, 22 Oct. 1883; House Judiciary Committee, *Organized Baseball,* 1440–41; Voigt, *American Baseball,* 1:130; and Voigt, "Cash and Glory," 505, 524, 529–30. On the Players' League, see Lee Lowenfish and Tony Lupien, *The Imperfect Diamond: The Story of Baseball's Reserve Clause and the Men Who Fought to Change It* (New York, 1980), pt. 1.

21. Seymour, *Baseball,* 1:229, 245; Levine, *Spalding,* 64.

22. Seymour, *Baseball*, 1:251–62.

23. *CDN*, 18 July 1918; *Dictionary of American Biography*, s.v. "Anson, Adrian C." Anson owned 130 shares when he retired and sold them in 1905 for about thirteen thousand dollars. *CT*, 31 Dec. 1899, 10 Dec. 1905; Albert N. Marquis, ed., *The Book of Chicagoans*, vol. 2 (Chicago, 1911), 439, 670; *SL*, 8 Jan. 1898, 21 Oct. 1899; *SN*, 17 Feb. 1900; *Chicago Times-Herald*, 15 Oct. 1899; *Annual Meeting of the National League and American Association of Professional Baseball Clubs, 1901* (New York, 1901), 148.

24. Gustav Axelson, *"Commy": The Life Story of Charles A. Comiskey* (Chicago, 1919), 33–35, 39; Richard C. Lindberg, *Stealing First in a Two-Team Town: The White Sox from Comiskey to Reinsdorf* (Champaign, Ill., 1994), 13.

25. *SL*, 17 Oct. 1900; Richard Lindberg, *Who's on Third? The Chicago White Sox Story* (South Bend, 1983), 17–22; Richard Lindberg, "Yesterday's City: The South Side's Baseball Factory," *Chicago History* 28 (Summer 1989): 61; Murdock, *Ban Johnson*, 44.

26. Peter M. Gordon, "The Greatest World Series of All Time," *NP* 10 (1990): 21–26.

27. Lindberg, *Who's on Third?* 17–22; Lindberg, "South Side's Baseball Factory, 61; Seymour, *Baseball*, 2:71; Murdock, *Ban Johnson*, 149, 154; *NYT*, 28 Sept. 1919. The Bards were organized in 1910, eventually had 250 members, and met at a lavish room Comiskey constructed at the ballpark.

28. *NYTr*, 16 July 1905; Woolley, "Business of Baseball," 245.

29. Woolley, "Business of Baseball," 245; *Dictionary of American Biography*, s.v. "Taft, Charles P."; Frank Graham, *The Brooklyn Dodgers* (New York, 1945), 28–29. Charles P. Taft corresponded almost daily with his brother, but almost never mentioned baseball. William Howard Taft Papers, Library of Congress, Washington, D.C.

30. Woolley, "Business of Baseball," 245.

31. G. H. Fleming, *The Unforgettable Season* (New York, 1981), 129, 206–8; Ray Robinson, *Matty—an American Hero: Christy Mathewson of the New York Giants* (New York, 1993), 94–97; Gershman, *Diamonds*, 78, 80.

32. *CT*, 24 Sept. 1908; Robinson, *Matty*, 98, 100. For Emslie's report to the NL president, see Emslie to Harry Pulliam, 23 Sept. 1908, National Baseball Library, in "A Letter from the Files," *Baseball Research Journal* 22 (1993): 32. Quote is from *New York Evening Telegram*, 8 Oct. 1908, cited in Gershman, *Diamonds*, 83.

33. Woolley, "Business of Baseball," 245; *CT*, 18 Mar. 1916. Four AL teams suffered heavy losses in 1915, and just two FL teams made any profit. Emil H. Rothe, "Was the Federal League a Major League?" *Baseball Research Journal* 10 (1981): 9. On the FL, see also Marc Okkonnen, *The Federal League, 1914–1915: Baseball's Third Major League* (Cooperstown, N.Y., 1989).

34. *CDN*, 23 Dec. 1911; *SN*, 11 Jan. 1912.

35. *Chicago Record-Herald,* 10 Oct. 1908; *AC,* 19 Dec. 1908; *Albany Times-Union,* 26 Mar. 1914. Typical scalping rates for a three-game set of 1915 World Series seats were $3.00 tickets being sold for $40.00, and $2.00 tickets for $30.00. *NYTr,* 8 Oct. 1915. Two years later average rates for three-game sets in Chicago were $1.50 tickets going for $35.00, and $5.00 tickets for $50.00. *AC,* 3 Oct. 1917.

36. Joe Tinker, "Putting across the Federal League," *Everybody's Magazine,* May 1914, 583; Seymour, *Baseball,* 2:34–36; Warren Brown, *The Chicago Cubs* (New York, 1946), 64–65.

37. *CT,* 2 Feb. 1914, 25 Feb. 1914, 7 Mar. 1914, 18 Mar. 1914; *CDN,* 7 Mar. 1914; Albert N. Marquis, ed., *The Book of Chicagoans,* vol. 3 (Chicago, 1917), 543, 674–75, 713.

38. Raymond D. Kush, "The Building of Chicago's Wrigley Field," *Baseball Research Journal* 10 (1981): 10.

39. Seymour, *Baseball,* 2:196–224; and Voigt, *American Baseball,* 2:14–33.

40. Seymour, *Baseball,* 2:420; *The Federal Baseball Club of Baltimore, Inc. v. The National League of Professional Baseball Clubs and the American League of Professional Baseball Clubs,* 259 U.S. 200 (1922).

41. *CT,* 16 Jan. 1916, 18 Jan. 1916, 23 Jan. 1916; *CDN,* 18 Jan. 1916, 20 Jan. 1916; Marquis, *Book of Chicagoans,* 3:455, 543; Seymour, *Baseball,* 2:232; William Zimmerman Jr., *William Wrigley, Jr: The Man and His Business, 1861–1932* (Chicago, 1935), 205–13. During the seventh inning stretch of the first game, the band played "The Star-Spangled Banner," which was played at every game during the series and thereafter became identified with baseball. *NYT,* 26 Sept. 1918. It became the national anthem in 1931.

42. *Dictionary of American Biography,* s.v. "Wrigley, William"; "Albert D. Lasker," Oral History Transcript, Oral History Research Department, Butler Library, Columbia University, New York; John Gunther, *Taken at the Flood: The Story of Albert D. Lasker* (New York, 1960), 98–125; Robert K. Murray, *The Harding Era: Warren G. Harding and His Administration* (Minneapolis, 1969), 47, 52, 283; Francis Russell, *The Shadow of Blooming Grove: Warren G. Harding and His Time* (New York, 1968), 563; Randolph C. Downes, *The Rise of Warren G. Harding, 1865–1920* (Columbus, 1970), 452–53, 463, 471–74; William Veeck, *The Hustler's Handbook* (New York, 1965), 267.

43. *NYT,* 26 Apr. 1924; James Farley, *Behind the Ballots: The Personal History of a Politician* (New York, 1938), 17, 191. On the New York machine, see Theodore Lowi, *At the Pleasure of the Mayor: Patronage and Power in New York City, 1898–1958* (New York, 1965); William L. Riordan, comp., *Plunkitt of Tammany Hall* (1905; repr., New York, 1963); Lincoln Steffens, *The Shame of the Cities* (New York, 1904); M. R. Werner, *Tammany Hall* (Garden City, N.Y., 1928). Recent scholars have pointed to the limitations on the powers of bosses from competing elites, municipal bureaucrats, and economic, social, and cultural interest groups. See David Hammack, *Power and*

Society: Greater New York at the Turn of the Century (New York, 1982), and Jon Teaford, *The Unheralded Triumph: City Government in America, 1870–1920* (Baltimore, 1984).

44. Adelman, *Sporting Time*, 158–61, 163–64; Kirsch, *Creation of American Team Sports*, 157, 245, 255; Vincent, *Mudville's Revenge*, 100–106.

45. *SL*, 8 Oct. 1883; John J. O'Malley, "Mutrie's Mets of 1884," *NP* 4 (Spring 1985): 41.

46. *New York World*, 12 Mar. 1903; Voigt, "Cash and Glory," 525; Blanche McGraw, *The Real McGraw*, ed. Arthur Mann (New York, 1953), 170; Seymour, *Baseball*, 1:164–65, 214–17; Benson, *Ballparks of North America*, 254; *NYTr*, 23 Sept. 1901; House Judiciary Committee, *Organized Baseball*, 1440; Burk, *Never Just a Game*, 104.

Baseball became increasingly profitable following the merger of the AA and the NL. In 1883 only two NL teams lost money. The biggest money-maker was Boston, which allegedly made over forty thousand dollars. See Burk, *Never Just a Game*, 73.

47. Seymour, *Baseball*, 1:214–16.

48. *NYTr*, 25 Jan. 1895; *NYT*, 26 Oct. 1904, 5 Dec. 1915, 13 Apr. 1917, 7 Apr. 1941; *BE*, 18 Jan. 1896; McGraw, *Real McGraw*, 90–91, 170; Seymour, *Baseball*, 1:238.

49. Seymour, *Baseball*, 1:244. Losses for 1892 were estimated at less than forty thousand dollars; *SN*, 12 Jan. 1895; *NYTr*, 23 Sept. 1901; House Judiciary Committee, *Organized Baseball*, 25; Voigt, *American Baseball*, 1:232, 234; James H. Hardy Jr., *The New York Giants Base Ball Club: The Growth of a Team and a Sport, 1870 to 1900* (Jefferson, N.C., 1996), 156.

50. *NYT*, 3 Dec. 1897, 7 Jan. 1904, 30 Mar. 1944; *SL*, 25 Dec. 1897; *New York American*, 5 Dec. 1915, in Tammany Newspaper Clippings File, 1913–34, Edwin P. Kilroe Collection of Tammaniana, Special Collections, Butler Library, Columbia University, N.Y.; *Dictionary of American Biography*, s.v. "Freedman, Andrew"; McGraw, *Real McGraw*, 169. On Freedman's financial dealings with Croker, see *NYTr*, 24 Jan. 1895, 25 Jan. 1895, 8 Dec. 1897; and *NYT*, 18 Apr. 1899, 29 June 1916. On rumors of Croker's financial involvement in the Giants, see *NYTr*, 27 July 1898.

Freedman was a member of nearly a dozen prestigious men's clubs, as well as on the boards of the Society for the Prevention of Cruelty to Animals, the Metropolitan Museum of Art, and the America Museum of Natural History. He donated his entire seven-million-dollar fortune to found a home for senior citizens. See Pat Edith Aynes, "The Andrew Freedman Story" (1976), Andrew Freedman Home for the Aged, Bronx, N.Y., i, 39.

51. *SN*, 24 Aug. 1895; *NYTr*, 23 Apr. 1896, 29 Apr. 1896; Seymour, *Baseball*, 1:296–98.

52. Seymour, *Baseball*, 1:296–98, 303; Voigt, *American Baseball*, 284 (quote).

53. *SN*, 24 Aug. 1895, 25 Dec. 1897, 6 Aug. 1898; *NYTr*, 23 Apr. 1896, 29 Apr. 1896, 4 June 1898, 7 July 1898, 15 Mar. 1899, 14 Dec. 1899, 6 July 1900, 23 Sept. 1901, 15 Dec. 1901, 2 Oct. 1902; *BE*, 26 May 1896. For Freedman's early rivalry with Brooklyn, see *BE*, 20 Nov. 1895. See also Seymour, *Baseball*, 1:296–98, 303; and Burk, *Never Just a Game*, 133–34, 140–41.

54. *SL*, 11 Nov. 1899, 26 Oct. 1901; *CDN*, 15 June 1901.

55. *CDN*, 7 Nov. 1901; *SN*, 9 Nov. 1901; *SL*, 16 Nov. 1901.

56. *NYT*, 14 Jan. 1902, 20 Jan. 1902; *Annual Meeting of the National League and American Association*; Seymour, *Baseball*, 1:317–22; *CDN*, 7 Nov. 1901; *SN*, 9 Nov. 1901; *SL*, 16 Nov. 1901; McGraw, *Real McGraw*, 177–78; Levine, *Spalding*, 66–69.

57. Murdock, *Ban Johnson*, 55–56; Seymour, *Baseball*, 1:321–22; Alexander, *McGraw*, 82–93.

58. *NYT*, 17 July 1902; *AC*, 17 July 1902; Murdock, *Ban Johnson*, 56–58; Seymour, *Baseball*, 1:321; Alexander, *McGraw*, 92.

59. *NYT*, 30 Sept. 1902; *CDN*, 30 Sept. 1902; *NYTr*, 2 Oct. 1902; *SN*, 25 Dec. 1897, 8 Jan. 1898, 4 Oct. 1902; *Cincinnati Enquirer*, 9 Jan. 1903; *New York World*, 8 Jan. 1903; *SL*, 17 Jan. 1903; "The Business Side of Baseball," 170; *NYT*, 11 Mar. 1916; McGraw, *Real McGraw*, 176–77, 179; Allen, *Giants and Dodgers*, 48. For Tammany's continuing connections with the team, see Henry Chadwick, Scrapbooks, vol. 18, p. 27, Albert G. Spalding Collection, New York Public Library.

60. Woolley, "Business of Baseball," 243; *Cincinnati Enquirer*, 17 Mar. 1903; Voigt, *American Baseball*, 2:108; Murdock, *Ban Johnson*, 35. Freedman had previously met with the New York gambler Frank Farrell, who supposedly agreed to help Brush obtain the Giants by getting his friend and racing stable partner, Cincinnati Mayor Julius Fleischmann, to acquire the Reds from Brush. In return, Farrell was promised Freedman's support in buying and moving the Baltimore Orioles to New York in 1902. McGraw, *Real McGraw*, 162.

61. McGraw, *Real McGraw*, 162; Woolley, "Business of Baseball," 243; *Cincinnati Enquirer*, 17 Mar. 1903; Voigt, *American Baseball*, 2:108; Murdock, *Ban Johnson*, 35. In 1891 the NL brought Brush in as Cincinnati owner to bolster its fight against the AA. The NL voted him a salary and five thousand dollars to maintain the Reds. By the time the war ended in 1892, Brush had received twenty-three thousand dollars. See *CT*, 4 Nov. 1900.

On the politics of Cincinnati ownership, see Norman Rose to William Gray, 19 Apr. 1911, Herrmann Papers. The bribe to permit Sunday baseball was exacted by police clerk Rudolph Hynicka, who eventually succeeded Cox as boss. After Cox and his friends bought the club, their agents raised money from local tavern keepers to pay for a parade to commemorate the purchase. See Louis Leonard Tucker, *Cincinnati's Citizen Crusaders: A History of the Cincinnatus Association, 1920–1965* (Cincinnati, 1965), 22, 53, 38.

62. *CT,* 17 Oct. 1912; Paul J. Zingg, *Harry Hooper: An American Baseball Life* (Urbana, Ill., 1993), 104–6; Robinson, *Matty,* 146–49; Seymour, *Baseball,* 2:71; *NYT,* 6 Apr. 1974.

63. *NYT,* 12 Feb. 1908, 13 Nov. 1923; *SN,* 15 Nov. 1923; *NYTr,* 17 Feb. 1919; Alexander, *McGraw,* 208–10; Seymour, *Baseball,* 2:72, 140, 309; Frank Graham, *McGraw of the Giants* (New York, 1944), 113; Tom Clark, *The World of Damon Runyon* (New York, 1968), 103–4; McGraw, *Real McGraw,* 265; Herbert Mitgang, *The Man Who Rode the Tiger: The Life of Judge Samuel Seabury and the Story of the Greatest Investigation of City Corruption in This Century* (New York, 1970), 189–90.

64. *SN,* 10 Jan. 1929, 21 Nov. 1929. The press reported that the Giants made $860,000 and the Yankees about $600,000 in 1920, far different from the actual profits compiled from tax returns. *CDN,* 31 Dec. 1920; House Judiciary Committee, *Organized Baseball,* 1599–1600. The Yankees' annual expenditures included $120,000 for salaries, $93,500 for daily expenses, $60,000 for rent, $75,000 for traveling, and $60,000 for overhead, or a grand total of $408,500, requiring attendance of about one million fans to make a profit. The only money earned on roadtrips was one-half of general admission tickets. "Inside Baseball," *Collier's,* 25 Mar. 1922, 29. Joe Vila of the *New York Morning Sun* judiciously estimated Giants' profits for 1921 at $400,000. Alexander, *McGraw,* 238.

Additional profits came from the rental of the field for boxing matches, particularly the Jack Dempsey–Louis Firpo heavyweight championship fight in 1923 that brought in $50,000 in rent and concession fees.

65. *New York World,* 26 Sept. 1902; *SL,* 11 Nov. 1902; Chadwick Scrapbooks, vols. 2, 5; Vincent, *Mudville's Revenge,* 107; Allen, *Giants and Dodgers,* 17–19; Voigt, "Cash and Glory," 530–31.

66. *New York World,* 26 Sept. 1902; *SL,* 11 Nov. 1902; Chadwick Scrapbooks, vols. 2, 5; Allen, *Giants and Dodgers,* 23; Stanley Cohen, *Dodgers! The First One Hundred Years* (New York, 1990), 4–8; Richard Goldstein, *Superstars and Screwballs: One Hundred Years of Brooklyn Baseball* (New York, 1991), 32.

67. On the problems of the AA, see Seymour, *Baseball,* 1:219–20. The Gladiators failed to complete the season and moved to Baltimore. Voigt, "Cash and Glory," 531; Philip Lowry, *Green Cathedrals* (Cooperstown, N.Y., 1986), 34, 39. The club was capitalized at $250,000 in 1891, but the value of its stock was only $80,000. See Andy McCue, "A History of Dodger Ownership: From Red Hook to the West Coast," *NP* 13 (1993): 35–36.

68. *NYT,* 19 Apr. 1925; Graham, *Brooklyn Dodgers,* 7; Tommy Holmes, *Dodger Daze and Knights* (New York, 1953), 23; Cohen, *Dodgers!* 8; Goldstein, *Superstars and Screwballs,* 69–72, 98; McCue, "Dodger Ownership," 36–37.

69. Seymour, "Rise of Major League Baseball," 446; *Clipper,* 1 Nov. 1890,

cited in ibid., 484 (quote); *BE*, 10 Jan. 1896, 3 Feb. 1898, 15 Mar. 1898; *NYTr*, 16 Mar. 1898; *SN*, 1 Dec. 1906; McCue, "Dodger Ownership," 37.

70. *NYT*, 19 Apr. 1925; Graham, *Brooklyn Dodgers*, 7; Holmes, *Dodger Daze and Knights*, 23; Cohen, *Dodgers!* 8–10; Seymour, *Baseball*, 1:302; Voigt, *American Baseball*, 1:272; Goldstein, *Superstars and Screwballs*, 72, 74.

71. *SL*, 13 Jan. 1900; *NYT*, 19 Apr. 1925; *NYTr*, 19 Apr. 1925; *SN*, 3 Jan. 1920. Both the *New York Times* and the *New York Tribune* inaccurately estimated profits in 1920 at over five hundred thousand dollars. Goldstein, *Superstars and Screwballs*, 98; McCue, "Dodger Ownership," 37.

72. On Sullivan, see *NYT*, 28 Sept. 1902; *SL*, 4 Oct. 1902, 8 Nov. 1902; Daniel Czithrom, "Underworlds and Underdogs: Big Tim Sullivan and Metropolitan Politics in New York, 1889–1913," *Journal of American History* 78 (Sept. 1991): 536–58; Riess, *City Games*, 82, 174–75, 183, 185–86, 198, 206; and Thomas M. Henderson, *Tammany Hall and the New Immigrants: The Progressive Years* (New York, 1976), 1–15.

73. *CDN*, 11 Mar. 1903; *New York World*, 8 Jan. 1903, 13 Mar. 1903, 14 Mar. 1903; *NYT*, 16 Oct. 1901, 15 Mar. 1903, 22 Nov. 1911; Woolley, "Business of Baseball," 254; Tammany Newspaper Clippings File, 1913–34, Edwin P. Kilroe Collection of Tammaniana; Al Fein, "New York Politics, 1897–1903: A Study in Political Party Leadership" (M.A. thesis, Columbia University, 1954), 81–91.

74. *Cincinnati Enquirer*, 17 Mar. 1903; *NYT*, 20 Oct. 1901, 28 Oct. 1901, 31 Aug. 1902, 22 Feb. 1926; *SN*, 18 Feb. 1926; Maxwell F. Marcuse, *This Was New York: A Nostalgic Picture of Gotham in the Gas Light Era*, rev. and enl. (New York, 1969), 170–71; Lloyd Morris, *Incredible New York: High Life and Low Life of the Last One Hundred Years* (New York, 1951), 226; Stephen Fox, *Big Leagues: Professional Baseball, Football, and Basketball in National Memory* (New York, 1994), 351–53.

75. On Farrell's improved image, see *NYTr*, 7 Sept. 1908, 18 Dec. 1911 (quote), 1 July 1912; *SN*, 4 Feb. 1909; *SL*, 21 Aug. 1909; and *New York American*, 26 Dec. 1907, quoted in Fleming, *Unforgettable Season*, 11–12.

Farrell's club was prepared to do whatever was necessary to win. On 25 September 1909 the Detroit Tigers' trainer found a cubby hole in center field with holes bored into the fence where a Highlander employee would sit with binoculars to steal signs from the opposing catcher. The operator would then flash signals to the batter so he would know what to expect. See Henry Tuthill to Ban Johnson, 4 Oct. 1909, Detroit Baseball Club Letterbooks, 1903–12, Ernie Harwell Collection, Detroit Public Library, quoted in Fox, *Big Leagues*, 356.

76. *NYT*, 5 Aug. 1902, 7 Sept. 1902, 21 June 1919; *New York Sun*, 21 June 1919; James F. Richardson, *The New York Police: Colonial Times to 1901* (New York, 1970), 271–72; Fox, *Big Leagues*, 351.

77. *NYT,* 9 Apr. 1899, 21 June 1919; *New York Sun,* 21 June 1919; Lincoln Steffens, *The Autobiography of Lincoln Steffens* (New York, 1931), 320 (quote).

After the 1901 election Devery broke from the regular organization because he felt he had been used as a scapegoat. Nevertheless, he was still elected district leader from the Ninth Aldermanic District. In 1903 he ran for mayor as an independent, but was soundly thrashed, getting fewer than three thousand votes. *NYT,* 4 Nov. 1903; Richard J. Butler and Joseph Driscoll, *Dock Walloper: The Story of "Big Dick" Butler* (New York, 1928), 487–91; Fein, "New York Politics," 128–29, 142–43.

78. *NYT,* 11 Feb. 1926; Frank Graham, *New York Yankees* (New York, 1943), 19–21; Woolley, "Business of Baseball," 245.

79. Graham, *New York Yankees,* 21; *NYT,* 1 Oct. 1897, 2 Oct. 1897, 10 Oct. 1897. Issues of *Tammany Times,* the machine's magazine in the late 1890s, carried a lot of Ruppert Beer ads.

80. Smelser, *The Life That Ruth Built,* 86–88, 97–101, 109, 127–28, 163; Marshall Smelser, "The Babe on Balance," *American Scholar* 44 (Spring 1975): 299–304; Robert Creamer, *Babe: The Legend Comes to Life* (New York, 1974); Seymour, *Baseball,* 2:426–33; Leverett T. Smith, *The American Dream and the National Game* (Bowling Green, Ohio, 1975); Tristam P. Coffin, *The Old Ball Game: Baseball in Folklore and Fiction* (New York, 1971).

81. Edgar B. Tolman, reviser, *The Revised Municipal Code of Chicago of 1905* (Chicago, 1905), 35, 38; Edward J. Brundage, reviser, *The Chicago Code of 1911* (Chicago, 1911), 7, 10.

82. *AC,* 8 May 1904; *SN,* 8 May 1897; *Chicago Record-Herald,* 5 Aug. 1909; John C. Thomson, *The Greater New York Charter of 1901* (New York, 1901), 838–39; notation penciled over letter from Barney Dreyfuss to A. Herrmann, 15 June 1912, Herrmann Papers; *CDN,* 17 Dec. 1909; *CT,* 18 Dec. 1909. One unfriendly member of the city council had previously called for a daily fee of two hundred dollars for the Chicago teams. *NYTr,* 7 Nov. 1909.

83. Parks seating 10,000–15,000 were assessed $1,000; 4,000–10,000, $350; and smaller fields, $75. *Journal of the Proceedings of the City Council of Chicago* (2 Apr. 1919): 1947, (29 Dec. 1919): 1689, (7 Apr. 1920): 2534.

84. License fees for other parks were not affected. *CDN,* 26 Jan. 1921, 3 Feb. 1921; *Journal of the Proceedings of the City Council of Chicago* (4 Feb. 1921): 1746; Alex Gottfried, "Anton J. Cermak, Chicago Politician: A Study in Political Leadership" (Ph.D. diss., University of Chicago, 1952), 175–76. Shortly thereafter Cermak operated a semiprofessional team, which played at Cermak Park in Pilsen, as a business venture and a vehicle to improve his public image by indicating his concern for the recreational options of his voters. Gottfried, "Anton J. Cermak," 284.

85. Voigt, *American Baseball,* 1:65; "The Chicago Base-ball Grounds,"

Harper's Weekly, 12 May 1883, 299; *Journal of the Proceedings of the City Council of Chicago* (1 May 1899): 281–82.

86. *NYT,* 5 Oct. 1906, 18 Sept. 1908, 10 Oct. 1911, 14 Oct. 1911, 6 Oct. 1913; Ring Lardner, "The Cost of Baseball," *Collier's,* 2 Mar. 1912, 28, 30; see also *Chicago Times,* 5 July 1885. Comiskey claimed that he paid the city $1.50 for every officer assigned to the ballpark. *CDN,* 4 Oct. 1919. On proposed legislation, see *Journal of the Proceedings of the City Council of Chicago* (4 Jan. 1920): 1897, (21 July 1921): 903, (19 Dec. 1928): 4139, (3 Jan. 1930): 1909. Bruce Smith, *Chicago Police Problems* (Chicago, 1931), 256.

87. *NYT,* 19 July 1889, 12 Apr. 1907; Chadwick Scrapbooks, vol. 5; *New York Globe,* 4 Apr. 1908, cited in Fleming, *Unforgettable Season,* 51.

88. *NYT,* 13 Apr. 1907; *SL,* 1 June 1907.

89. *NYT,* 13 Apr. 1907; John J. Hickey, *Our Police Guardians* (New York, 1925), 152–53; *New York Globe,* 24 Apr. 1908. For instances of disorder with which the special police failed to cope, see the newspaper clippings for 30 May 1907, in Henry Chadwick Diaries, Albert G. Spalding Collection; *Chicago Record-Herald,* 22 May 1907; *NYT,* 23 Apr. 1908, 28 June 1911, 10 Oct. 1911, 12 Oct. 1911, 16 Aug. 1920; *NYTr,* 17 Apr. 1911; *BE,* 13 Apr. 1912; *AC,* 31 Aug. 1919. On the Giants' special police, see R. G. Wilson, "Policing the Greatest Baseball Stadium in the World," *BM,* May 1913, 65. George Dougherty was also a former Pinkerton who went on to become a deputy police commissioner. See *Who's Who in New York, 1929,* s.v. "Dougherty, George."

90. *NYT,* 18 Sept. 1908, 19 Sept. 1908, 20 Sept. 1908, 21 Sept. 1908, 22 Sept. 1908; *CDN,* 18 Sept. 1908, 19 Sept. 1908, 20 Sept. 1908, 21 Sept. 1908, 22 Sept. 1908; Fleming, *Unforgettable Season,* 226–27, 303, 305, 314. See also *BE,* 30 Apr. 1912. In 1920 Charles Ebbets managed to get volunteer off-duty uniformed police to patrol Ebbets Field in return for a donation to the police pension fund. *NYT,* 1 June 1920; New York Board of Aldermen, *Proceedings* (15 June 1920): 456.

91. *Chicago Record-Herald,* 15 Oct. 1911; *NYTr,* 17 Oct. 1911; "Working the Baseball Public," *Literary Digest* 42 (28 Oct. 1911): 726–27; *NYT,* 8 Oct. 1912; *New York Globe,* 8 Oct. 1912, quoted in *SN,* 17 Oct. 1912. See also *NYTr,* 9 Oct. 1916.

92. *Chicago Record-Herald,* 15 Oct. 1906, 22 May 1907; *NYTr,* 17 Apr. 1911; *BE,* 12 Apr. 1912, 16 Aug. 1920; *AC,* 31 Aug. 1919; *SN,* 6 May 1920.

93. T. B Collier to A. Herrmann, 14 July 1914, Herrmann Papers. On overflow crowds, see the photographs in Voigt, *American Baseball,* 2:36; and Seymour, *Baseball,* vol. 2, photo pages following 152.

94. *NYT,* 12 Apr. 1912; *BE,* 13 Apr. 1912; *NYTr,* 15 Apr. 1912.

95. *NYTr,* 28 Oct. 1919; *CDN,* 25 Sept. 1920; Woolley, "Business of Baseball," 251; Seymour, *Baseball,* 2:54, 300, 308, 389; Graham, *New York Yankees,* 21; Clark, *World of Damon Runyon,* 103–4; Mitgang, *The Man Who Rode the Tiger,* 190. Rothstein was not only in business with Stoneham but

also had previously been John McGraw's partner in a pool hall. Seymour, *Baseball*, 2:308.

96. For an in-depth study of sport and gambling, see Hugh Fullerton, "American Gambling and Gamblers," *American Magazine*, Feb. 1914, 33–38. On baseball gambling, see *AC*, 16 July 1903; *NYTr*, 30 July 1913; Seymour, *Baseball*, 2:278–81.

97. Riess, *City Games*, 182; *AC*, 18 July 1907, 16 Apr. 1911; *NYTr*, 28 Feb. 1911, 14 Oct. 1911, 10 Dec. 1911; *CDN*, 28 May 1915, 27 Sept. 1919, 3 Oct. 1919, 4 Oct. 1919; Seymour, *Baseball*, 2:280. On the early pools, see Spalding, *America's National Game*, 190–91.

98. *CDN*, 28 Dec. 1901; Voigt, *American Baseball*, 1:71–75; Seymour, *Baseball*, 2:274–76, 281–93; Stephan S. Hall, "Scandals and Controversies," in *Total Baseball*, ed. John Thorn and Pete Palmer (New York, 1989), 435–37; Murdock, *Ban Johnson*, 209. William M. Spink of the *St. Louis Globe Democrat* averred that the game between Chicago and St. Louis on 24 August 1877 had been fixed by two Browns players who made important errors. He claimed that detectives followed them to a saloon where they met an agent of Mike McDonald, the head of organized crime in Chicago, and money changed hands. *SN*, 10 Nov. 1894.

99. Seymour, *Baseball*, 2:288–92; quote from *SN*, 17 Apr. 1947, cited in Fox, *Big Leagues*, 354.

100. Lieb, *Baseball as I Have Known It*, 97–103, 98 (quote); *Dictionary of American Sports, Baseball*, s.v., "Chase, Hal"; Robert C. Hoie, "The Hal Chase Case," *Baseball Historical Review*, ed. L. Robert Davids (Washington, D.C., 1981), 34–41. Rookie shortstop Roger Peckinpaugh was originally mystified by his poor throws to first base that too frequently ended up in the stands. Years later he realized that Chase "was tangling up his feet and then making a fancy dive after the ball, making it look like a wild throw." See John Tullius, *I'd Rather Be a Yankee: An Oral History of America's Most Loved and Most Hated Team* (New York, 1986), 10–14 (quote on 11).

101. Hoie, "Hal Chase Case," 34–41 (quote on 38); Seymour, *Baseball*, 2:209–10, 288–93; Lieb, *Baseball as I Have Known It*, 102; Murdock, *Ban Johnson*, 185 (second quote).

102. Seymour, *Baseball*, 2:288–92; Hoie, "Hal Chase Case," 34–40; Alexander, *McGraw*, 206–7, 214–16.

103. Fleming, *Unforgettable Season*, 185; Seymour, *Baseball*, 2:280; Adomites, "Fans," 667. See also *NYT*, 28 May 1914.

104. *NYTr*, 6 Aug. 1908; *SN*, 17 Aug. 1895; *Philadelphia Inquirer*, 11 Sept. 1903; *AC*, 16 July 1903, 23 Jan. 1904, 18 July 1907; *New York Telegram*, 16 June 1913; *NYT*, 14 May 1913, 17 June 1913, 18 June 1913; *CDN*, 27 Sept. 1919; Fleming, *Unforgettable Season*, 152, 154; Seymour, *Baseball*, 2:278–79; Murdock, *Ban Johnson*, 184–85. Quote is from *St. Louis Post-Dispatch*, 14 Feb. 1929, cited in Murdock, *Ban Johnson*, 185.

105. *AC*, 18 July 1907, 5 May 1912; *NYTr*, 30 Sept. 1912, 27 June 1914; *NYT*, 17 June 1913. The *New York Times* had articles during this period entitled "Gamblers Ejected from the Game" (1913); "Gambling Pools Barred" (1914); "Arrests for Gambling" (1915); and "Gambling Stopped at All Ball Parks" (1919) (this was simply not true). In 1920 six people were arrested for gambling at a game in Boston, four and five at two games at the Polo Grounds, and ten at a Pacific Coast League game. See Adomites, "Fans," 667.

106. *AC*, 20 Mar. 1920; *NYT*, 25 May 1920, 26 May 1920. When Louis Hirsch got up and moved out of his seat, he was ejected as a suspected gambler. Hirsch sued the Yankees for his mistreatment, which helped discourage strong efforts at fighting gambling. *NYT*, 28 May 1920.

107. On the scandal, see Eliot Asinof, *Eight Men Out: The Black Sox and the 1919 World Series* (New York, 1963); Victor Luhrs, *The Great Baseball Mystery: The 1919 World Series* (South Brunswick, N.J., 1966); Seymour, *Baseball*, 2:164, 294–339; Robert I. Goler, "Black Sox," *Chicago History* 17 (Fall–Winter 1988–89): 42–69; *Eight Men Out*, produced by John Sayles, 1988; Murdock, *Ban Johnson*, 185–89; Leo Katcher, *The Big Bankroll: The Life and Times of Arnold Rothstein* (New York, 1959), 148; Ward, *Baseball*, 133–45.

108. Seymour, *Baseball*, 1:334; Ward, *Baseball*, 133.

109. *SN*, 12 Dec. 1915; *SL*, 12 Dec. 1915; Richard Lindberg, "Yesterday's City: The Southside Baseball Factory," *Chicago History* 28 (Summer 1989): 61; Murdock, *Ban Johnson*, 79–80; Charles Fountain, *Sportswriter: The Life and Times of Grantland Rice* (New York, 1993), 171; Ban Johnson, "The Inside of the Collins Deal" *BM*, Mar. 1913, 31–32. John Sayles, in Ken Burn's documentary *Baseball*, and repeated in Ward, *Baseball*, 133, claimed that in 1918 the ballplayers nicknamed themselves the "Black Sox" during their laundry strike. This whimsical anecdote is discounted by the veteran baseball journalist Jerome Holtzman, who could find no corroboration for the tale. *CT*, 25 Sept. 1994.

110. On salaries, see Seymour, *Baseball*, 2:334; Lindberg, *Stealing First*, 104, reported higher salaries. On the mistreatment of players, see Zingg, *Hooper*, 188–89.

111. The Cicotte legend has been examined by the historian Lowell Blaisdell, who questioned that the miserly Comiskey would have ever promised anyone a ten-thousand-dollar bonus. Of course, he might have promised it, never expecting that Cicotte would come close to winning that many games, although he had won twenty-nine games in 1917. When Cicotte confessed to the grand jury about his complicity, he did not claim that the lost bonus was a motivating factor. Blaisdell concurs with the judgment of the *New York Times*. See Lowell D. Blaisdell, "Legends as an Expression of Baseball Memory," *Journal of Sport History* 19 (Winter 1992): 231, 233–34.

112. Seymour, *Baseball*, 2:303, 334. Gropman argues that Jackson did not understand what the fix was all about and was innocent of any wrongdoing. Donald Gropman, *Say It Ain't So, Joe! The Story of Shoeless Joe Jackson* (Boston, 1979), 170–211, 220–27.

113. Quote is cited in Ward, *Baseball*, 135. On Lardner's ditty, see Asinof, *Eight Men Out*, 94.

114. *SN*, 16 Oct. 1919; Ward, *Baseball*, 141. The Comiskey-Hoyne meeting is nicely recounted in Asinof, *Eight Men Out*, 130–31.

115. Bill Felber, "Under Pallor, Under Shadow," *Baseball History*, premier ed., 29, 34–35; Seymour, *Baseball*, 2:334–35.

116. Seymour, *Baseball*, 2:297–98. A sports editor subsequently wrote a letter to AL President Ban Johnson indicating that on 31 August a gambler named Frog Thompson had received a telegraph message, presumed to be from Claude Hendrix, in which the sender bet five thousand dollars against the Cubs. The editor also claimed that Hal Chase had wired Thompson that the game was fixed. Hendrix was blacklisted from baseball in 1921. Seymour, *Baseball*, 2:301.

117. Hall, "Scandals and Controversies," 437; Asinof, *Eight Men Out*, 149–52; Seymour, *Baseball*, 2:298–305; "The Confession of Joe Jackson before the Grand Jury of Cook County," 28 Sept. 1920, in author's possession.

118. On the cultural significance of the Black Sox scandal, see Roderick Nash, *The Nervous Generation: American Thought, 1917–1930* (Chicago, 1970), 130–32. In the fall of 1919, when the fix was just a rumor, the *Sporting News* suspected Jewish gamblers behind it attempting to undermine the national pastime. *SN*, 9 Oct. 1919, 16 Oct. 1919. Rothstein was never even indicted for any crime, but most Americans believed he had masterminded the fix. Anti-Semites like the American icon Henry Ford blamed Jews for the Black Sox scandal. His *Dearborn Independent* published articles in September 1921 entitled "Jewish Gamblers Corrupt American Baseball" and "The Jewish Degradation of American Baseball." The scandal exemplified to anti-Semites how Jews were insidiously destroying the inner fabric of American society by ruining the national pastime (not to mention motion pictures and Wall Street), and thereby subverting American institutions and undermining morality. Rothstein was fictionalized as Meyer Wolfsheim in F. Scott Fitzgerald's *The Great Gatsby* (1925). Another Jewish "presumed" participant in the scandal was former bantamweight champion Abe Attell, who tried to interest Rothstein in fixing the series and then independently helped finance it. He was indicted, but never convicted. On the periphery were Alfred Austrian, the Sox attorney, who expedited the grand jury confessions, and team secretary Harry Grabiner, who helped Austrian with damage control. See Peter Levine, *Ellis Island to Ebbets Field: Sport and the American Jewish Experience* (New York, 1992), 116–18; Daniel A. Nathan, "Anti-Semitism

and the Black Sox Scandal," *Nine* 4 (Dec. 1995): 94–100; Arnd Kruger, " 'Fair Play for American Athletes': A Study in Anti-Semitism," *Canadian Journal of the History of Sport and Physical Education* 9 (May 1978): 55.

119. *The People of the State of Illinois v. Edward V. Cicotte et al.*, Criminal Court of Cook County, Mar. 26, 1921; Seymour, *Baseball*, 2:308–10, 324–30.

120. Seymour, *Baseball*, 2:330–31. On Landis, see J. G. Taylor Spink, *Judge Landis and Twenty-Five Years of Baseball* (New York, 1947); Seymour, *Baseball*, 2:312–13, 317–25, 330–31, 376–96. For an excellent revisionist analysis of Landis's relationship with the owners, see Clark Nardinelli, "Judge Kenesaw Mountain Landis and the Art of Cartel Enforcement," *Baseball History*, premier ed., 103–14.

121. For the political connections of major league owners, see Steven A. Riess, "Professional Baseball and American Culture in the Progressive Era: Myths and Realities, with Special Emphasis on Atlanta, Chicago, and New York" (Ph.D. diss., University of Chicago, 1974), appendixes A and B; Voigt, *American Baseball*, 1:234–35, 246, 259. On profitability, see Burk, *Never Just a Game*, 134–36. On the minors, see Warnock, "Entrepreneurs and Progressives," 92–100.

122. *SL*, 11 Nov. 1898; *SN*, 12 Nov. 1898; Burk, *Never Just a Game*, 135–36. The *Sporting News* estimated that an average team cost $61,000 to operate, of which $35,700 (58.5 percent) went to players' salaries. *SN*, 17 Feb. 1900.

123. *NYT*, 30 Dec. 1906, 10 Sept. 1908, 3 Feb. 1920; Woolley, "Business of Baseball," 251–55; George Ethelbert Walsh, "The Gilt-Edged Diamond," *Independent*, 31 July 1913, 261–63. The Giants made at least $200,000 in 1908. See Alexander, *McGraw*, 139.

124. The article reported that 55.5 percent of the income came from home game ticket sales, 2.6 percent from the sale of concession privileges, and the rest, 41.9 percent, from road games. The latter number is questionable since teams received only a small fraction of revenue from away games. This estimate failed to take into account many other sources of profit, such as rental of the ballpark and revenue from exhibition games. Other major expenses were $24,000 for losses incurred by postponed games, $20,000 to rent the site of the ballpark, and $12,000 for travel. *SN*, Aug. 1910, cited in David Pietrusza, *Major Leagues: The Formation, Sometimes Absorption, and Mostly Eventual Demise of Eighteen Professional Baseball Organizations, 1871 to Present* (Jefferson City, N.C., 1991), 183–84.

125. Compiled from table entitled "Margin of Profit on Gross Operating Income, Major League Clubs, 1920–1950," House Judiciary Committee, *Organized Baseball*, 1615.

126. On Jewish baseball executives, see Stanley B. Frank, *The Jew in Sport* (New York, 1936), 75–91; *Encyclopedia Judaica*, 1st ed., s.v. "Sports"; Bernard Postal, Jesse Silver, and Roy Silver, eds., *Encyclopedia of Jews in Sports* (New York, 1965). On Jews in the motion picture industry, see May, *Screen-*

ing Out the Past, 167–77; Neal Gabler, *An Empire of Their Own: How the Jews Invented Hollywood* (New York, 1988); Ben B. Seligman, *The Potentates* (New York, 1971), 260–61.

127. Buenker, *Urban Liberalism,* 118–22; Oscar Handlin, *The Uprooted* (Boston, 1951), 195–97, 243; John Higham, *Strangers in the Land* (New Brunswick, N.J., 1963), 116–18; Hofstadter, *Age of Reform,* 60–61, 75, 167, 176; J. Joseph Huthmacher, "Urban Liberalism and the Age of Reform," *Mississippi Valley Historical Review* 49 (Sept. 1962): 231–41. The relationship between ball clubs and politicians can be seen as an example of honest graft by which insiders used their information to make lucrative investments or enhance their enterprises. See Riordan, *Plunkitt of Tammany Hall,* 3–6.

Chapter 3: Politics, Ballparks, and the Neighborhoods

1. A wealth of data on ballparks can be found in Lowry, *Green Cathedrals,* Gershman, *Diamonds,* and Benson, *Ballparks of North America.* Also useful are Bill Shannon and George Karlinsky, *The Ballparks* (New York, 1975); and Lowell Reidenbaugh, *Take Me Out to the Ball Park* (St. Louis, 1983). For superb locator maps, ballpark drawings that include each field's principal neighbors, and rare photographs from the early 1900s, see Marc Okkonen, *Baseball Memories: 1900–1909* (New York, 1992).

2. Federal Writers Project, *Baseball in Old Chicago,* 11–13, 22; Voigt, "Cash and Glory," 106; Charles S. Winslow, *Historical Events of Chicago in Three Volumes* (Chicago, 1937), 2:101, 103; *CT,* 25 June 1884; Benson, *Ballparks of North America,* 80–81.

3. Lowry, *Green Cathedrals,* 42; Benson, *Ballparks of North America,* 81–83; Levine, *Spalding,* 45–46.

4. "Chicago Base-Ball Grounds," 299; *CT,* 25 June 1884; Winslow, *Historical Events,* 2:156; Pierce, *A History of Chicago,* 3:477; Gershman, *Diamonds,* 37; Benson, *Ballparks of North America,* 83. Spalding made extra money by renting out Lake Front Park to other outdoor recreations ranging from the Calumet Lacrosse Club to the Barnum and Bailey Circus, which paid twenty-five hundred dollars. Levine, *Spalding,* 38.

5. *CT,* 25 Feb. 1885, 31 May 1885, 7 June 1885; *Mirror of American Sport, Supplement,* 6 June 1885, R. C. Kuhn Scrapbooks, 1885, and clipping from *Mirror of American Sport,* 1887, both in R. C. Kuhn Collection, Chicago Historical Society; Benson, *Ballparks of North America,* 85; Pierce, *A History of Chicago,* 3:477–78 (quote on 478). For a description of the neighborhood, see U.S. Census Office, *Report on Vital and Social Statistics, Cities of One Hundred Thousand Population and Upward,* comp. John S. Billings (Washington, D.C., 1896), 168.

6. *Chicago Herald,* 22 May 1891; *SN,* 9 Jan. 1892; *CT,* 20 Mar. 1892, 4 Apr. 1892; *CDN,* 21 Mar. 1892; Joseph Burke, "Chicago National League Baseball

Club Played at Thirty-Fifth and Wentworth," 1950, typescript, 1–4, Chicago Historical Society; Homer Hoyt, *One Hundred Years of Land Values in Chicago, 1830–1933* (Chicago, 1933), 137, 146. On the brotherhood's quest for a Chicago ballpark, see Riess, "Professional Baseball," 129–32.

7. *CT,* 4 Apr. 1892, 6 Aug. 1894; Lowry, *Green Cathedrals,* 43; Benson, *Ballparks of North America,* 86–87; *SN,* 23 Nov. 1889, 18 Dec. 1892, 11 Feb. 1893, 22 Apr. 1893; U.S. Census Office, *Report on Cities,* 172. The lease on the abandoned South Side Park ran to 1897, and Spalding rented it out to other amusements, including professional cycling races, college football games, and Bedouin Wild East shows. Burke, "Chicago National League Baseball Club," 1–4. The Congress Street bleachers were enclosed with barbed wire in 1892 after fans had rushed the field to curse the umpire, who responded by forfeiting the game to the visiting team. Gershman, *Diamonds,* 54.

8. *CT,* 6 Aug. 1894; *Chicago Times,* 6 Aug. 1894; *BE,* 8 Aug. 1894; undated newspaper article, Henry Chadwick Diaries, vol. 17; Voigt, *American Baseball,* 1:259. The *Chicago Tribune* estimated the loss at $5,000, while President Hart in the *Chicago Times* estimated it at $30,000–$35,000, a substantial disparity. The Twenty-Third Street Grounds caught on fire on 15 July 1874. Lowry, *Green Cathedrals,* 42.

9. *Chicago Times-Herald,* 9 Mar. 1900, 25 Mar. 1900; *SL,* 7 Apr. 1900, 14 Apr. 1900, 21 Apr. 1900, 28 Apr. 1900; Frank Young, "More about Foster's Baseball Team," *Half Century Magazine,* June 1919, 8; Axelson, *"Commy,"* 150; Richard Lindberg, "Yesterday's City: The South Side's Baseball Factory," *Chicago History* 28 (Summer 1989): 62; U.S. Census Office, *Report on Cities,* 155; Louis Wirth, ed., *Local Community Fact Book, 1938* (Chicago, 1938), 34, 37; Lowry, *Green Cathedrals,* 43; Benson, *Ballparks of North America,* 84; Okkonen, *Baseball Memories,* 41; John Thorn and Pete Palmer, *The Hidden Game of Baseball: A Revolutionary Approach to Baseball and Its Statistics* (Garden City, N.Y., 1984), 89. The Philadelphia Athletics' Columbia Park cost just seven thousand dollars to build in 1901. Gershman, *Diamonds,* 66.

10. Gershman, *Diamonds,* 40; Lowry, *Green Cathedrals,* 62–63. On 28 May 1883 heavyweight champion John L. Sullivan played an exhibition game for the Mets for which he was paid twelve hundred dollars. Four thousand fans attended, paying double the normal admission price for a baseball game. *NYT,* 29 May 1883. Panoramic photographs of opening day in 1886 at the old Polo Grounds show advertisements on the outfield walls for A. G. Spalding & Bros., cigars and cigarettes, and the *Evening Telegram,* plus a sign: "No Betting Allowed on These Grounds." See "Baseball in the Nineteenth Century: A Special Pictorial Issue," *NP* 3 (Spring 1984): 50–51.

11. Gershman, *Diamonds,* 40; Lowry, *Green Cathedrals,* 62–63; O'Malley, "Mutrie's Mets," 40 (quote).

12. *NYT,* 10 July 1888, 15 July 1888, 9 Feb. 1889, 4 Apr. 1889, 8 Apr. 1889, 13 Apr. 1889; Voigt, "Cash and Glory," 285. For an illustration depicting the

Staten Island field, see Official Scorecard for the New York Metropolitans, 1886, Bradshaw Swales Collection, New York Public Library; Gershman, *Diamonds*, 39. The Polo Grounds had a positive impact on local property values. An adjacent saloon paid $420 in rent when the field opened, and this amount rose to $2,500 in 1888. *Chicago Times*, 21 Feb. 1889.

13. *NYT*, 10 July 1888, 15 July 1888, 9 Feb. 1889, 4 Apr. 1889, 8 Apr. 1889, 13 Apr. 1889.

14. *NYT*, 4 Apr. 1889, 8 Apr. 1889, 13 Apr. 1889, 30 May 1889, 12 June 1889, 22 June 1889, 25 June 1889; *Chicago Times*, 11 Feb. 1889; Manhattan Field was not ready until July, so the Giants played their first two games in Jersey City and the next twenty-three on Staten Island at the St. George Cricket Grounds. Voigt, "Cash and Glory," 285; McGraw, *Real McGraw*, 185–86; Allen, *Giants and Dodgers*, 32; Fleming, *Unforgettable Season*, 236; Lowry, *Green Cathedrals*, 63–64; Benson, *Ballparks of North America*, 258; Gershman, *Diamonds*, 101; Clark C. Griffith, "Twenty-Five Years in Baseball," *Outing* 64 (Apr.–May 1914): 169. The park site belonged to James J. Coogan, a former mayoralty candidate and future borough president. *NYT*, 25 June 1889. In 1908 the park had as few as five hundred quarter seats. *NYT*, 10 Sept. 1908.

15. Kirsch, *Creation of American Team Sports*, 235; Seymour, *Baseball*, 1:48–49; Benson, *Ballparks of North America*, 57, 59–62; George Buckley, "The Day the Reds Lost," *NP* 2 (1983): 6.

16. In 1883 the Brooklyn Grays (the future Dodgers) began at Prospect Park because Washington Park was not ready. The one thousand spectators watched for free because the game was played in a municipal park. Allen, *Giants and Dodgers*, 17–18; *NYT*, 10 Jan. 1890, 31 Jan. 1898; Chadwick Scrapbooks, vol. 2; Goldstein, *Superstars and Screwballs*, 55; Gershman, *Diamonds*, 58; John S. Billings, *Vital Statistics of New York City and Brooklyn Covering a Period of Six Years Ending May 31, 1890* (Washington, D.C., 1894), 225–29; *SL*, 15 June 1895, 9 Jan. 1897, 23 Jan. 1897, 22 May 1897; *BE*, 10 Jan. 1896, 21 Jan. 1897, 17 Feb. 1897, 2 Apr. 1897; *NYT*, 11 Jan. 1896, 21 Jan. 1897; Benson, *Ballparks of North America*, 59–61.

17. Allen, *Giants and Dodgers*, 22–23; *NYT*, 31 Jan. 1898; Chadwick Scrapbooks, vol. 2; Goldstein, *Superstars and Screwballs*, 61–63; Billings, *Vital Statistics of New York City and Brooklyn*, 225–29; *SL*, 22 May 1897, 15 Jan. 1898, 5 Feb. 1898, 9 Feb. 1898, 19 Nov. 1898; *BE*, 21 Jan. 1897, 17 Feb. 1897, 2 Apr. 1897, 22 Jan. 1898, 15 Mar. 1898, 10 Jan. 1899; *NYTr*, 21 Jan. 1897, 16 Mar. 1898; *SN*, 26 Mar. 1898; Benson, *Ballparks of North America*, 61–62.

18. *SL*, 17 Aug. 1901, 16 Nov. 1901, 4 Oct. 1902, 8 Nov. 1902, 15 Nov. 1902; *SN*, 28 Mar. 1903; *NYTr*, 25 Sept. 1902; *BE*, 27 Sept. 1902; *NYT*, 28 Sept. 1902, 7 Mar. 1903; *New York Sun*, 29 Oct. 1902; *CDN*, 12 Dec. 1902; *Cincinnati Enquirer*, 7 Mar. 1903, 8 Mar. 1903; *New York Evening Journal*, 7 Mar. 1903; Chadwick Scrapbooks, vol. 4; McGraw, *Real McGraw*, 155.

19. *CDN*, 13 Mar. 1903; *New York World*, 13 Mar. 1903; *NYT*, 22 Nov. 1911.

20. *Cincinnati Enquirer*, 4 Mar. 1903, 13 Mar. 1903; *New York World*, 13 Mar. 1903, 14 Mar. 1903; *NYTr*, 14 Mar. 1903, 14 Apr. 1906; *NYT*, 15 Mar. 1903, 6 Sept. 1903; *SN*, 18 Apr. 1903, 30 Nov. 1916, 17 Feb. 1921; James Blaine Walker, *Fifty Years of Rapid Transit, 1864–1917* (New York, 1918), 190.

21. *NYT*, 17 Mar. 1903, 26 Mar. 1903, 31 Mar. 1903, 1 Apr. 1903; *New York World*, 1 Apr. 1903; *NYTr*, 10 Apr. 1903; *CDN*, 7 Oct. 1903; *SN*, 28 Mar. 1903, 4 Apr. 1903, 11 Apr. 1903, 18 Apr. 1903, 23 Nov. 1903; *SL*, 11 Apr. 1903, 18 Apr. 1903; *Cincinnati Enquirer*, 14 Dec. 1903.

22. *New York Sun*, 6 Apr. 1903; *NYT*, 6 Apr. 1903. For outfield advertisements at Hilltop Park, see the photograph of the field in Seymour, *Baseball*, 2:facing 153; Lowry, *Green Cathedrals*, 64; Richard L. Miller, "The Baseball Parks and the American Culture," in *Cooperstown Symposium on Baseball and the American Culture (1990)*, ed. Alvin L. Hall (Westport, Conn., 1991), 177.

23. *AC*, 8 Mar. 1885, 12 Mar. 1885, 7 Mar. 1886, 15 Apr. 1888, 6 Apr. 1889, 10 May 1889, 19 June 1889, 22 June 1889, 6 Mar. 1892, 10 Mar. 1892, 16 Mar. 1892, 24 Apr. 1892, 20 Mar. 1894, 29 Mar. 1896; *SN*, 10 May 1889, 29 July 1893, 29 Dec. 1894, 11 Feb. 1899; "Atlanta Transit and Location of Ball Park," *Looking Glass* 4 (11 Apr. 1896): 7; Thomas M. Deaton, "Atlanta during the Progressive Era" (Ph.D. diss., University of Georgia, 1969), 310; Edward L. Grant, "When Town Ball Was the Big Game Here," *Atlanta Journal Sunday Magazine*, 9 Mar. 1924, 11; *AJ*, 5 May 1971; Doreen McMahon, "Pleasure Spots of Old Atlanta," *Atlanta Historical Bulletin* 7 (Oct. 1944): 229–31; *Atlanta City Directory*, 1892, 1894, 1896, 1899, 1902; *Sanborn Fire Insurance Maps of Atlanta, 1911, Revised to 1923* (New York, 1923); National Municipal League, *The Governments of Atlanta and Fulton County, Georgia* (Atlanta, 1938), 137–38. Residents near Brisbine Park sent a petition to the city council declaring their opposition to the field. E. P. Shropshire et al. to the Atlanta City Council, 21 Jan. 1897, Atlanta City Council Proceedings, Office of the City Clerk, Atlanta City Hall.

24. *AJ*, 26 May 1898, 15 Jan. 1902, 7 Feb. 1902, 7 Feb. 1903, 25 Mar. 1903; *AC*, 14 Jan. 1902, 9 Mar. 1903; Minutes of the Atlanta City Council, 16 May 1904, typescript, Office of the City Clerk, Atlanta City Hall; Garrett, *Atlanta and Environs*, 2:454.

25. *AJ*, 27 June 1904, 2 Nov. 1906, 2 Feb. 1907, 18 Feb. 1907, 9 May 1907, 23 May 1907, 24 May 1907, 27 Oct. 1908; *AC*, 4 Nov. 1904; Deaton, "Atlanta during the Progressive Era," 315–17; Wright, *History of the Georgia Power Company*, 87–88; Norman Macht, "His Forty-Ninth Opening Game," *AJ*, 11 Apr. 1947; *Sanborn Fire Insurance Maps of Atlanta*. On the destruction of Ponce De Leon Park and the building of Spiller Park, see *AJ*, 8 Sept. 1923,

29 Mar. 1924; Guy Butler, "Best Baseball Park in South for Atlanta," *Atlanta Journal Sunday Magazine,* 16 Mar. 1924, 7; and Garrett, *Atlanta and Environs,* 2:798. Atlanta's building codes were revised in December 1923 to require fireproof construction for the ballpark except for wooden seats. James L. Mayson, *The Charter of the City of Atlanta for 1924* (Atlanta, 1924), 23.

26. *CDN,* 20 Feb. 1901.

27. Rich Westcott, *Philadelphia's Old Ballparks* (Philadelphia, 1996), 28–31, 49; Kuklick, *To Every Thing a Season,* 19–30; Benson, *Ballparks of North America,* 101, 297–98; Gershman, *Diamonds,* 56, 71–74; Richard Miller and Gregory L. Rhodes, "The Life and Times of the Old Cincinnati Ballparks," *Queen City Heritage* 46 (Spring 1988): 25–41; Peter S. Craig, "Organized Baseball: An Industrial Study of a $100 Million Spectator Sport" (B.A. paper, Oberlin College, 1950), 99. See also Peter Carino, " 'The Ballparks Are like Cathedrals': Stadia as Signifiers in American Culture," *NINE* 1 (Fall 1992): 1–18; Rolando Llanes, "The Urban Ballpark: Fundamental Qualities of an American Original," *NINE* 3 (Fall 1994): 168–79.

28. Kuklick, *To Every Thing a Season,* 19–30; Westcott, *Philadelphia's Old Ballparks,* 99–112; Benson, *Ballparks of North America,* 101, 297–98; Gershman, *Diamonds,* 88; Ralph E. L. Weber, ed., *The Toledo Baseball Guide of the Mud Hens, 1883–1943* (Rossford, Ohio, 1944), 97; Opening of Ewing Field (S.F.), Souvenir Program, Chicago Historical Society. For a discussion of the ballpark as a major American contribution to the building arts, see Simeon Strunsky, "The Game," *Atlantic Monthly,* Aug. 1914, 248–56; and Daniel L. Bonk, "Ballpark Figures: The Story of Forbes Field," *Pittsburgh History* 76 (Summer 1993): 55–57, 64–65.

29. Seymour, *Baseball,* 2:49–51. On overcrowded accommodations for the 1903 World Series, see "Ball Grounds Too Small," *CT,* 25 Oct. 1903. In 1908 the columnist W. A. Phelon pointed out certain fields' seating capacity, like West Side Park, was already seriously taxed, and recommended building new multilevel structures that could seat up to sixty thousand. *SL,* 8 Aug. 1908.

30. Seymour, *Baseball,* 2:49; David John Kammer, "Take Me Out to the Ball Game: American Cultural Values as Reflected in the Architectural Evolution and Criticism of the Modern Baseball Stadium" (Ph.D. diss., University of New Mexico, 1982), 86; Kuklick, *To Every Thing a Season,* 25; Spalding, *America's National Game,* 497. For the views of the sportswriter John Sheridan on the need for improved park amenities in the 1920s, see Kammer, "Take Me Out to the Ball Game," 123–33.

On popular entertainment, see Kasson, *Amusing the Million,* 57–86; Robert Sklar, *Movie-Made America* (New York, 1975), 45–46; May, *Screening Out the Past;* Albert F. McLean, *American Vaudeville as Ritual* (Lexington, Ky., 1965), 193–210; and Snyder, *Voice of the City.*

31. Benson, *Ballparks of North America;* Gershman, *Diamonds,* 55–59. The sporting press circulated rumors that certain fires had been set by arson-

ists, possibly Sabbatarians trying to block the establishment of Sunday base-ball. The Boston fire at the South End Grounds was the result of a prank by boys who set fire to garbage under some seats. Gershman, *Diamonds*, 53, 55. For evidence of public officials' concern for the safety of spectators, see *SN*, 15 Aug. 1911; *Journal of the Proceedings of the City Council of Chicago* (8 May 1899): 281–82; New York Board of Aldermen, *Proceedings* (13 July 1909): 453; Seymour, *Baseball*, 2:50.

In 1898 after one of its several fires, Sportsman's Park's grandstand was redesigned with an elevated stand designed to give fans an excellent view of the Shoot-the-Chutes roller coaster that surrounded the park. *Sporting News* described this as "prostitution of a ballpark." Quoted in Gershman, *Diamonds*, 60.

32. *CDN*, 28 May 1900; *SN*, 29 Apr. 1909; *NYT*, 15 Apr. 1911; Seymour, *Baseball*, 2:50–51; *NYTr*, 26 Aug. 1897. Minor league structures were even more poorly constructed. Syracuse's minor league grandstand collapsed in 1885 and in 1890. *SN*, 26 Mar. 1887; Chadwick Scrapbooks, vol. 2.

33. Seymour, *Baseball*, 2:50; *Journal of the Proceedings of the City Council of Chicago* (8 May 1899): 281–82; *SN*, 15 Aug. 1891; New York Board of Aldermen, *Proceedings* (13 July 1909): 453; *CT*, 24 Dec. 1910.

34. Voigt, "Cash and Glory," 265; *SN*, 29 July 1893, 10 Sept. 1898, 1 May 1899; *CDN*, 31 Aug. 1907, 19 Jan. 1910; *Chicago Record-Herald*, 18 July 1908; *Journal of the Proceedings of the City Council of Chicago* (6 July 1899): 935, (25 June 1900): 749, (5 Oct. 1908): 1361, (20 Dec. 1909): 2228–29; *Olcott's Land Values Blue Book of Chicago, 1909* (Chicago, 1909), 52; Kuklick, *To Every Thing a Season*, 73–76; Moss, *Tiger Stadium*, 8, 9.

35. In 1912 Charles Murphy was fined six hundred dollars for letting in too many spectators to a Cubs game. *NYTr*, 13 Aug. 1912; *NYT*, 22 Sept. 1912.

36. *Journal of the Proceedings of the City Council of Chicago* (23 June 1919): 391, (10 Mar. 1920): 2176; George K. Kuhlman to A. Herrmann, Herrmann Papers; *Chicago Record-Herald*, 24 Apr. 1909.

37. *Chicago Record-Herald*, 24 Apr. 1909, 26 Apr. 1909.

38. *Chicago Record-Herald*, 29 Dec. 1908, 9 Mar. 1910, 2 July 1910; *SN*, 13 May 1909; Lindberg, *Stealing First*, 83.

39. *Chicago Record-Herald*, 29 Dec. 1908, 9 Mar. 1910, 2 July 1910; *SN*, 13 May 1909; *NYT*, 28 Sept. 1919; Young, "More about Foster's Baseball Team," 8; L. H. Constans, "Major League Parks Built," *BM*, May 1913, 89–90; Lindberg, *Who's on Third?* 32–33; Lindberg, "South Side's Baseball Factory," 61, 63, 65; Jordan Deutsch, Richard Cohen, Roland T. Johnson, and David S. Neft, *The Scrapbook History of Baseball* (Indianapolis, 1975), 72; Robin F. Bachin, "Cultural Boundaries: Constructing Urban Space and Civic Culture on Chicago's South Side, 1890–1919" (Ph.D. diss., University of Michigan, 1996), 295 (quote), 322–24.

40. *Chicago Record-Herald*, 29 Dec. 1908, 9 Mar. 1910, 2 July 1910; *SN*, 13

May 1909; *NYT*, 28 Sept. 1919; Young, "More about Foster's Baseball Team," 8; Constans, "Major League Parks Built," 89–90; Lindberg, *Who's on Third?* 32–33; Lindberg, "South Side's Baseball Factory," 61, 63, 65; Deutsch, Cohen, Johnson, and Neft, *Scrapbook History of Baseball*, 72.

41. The first night game occurred on 2 September 1880 in Hull, Mississippi, between teams representing Boston department stores and was illuminated with carbon arc lamps made by the newly formed Northern Electric Light Company of Boston. Players felt the lighting was insufficient. Three years later a second night game was staged in Fort Wayne between Quincy (Northwestern League) and a local college team. The lighting was either too bright or inadequate, especially when the ball got dirty. In 1887 Erastus Wiman tried night ball at his St. George's Field, but it was a failure. The first professional night game occurred on 4 July 1896 between teams from Paterson, New Jersey, and Wilmington, Delaware, at the latter's Union Street Grounds. They used a softball, and visibility was very poor. David Pietrusza, *Lights On! The Wild Century-Long Saga of Night Baseball* (Lanham, Md., 1997), 3–7, 9, 11, 12; Gershman, *Diamonds*, 55; Edward G. Barrow, *My Fifty Years in Baseball* (New York, 1951).

A night game between local Elk lodges was played on 19 June 1909 at Cincinnati's Palace of the Fans using George F. Cahill's new portable lighting system. Three thousand fans attended, including the Reds and Phillies who had played that afternoon, and everyone seemed impressed. But Cahill was too far ahead of his time and the idea did not catch on. Benson, *Ballparks of North America*, 101.

42. Wirth, *Community Fact Book, 1938*, 34, 37; Ernest W. Burgess and Charles Newcomb, eds., *Census Data of the City of Chicago, 1920* (Chicago, 1931), 331; Allen H. Spear, *Black Chicago: The Making of a Negro Ghetto, 1890–1920* (Chicago, 1967), 14–15, 116–19, 183. On use of the old Sox site by African Americans, see Jerry Malloy, "Rube Foster and Black Baseball in Chicago," in *Baseball in Chicago*, ed. Emil H. Rothe (Cooperstown, N.Y., 1986), 25; Lowry, *Green Cathedrals*, 43.

43. See James T. Farrell, *A World I Never Made* (New York, 1936), 32.

44. Author interview with urban economist George Hilton, 15 Aug. 1971, Chicago.

45. Hoyt, *One Hundred Years of Land Values in Chicago*, 137, 144–48, 206, 231, 237, 249; see the map on page 101 for each edition of *Olcott's Land Values Blue Book of Chicago* from 1909 to 1930. *Olcott's Land Values Blue Book of Chicago* provides an annual report of property values in the city of Chicago. The maps are arranged by geographic locality, and the map of a particular locale always can be found year after year on the same page. This makes it convenient to chart annual changes in property valuations.

46. Harold M. Mayer and Richard C. Wade, *Chicago: Growth of a Metropolis* (Chicago, 1969), 212; *Chicago Times-Herald*, 25 Mar. 1900; *Chicago*

Record-Herald, 18 Dec. 1907; *Chicago North Shore News*, 27 Aug. 1909; Ray Schmidt, "The Semi-Pro Team That Beat the Champs," in *Baseball in Chicago*, ed. Rothe, 22–23.

47. *AC*, 24 Oct. 1909; *CT*, 23 May 1913, 24 May 1913, 23 Jan. 1914; *CDN*, 29 Dec. 1913; *Sanborn Fire Insurance Map for Chicago: Lakeview (1894)* (Chicago, 1894); see the map on page 52 for each edition of *Olcott's Land Values Blue Book of Chicago* from 1909 to 1914.

48. *CT*, 23 Jan. 1914, 29 Jan. 1914, 30 Jan. 1914 (quote), 14 Mar. 1914; *CDN*, 30 Dec. 1913, 21 Feb. 1914.

49. *CT*, 5 Jan. 1914, 8 Jan. 1914; Kush, "Building of Chicago's Wrigley Field," 11; Gershman, *Diamonds*, 120.

From home, the original left field was 310 feet and it was 345 feet to right field. After two homers were hit over the short left field fence, it was pushed back to 327 feet. A second bleacher section, twice as large as the first one, was built in left field for the 1915 season. Seats there went for a dime. Only in 1923 was the grandstand extended down the foul lines and two larger steel-framed bleachers were built to replace those already in place. Kush, "Building of Chicago's Wrigley Field," 12, 14–15.

50. Only Kansas City and Pittsburgh used the same edifices in 1914 that they had used while operating as minor league teams in 1913. Okkonen, *Federal League*, 50–63. On the relationship between big business and social reform, see James Weinstein, *The Corporate Ideal in the Industrial State* (Boston, 1968); and Kolko, *Triumph of Conservatism*.

51. Burgess and Newcomb, *Census Data of Chicago*, 127, 331, 421; Zimmerman, *William Wrigley*, 206; *CDN*, 14 Nov. 1914; *CT*, 21 Dec. 1915. Few West Side fans followed their Cubs to the North Side. *SN*, 13 Sept. 1917. For a sketch of Wrigley Field in 1929 and the making of the ivy wall, see Gershman, *Diamonds*, 135, 149–50; and Bill Veeck, *Veeck as in Wreck* (New York, 1962), 42–43.

52. *Sanborn Insurance Map: Lakeview, 1894*; U.S. Works Progress Administration, Illinois, *Report of the Chicago Land Use Survey: Land Use in Chicago*, vol. 2 (Chicago, 1943), 98–99, 188–89, 234–35; *Olcott's Blue Book, 1909 . . . 1930*, 52; Hoyt, *Land Values in Chicago*, 237. The physical neighborhood has not changed much since the 1920s, although the ethnicity and social status of Lakeview residents has. A neighborhood that had declined was gentrified in the 1980s, especially on Sheffield and Waveland Avenues, where people still watch games from rooftops.

53. *NYT*, 2 Apr. 1909, 3 Feb. 1910, 15 Apr. 1911, 6 Nov. 1914; McGraw, *Real McGraw*, 185–86; Lowry, *Green Cathedrals*, 65.

54. *NYT*, 15 Apr. 1911; *NYTr*, 15 Apr. 1911, 23 Apr. 1911; *SL*, 22 Apr. 1911; Griffith, "Twenty-Five Years in Baseball," 169; Brush to A. Herrmann, 4 Aug. 1911, Herrmann Papers; Seymour, *Baseball*, 2:51.

55. John Montgomery Ward, "Making a Baseball Team," *Collier's*, 14 May

1910, 28–29; *NYT,* 15 Oct. 1911; Allen, *Giants and Dodgers,* 83; Gershman, *Diamonds,* 101, 103–4; Lowry, *Green Cathedrals,* 64–66.

56. *NYT,* 10 Sept. 1908; Voigt, "Out with the Crowds," 111; Seymour, *Baseball,* 2:68–71; Veeck, *Hustler's Handbook,* 40; Paul Angle, *Philip K. Wrigley: A Memoir of a Modest Man* (Chicago, 1975), 58, 61; Paul Angle, "Mr. Wrigley's Cubs," *Chicago History* 5 (Summer 1976): 105–15.

57. Seymour, *Baseball,* 2:68–71; Frank H. Behle to A. Herrmann, 3 Feb. 1909, 16 Feb. 1909, Herrmann Papers; *CT,* 5 Sept. 1911; *NYT,* 23 June 1914; *NYTr,* 1 June 1915.

58. Lee A. Lendt, "A Social History of Washington Heights," 1960, mimeograph, 13, 16–17, New York Historical Society; Department of Church Planning and Research of the Protestant Council of New York, "Upper Manhattan—A Community Study of Washington Heights," 1954, mimeograph, 2, New York Historical Society. On land uses, see George W. Bromley and Walter S. Bromley, *Atlas of the City of New York, Borough of Manhattan* (Philadelphia, 1905); *Atlas of the Borough of Manhattan* (New York, 1912); *Manhattan Land Book, City of New York* (New York, 1934); *Manhattan Land Book of the City of New York* (New York, 1955–71); and Okkonen, *Baseball Memories,* 58.

59. Edwin Spengler, *Land Values in New York in Relation to Transit Facilities* (New York, 1930), 143, 158–62, 165. For New York City real estate values, I relied heavily on New York City, City Record Office, *Annual Record of Assessed Valuations of Real Estate in the City of New York: Supplement to the City Record,* 1904–30. This publication listed all city lots by borough with their assessed land value and the value of any improvements. Samples were taken for the years 1904, 1910, 1920, and 1930, as well as the years when ballparks were either demolished or constructed.

60. *SL,* 20 Jan. 1912; Graham, *Brooklyn Dodgers,* 22–23.

61. Ebbets to Herrmann, 12 May 1912, Herrmann Papers; *NYT,* 7 Apr. 1912, 21 Feb. 1913, 19 Apr. 1925; *NYTr,* 3 Jan. 1912; *SL,* 13 Jan. 1912, 20 Jan. 1912, 2 Mar. 1912; *BE,* 17 Feb. 1912, 5 Apr. 1912, 6 Apr. 1912; Graham, *Brooklyn Dodgers,* 23–24; Benson, *Ballparks of North America,* 63.

62. *BE,* 1 Feb. 1912, 2 Feb. 1912, 5 Apr. 1912, 20 Aug. 1912; Ebbets to Herrmann, 2 Jan. 1912, Herrmann Papers; Allen, *Giants and Dodgers,* 89; Graham, *Brooklyn Dodgers,* 31–32; Goldstein, *Superstars and Screwballs,* 98, 99.

63. *NYT,* 6 Apr. 1912, 7 Apr. 1912, 17 Mar. 1913; *SL,* 13 Jan. 1913; *BE,* 1 Feb. 1913; *NYTr,* 26 Mar. 1913; Goldstein, *Superstars and Screwballs,* 100.

64. *NYT,* 7 Apr. 1912, 17 Mar. 1913; *SL,* 13 Jan. 1913; *BE,* 1 Feb. 1913; *NYTr,* 26 Mar. 1913; Robert F. Bluthardt, "Fenway Park and the Golden Age of the Baseball Park," *Journal of Popular Culture* 21 (Summer 1987): 46; Lowry, *Green Cathedrals,* 40–41; Benson, *Ballparks of North America,* 63–65.

65. *BE,* 9 Apr. 1913; George W. Bromley and Walter S. Bromley, *Atlas of the*

City of Brooklyn (Philadelphia, 1893); *Belcher Hyde Atlas of Brooklyn* (New York, 1908); E. Belcher Hyde, *Miniature Atlas of the Borough of Brooklyn* (Brooklyn, 1912); *Desk Atlas of the Borough of Brooklyn, City of New York* (Brooklyn, 1920); E. Belcher Hyde, *Desk Atlas, Borough of Brooklyn, City of New York* (New York, 1929); Kuklick, *To Every Thing a Season*, 40–41. On the Brooklyn Feds, see Okkonen, *Federal League*, 7, 42; and Lowry, *Green Cathedrals*, 40.

66. Spengler, *Land Values in New York*, 143; New York, *Record of Assessed Valuations*, 1904–30.

67. *NYT*, 11 Jan. 1913.

68. *NYT*, 25 Dec. 1909, 11 Jan. 1913, 18 Jan. 1913, 23 Jan. 1913, 11 Apr. 1913, 31 July 1913; *NYTr*, 31 Mar. 1912.

69. *NYT*, 12 Dec. 1914; *SL*, 30 Jan. 1915.

70. *SL*, 30 Jan. 1915, 20 Feb. 1915, 16 Oct. 1915; *SN*, 29 July 1915; *NYT*, 3 Oct. 1915, 8 Dec. 1915.

71. *NYT*, 11 Feb. 1915, 13 May 1915; *Bronx Evening Star*, 13 Mar. 1915, 3 Apr. 1915; *SL*, 27 Mar. 1915; *NYTr*, 13 Apr. 1915; Bronx business owners also tried to secure a team in the minor International League, but could not get the necessary approval of Giants' president Harry Hempstead, which was needed because the borough was within the Giants' geographic monopoly. *NYT*, 7 Feb. 1915, 11 Feb. 1915, 15 Mar. 1915.

72. *NYTr*, 1 Nov. 1915; *SL*, 27 Nov. 1915, 11 Dec. 1915; *NYT*, 30 Nov. 1915, 1 Dec. 1915; *Federal Baseball Club of Baltimore, Inc., v. National League of Professional Baseball Clubs and American league of Professional Baseball Clubs*, 259 U.S. 200 (1922), brief of respondents, 340, 388, 393.

73. *SL*, 11 Dec. 1915, 2 Dec. 1916; *NYT*, 24 Nov. 1916, 15 May 1920, 17 May 1920, 14 Sept. 1920.

74. *CDN*, 11 Nov. 1919; *NYT*, 15 May 1920, 17 May 1920, 22 May 1920; Durso, *Days of Mr. McGraw*, 125. The historian David Kammer points out that with the legalization of boxing in 1920 under the Walker Act, Stoneham wanted to free up summer dates for his Republic Athletic Club, the exclusive promoter for Ebbets Field and the Polo Grounds. Kammer, "Take Me Out to the Ball Game," 119.

75. Veeck, *Hustler's Handbook*, 188–89; Seymour, *Baseball*, 2:270–71; Murdock, *Ban Johnson*, 175–76; Smelser, *The Life That Ruth Built*, 270; Kammer, "Take Me Out to the Ball Game," 115, 117–20; Alexander, *McGraw*, 220.

76. *SN*, 18 Nov. 1915, 7 Feb. 1918, 28 Feb. 1918, 2 Sept. 1920; *NYT*, 17 May 1920; Frederick C. Lane, "Big Business Reforms in Immediate Prospect," *BM*, Jan. 1919, 137–39; Kammer, "Take Me Out to the Ball Game," 78–79.

77. *NYT*, 7 Feb. 1921; *SN*, 10 Feb. 1921, 17 Feb. 1921; Kammer, "Take Me Out to the Ball Game," 122, 125–27.

78. *NYT*, 20 May 1920, 21 Apr. 1922, 19 Apr. 1923, 17 May 1923; *SN*,

17 Feb. 1921. On the process of construction, see Kammer, "Take Me Out to the Ball Game," 117–28, 146–50, 155, 159–62, and on inadequate parking, see 129, 132, 134–36.

79. *Stadium* comes from the Greek *stade,* referring to the length of a footrace of about two hundred yards as well as to the seating area where track events were staged. The term was used first in England in 1834, and then in the United States in 1901, when the athletic building at the Pan-American Exposition in Buffalo was so designated. Harvard Field built in 1903 was sometimes referred to as Harvard Stadium. Kammer, "Take Me Out to the Ball Game," 63–65, 189–90; Riess, *City Games,* 208.

80. *NYT,* 30 June 1912, 12 Apr. 1971; *SN,* 7 Feb. 1929; *Atlas of the Borough of the Bronx, Sections 9 to 13* (New York, 1912); *Land Book of the Bronx, Sections 9, 10, 11, 12, and 13, City of New York* (New York, 1928).

81. *NYT,* 12 Apr. 1971; Edward G. Barrow to A. Herrmann, 23 Dec. 1913, Herrmann Papers; *Atlas of the Bronx* (1912); *Land Book of the Bronx* (1928); *Atlas of the City of New York, Borough of the Bronx* (Philadelphia, 1934); *Bronx Land Book of the City of New York* (New York, 1960–71).

82. *SN,* 17 Jan. 1929; New York, *Record of Assessed Valuations,* 1904–30; Spengler, *Land Values in New York,* 90–91, 165.

83. New York, *Record of Assessed Valuations,* 1904–30.

84. Cincinnati's Redland Field (Crosley Park), built in 1912, was in an industrial area where major league baseball had been played since 1884. At that time most nearby lots were vacant, but the area rapidly industrialized. Elisha H. Robinson and Roger H. Pidgeon, *Atlas of the City of Cincinnati, Ohio* (New York, 1883–84); U.S. Census Office, *Report on Cities,* 193; *SN,* 8 Feb. 1934. Washington's ballpark was in a primarily black neighborhood. John S. Billings, *Vital Statistics of the District of Columbia and Baltimore Covering a Period of Six Years Ending May 31, 1890* (Washington, D.C., 1893), 44–45, 52–53. Detroit's Navin Field (later Briggs Stadium), where the Tigers had played since they joined the AL in 1901, was often referred to as the only downtown major league park. However, it was originally in the midst of a residential neighborhood, and from photographs and personal experience, it seems well beyond walking distance from the central business district. For Detroit, see U.S. Census Office, *Report on Cities,* 222–23; Michael Betzold and Ethan Casey, *Queen of Diamonds: The Tiger Stadium Story* (West Bloomfield, Mich., 1992); Lieb, *Detroit Tigers,* 4; and Moss, *Tiger Stadium,* 15, 17, which has a 1937 photograph of the homes behind left field and an aerial view in 1945 that shows the business district located far from the field. For Baltimore, see Billings, *Statistics of the District of Columbia and Baltimore,* 77; and Frederick Lieb, *The Baltimore Orioles: A History of a Colorful Team in Baltimore and St Louis* (New York, 1955), 24. For Boston, see *SN,* 10 Dec. 1914, 24 Oct. 1918. For Cleveland, see U.S. Census Office, *Report on Cities,* 207; and Franklin Lewis, *The Cleveland Indians* (New

York, 1949), 13. For Philadelphia, see John S. Billings, *Vital Statistics of Boston and Philadelphia Covering a Period of Six Years Ending May 31, 1890* (Washington, D.C., 1895), 110, 113; Westcott, *Philadelphia's Old Ballparks,* 151–52; and Kuklick, *To Every Thing a Season,* 21–25. For Pittsburgh, see *NYT,* 10 Oct. 1908; Bonk, "Ballpark Figures," 55–57; and Frederick Lieb, *The Pittsburgh Pirates* (New York, 1948), 109. For St. Louis, see *SN,* 1 Mar. 1934.

85. On the misguided belief that ballparks had a beneficial impact on their surrounding localities and how that idea justified municipal sponsorship and support for the construction of multimillion-dollar sports complexes, see Riess, *City Games,* 234–45. A classic case was New York, whose council, anticipating the revival of the neighborhood, allocated $25 million in 1972 to refurbish Yankee Stadium. The final cost was $100 million and the neighborhood did not improve. *NYT,* 27 Aug. 1971, 24 Mar. 1972, 17 Aug. 1972, 17 July 1975. Scholars who examine the economic and psychological relationship between ballparks and their cities include Charles C. Euchner in *Why Sports Teams Move and Cities Fight to Keep Them* (Baltimore, 1993); Roger G. Noll and Andrew Zimbalist, eds., in *Sports, Jobs, and Taxes: The Economic Impact of Sports Teams and Stadiums* (Washington, D.C., 1997); and Mark Rosentraub in *Major League Losers: The Real Cost of Sports and Who's Paying for It* (New York, 1997).

Chapter 4: Professional Sunday Baseball and Social Reform

1. Roy Z. Chamblee, "The Sabbatarian Crusade in the United States, 1810–1920" (Ph.D. diss., George Washington University, 1969), 263, 317–18, 341–42; Dulles, *America Learns to Play,* 207–9; Vincent, *Mudville's Revenge,* 117. For a comparison between pietistic and liturgical perspectives, see Richard Jensen, *The Winning of the Midwest: Social and Political Conflict, 1888–1896* (Chicago, 1971), 63–66; and Paul Kleppner, *The Cross of Culture: A Social Analysis of Midwestern Politics, 1850–1900* (New York, 1970), 73–74.

2. Seymour, *Baseball,* 1:91–93; Voigt, *American Baseball,* 1:125; *Palladium of Labor,* 10 Apr. 1886.

Despite league proscriptions, in 1879 the Syracuse Stars did play several Sunday games at a site outside the county limits. Gershman, *Diamonds,* 34.

3. Seymour, "Rise of Major League Baseball," 379; Wilbur F. Crafts, *The Sabbath for Man: A Study of the Origin, Obligation, History, Advantages, and Present State of Sabbath Observance, with Special Reference to the Rights of Workingmen* (New York, 1885), 121, 386–88, 488n; Chamblee, "Sabbatarian Crusade," 233; U.S. Census Office, *Report on Population of the United States at the Eleventh Census: 1890,* vol. 1, part 1 (Washington, D.C., 1895), clxxii. For Irish and German political influence in Chicago, see Jensen, *Winning of the Midwest,* 119–21, 296–98.

4. *Chicago Evening Journal,* 30 Apr. 1887, in R. C. Kuhn Scrapbooks, R. C. Kuhn Collection, Chicago Historical Society.

5. Vincent, *Mudville's Revenge,* 115.

6. "Editorial," *Spalding's Official Base Ball Guide, 1891* (New York, 1891), 38; *SN,* 24 Dec. 1892; *CDN,* 31 Jan. 1900, 14 Feb. 1900, 12 Feb. 1903. In 1893 the Louisville Colonels opened a new ballpark in Parkland, a suburb that banned Sunday ball and liquor sales. The state legislature let the city annex the field, and Sunday ball and beer sales soon followed. Sullivan, "Growth of Sport in a Southern City," 109.

7. *Chicago Times,* 18 Dec. 1892; *SN,* 24 Dec. 1892.

8. *CDN,* 18 Feb. 1892, 19 Apr. 1892, 26 Apr. 1892; *SN,* 24 Dec. 1892.

9. *SN,* 25 Mar. 1893; *CT,* 14 May 1893, 11 Aug. 1894, 12 Aug. 1894, 20 Aug. 1894; *CDN,* 11 Aug. 1894; *NYTr,* 12 Aug. 1894. On Sundays and the fair, see Chamblee, "The Sabbatarian Crusade," 273–83; David F. Burg, *Chicago's White City of 1893* (Lexington, Ky., 1976), 86; James Gilbert, *Perfect Cities: Chicago's Utopias of 1893* (Chicago, 1991), 127.

10. *Chicago Times,* 30 Apr. 1895, 1 May 1895, 6 May 1895, 24 June 1895; *NYT,* 24 June 1895; *SN,* 1 June 1895; *Chicago Times-Herald,* 14 Jan. 1896; *BE,* 14 Jan. 1896; *SL,* 25 Jan. 1896. On political pressure and Sunday ball, see *Chicago Times,* 19 June 1897; *Chicago Record-Herald,* 10 June 1897; *SL,* 26 Jan. 1907, 16 Feb. 1907; Illinois, General Assembly, House of Representatives, *Journal, 1897* (10 Feb. 1897): 153, (19 Feb. 1897): 204, (10 Mar. 1897): 270; *Journal of the Proceedings of the City Council of Chicago* (8 June 1897): 326–27, (28 June 1897): 513; Charles W. Murphy, "The Pros and Cons of Sunday Baseball," *BM,* June 1919, 119.

11. Chamblee, "Sabbatarian Crusade," 248, 318, 375; *Eleventh Census, 1890,* 1:clxii–clxiii; *SN,* 19 Aug. 1893. In 1909, to prevent passage of a bill to prohibit Sunday baseball, the owners of the St. Louis Browns and the Cardinals gave season passes worth $52.50 to each of the 176 state legislators. *St. Louis Post-Dispatch,* 14 Apr. 1909. On Detroit, see Frederick C. Lane, The Critical Situation in Sunday Baseball," *BM,* Oct. 1911, 21–28; Malcolm W. Bingay, *Detroit Is My Home* (New York, 1946), 185; Benson, *Ballparks of North America,* 133. A compilation of various state laws on Sunday baseball can be found in James Hodgson, "Digest of Laws Prohibiting Sports or Baseball on Sunday," report for the New York State Reference Library, Feb. 1917, mimeograph, New York Public Library.

12. In 1888 the Spiders played on Sundays at Beyerle's Park, just outside the city limits. Benson, *Ballparks of North America,* 105. On the liquor question, see *SN,* 2 Mar. 1895; *SL,* 13 Feb. 1897, 13 Mar. 1897. Mayor Tom Johnson originally opposed Sunday sport, but changed his mind by 1906. See *SL,* 22 Mar. 1902; Hoyt Landon Warner, *Progressivism in Ohio, 1897–1917* (Columbus, 1964), 175. On the Indians' lobbying efforts, see E. S. Barnard to A. Herrmann, 6 May 1910, 17 May 1911, 8 June 1911, 10 June 1911, Herr-

mann Papers. On the ultimate passage of a reform bill, see *NYT,* 9 May 1911; and Warner, *Progressivism in Ohio,* 237.

13. *NYT,* 16 July 1887; *St. Louis Post-Dispatch,* 16 July 1887.

14. *NYT,* 16 July 1887; *St. Louis Post-Dispatch,* 16 July 1887. *Ex Parte Joseph Neet,* 157 Mo. 527 (1900) influenced such cases as *State v. Prather,* 79 Kans. 513 (1907); *New Mexico v. T. M. Davenport,* 17 N.M. Rept. 214 (1912); and *State v. Nashville Baseball Association,* 14 Tenn. 456 (1918).

15. Chamblee, "Sabbatarian Crusade," 369–79.

16. Ibid., 217–29, 344–49. Consult also the *Lord's Day Leader,* vols. 3–6 (1915–19); New York Sabbath Committee, *Report,* vols. 40–56 (1897–1913); and U.S. Census Office, *Twelfth Census of the United States Taken in the Year 1900: Population,* vol. 1, part 1 (Washington, D.C., 1901), clxxxviii.

17. Lowry, *Green Cathedrals,* 39. In 1890 Syracuse scheduled a Sunday game against Louisville even though police were expected to halt the game. Syracuse took the field, but the visitors did not play because they feared the sheriff would arrest them. The umpire forfeited the game to Syracuse. Vincent, *Mudville's Revenge,* 116. Sunday minor league games were played in Buffalo and Rochester, but were soon curtailed. New York Sabbath Committee, *Report,* vols. 32–33 (1889–90): 9–10.

18. *SL,* 6 Feb. 1897; *NYTr,* 7 Apr. 1897.

19. *NYT,* 17 Dec. 1897 (quote); *SN,* 18 Dec. 1897.

20. Betts, "Organized Sport in Industrial America," 389–91.

21. *NYT,* 8 Feb. 1904, 26 Apr. 1904.

22. *NYTr,* 22 Mar. 1898.

23. *SN,* 18 Dec. 1897; Lyman Abbott, "Letters to Unknown Friends," *Outlook,* 25 Jan. 1913, 159.

24. *CDN,* 14 Nov. 1902; *SL,* 25 Apr. 1903; *SN,* 1898 to 1903. It is not clear why teams in smaller New York cities played regularly on Sundays but those in Buffalo, New York, and Rochester did not, since native-born pietists were much more dominant in smaller cities. On Rochester, see Blake McKelvey, *Rochester: The Quest for Quality* (Cambridge, Mass., 1956), 176, 178; New York Sabbath Committee, *Report,* vols. 42–43 (1899–1900): 3–4.

25. *NYT,* 12 Aug. 1894, 4 Sept. 1894; *NYTr,* 4 June 1902. Examples of subterfuge are documented in New York Sabbath Committee, *Bulletin* 1 (Apr. 1914): 29–30. Enforcement of the blue laws regarding baseball was a big police problem. See William G. McAdoo, *Guarding a Great City* (New York, 1906), 11–12; and Harold Seymour, *Baseball,* 3:261.

26. Lowry, *Green Cathedrals,* 157; *NYT,* 5 Oct. 1903; *SN,* 1898 and 1899.

27. *SN,* 21 Nov. 1903; *SL,* 9 Jan. 1904, 16 Jan. 1904.

28. *NYTr,* 17 Apr. 1904, 23 Apr. 1904; *NYT,* 18 Apr. 1904; *SN,* 23 Apr. 1904. On Farrell's efforts to play at Ridgewood, see *NYT,* 3 Mar. 1904, 19 Apr. 1904.

29. *NYTr,* 25 Apr. 1904, 2 May 1904; *In Re Rupp,* 53 NYS 927 (1898).

30. *NYT,* 3 May 1904; Louis H. Pink, *Gaynor: The Tammany Mayor Who Swallowed the Tiger* (New York, 1931), 95; Lately Thomas, *The Mayor Who*

Mastered New York: The Life and Opinions of William J. Gaynor (New York, 1969), 91, 115–16, 467–68.

31. *NYT*, 4 May 1904, 19 May 1904, 30 May 1904, 19 June 1904; *People v. Poole*, 89 NYS 773 (1904); *NYTr*, 13 Sept. 1905.

32. *NYTr*, 24 May 1905, 24 June 1905 (quote); *NYT*, 24 May 1905.

33. *NYTr*, 16 Apr. 1906; *NYT*, 23 Apr. 1906, 9 June 1906, 11 June 1906, 25 June 1906; *SL*, 5 May 1906, 23 June 1906, 14 July 1906.

34. Chadwick Scrapbooks, vol. 7; Governor Hughes instructed local police authorities in 1910 that it was illegal to play Sunday baseball if admission was charged. C. P. Stack, "The Future of the New York State League," *BM*, Jan. 1911, 75–78.

35. *NYT*, 17 Jan. 1907; *SN*, 26 Jan. 1907, 16 Feb. 1907.

36. *NYT*, 16 Apr. 1907; New York Sabbath Committee, *Occasional Papers* 3 (July 1907): 1–14.

37. On Sunday closing, see *SN* and sundry New York papers from 1897 to 1920.

38. Stack, "New York State League," 75–78; *AC*, 2 Oct. 1910; *SN*, 13 Aug. 1910.

39. *SN*, 18 Jan. 1912 (quote); *NYTr*, 15 July 1913.

40. Gerald Zahavi, *Workers, Managers, and Welfare Capitalism: The Shoeworkers and Tanners of Endicott Johnson, 1890–1950* (Urbana, Ill., 1988), 26–27. In the 1920s Johnson led the fight for Sunday movies, drinking, and horse racing. Zahavi, *Workers, Managers, and Welfare Capitalism*, 51–52; *NYT*, 18 Sept. 1913; *SN*, 23 Oct. 1913. See also New York Sabbath Committee, *Bulletin* 1 (Apr. 1914): 5.

41. *NYT*, 5 July 1909, 20 May 1917, 23 May 1917, 25 May 1917. The benefit for the Titanic on 21 April 1912 raised nearly ten thousand dollars from the sale of programs. See "Titanic Benefit Game," *BM*, June 1912, 15–16; "Report of the Secretary to the Board Meeting of Lord's Day Alliance," 13 May 1912, Files of the Lord's Day Alliance, Atlanta.

42. *NYTr*, 18 June 1917; *NYT*, 1 July 1917, 2 July 1917; "The Meaning of the Ebbets Decision," New York Sabbath Committee, *Bulletin* 4 (Aug.–Sept. 1917): 14.

43. *NYT*, 21 Aug. 1917, 22 Aug. 1917, 21 Dec. 1919.

44. *NYT*, 1 Nov. 1917, 3 Nov. 1917; *SN*, 23 Aug. 1917, 1 Nov. 1917, 8 Nov. 1917.

45. *NYT*, 20 Mar. 1918; *Albany Times-Union*, 18 Mar. 1918, 20 Mar. 1918. On women's opposition to Sunday baseball, see *Cincinnati Enquirer*, 5 Feb. 1903; and "Letters, Comments, and Editorials Endorsing Sunday Baseball," in Charles Ebbets File, National Baseball Library.

46. *NYT*, 5 Apr. 1918, 11 Apr. 1918, 13 Apr. 1918; *NYTr*, 18 Mar. 1918, 14 Apr. 1918, 15 Apr. 1918; *SN*, 14 Mar. 1918, 11 Apr. 1918, 18 Apr. 1918, 9 Aug. 1917.

47. *NYTr*, 13 Jan. 1918; *SN*, 14 Nov. 1918, 27 Feb. 1919.

48. Republicans, who controlled the Senate, cast all the negative votes on the Sunday bill. The Assembly had 94 Republicans, 54 Democrats, and 2 Socialists. Fifty-one Democrats voted in favor of the bill and 3 abstained; they were supported by 30 Republicans and 1 Socialist. *NYTr*, 6 Mar. 1919; *NYT*, 8 Apr. 1919; New York Legislature, Senate, *Journal, 1919* (Albany, 1919), 1:866–67, 2:1701–2; James Malcolm, ed., *The New York Red Book, 1919* (Albany, 1919), 125, 185.

49. Alfred E. Smith, "Memorandum Accompanying Approval of Optional Sunday Baseball," in *Progressive Democracy: Addresses and State Papers of Alfred E. Smith* (New York, 1928), 304–6.

50. New York Sabbath Committee, *Bulletin* 6 (Apr.–May 1919): 5–7, (June–July 1919): 14–16, (Aug.–Sept. 1919): 8–11. Schenectady's mayor, who had opposed a liberalized Sunday, was defeated for reelection by a pro-Sunday candidate. *NYT*, 5 Nov. 1919. On legalizing Sunday ball in New York City, see *NYTr*, 30 Apr. 1919, and for estimates of Sunday crowds throughout the season, consult the spring and summer Monday editions of the *NYT.*

51. *NYTr*, 5 May 1919.

52. On power and Tammany Hall, see Hammack, *Power and Society*; and Thomas M. Henderson, *Tammany Hall and the New Immigrants: The Progressive Years* (New York, 1976).

53. The first team from an important eastern city to play on Sunday after 1900 was probably Providence of the Eastern League, which played in its Rocky Point suburb. Lane, "Critical Situation in Sunday Baseball," 21–28. Clout in New Jersey helped protect violators. A witness in a case against Sunday ball in Bayonne contradicted his previously incriminating testimony after several prominent politicians threatened to have him fired. *NYT*, 27 May 1904.

54. Wiebe, *Search for Order*, 176; Buenker, *Urban Liberalism*, 36, 65–70; Kuklick, *To Every Thing a Season*, 70.

55. *CDN*, 4 Mar. 1903; *NYT*, 25 Dec. 1918, 25 Dec. 1928; *SN*, 15 Apr. 1920, 15 Dec. 1928; *Twelfth Census, 1900,* 1:clxxxvii–cxc; "Votes on Acceptance of the Law Proposed by Initiative Petitions," 6 Nov. 1928, Sunday Baseball Files, National Baseball Library; Harold Kaese, *The Boston Braves* (New York, 1948), 207.

56. *SN*, 6 Apr. 1918, 18 Mar. 1920; *CDN*, 15 June 1918; Edward M. Ashenback, *Humor in the Minor Leagues: True Tales from the Baseball Brush*, ed. Jack Ryder (Chicago, 1911), 82–84; William C. Whyte, "Bye Bye, Blue Laws," *Scribner's Magazine*, Aug. 1933, 107–9. Factory teams played on Sundays, as did minor league clubs. In Wilkes-Barre clerical opposition resulted in a temporary halt of industrial baseball on Sunday. Seymour, *Baseball*, 3:226.

57. On Pennsylvania blue laws, see J. Thomas Jable, "Sports, Amusements, and Pennsylvania Blue Laws, 1682–1973" (Ph.D. diss., Pennsylvania State University, 1974). On the efforts of black teams to play on Sundays in the early 1920s, see Lanctot, *Fair Dealing and Clean Playing*, 66–69.

Certain politicians in the mid-1920s allegedly convinced religious leaders to oppose Sunday reform in return for silence on political corruption. *SN*, 26 Aug. 1926, 15 Nov. 1928. On the Sunday baseball fight, see John A. Lucas, "The Unholy Experiment: Professional Baseball's Struggle against Pennsylvania Sunday Blue Laws, 1926–1934," *Pennsylvania History* 38 (Apr. 1971): 163–75; Kuklick, *To Every Thing a Season*, 70–72; *Philadelphia Bulletin*, 26 Apr. 1933, in Kuklick, *To Every Thing a Season*, 209n70 (quote). Incidentally, even after Sunday ball was approved, Mack continued to break up his great team.

58. Kenneth K. Bailey, *Southern White Protestantism in the Twentieth Century* (New York, 1964), 32–37; Chamblee, "Sabbatarian Crusade," 248, 333.

59. *Twelfth Census, 1900*, 1:clxxxvii; David R. Goldfield and Blaine Brownell, *Urban America: From Downtown to No Town* (Boston, 1979), 260; "Motion Pictures in Atlanta on Sunday," *Lord's Day Leader* 3 (Mar.–Apr. 1917): 36; Charles Howard Candler, *Asa Griggs Candler* (Atlanta, 1950), 331; *Atlanta Life*, 2 Feb. 1927, (quote) in Blaine A. Brownell, *The Urban Ethos in the South, 1920–1930* (Baton Rouge, 1975), 14. For Sunday behavior in industrialized Birmingham, see Blaine A. Brownell, "Birmingham, Alabama: New South City in the 1920s," *Journal of Southern History* 38 (Feb. 1972): 38–39.

60. *AC*, 23 June 1903, 13 June 1904, 18 Apr. 1905, 22 Mar. 1919, 28 Mar. 1919, 16 May 1919; *AJ*, 26 Feb. 1907, 7 Sept. 1919, 8 Sept. 1919.

61. *SN*, 4 Apr. 1929; *AC*, 10 Mar. 1933, 17 Mar. 1933, 19 Mar. 1933, 25 July 1933.

62. *AC*, 25 July 1933; *Atlanta Georgian*, 25 July 1933.

63. *AC*, 7 Aug. 1933; *Atlanta Georgian*, 8 Aug. 1933, 10 Aug. 1933; Atlanta, Minutes of the Atlanta City Council, 7 Aug. 1933, typescript, 211, Office of the City Clerk, Atlanta City Hall.

64. *AJ*, 15 Aug. 1933, 31 Aug. 1933.

65. *Atlanta Georgian*, 20 Aug. 1933.

66. *Atlanta Georgian*, 21 Sept. 1933, 3 Oct. 1933.

67. *AJ*, 17 Oct. 1933, 18 Oct. 1933, 19 Oct. 1933; author interview with Jasper Donaldson, Atlanta Crackers general manager in the 1930s, 13 Sept. 1971, Atlanta; author interview with Dr. Louie Newton, 15 Sept. 1971, Atlanta; author interview with baseball fan Jesse Pittard, 15 Sept. 1971, Atlanta; *AC*, 15 Mar. 1934, 31 Mar. 1934. The first exhibition game drew 3,941 spectators. *AC*, 2 Apr. 1934. For the regular season game on 13 May 1934, 13,628 turned out. *AC*, 14 May 1934; Minutes, Atlanta City Council, 5 Nov. 1934, 349; Earl Mann, "Another Great Team," *Atlanta Journal Sunday Magazine*, 21 Jan. 1936, 4.

68. See *SN*, 1895–1910; William B. Ruggles, *The History of the Texas League of Professional Baseball Clubs* (Dallas, 1951), 98; *Twelfth Census, 1900*, 1:clxxxvii–cxc.

69. Dale Somers, *The Rise of Sports in New Orleans, 1850–1900* (Baton Rouge, 1972), 10–14.

70. *Cincinnati Enquirer*, 18 Mar. 1903; William D. Miller, *Memphis during the Progressive Era, 1900–1917* (Memphis, 1957), chap. 1; William D. Miller, *Mr. Crump of Memphis* (Baton Rouge, 1964), 108–9; *Twelfth Census, 1900*, 1:clxxxvii; U.S. Census Office, *Religious Bodies: 1906*, vol. 1 (Washington, D.C., 1910), 402–4. Sunday ball in Memphis encouraged Nashville's owners to introduce Sunday ball in 1912. One of the chief owners was a state legislator, and the club evidently felt he had enough clout to protect the franchise against the wrath of the God-fearing citizenry. Nashville was more conservative than Memphis, but was a "wide-open town" by William Jennings Bryan's standards. In 1912 and 1918, Nashville's team went to court to defend Sunday baseball, winning both times. In 1918 the courts ruled that the 1803 status prohibiting Sunday sports could not have been intended to proscribe Sunday baseball since that sport had not yet been invented and the legislators had intended to eliminate only blood sports. See *SN*, 13 June 1912, 16 Nov. 1916, 24 Apr. 1919; *AC*, 1 Sept. 1911; George B. Tindall, *The Emergence of the New South, 1913–1946* (Baton Rouge, 1967), 200; *State ex rel J. A. Pitts*, 127 Tenn 292 (1912); *Tenn. v. Nashville Baseball Club*, 141 Tenn. 456 (1918).

71. *AJ*, 18 Jan. 1907; *AC*, 16 Jan. 1908, 2 Mar. 1908, 11 Apr. 1908, 14 Apr. 1908, 28 Apr. 1908, 23 May 1908, 14 Apr. 1900; *Twelfth Census, 1900*, 1:clxxix; *Nashville Banner*, 15 Apr. 1911. Sunday ball was also briefly played in Montgomery in the early 1900s because the team had a lot of political influence. The city council passed an ordinance against Sunday sports, but levied just a token fine for any violation. This enabled the team to evade the stiffer state laws since it could be tried only once for the same crime. The owners would be indicted and convicted, pay their fine, and continue staging Sunday games. Rural opponents, however, secured new state laws that effectively stopped Sunday ball in Montgomery. See *AC*, 30 Mar. 1903, 15 Dec. 1903, 16 Dec. 1903, 13 May 1904, 25 June 1904, 20 Oct. 1904; *AJ*, 16 Feb. 1904.

72. For a critique of the "solid" urban South theory, see Blaine Brownell, "Urbanization in the South: A Unique Experience?" *Mississippi Quarterly* 26 (Spring 1973): 120.

Chapter 5: Professional Baseball as a Source of Social Mobility

1. Leonard Dinnerstein and David M. Reimers, *Ethnic Americans: A History of Immigration and Assimilation* (New York, 1975), 136–37. For a historical analysis of sport and social mobility, see Steven A. Riess, "Professional Sports as an Avenue of Social Mobility in America: Some Myths and Realities," in *Essays on Sport History and Sport Mythology*, ed. Donald G. Kyle and Gary D. Stark (College Station, Tex., 1990), 83–117.

2. Seymour, *Baseball*, 1:47–48, 52; Adelman, *Sporting Time*, 133.

3. Adelman, *Sporting Time*, 157–61, 164–65; Levine, *Spalding*, 8–9; Kirsch, *Creation of American Team Sports*, 206–7, 233, 240–43, 255; *Brooklyn Union*, 29 Nov. 1868, in Chadwick Scrapbooks, vol. 1, p. 21; Voigt, "Cash and Glory," 66–67; H. C. Palmer, *Athletic Sports in America, England, and Australia* (Philadelphia, 1889), 35.

4. Adelman, *Sporting Time*, 152–54; Kirsch, *Creation of American Team Sports*, 239. On the distinction between baseball as play and as work, see Goldstein, *Playing for Keeps*, 4–6, 17–31, 120–26.

5. Kirsch, *Creation of American Team Sports*, 242. A survey of contemporary Brooklyn professionals who averaged twenty-three years of age revealed that three had been compositors and the rest included a glass blower, a stonemason, a shipping clerk, and a postal worker. Seymour, *Baseball*, 1:56–57; Voigt, *American Baseball*, 1:19.

6. Seymour, *Baseball*, 1:56–57; Voigt, *American Baseball*, 2:23–34; Federal Writers Project, *Baseball in Old Chicago*, 9.

7. Voigt, *American Baseball*, 1:14–34; Seymour, *Baseball*, 1:57–61; Adelman, *Sporting Time*, 167–68.

8. *NYT*, 22 Mar. 1875.

9. William Ryczek, *Blackguards and Red Stockings: A History of Baseball's National Association* (Jefferson, N.C., 1992); Voigt, *American Baseball*, 1:35–59; Gershman, *Diamonds*, 21.

10. Compiled and computed from *The Baseball Encyclopedia: The Complete and Official Record of Major League Baseball* (New York, 1969), 467–91.

11. Computed from ibid.

12. Adelman, *Sporting Time*, 156, 175, 177, 179.

13. Seymour, *Baseball*, 1:104–19. For comments on players as wage slaves, see *Sporting and Theatrical Journal*, 15 Mar. 1884, 286. There are relatively little data on salaries during the early years of the major leagues. On average salaries, see *CDN*, 13 Oct. 1881. In 1881 Providence paid its eleven players an average of $1,161. Morse, *Sphere and Ash*, 58. In 1882 its sixteen men averaged $1278.51 and one year later averaged $1446.66. Cincinnati in the mid-1880s paid its players from $500 to $2,000, an average of $1,620. Seymour, *Baseball*, 1:117.

A considerable amount of data on salaries can be found in Burk, *Never Just a Game*, but the data must be used with caution since Burk employs some studies uncritically. By 1929 salaries had declined to 35.3 percent of expenditures and were down to 20.5 percent in 1969. See Smelser, *The Life That Ruth Built*, 564.

14. The National Agreement signed by the NL, the AA, and the Northwestern League guaranteed minimum salaries of $1,000 for veteran players in the majors. Some players earned as little as $500, however. Seymour,

Baseball, 1:117–20; Voigt, *American Baseball*, 1:140–41; Voigt, "Cash and Glory," 525; *CDN*, 18 Sept. 1885; *Chicago Times*, 25 July 1888; Palmer, *Athletic Sports*, 38. House Judiciary Committee, *Organized Baseball*, 1439; Burk, *Never Just a Game*, 79. To prove how well players were compensated, the owners compiled a list of fourteen stars who in 1889 averaged $3,695. Computed from A. H. Tarvin, *A Century of Baseball, 1839–1939* (Louisville, Ky., 1938), 70.

Burk argues that owners tried to manipulate rules to curtail offense and keep down salaries. Burk, *Never Just a Game*, 68, 98, 254n21.

15. Gorn and Goldstein, *A Brief History of American Sports*, 101; *NYT*, 8 Mar. 1872, 8 Sept. 1897; *SN*, 18 Mar. 1905; Connie Mack, *My Sixty-Six Years in the Big Leagues* (Philadelphia, 1950), 20; Durso, *The Days of Mr. McGraw*, 99; Seymour, *Baseball*, 1:336.

16. "The Professional Player," *NYT*, 8 Mar. 1872.

17. Seymour, *Baseball*, 1:53; Voigt, *American Baseball*, 1:72–75; Federal Writers Project, *Baseball in Old Chicago*, 24–25; Gershman, *Diamonds*, 21; *Beadle's Dime Base Ball Player* (1875), quoted in Ward, *Baseball*, 25.

18. See also Mike Kelly, *"Play Ball": Stories of the Diamond Field* (Boston, 1888), written, according to the *Trenton Daily True American*, 7 July 1890, by his friend John J. Drohan; Marty Appel, *Slide, Kelly, Slide: The Wild Life and Times of Mike "King" Kelly, Baseball's First Superstar* (Lanham, Md., 1996), 114, 136–37; Fox, *Big Leagues*, 155–67. Quote is from Ward, *Baseball*, 34.

19. Coffin, *The Old Ball Game*, 36–37.

20. Voigt, *American Baseball*, 1:80–84, 91.

21. Quoted in Moore, "Great Base Ball Tour," 440.

22. *Chicago Times*, 23 July 1886; Spalding, *America's National Game*, 184 (quote), 525, 526. In contrast, outfielder Billy Sunday, a future evangelist, got a positive report. Eddie Gold and Art Ahrens, *The Golden Era Cubs: 1876–1940* (Chicago, 1985), 26, relates the story of a great catch by Sunday that strengthened his faith.

23. Voigt, *American Baseball*, 1:54, 79, 84, 103, 111; Appel, *Slide, Kelly, Slide*, 84; Moore, "Great Baseball Tour," 442; *Chicago Evening Journal*, 26 Apr. 1887, cited in Moore, "Great Baseball Tour," 442. The *Sporting and Theatrical Journal* often reported on players losing their jobs for drunkenness.

24. *SL*, 14 May 1892; Voigt, *American Baseball*, 1:66–68, 282–83; Seymour, "Rise of Major League Baseball," 567; Mack, *My Sixty-Six Years*, 20; David L. Porter, ed., *Biographical Dictionary of American Sports: Baseball* (Westport, Conn., 1987), s.v., "Lange, Bill."

25. Data drawn from Porter, *Biographical Dictionary of American Sports: Baseball*.

26. *SN*, 17 Apr. 1897; Voigt, *American Baseball*, 1:158–59; Seymour, *Baseball*, 1:224. On the Brotherhood, see Voigt, *America through Baseball* (Chicago, 1976), chaps. 9, 14; and Lowenfish and Lupien, *Imperfect Diamond*.

27. Voigt, "Cash and Glory," 518; Voigt, *American Baseball*, 1:156, 162–63 (quote).

28. *CT*, 2 Dec. 1891; Tarvin, *Century of Baseball*, 70; Voigt, *American Baseball*, 1:233–34; Seymour, *Baseball*, 1:266–70, 297–98.

29. Voigt, *American Baseball*, 1:233–35; *SN*, 12 Nov. 1898, 4 Feb. 1899, 17 Feb. 1900.

30. Voigt, *American Baseball*, 1:281.

31. Ibid.; Stephan Thernstrom, *The Other Bostonians: Poverty and Progress in the American Metropolis, 1880–1970* (Cambridge, Mass., 1973), 234. A control sample based on 116 nineteenth-century "stars" whose biographies appear in Robert L. Tiemann and Mark Rucker, eds., *Nineteenth Century Stars* (Cooperstown, N.Y., 1989) produced different results. Of the 66 players active in 1882 or earlier, 71.1 percent ended up in white-collar occupations (64.6 percent if men for whom no data were found are included). Stars who began their careers in 1883 or later fared better, with 79.1 percent becoming white-collar (66.7 percent if subjects with no data are included).

32. *SN*, 12 Nov. 1908; *Dictionary of American Biography*, s.v. "Anson, Adrian C."

33. *NYT*, 28 Dec. 1912; *NYTr*, 6 Jan. 1913.

34. On players and bars, see *SN*, 24 Dec. 1887. The most notable bookmaker to come out of baseball was "Honest John" Kelly, who briefly played in the majors in 1879 for Syracuse and Troy and then became an umpire. Kelly was given his nickname in 1888 by NL president Nick Young after he had refused a ten-thousand-dollar bribe. He went into the gambling business in the 1890s and ended the decade as a leading New York gambler with an elegant midtown gambling hall that he operated until 1922. Kelly was protected by an old sandlot teammate, Charles F. Murphy, the boss of Tammany Hall. See James D. Smith III, "Honest John Kelly," *Baseball Research Journal* 14 (1985): 7–9.

35. *SN*, 17 Oct. 1896; Seymour, *Baseball*, 1:336.

36. Seymour, *Baseball*, 1:326, 331, 336, 2:97–99, 104; Voigt, *American Baseball*, 1:292, 2:68–71, 80; Alexander, *Ty Cobb*.

37. Voigt, *American Baseball*, 1:285, 2:65, 80; Seymour, *Baseball*, 2:194–95; *SN*, 5 Jan. 1913; Voigt, *America through Baseball*, chap. 9; Seymour, *Baseball*, 2:223–30, 236–42; Lowenfish and Lupien, *Imperfect Diamond*, chaps. 3, 4; Burk, *Never Just a Game*, 143–47. On the improved conduct and demeanor of players, see *AC*, 9 Apr. 1904.

38. Durso, *Days of Mr. McGraw*, 69; quote is cited in Ward, *Baseball*, 108; Alexander, *McGraw*, 112–15.

39. *CDN*, 24 July 1903; *NYTR*, 11 Oct. 1911, 14 Apr. 1912; Ritter, *Glory of Their Times*, 164; Clark, *World of Damon Runyon*, 55–56; Kuklick, *To Every Thing a Season*, 37–38.

40. *SN*, 17 Oct. 1896. Little data exist on marital rates. In 1906 a smaller

proportion of the world champion White Sox were married, 7 of 18 (38.9 percent), compared with 13 of 24 men (54.2 percent) on the Class A Atlanta Crackers. *CDN*, 4 Oct. 1906; *AC*, 25 Mar. 1906.

41. *SN*, 26 Jan. 1895; Weir, "Baseball," 761 (quote).

42. *SN*, 22 Jan. 1908; Ritter, *Glory of Their Times*, 88.

43. Joe Durso, *Casey: The Life and Legend of Charles Dillon Stengel* (Englewood Cliffs, N.J., 1967), 5, 57–58.

44. Ban Johnson, "What the American League Has Done for Baseball," *Illustrated Sporting News*, 21 May 1904, 16; Ward, *Baseball*, 65; Burk, *Never Just a Game*, 243; Alan Tractenberg, *The Incorporation of America: Culture and Society in the Gilded Age* (New York, 1982), 90–91; Long, *Wages and Earning*, 4; Rees, *Real Wages in Manufacturing*, chap. 3; Seymour, *Baseball*, 1:314, 2:172–73; *NYT*, 8 Mar. 1903; Handlin, *The Uprooted*, 76.

45. *AC*, 16 July 1904; Weir, "Baseball," 759; Voigt, *American Baseball*, 2:65–68. Lieb, *Baseball as I Have Known It*, 265; Burk, *Never Just a Game*, 159–60, 243.

46. *SN*, 5 Jan. 1913; Voigt, *American Baseball*, 2:65, 80; Seymour, *Baseball*, 2:194–99, 223–30, 237–42; *AC*, 16 July 1904; New York Yankees Ledger Book, George Weiss Collection, National Baseball Library. On Clarkson's eligibility at Harvard, see Ronald A. Smith, *Sports and Freedom: The Rise of Big-Time College Athletics* (New York, 1988), 64–65.

47. Seymour, *Baseball*, 2:206–7.

48. Zingg, *Harry Hooper*, 123; Yankees Ledger Book; Voigt, *American Baseball*, 2:66.

49. Computed from Philadelphia Phillies Ledger Book, 1913–20, National Baseball Library; *NYT*, 25 Feb. 1917; Seymour, *Baseball*, 2:334.

50. Paul M. Gregory, *The Baseball Player: An Economic Study* (Washington, D.C., 1956), 93. Excellent data on team salaries appear in House Judiciary Committee, *Organized Baseball*, 1610–11, although 1929 salaries are probably inaccurate since there were just four hundred players but the total major league payroll was divided by five hundred, which may have included coaches and managers.

51. Black Sox salaries were computed from Seymour, *Baseball*, 2:334.

52. Voigt, *American Baseball*, 2:279. Surprisingly, the pennant-winning Columbus, Georgia, club of the South Atlantic League in 1910 averaged 25.9 years of age, with only two as young as 22. *AC*, 28 Aug. 1910. There are data on the wages of certain minor leaguers like Charles Pick, who had a brief stay in the majors, in the George Weiss Scrapbooks, Weiss Collection, National Baseball Library.

53. *AC*, 16 July 1904. Schoolteachers in Atlanta earned from fifty to seventy-five dollars a month. *AC*, 7 June 1918.

54. House Judiciary Committee, *Organized Baseball*, 1612; *Dictionary of American Biography*, s.v., "Heilmann, Harry."

55. *AC*, 31 Dec. 1908, 19 Sept. 1909. In 1911 the winners got $875 and the losers $631. *NYT*, 15 Oct. 1912; Arthur A. Ahrens, "Chicago's City Series," *Chicago History* 5 (Winter 1976–77): 243–52; Robinson, *Matty*, 120.

56. *NYTr*, 13 Oct. 1910, 19 Jan. 1911; *NYT*, 22 Oct. 1916, 16 Oct. 1917; Seymour, *Baseball*, 2:79–90, 392–93. Major leaguers sometimes played Sunday games under pseudonyms with local semipro teams. See *CDN*, 20 Aug. 1906.

57. *SN*, 24 Oct. 1912; Lieb, *Pittsburgh Pirates*, 57–58; *NYTr*, 5 Feb. 1904; *CDN*, 20 Jan. 1909; *AC*, 4 Jan. 1906, 21 Jan. 1906, 23 Jan. 1906; Seymour, *Baseball*, 1:333, 2:117–19; *BE*, 26 Nov. 1895; Alexander, *McGraw*, 166–67.

58. *NYTr*, 7 Mar. 1913, 9 Mar. 1913.

59. *CDN*, 5 July 1913, 7 July 1913; Henry B. Needham, "The Jinx," *Collier's*, 7 Feb. 1914, 7–8, 27–28; Robinson, *Matty*, 132–33, 152–53.

60. *NYTr*, 20 Apr. 1913.

61. *SN*, 24 Oct. 1912; McGraw, *Real McGraw*, 251; Durso, *Days of Mr. McGraw*, 79; Frederick C. Lane, "Winter Occupations of Famous Baseball Celebrities," *BM*, Mar. 1920, 575; Frederick C. Lane, "Gamest Player in Baseball," *BM*, Oct. 1913, 54–55. See also Jake Daubert, "Why Business Is Bad for a Ball Player," *BM*, Sept. 1922, 441–42.

62. Steven A. Riess, *Touching Base: Professional Baseball and American Culture in the Progressive Era* (Westport, Conn., 1980), 168–70; *CDN*, 31 Mar. 1908; *Detroit Daily News*, 13 Jan. 1914; Gregory, *Baseball Player*, 129.

63. Al Durant, "The Professional Minor Leaguer," *BM*, Apr. 1914, 57–58; author interview with Clement Wade, attorney for Dubuque, Iowa, minor league team, 13 Oct. 1971, Winnetka, Ill.

64. *AC*, 21 Sept. 1914, 20 Sept. 1917, 20 Apr. 1904, 27 Sept. 1905, 30 Oct. 1905, 18 Dec. 1905, 27 Jan. 1916.

65. The sample was based on a confidential questionnaire sent to 403 major leaguers active between 1900 and 1919 who were purported to be alive in 1971. I received 117 usable responses. See the appendix for the methods of compiling the questionnaire and computing the data. As a control, I prepared a second sample of 52 star players born between 1880 and 1899. Most of those players were also sons of white-collar fathers (38.5 percent), however over one-third (36.5 percent) were sons of farmers. Merely one-fourth (25.0 percent) were sons of blue-collar workers. Computed from biographical data in *Biographical Dictionary of American Sports: Baseball.*

66. Computed from raw data generously provided by Rudolph K. Haerle Jr., based on a 1958 questionnaire sent to 876 former major leaguers, of whom 335 (38.2 percent) responded. See Rudolph K. Haerle Jr., "Career Patterns and Career Contingencies of Professional Baseball Players: An Occupational Analysis," in *Sport and Social Order: Contributions to the Sociology of Sport*, ed. Donald W. Ball and John W. Loy (Reading, Mass., 1975), 510n4. Conclusions about the geographic origins of players were based on a sample

of 353 major leaguers who played in Chicago or New York between 1920 and 1939. The source for birthplaces was *Baseball Encyclopedia*. See also Steven A. Riess, "Professional Sports," 102–10.

67. Seymour, *Baseball*, 2:119. Computed from the weighted sample of 117 respondents. For the variables Player's Education x Wife's Education, Gamma = 0.53; for Player's Father's Job x Wife's Father's Job, Gamma = 0.32.

68. Laurence R. Veysey, *The Emergence of the American University* (Chicago, 1965), 2. Educational data are based on a sample of 593 major leaguers who played at least one year (defined operationally as one hundred at-bats or fifty innings pitched) in either Chicago or New York, from Lee Allen, Notebooks Containing Statistical Data on Baseball Players, Office of the Historian, National Baseball Library, Baseball Hall of Fame, Cooperstown, N.Y.

69. Data from 1971 questionnaire.

70. Smith, *Sports and Freedom*, chap. 5. As late as 1900 Princeton's profits from baseball still exceeded those from football. *NYT*, 27 Sept. 1900. On collegiate baseball stars, see *AC*, 1 Mar. 1908, 23 Oct. 1910, 13 Nov. 1910; C. P. Beaumont, "A Training School for Baseball Stars," *BM*, Nov. 1916, 73–76. On Beebe, see *CDN*, 6 Oct. 1910. The leading producers of major league ballplayers from 1871 to 1910 were Notre Dame (twenty), Holy Cross (eighteen), and Georgetown (seventeen), all Catholic institutions. Zingg, *Hooper*, 228.

71. *AC*, 31 Oct. 1910.

72. Hugh Fullerton, "Seeking the .300 Hitter," *American Magazine*, Nov. 1910, 90; *CDN*, 5 July 1907, 14 Mar. 1918; Ritter, *Glory of Their Times*, 30; Seymour, *Baseball*, 3:267; *Spalding's Chicago Amateur Baseball Annual and Intercity Baseball Association Yearbook* (New York, 1906). On Callahan, see Clark, *World of Damon Runyon*, 81, 82.

73. "Mysterious Fate of the Minor Leaguer," *Literary Digest* 51 (7 Aug. 1915): 268; *NYTr*, 31 Aug. 1915; Beaumont, "Training School," 73–76; *CDN*, 6 Oct. 1910, 9 Oct. 1910; Ritter, *Glory of Their Times*, 37, 144–45; Joseph M. Overfield, "The Other George Davis," *Baseball Research Journal* 18 (1989): 33–35.

74. Zingg, *Hooper*, 229; Smith, *Sports and Freedom*, 60–61; *SL*, 19 Nov. 1898, 23 Dec. 1899; Allen, Notebooks.

75. Allen, Notebooks; *NYT*, 8 Oct. 1905; Fred Tenney, "The Dearth of Batsmen—Some Star Players," *Illustrated Sporting News*, 10 June 1905, 4. The proportion of collegians in the majors rose from 22.1 percent of rookies in 1901–10 to 27.9 percent in 1911–20. Zingg, *Hooper*, 229.

76. Zingg, *Hooper*, 230; John J. McGraw, *My Thirty Years in Baseball* (New York, 1923), 237; Thomas L. Lynch, "The College Player in the Big Leagues," in *Spalding's Official College Baseball Annual, 1911*, ed. Edward B. Moss (New York, 1911), 15; Seymour, *Baseball*, 2:98–99; T. Paul McGannon to Herrmann, 2 June 1908, 10 June 1908, 14 July 1908, 1 Sept. 1908, 5 Sept. 1908, Herrmann Papers.

77. *NYT,* 30 Oct. 1919. For a fictional account, see Charles Van Loan, "The Bush League Demon," *SN,* 18 Dec. 1919.

78. *AC,* 13 Nov. 1913, 20 Sept. 1917; Howard J. Savage, *American College Athletics* (New York, 1929), 28–29; James Hugh Moffat, "Summer Baseball," *Independent,* 1 Sept. 1907, 752–53; *SN,* 7 Mar. 1912; *AC,* 29 May 1905; Needham, "College Athlete," 115–28. On "tramp" athletes who became major leaguers, see *SL,* 24 Aug. 1901; and *SN,* 7 Jan. 1915.

79. *NYTr,* 16 Oct. 1913; see also *Illustrated Sporting News,* 18 June 1904, 2. When Hugo Bezdek, a former football star at the University of Chicago, accepted an offer to manage the Pittsburgh Pirates in 1917, his friends found it incongruous that "a man of some education and intelligence should deliberately devote his career to athletic sport." *BM,* June 1919, 73.

80. Robin Lester to author, July 23, 1972, author's possession.

81. *NYTr,* 3 Jan. 1909.

82. Smith, *Sports and Freedom,* 62–66; *SN,* 8 Feb. 1917. Eddie Collins, the great second baseman for the Athletics and the White Sox, played briefly in the majors under the name Sullivan while a student at Columbia. *NYTr,* 6 Apr. 1908. See also Henry Beach Needham, "The College Athlete: His Amateur Code: Its Evasion and Administration," *McClure's,* July 1905, 260–69; "Menace to Amateur Sport," *Outlook,* 24 Feb. 1915, 413–14; and "The Amateur," *Outlook,* 8 Feb. 1913, 293–95.

83. *NYT,* 27 Mar. 1910.

84. "Menace to Amateur Sport," 413.

85. *CDN,* 8 Feb. 1904.

86. *CDN,* 9 Feb. 1904; *AC,* 24 Dec. 1903, 13 Dec. 1908, 5 Dec. 1915, 11 Dec. 1916.

87. "Why Is a Baseball Player?" *Literary Digest* 50 (12 June 1915): 1408; Arthur McDonald, "Scientific Study of Baseball," *American Physical Educational Review* 19 (Apr. 1914): 240; *SN,* 13 May 1916. See also "'Hick' Baseball as the Basis of the Game," *Literary Digest* 77 (19 May 1923): 64–66. Data computed from biographical information in *Baseball Encyclopedia;* and U.S. Bureau of Census, *Statistical Abstract of the United States, 1938* (Washington, D.C., 1939), 6–7. Voigt pointed out that the average big leaguer came from a small town. The typical player did come from a town of under 8,000 inhabitants, but there was a large deviation from the mean. Voigt, *American Baseball,* 2:64. More important is that nearly half (46.8 percent) of the players came from cities of 8,000 or more, whereas only 29.4 percent of the national population dwelled in cities of over 8,000 inhabitants in 1890.

88. *St. Louis Post-Dispatch,* 4 June 1905.

89. *AC,* 31 Oct. 1910. Chicago had 194 registered teams in 1906, and over 550 in 1910, including 26 semipro teams. *Spalding's Chicago Amateur Baseball Annual,* 13; Evers and Fullerton, *Touching Second,* 15. On St. Louis, see

Clarence F. Lloyd, "Baseball in St. Louis," in *Spalding's Official Baseball Guide, 1906*, 1215–29.

90. Computed from biographical information in *Baseball Encyclopedia*. There were about 2,750 big leaguers in this era. Voigt, *American Baseball*, 2:64.

91. Harvey Lehman, "The Geographic Origin of Professional Baseball Players," *Journal of Educational Research* 34 (Oct. 1940): 131–34.

92. *NYT*, 20 July 1919; Thomas H. Jenkins, "Changes in Ethnic and Racial Representation among Professional Boxers: A Study in Ethnic Succession" (M.A. thesis, University of Chicago, 1955), 15, 21; S. Kirson Weinberg and Henry Avond, "The Occupational Culture of the Boxer," *American Journal of Sociology* 57 (Mar. 1952): 460–69. For players' ethnic origins, see Allen, *Notebooks*. Using this source, Burk found occupational information on the ethnic backgrounds of 275 out of 2,204 players active in the nineteenth century. By his tabulation, WASPs comprised 48 percent of the NA, one-third of the NL from 1876 to 1890, and 40 percent of the NL 1891–1915. Burk, *Never Just a Game*, 44, 67, 90, 131, 171, 204, 223, 244. For a thorough analysis of baseball and ethnicity, especially the democratic myth, see White, *Creating the National Pastime*, chap. 8.

93. Thernstrom, *Other Bostonians*, 131–35.

94. Jenkins, "Changes in Ethnic and Racial Representation," 15; Michael Isenberg, *John L. Sullivan and His America* (Urbana, Ill., 1988).

95. Ritter, *Glory of Their Times*, 30.

96. *SN*, 8 Oct. 1892; *NYTr*, 24 Feb. 1915, 25 Feb. 1915, 4 Mar. 1915, 8 Mar. 1915, 26 Mar. 1915. As late as 1923 Fred Lieb, one of the greatest baseball writers, estimated that one-half of the players and three-fourths of the stars were Irish. Fred Lieb, "Baseball—The Nation's Melting Pot," *BM*, Aug. 1923, 393–95.

Using Lee Allen's notebooks, Burk found that the Irish were most prominent in the majors in the periods 1876–84 and 1885–90, when they comprised, respectively, 41 percent and 36 percent of the first-year players, and thereafter comprised about one-fifth of the rookies. Burk, *Never Just a Game*, 44, 67, 90, 131, 171, 204, 223. However, Allen did not have ethnic data for most of the players, plus there were errors in his ethnic identifications.

97. Thernstrom, *Other Bostonians*, 131–34; Hartmut Keil, ed., *German Workers' Culture in the United States, 1850 to 1920* (Washington, D.C., 1988); Rudolph A. Hofmeister, *The Germans of Chicago* (Champaign, Ill., 1976); E. Allen McCormick, *Germans in America: Aspects of German-American Relations in the Nineteenth Century* (Brooklyn, 1983); Henry Metzner, *A Brief History of the American Turnerbund* (Pittsburgh, 1924); Carl Wittke, *Refugees of Revolution: The German 48ers in America* (Philadelphia, 1952).

98. Burk argues that 30 percent of players in the NA were German. In

1876–90 they comprised 21–24 percent of players, and in 1890–1920, around 30 percent. See Burk, *Never Just a Game*, 44, 67, 90, 131, 171, 204, 223.

99. *Denni Hlasatel*, 16 Sept. 1911, Chicago Foreign Language Press Survey.

100. Compiled from admittedly incomplete data in Allen, *Notebooks*, although these ethnic names (if not pseudonyms), were fairly easy to pick out; *NYTr*, 28 Sept. 1918; *AC*, 6 Mar. 1910; Leitner, *Baseball*, 205. For an opposite view of new immigrants, see *NYTr*, 9 Mar. 1915.

101. Joseph Gerstein, "Anti-Semitism in Baseball," *Jewish Life* 6 (July 1952): 21–22; Frank, *Jew in Sport*, 75–91; *Encyclopedia Judaica*, 1st ed., s.v. "Sports"; Postal, Silver, and Silver, *Encyclopedia of Jews in Sports*. On an early Jewish minor leaguer, see Joel S. Franks, "Rube Levy: A San Francisco Shoe Cutter and the Origin of Professional Baseball in California," *California History* 70 (Summer 1991): 174–91.

102. Susan A. Glenn, *Daughters of the Shtetl: Life and Labor in the Immigrant Generation* (Ithaca, N.Y., 1990), 13, 20; Thernstrom, *Other Bostonians*, 131, 136–37; Thomas Kessner, *The Golden Door: Italian and Jewish Immigrant Mobility in New York City, 1880–1915* (New York, 1977), 36–37, 59–65, 87–93, 167–68.

103. Thernstrom, *Other Bostonians*, 171–73; Kessner, *Golden Door*, 94–99, 124–26, 172–73. On Jewish life in New York, see Irving Howe, *World of Our Fathers* (New York, 1976).

104. Steven A. Riess, "Tough Jews: The Jewish-American Boxing Experience, 1890–1950," *Sports and the American Jew* (Syracuse, 1998), 60–104; Howe, *World of Our Fathers*, 141. On street fighting as a training ground for future careers, see Mark Haller, "Organized Crime in Urban Society: Chicago in the Twentieth Century," *Journal of Social History* 5 (Winter 1971–72): 221–27; Daniel Bell, *The End of Ideology* (Glencoe, Ill., 1960), 127–50.

105. Riess, "Tough Jews"; Jenkins, "Changes in Ethnic and Racial Representation," 85–89.

106. Barry McCormick quoted in *Cincinnati Enquirer*, 17 Nov. 1903. See also *SN*, 13 June 1897; Frederick C. Lane, "Why Not More Jewish Ball Players?" *BM*, Jan. 1926, 341; Leitner, *Baseball*, 205; and David Spaner, "From Greenberg to Green: Jews in American Baseball," in *Total Baseball: The Official Encyclopedia of Major League Baseball*, ed. John Thorn and Pete Palmer (New York, 1997), 171–80.

107. Frederick C. Lane, "He Can Talk Baseball in Ten Languages," *BM*, Mar. 1928, 440; Moses Rischin, *The Promised City: New York Jews, 1870–1914* (Cambridge, Mass., 1962), 93; Riess, *City Games*, 63–64, 100–101, 104–6, 109–11.

108. William Carlson Smith, *Americans in the Making: The Natural History of the Assimilation of Immigrants* (New York, 1939), 116–19. Quotes are taken from Howe, *World of Our Fathers*, 182, 259; and Irving Howe and Kenneth Libo, *How We Lived, 1880–1930* (New York, 1979), 51–52.

109. Leitner, *Baseball*, 205.

110. Gerstein, "Anti-Semitism in Baseball," 21–22; Lieb, "Baseball—The Nation's Melting Pot," 395; Harry Golden, *The Right Time; An Autobiography* (New York, 1969), 55; Seymour, *Baseball*, 2:82–83; *Encyclopedia Judaica*, s.v. "Sports." For a player's personal experiences with anti-Semitism, see Alexander Schacht, *My Own Particular Screwball* (Garden City, N.Y., 1955), 79, 81, 117. On the continuing problem with anti-Semitism in baseball, see Hank Greenberg, *Hank Greenberg: The Story of My Life*, ed. Ira Berkow (New York, 1989), 52–53, 82–84, 102–4, 106–7, 155, 190–91, 254–55; Cal Abrams interview, Weiner Collection, American Jewish Committee, Jewish Collection, New York Public Library, 91, 94–95, 160, 234–35, 240.

111. *SN*, 6 Sept. 1923 (quote), 26 Apr. 1928; Samuel S. Merin, "A Close-Up of Andy Cohen," *BM*, July 1928, 358; Golden, *Right Time*, 55; Allen, *Giants and Dodgers*, 122; Seymour, *Baseball*, 2:83. Solomon was born on the Lower East Side of New York, but grew up in poverty in Columbus, Ohio. Earning twelve letters in high school, he had been offered a football scholarship by Ohio State, but went to work to help support his family. After the 1923 season McGraw wanted Solomon to stay with the club during the World Series, for which Solomon was not eligible and would not be paid. Instead Solomon joined the Portsmouth Spartans of the NFL, despite McGraw's warning him that if he left the ball club, the Giants would not bring him back the next season. Solomon later played with the Oorong Indians in the NFL, using a pseudonym while with the supposedly all-Indian squad. His parents never respected his work as a professional athlete. Louis Jacobson, "Will The Real Rabbi of Swat Please Stand Up?" *Baseball Research Journal* 18 (1989): 17–18; Levine, *Ellis Island*, 110.

112. Tilden G. Edelstein, "Cohen at the Bat," *Commentary* 76 (Nov. 1983): 53–56; Bill Simons, "Andy Cohen: Second Baseman as Ethnic Hero," *NP* 10 (1990): 83–87; Charles C. Alexander, *Rogers Hornsby* (New York, 1991), 141–45. When Cohen was in the minor leagues, one fan called him "Christ Killer." He responded by grabbing a bat and yelling back, "Yes and I'll kill you too." When he got to the majors, he was called "showy sheenie," "cocky Kike," and "Stupid Hebe." Andrew Howard Cohen interview, 21–23, Oral History Collection, Weiner Archives, American Jewish Committee, Jewish Collection, New York Public Library; Simons, "Andy Cohen," 83–87.

113. Charles J. Sanders, "In Search of the Great American Baseball Dream," *Baseball Digest*, Feb. 1985, 36–45; Abrams interview, 47. There were 15 Jewish ballplayers active in the 1920s, 25 in the 1930s, and 26 in the 1940s. Overall, there were 137 Jewish major leaguers through 1997. For a definitive listing of Jewish ballplayers, see Spaner, "From Greenberg to Green," 179–80. His extensive research is a valuable corrective to the list in Peter C. Bjarkman, "Baseball and the American Jewish Experience," in *Cooperstown: Symposium on Baseball and the American Culture, 1990*, ed. Alvin L. Hall (Westport, Conn., 1991), 343.

114. Marazzi, "Al Schacht," 34–35 (quote). Computed from data in Postal, Silver, and Silver, *Encyclopedia of Jews in Sports* and *Baseball Encyclopedia*. By the 1930s Jewish players from New York, such as Hank Greenberg, were coming from the more outlying boroughs, where the economically prosperous and more assimilated Jews lived and where there was more space to play.

115. Thernstrom, *Other Bostonians*, 136–37, 162–63, 168–73. On Italian immigrant life, see Richard Gambino, *Blood of My Blood: The Dilemma of the Italian-Americans* (New York, 1974); Humbert Nelli, *The Italians in Chicago, 1880–1930* (New York, 1970); and Humbert Nelli, *The Business of Crime: Italians and Syndicate Crime in the United States* (New York, 1976). On Polish Americans, see Edward Kantowicz, *Polish-American Politics in Chicago, 1880–1940* (Chicago, 1975); and Dominic A. Pacyga, *Polish Immigrants and Industrial Chicago: Workers on the South Side, 1880–1922* (Columbus, 1991).

116. Jenkins, "Changes in Ethnic and Racial Representation," 15, 98; Randy Roberts, *Papa Jack: Jack Johnson and the Era of White Hopes* (New York, 1983), 131.

117. Allen, Notebooks. On Italian intergenerational conflicts over baseball, see National Commission on Law Observance and Enforcement, *Report on the Causes of Crime*, vol. 2, no. 13 (Washington, D.C., 1931), 4–5, cited in Smith, *Americans in the Making*, 312.

118. White, *Creating the National Pastime*, 255–58. In 1930–32 there were four Italian rookies each year and six in 1934. In 1936 Joe DiMaggio was one-third of all the Italian-American rookies. There was only one Polish rookie in 1930, but seven in 1932 (out of ninety-three rookies total). Ethnic data drawn from Harold Johnson, *Who's Who in the National League, 1935* (Chicago, 1935); John G. T. Spink, comp., *Baseball Register, 1941* (St. Louis, 1941); and Allen, Notebooks. Population data drawn from U.S. Bureau of the Census, *Statistical Abstract of the United States, 1943* (Washington, D.C., 1944), 28.

119. "Indians Who Played in the Big Leagues," *BM*, July 1921, 355; Seymour, *Baseball*, 2:81–82; Stephen I. Thompson, "The American Indian in the Major Leagues," *Baseball Research Journal* 3 (1983): 1–7.

120. *CDN*, 19 Oct. 1910.

121. *AC*, 10 Jan. 1909, 2 Jan. 1916; *NYTr*, 3 Dec. 1909, 26 Dec. 1911, 15 Apr. 1917; *New York Age*, 8 Dec. 1910, 22 Dec. 1910; Seymour, *Baseball*, 2:83–85; Samuel O. Regalado, *Viva Baseball! Latin Major Leaguers and Their Special Hunger* (Urbana, Ill., 1998), 6, 10; Michael M. Oleksak and Mary Adams Oleksak, *Béisbol: Latin Americans and the Grand Old Game* (Grand Rapids, 1991); Louis A. Perez Jr., "Between Baseball and Bullfighting: The Quest for Nationality in Cuba, 1868–1898," *Journal of American History* 81 (Sept. 1994): 493–517.

In 1911 the National Commission banned barnstorming by league champions after the world champion Philadelphia Athletics barely won its exhibition series in Cuba. This ruling largely ended major league tours to Cuba. Lanctot, *Fair Dealing and Clean Playing*, 35, 167–68.

122. *NYTr*, 13 Oct. 1912, 26 Feb. 1914; Seymour, *Baseball*, 2:84–85; Oleksak and Oleksak, *Béisbol*, 25; Peter C. Bjarkman, "Cuban Blacks in the Majors before Jackie Robinson," *NP* 12 (1992): 60–61.

123. *Chicago Defender*, 16 Jan. 1915; *CDN*, 27 Nov. 1915; Bowman and Zoss, *Diamonds in the Rough*, 146–47.

124. Peterson, *Only the Ball Was White*, 18, 23; Larry Bowman, "Moses Fleetwood Walker: The First Black Major League Baseball Player," in *Baseball History 2*, 61–74; David W. Zang, *Fleet Walker's Divided Heart: The Life of Baseball's First Black Major Leaguer* (Lincoln, 1995); Seymour, *Baseball*, 3:chaps. 33, 34; Lanctot, *Fair Dealing and Clean Playing*, 240n13.

125. *Sporting News* quoted in Peterson, *Only the Ball Was White*, 41; Bowman and Zoss, *Diamonds in the Rough*, 140–42; Seymour, *Baseball*, 3:550–51. On the efforts of Syracuse's squad to sabotage their black pitcher Bob Higgins, see Jerry Malloy, "Out at Home: Baseball Draws the Color Line, 1887," *NP* 2 (1983): 22–23.

126. Quoted in Malloy, "Out at Home," 23.

127. "Letters to the Editor," *NP* 4 (Spring 1985): 87–88; *Toledo Blade*, 11 Aug. 1883.

128. John Brown to C. H. Morton, 11 Apr. 1884, Chicago Baseball Club Letterpress Records, Chicago Historical Society, quoted in Levine, *Spalding*, 47; Malloy, "Out at Home," 25; Bowman and Zoss, *Diamonds in the Rough*, 136–38; Seymour, *Baseball*, 3:552–53, 554–55. Anson again drew the color line in an exhibition game on 27 September 1888 against Syracuse, keeping Walker off the field. Drawing the color line had become so commonplace by then that the white press did not report the incident. Malloy, "Out at Home," 28.

In 1886 John M. Ward of the New York Giants reportedly tried to hire the light-complexioned George Stovey, then of the Cuban Giants, to pitch in a key series against Anson's Chicago White Stockings, but the players objected. Stovey pitched that season for Jersey City of the Eastern League, going 16-15 with a 1.13 ERA. Jerry Malloy, "The Cubans' Last Stand," *NP* 11 (1992): 11–12; Burk, *Never Just a Game*, 97.

129. Quoted in Malloy, "Out at Home," 26.

130. Peterson, *Only the Ball Was White*, 23, 54–56; Seymour, *Baseball*, 3:554–57; Bowman and Zoss, *Diamonds in the Rough*, 142–44; Lanctot, *Fair Dealing and Clean Playing*, 166. Celoron brought in white players as replacements, with little success. The club went 10-37 for the season. Greg Peterson, "The Celoron Acme Colored Giants," *NP* 16 (1996): 101–3.

Comiskey's action in the Grant case has often been cited as evidence of his racism. However, he was one of only two St. Louis Browns who did not sign a petition in 1887 against playing an African-American team and recognized the quality of black ballplayers. Following the games between the Leland Giants and the Donlin All-Stars in 1907, Comiskey indicated that he would have signed three of the Leland players had they been white. Comiskey employed African-American equipment managers and groundskeepers, donated money to black charities, rented his park to African-American teams, and maintained cordial relations with Rube Foster. The proximity of a black neighborhood to his ballpark, however, might have influenced some of his public actions. Lanctot, *Fair Dealing and Clean Playing*, 165, 166, 169–70, 185.

131. *CDN*, 15 July 1905 (quote); Karl Lindholm, "William Clarence Matthews," *NP* 17 (1997): 67–72. On the racism Matthews encountered in college sports, see Arthur R. Ashe Jr., *A Hard Road to Glory: A History of the African-American Athlete, 1619–1918* (New York, 1988), 78, 92, 95.

132. *AC*, 4 Mar. 1910; *New York Age*, 10 Mar. 1910; *NYT*, 3 Mar. 1910.

133. John Hope Franklin, *From Slavery to Freedom*, 2d ed., rev. and enl. (New York, 1956), 393; Marshall W. Taylor, *The Fastest Bicycle Rider in the World* (Worcester, Mass., 1928); David Wiggins, "Isaac Murphy: Black Hero in Nineteenth Century American Sport, 1861–1896," *Canadian Journal of the History of Sport and Physical Education* 10 (May 1979): 15–32; David Wiggins, "Peter Jackson and the Elusive Heavyweight Championship: A Black Athlete's Struggle against the Late Nineteenth Century Color Line," *Journal of Sport History* 12 (Summer 1985): 143–68; Roberts, *Papa Jack*; Al-Tony Gilmore, *Bad Nigger! The National Impact of Jack Johnson* (Port Washington, N.Y., 1975); David L. Porter, *Biographical Dictionary of American Sports: Basketball and Other Indoor Sports* (Westport, Conn., 1989), s.v., "Gans, Joe."

134. Seymour, *Baseball*, 3:533–45; Lanctot, *Fair Dealing and Clean Playing*, 12–13, 165; Malloy, "Cubans' Last Stand," 11–12. In 1886 the Cuban Giants defeated Cincinnati and Kansas City in exhibitions. The first African-American league was the short-lived Southern League of Colored Baseballists (1886). See William Plott, "The Southern League of Colored Baseballists," *Baseball Historical Review* 1 (1981): 75–78.

135. Seymour, *Baseball*, 3:533–45; Lanctot, *Fair Dealing and Clean Playing*, 165 (quote), 173–74; *New York Age*, 26 Jan. 1911, 11 Jan. 1919.

136. Quoted in *New York Age*, 28 Sept. 1911.

137. *Chicago Defender*, 13 Dec. 1919; Voigt, *American Baseball*, 1:279; Peterson, *Only the Ball Was White*, 7, 57, 63, 67, 70, 77, 107, chap. 16; Sol White, *Sol White's Official Baseball Guide* (Philadelphia, 1907), 65, 67.

138. Lomax, "Black Baseball," 212–14, 226; Lanctot, *Fair Dealing and Clean Playing*, 29–30; *NYT*, 11 Jan. 1935.

139. *New York Age*, 2 May 1912, 13 Mar. 1913; Peterson, *Only the Ball Was White*, 76; Seymour, *Baseball*, 3:261, 280; Lanctot, *Fair Dealing and*

Clean Playing, 29–30; Lomax, "Black Baseball," 221–22, 229–33, 235–36; Fox, *Big Leagues*, 309–10.

140. *New York Age*, 18 June 1918; *Chicago Defender*, 19 Apr. 1919, 4 Oct. 1919; Dixon, *Negro Baseball Leagues*, 121. On the black leagues, see Peterson, *Only the Ball Was White*, 53–181; John Holway, *Voices from the Great Black Baseball Leagues* (New York, 1975); Janet Bruce, *The Kansas City Monarchs: Champions of Black Baseball* (Lawrence, 1985); Donn Rogosin, *Invisible Men: Life in Baseball's Negro Leagues* (New York, 1985); Rob Ruck, *Sandlot Seasons: Sport in Black Pittsburgh* (Urbana, Ill., 1987); Lanctot, *Fair Dealing and Clean Playing*. Players in the black leagues made from $150 to $200 a month in the early 1920s. Peterson, *Only the Ball Was White*, 98.

141. *New York Age*, 28 Sept. 1911.

142. David Quentin Voigt, *Baseball: An Illustrated History* (University Park, Pa., 1987), 197.

143. The tenure data for a sample of 593 men who played at least one season in Chicago or New York are drawn from *Baseball Encyclopedia*. A sample of 501 Yankees active before 1947 averaged slightly over two years in tenure. House Judiciary Committee, *Organized Baseball*, 872; Voigt, *American Baseball*, 2:80.

144. *SN*, 22 Mar. 1902; *AC*, 28 Apr. 1904, 9 June 1918, 9 Feb. 1919, 18 Apr. 1919; *Atlanta City Directory*, 1910, 1920, 1925, 1930, and 1935; author interview with Joe Gerson, local fan, 14 Sept. 1971, Atlanta.

145. *SN*, 18 Mar. 1905; *AC*, 14 Feb. 1912.

146. Of the 593 players in the sample, 22 died while still playing professional ball or shortly after retirement. No occupational data were found on 93 men.

147. This percentage is slightly smaller than the percentage of questionnaire respondents (7.1 percent) who held professional jobs; Ritter, *Glory of Their Times*, 37.

148. *CDN*, 27 Jan. 1917; Axelson, *"Commy,"* 130; Robinson, *Matty*, 210–12; *Dictionary of American Biography*, s.v. "Mathewson, Christy"; Durso, *Casey*, 82–83; Robert Creamer, *Stengel: His Life and Times* (New York, 1984), 172–73.

149. Fred W. Odwell requested August Herrmann's help in securing him a postmastership. Odwell to Herrmann, 18 Nov. 1912, Herrmann Papers.

150. *Los Angeles Times*, 19 June 1917.

151. Smelser, *The Life That Ruth Built*, 420, 473–74, 485–91, 512–14, 521–22.

152. Rich Eldred, "Umpiring in the 1890's," *Baseball Research Journal* 18 (1989): 75–78; Murdock, *Ban Johnson*, 105.

153. Eldred, "Umpiring in the 1890's," 78; Voigt, *American Baseball*, 2:103–4, 227; Murdock, *Ban Johnson*, 25–27, 39–41, 51–52, 98–108.

154. *NYT*, 28 Dec. 1912; *NYTr*, 6 Jan. 1913.

155. Merely 6.4 percent of questionnaire respondents were farmers. Some ballplayers for whom no occupational data were found may have been farmers because obscure players who lived and died in rural communities were less likely to have obituaries.

156. One-fifth (19.3 percent) of the respondents to my questionnaire were blue-collar workers.

157. *SN*, 26 Sept. 1918, 8 July 1920; *AC*, 1 Feb. 1919; Seymour, *Baseball*, 2:249–51, 3:chaps. 14–16; Lanctot, *Fair Dealing and Clean Playing*, 50, chap. 3; Tamara Hareven and Randolph Langenbach, *Amoskeag: Life and Work in an American Factory-City* (New York, 1978), 179. On industrial recreation, see Riess, *City Games*, 83–86; Wilma Pesavento, "Sport and Recreation in the Pullman Experiment, 1880–1900," *Journal of Sport History* 9 (Summer 1982): 38–62; Wilma Pesavento and Lisa C. Raymond, "'Men Must Play, Men Will Play': Occupations of Pullman Athletes, 1880 to 1900," *Journal of Sport History* 11 (Summer 1984): 233–51; Betts, *America's Sporting Heritage*, 314–19; Frederick Cozens and Florence S. Stumpf, *Sports in American Life* (Chicago, 1953), 52–62; and John R. Schleppi, "'It Pays': John H. Patterson and Industrial Recreation at the National Cash Register Company," *Journal of Sport History* 6 (Winter 1979): 20–28.

158. Seymour, *Baseball*, 2:288.

159. Ibid., 2:288–92; Hoie, "Hal Chase Case," 34–40.

160. Tenure computed for sample of 593 Chicago and New York major leaguers from data in *Baseball Encyclopedia*. Haerle, "Professional Baseball Players," 504–7nn4, 5; Rudolph K. Haerle Jr., "Education, Athletic Scholarships, and the Occupational Career of the Professional Athlete," *Sociology of Work and Occupations* 2 (Nov. 1975): 373–403.

161. Computed from 117 respondents to questionnaire. On education and class, Gamma = 0.66. On father's status and player's future status, Gamma = 0.48.

162. Seymour, *Baseball*, 1:121–23, 2:104.

163. Thernstrom, *Other Bostonians*, 234.

Conclusion

1. Edwards, *Sociology of Sport*, 269–70.

2. See ibid., 242–45, 318–29; Allen G. Ingham, "Occupational Subcultures in the Work World of Sport," in *Sport and Social Order*, ed. Donald W. Ball and John W. Loy (Reading, Mass., 1975), 362–67.

3. Freedman, "The Baseball Fad in Chicago," 44–53; Robin Lester, "American Intercollegiate Football: An Overview," 2, 13–14, paper presented at the Ninetieth Annual Meeting of the American Historical Association, Atlanta, 29 Dec. 1975.

4. Dulles, *America Learns to Play*, ix, 4–21; Nancy Struna, "Puritans and

Sport: The Irretrievable Tide of Change," *Journal of Sport History* 4 (Spring 1977): 1–21; Breen, "Horses and Gentlemen," 329–47.

5. Betts, "Mind and Body in Early American Thought," 787–805; John A. Lucas, "A Prelude to the Rise of Sport: Ante-bellum America, 1850–1860," *Quest* 11 (Dec. 1968): 50–57; George M. Fredrickson, *The Inner Civil War* (New York, 1965), 221–24; Daniel F. Rodgers, *The Work Ethic in Industrial America, 1850–1920* (Chicago, 1978), 11–12, 105.

6. Kuklick, *To Every Thing a Season,* 192.

7. Edwards, *Sociology of Sport,* 5, 242–45, 320; James A. Michener, *Sports in America* (New York, 1976), 382; Paul Hoch, *Rip Off: The Big Game* (New York, 1972), 82–83; Robert Lipsyte, *SportsWorld: An American Dreamland* (New York, 1975), 39–40, 46–49; Michael Roberts, *Fans! How We Go Crazy over Sports* (Washington, D.C., 1976), 102–3.

8. Jeffrey Goldstein and Robert Arms, "Effects of Observing Athletic Contests on Hostility," *Sociometry* 34 (Mar. 1971): 83–90; Leonard Berkowitz, "Experimental Investigations of Hostility Catharsis," in *Social Conflict,* ed. Philip Brickman (Lexington, Mass., 1974), 91–99; Ashley Montagu, *The Nature of Human Aggression* (New York, 1976), 276–82; Konrad Lorenz, *On Aggression* (New York, 1966), 281.

9. Bruce C. Ogilvie and Thomas A. Tutko, "Sports: If You Want to Build Character, Try Something Else," *Psychology Today,* Oct. 1971, 61; Edwards, *Sociology of Sport,* 79, 139. The psychologist Julian Morrow has found that contemporary professional baseball and football players have higher levels of aggression than the general public does. Jeffrey R. Benedict's research into police and court records convinced him that sports might condition male athletes to antagonistic actions. See Robert Lipsyte, "The Emasculation in Sports," *New York Times Magazine,* 2 Apr. 1995, 53–54.

10. On the diffusion of American baseball, see Perez, "Between Baseball and Bullfighting," 493–517.

On records, see Allen Guttmann, *From Ritual to Record: The Nature of Modern Sports* (New York, 1978), 51–55, 109–12, 129; and Richard D. Mandell, "The Invention of the Sports Record," *Stadion* 2 (1976): 250–64.

11. Frederick J. Turner, "The Significance of the Frontier in American History," in American Historical Association, *Annual Report for the Year 1893* (Washington, D.C., 1894), 197–227; George Mowry, *The Urban Nation, 1920–1960* (New York, 1965), 2; Hofstadter, *Age of Reform,* 24.

12. Peter Schmitt, *Back to Nature: The Arcadian Myth in Urban America* (New York, 1969), xvii.

13. Wiebe, *Search for Order,* chaps. 2, 3, 7, 8.

14. Higham, *Strangers in the Land;* William E. Leuchtenburg, *The Perils of Prosperity, 1914–1932* (Chicago, 1958); Nash, *Nervous Generation.*

15. Nash, *Nervous Generation,* 126–63; John W. Ward, "The Meaning of Lindbergh's Flight," *American Quarterly* 10 (Spring 1958): 3–16.

16. Rader, *American Sports*, 135. For an interesting discussion of the typology of baseball's folklore heroes, see Coffin, *The Old Ball Game*, chap. 4.

Appendix

1. Addresses were taken from Jack Smalling, "Address List of Past and Present Major Leaguers," 1971, mimeograph, author's possession.

2. Adds up to 100.1 percent because of rounding.

3. Clifford Kachline, archivist at the National Baseball Library, to the author, 3 Sept. 1975, author's possession. David Quentin Voigt had earlier reported that 493 men had attended college in this era. Voigt, *American Baseball*, 2:64.

4. Thernstrom, *Other Bostonians*, 290–92.

5. Alba Edwards, *Comparative Occupational Statistics for the United States, 1870 to 1940* (Washington, D.C., 1942), 187.

Index

Steven A. Riess is the author or editor of many articles and books on sport history, including *City Games: The Evolution of American Urban Society and the Rise of Sports.* He is a professor of history at Northeastern Illinois University.

Sport and Society

Touching Base: Professional Baseball and American Culture in the Progressive
Era (rev. ed.) *Steven A. Riess*

Reprint Editions
The Nazi Olympics *Richard D. Mandell*
Sports in the Western World (2d ed.) *William J. Baker*

Typeset in 9.5/13 Trump Mediaeval
with Trump Mediaeval display
Designed by Paula Newcomb
Composed by Keystone Typesetting, Inc.
Manufactured by Thomson-Shore, Inc.